THROUGH THE EYES
OF DESCARTES

STUDIES IN CONTINENTAL THOUGHT

John Sallis, *editor*

Consulting Editors

Robert Bernasconi
John D. Caputo
David Carr
Edward S. Casey
David Farrell Krell
Lenore Langsdorf

James Risser
Dennis J. Schmidt
Calvin O. Schrag
Charles E. Scott
Daniela Vallega-Neu
David Wood

THROUGH THE EYES OF DESCARTES
Seeing, Thinking, Writing

Cecilia Sjöholm and
Marcia Sá Cavalcante Schuback

Indiana University Press

This book is a publication of

Indiana University Press
Office of Scholarly Publishing
Herman B Wells Library 350
1320 East 10th Street
Bloomington, Indiana 47405 USA

iupress.org

© 2024 by Cecilia Sjöholm and Marcia Sá Cavalcante Schuback

All rights reserved
No part of this book may be reproduced or utilized in any form or by any means, electronic or mechanical, including photocopying and recording, or by any information storage and retrieval system, without permission in writing from the publisher. The paper used in this publication meets the minimum requirements of the American National Standard for Information Sciences—Permanence of Paper for Printed Library Materials, ANSI Z39.48-1992.

Manufactured in the United States of America
First printing 2024

Cataloging information is available from the Library of Congress.

ISBN 978-0-253-06822-4 (hardback)
ISBN 978-0-253-06823-1 (paperback)
ISBN 978-0-253-06825-5 (ebook)

For Jean-Luc Nancy

Contents

Preface ix

Introduction 1

1 Descartes's Visceral Aesthetics: The Violence of the Beautiful and the Ugly / Cecilia Sjöholm 10

2 Philosophical Emotion: Descartes and the Aesthetics of Thought / Marcia Sá Cavalcante Schuback 34

3 Descartes's Performative *Cogito* / Marcia Sá Cavalcante Schuback 55

4 Rhythms of Snow: Figures of Differentiation in Descartes's *Meteorology* / Cecilia Sjöholm 74

5 Thinking through Lines with Descartes / Marcia Sá Cavalcante Schuback 98

6 The Gaze, Images, and Drives / Cecilia Sjöholm 123

7 The Thinking Fetus / Cecilia Sjöholm 145

8 The Love between Body and Soul / Marcia Sá Cavalcante Schuback 163

Notes 173
Bibliography 207
Subject Index 215
Names Index 223

Preface

THE PRESENT BOOK presents a study done by two authors, Cecilia Sjöholm and Marcia Sá Cavalcante Schuback. As authors, we have signed our chapters individually. But our work has developed in a close aesthetic-philosophical conversation over the past few years. In this way, the chapters intersect.

The research that moved our thoughts has been about the question of aesthetics in Descartes's thought. The ambition has not only been to find out how a Cartesian aesthetics is interwoven in his thought, but above all to show its prismatic reach. This has required a consideration of a variety of materials that is not always considered together; the metaphysical writings as well as the essays in natural philosophy, the anthropology of the *Passions*, retrieved in letters as well as drawings and printed images and so on.

It required, also, steps not only into a contemporary phenomenology that has been much influenced by the Cartesian meditations but also into a contemporary psychoanalytic thought. The prismatic reach means that the book stretches between questions and phenomena that are not symmetrical but are varieties of what we consider as aesthetic inquiries. To this belong the way in which perception interacts with emotions and thought, the way in which our gaze is directed toward limit-phenomena of beauty and fascination; the way in which pictures and images cross inside and outside; and the way in which a snowy landscape does it; the way in which beauty raises our instinct of love through body and soul, and the way in which infantile life fosters the reverse, hatred and revulsion.

In order to open the paths toward a Cartesian aesthetics, we organized an evening in Stockholm in 2018, a soirée with talks and music on the topic. For a country that has seen the death of one of the world's greatest philosophers, attached to queen Christina, such events have been surprisingly few. But the event was noteworthy above all for another reason: it received the presence and contribution of Jean-Luc Nancy.

This book is dedicated to the memory of Jean-Luc Nancy, whose work on philosophy and on Descartes has greatly inspired what we have tried to achieve. It is also dedicated to his memory as a thanks for his contribution to this project, incorporated in our reflections.

A few of the chapters have been published as articles in other versions; Cecilia Sjöholm: "Descartes, Emotions and the Inner Life of the Subject," in *The Palgrave Handbook of Affect Studies and Textual Criticism*, ed. Donald Wehrs

(London: Palgrave, 2017); "Figures of Snow: Preconceptual Dimensions of Descartes's *Meteorology*," in *Epoché: A Journal for the History of Philosophy* (2022); and "The Thinking Fetus: Descartes at the Brink of Psychoanalysis," in *Emotions: History, Culture, Society* 5 (2021).

For the completion of this book, we wish to thank the Swedish Research Council, which graciously granted us funding for the project.

THROUGH THE EYES
OF DESCARTES

Introduction

THE STANDARD PHILOSOPHICAL portrait of Descartes is that of a thinker of universal claims, standing without any worldly background and holding the hand only on himself (fig. Intro.1, portrait by David Beck). Another portrait is by Frans Hals (fig. Intro.2), who depicts Descartes, without any background, holding a hat on the hand and thereby emerging as the philosopher who departs from solid prejudices, inaugurating philosophy as a journey through one's own thoughts.

Descartes with a hat on the hands became a usual motive, as one can see in Jonas Suyderhoff's engraving after Frans Hals's painting (fig. Intro.3).

Another portrait that became typical, painted by Jan Baptist de Weenix in 1647 (fig. Intro.4), depicts Descartes holding a book in which the phrase "*mundus est fabula*" ("the world is a fable") is written.

As a fable, the Cartesian world has been seen as one disconnected from the cosmos and from nature, acosmic and unnatural. Descartes has been charged with the separation between body and soul in the name of the freedom of spirit and for the sake of mastering the body. Living in the era of the Europeanization of the world, he has been seen as making humankind the lord and master of all possible natures, imposing rationality as its main instrument.

However, among the many portraits of Descartes—and Descartes is indeed one of the most portrayed philosophers in modern times—there is one rarely seen and discussed—namely, the one in which we can see Descartes as a philosopher of aesthetics. That is the portrait developed in this book. It unravels a Descartes of the arts, sketching an "aesthetic machine"[1] of inner images and imagination, where metaphysics and autoanalysis intertwine with aesthetic sensibility. The main thesis of this book is that there is an aesthetics in Descartes—both in terms of a theory of the aesthetic as an experience of the senses and in terms of an aesthetic experience operating in philosophical thought. By proceeding from his first treatise on music, which formulates an idea of aesthetic taste over the extraordinary images of his natural philosophy and into his metaphysics and ethics, this book identifies a Cartesian baroque aesthetics in the movements between reason and passion, image and thought, inner and outer, sleep and wakefulness, consciousness and repressed traces and memories that make up Descartes's work. A baroque aesthetics creates an intense interaction between figures and images and writing, as well as between works—the visceral anatomy inherent to the theory of memory traces in *The Passions of the Soul* intersects

Figure Intro.1. *René Descartes, 1596–1650, fransk filosof.* Copy after David Beck, Nationalmuseum, Stockholm. Photographer: Christophe Laurentin.

Figure Intro.2. *Portrait of Descartes*, by Frans Hals, Musée du Louvre, Paris.

Figure Intro.3. *Portrait of Descartes, the philosopher with a hat on the hands*, by Jonas Suyderhoff's engraving after Frans Hals's painting.

Figure Intro.4. *Portrait of Descartes* by Jan Baptist de Weenix, Centraal Museum, Holland.

with the sensual experiences of the *Meditations*, the optical descriptions of *Dioptrics* intersects with the figurative imagery in *Rules for the Direction of the Mind*, as does the natural philosophy of the *Meteorology*, and so on. To the features of a baroque aesthetics belong also a strand of the philosophically uncontained—the act of thinking is an aesthetic act to Descartes, who profoundly seized upon what a philosophical emotion might be.

* * *

For centuries the name of Descartes has been connected to the advantages and disadvantages of upholding a certain definition of reason as the guiding principle of philosophy. He is known and acknowledged as the father of modern rationalism and idealism. The famous Cartesian figure of the mind, rendered archetypically, frames modern rationality and sensibility with a spatial-temporal relation through which it has become possible to abduct the body from time and the soul from space. In the same spirit, Descartes is also known for his ambition to construe a "general science," a *mathesis universalis* that would cover everything that entitles "other sciences to be called branches of mathematics."[2] Descartes did indeed formulate new principles of mathematics, arithmetic, and perspective. His treatises on optics, physics, and meteors, as well as the modern foundation of metaphysics and cosmology and the intensive studies dedicated to anatomy and medicine, have often been seen in this vein. The legacy of Cartesian philosophy has been defined as the introduction into a technical and modern world that objectifies the human body for the promotion of scientific knowledge and economic exchanges.

To this view belongs also the idea that Descartes construed a subject ruled and regulated by a rational intellect that does not need sensibility to think nor the senses to take part in its adventures. The rational intellect is seen as disembodied and disincarnated, ruling the world from a point of view outside the world, from a worldless perspective or a perspective alienated from the world and from the earth, much like Hannah Arendt's conception[3] of a world alienated from finitude.[4]

Descartes was indeed explicitly looking for a fabulous Archimedean point, "one firm and immovable point in order to shift the entire earth."[5] Kafka described it as a point that was used against itself in a paradoxical conditioning of its own discovery.[6] The notion of "used against itself" can be seen as the price a modern rational intellect has to pay for its presumed freedom and autonomy, considering its own origins in a "will to attention" and "the act of judgment."[7] The Cartesian world is usually portrayed as a world of a rational intellect completely encapsulated in itself, detached from all exteriority, emerging from itself and nourishing itself by itself. Indexed by the Cartesian use of the pronoun *je* (in Latin, *ego*), *I*, when spoken aloud, becomes even more Cartesian in English: an "eye," or a gaze *to* the world that no longer needs to be *of* the world. Understood in this way, the Cartesian modern rational intellect obliges human existence to isolate itself from the universe, to metaphysical solipsism and egoism, through an alienation of the senses and of sensibility, of aisthesis, to use a Greek word. However, what this book will demonstrate is, from such a perspective, a return of the oppressed, which is inherent in Descartes's own reflections: a model of anatomy in which childhood memories of love and desire are retained as physiological traces and affect the mind at any time; and a metaphysics of thought in which emotions can at all times be retrieved. In this way, the in-betweens of Descartes's baroque aesthetics precedes not only the psychoanalytical experience of today but also the many turns that have been undertaken in contemporary phenomenology.

Both the analytic and the continental philosophical traditions have presented efforts in the last few decades to overcome the abyss between the intelligible and the sensible sustained by the Cartesian tradition.[8] Studies have shown that Descartes himself presents a solution to dualism in the six *Meditations of First Philosophy*, *Passions of the Soul*, and in his correspondence with Princess Elisabeth of Bohemia.[9] Others have tried to scrutinize the philosophical and metaphysical errors in Descartes's philosophy for the sake of reembodying and reincarnating Cartesian reason, laying ground for an indissoluble bond between mind and body, intellect and sensibility.[10] It is, for instance, fairly well known today that Descartes overcomes dualism by showing that body and mind are connected in everyday life and through the habits of a person. In addition, contemporary research has shown that Descartes problematized dualism within his own system.[11]

But the portrait of Descartes and Cartesian thought presented in this book wishes to show something else. Rather than solving the mind-body problem, from within Cartesian thought or beyond, this book delves into territories that have been given little attention: the baroque aesthetics through which emotions and affects, performative claims of thoughts and desires and instincts, are given expression and philosophical body. In recent years, there has been an increasing interest in Descartes's position regarding the literature, theater, and painting of his own times.[12] But no study has hitherto been published that solely focuses on Descartes as a writer who not only theorizes about aesthetic problems or experiences but also integrates an aesthetics in the layers of thought.

We have chosen to consider features in Descartes's images and writing that we designate as baroque. Baroque thought can be seen as an "invention of a language that allows to order the elements in a signifying system."[13] It can be seen as the "transcription" or "translation" of things,[14] through which a human intellect can think or sense what it has constructed by itself, to itself. Rather than presenting a baroque of the fold, as Deleuze did in his famous book on Leibniz, Descartes's rationalism opens an avenue to the baroque through a "liberation of forms" and an "infidelity" to the seen and the sensed. As such it fits right into contemporary aesthetic thought, opening avenues for a critical view on ideas of mimetic reproduction. This operates not only in Cartesian theories of the image but also in the experience of how thought moves and reflects itself. This book suggests that a Cartesian baroque aesthetics is not to be understood as a simple response to sensible afflictions. It is also not what overcomes the mind-body dualism. It is rather what lies between the dualisms that Descartes formulates throughout his writings. Therefore, the natural philosophy and the metaphysics are regarded as two wings of the same bird. Descartes is not only challenging his own dualism between mind and body but also passive and active, physical and metaphysical, inside and outside, child and adult, and so on.

The numerous states of in-between are an intrinsic feature of the Cartesian baroque. Cartesian thought manifests itself between imagery and writing, between different states of consciousness, between body and mind, even between the unborn fetus and the child. His writings construe an aesthetic machine of the physical, sensual, affective, and thinking body. This thinking body is a tool for empirical observation in studies such as *Optics* and *Meteorology*. But it is also a tool for aesthetic experiences of beauty and ugliness, pleasure, wonder, and shock in which the body is turned inside and out. We can detect a visceral aesthetics that surpasses any intellectual concept of judgment. Inside becomes outside, dream and reality shift places, love and hate trigger each other, and their origins are seen to be as fantasmatic as they are real. The visceral aesthetics also affects the metaphysics of Descartes. Cartesian thought has been construed as a thinking in images. However, as a form of reflection, the Cartesian experience of thinking being thought, the very movement of being thinking, produces what can be called a "philosophical emotion." Reading Descartes with critical attention to the movements of his thoughts means experiencing the emotion of a thought being thought—a philosophical emotion. Not only do emotions give rise to thoughts but also the movement of thinking arouses a particular emotion that has rarely been acknowledged. Through such movements, we approach a physical body in which affects and emotions have been inscribed in different layers—the aesthetic machine of a visceral aesthetics, of childhood memories, desires, and drives. The "aesthetic machine" intrudes also in the metaphysical subject. In this way, a baroque aesthetics is formed through the reflection of metaphysical thought sensing itself, as well as through the way in which the passions, or thought as "confused," to use Descartes' own expression, is seen to be afflicted by desires, instinct, and repressed memories that take body in the natural philosophy. In Cartesian baroque aesthetics, aesthetics is a domain of philosophical emotions, dreams, fantasies, and instincts. In this way, the metaphysics, the natural philosophy and the ethics of Descartes are deeply intertwined.

In chapter 1, Cecilia Sjöholm argues that the Cartesian baroque aesthetic passes through the visceral; an intertwinement of bodily fluids and traces of perception. States of consciousness (the "soul"), such as taking pleasure in beauty, are affected directly by traces of perception, some of which return to memories of infancy. In this way, beauty is not just a formal quality in objects; it can also be a subjective experience that appears contingent and surprising. Such an experience is attached to inscriptions of the mind that are not readily attainable to consciousness and are often directed toward a person. Descartes inscribes a breaking point between a scopic drive of fascination and a desire for the beautiful. An aesthetic experience derives as much from physical desire or drives of abhorrence (or an ambivalent mixture) as from a spark of spirit touching the senses. The experience of aesthetic phenomena—the beautiful and the ugly—originates in a corporeal inside that has been depicted in anatomical writings and imagery. In this way, Descartes's baroque aesthetics is situated at the roots of a tradition that includes later proponents such as Baudelaire, the surrealists, and psychoanalytic theory.

In chapter 2, Marcia Sá Cavalcante Schuback departs from some key passages from *Passions of the Soul* to show that the Cartesian *cogito* can hardly be understood without paying attention to the emotion of the soul, the philosophical emotion. She argues that the reflexivity that has been the key concept for centuries in the discussion of the cogito unveils rather a description of this emotion, the way it moves and is moved by the act and experience of thinking. Discussing some dominant views on immediate reflexivity and being in Descartes's philosophy, she pays attention to the gerundive mode in which the cogito is enounced and proposes some lines to reread in the central passages of the *Meditations on First Philosophy*.

In chapter 3, Marcia Sá Cavalcante Schuback develops the preceding discussions on Descartes's attention to the movement of thinking while thinking. The main claim is that Descartes's cogito is a performative thinking gesture. This attention involves a particular way of seeing, which Descartes conceives of as seeing the seeing. The author shows what kind of vision it is that sees the seeing and how it reveals the baroque aesthetics of Descartes's doctrine of vision. Descartes's theory of the eye and the spirit differs from Maurice Merleau-Ponty's, not by being too physical, as Merleau-Ponty argues, but on the contrary, by being deeply aesthetic but in a baroque mode. In this chapter, the author also presents a brief unwritten treatise on painting that lies encrypted in Descartes's thoughts.

In chapter 4, Cecilia Sjöholm reads *The Meteorology* (*Les Météores*) from 1637, one of the least commented works of Descartes. In grappling with atmospheric phenomena such as weather, light, and minerals, it evokes experimental perspectives on weather and climate. Human subjects cannot master the elements or predict the weather, Descartes tells us. It hits us, and we are subject to its vicissitudes. While offering a key to the composites of nature, Descartes's essay also pushes up against the limits of reason. In times of climate change and unpredictable variations in weather conditions, not least in the climate of the North, Descartes's treatise, written during the Little Ice Age, has gained newfound relevance. He presents us with the kind of transformations that a northern climate in particular materializes: weather consisting of small particles changing shape and movement, intertwining, interfering, and reorganizing. The discourses on snow, rain, and hail analyze drops in temperature dramatic enough to cause distinct shifts in size, movement, and organization. Through affects, flows, and rhythm, Descartes relies on lived experience and approaches the atmosphere as an aesthetic kind of organization, like music or painting. Rhythmic figurations in image and narrative intersect with sensual experience. Descartes posits a "full" universe of an infinite variety of aquatic shapes that move and transform. This semiontological version of a natural philosophy does not construe rhythmic figurations as illustrations of what it says. Rather, it relies on a rhythmic conception inherent in the description of the experience of weather and other atmospheric phenomena that belong to it.

In chapter 5, Marcia Sá Cavalcante Schuback argues that Descartes's cogito is a thinking view that is very close to what André Gide called "mise en abime" and that Flemish painters from Descartes's time used in sophisticated ways in their painting practices. In this chapter, the author proposes that Descartes's cogito perspective, which is the cogito of the thinking *while* thinking, cannot be central but must instead be considered anamorphic. Indeed, anamorphic in the sense of seeing very closely, as when hands drawing see lines being drawn while drawing. In reading passages from Descartes's work that connect the thinking movement to writing, the author also claims that Descartes's philosophical way of thinking is a thinking through writing hands. She presents the thesis that Descartes's philosophical thought should be understood in connection to writing, showing how writing is a form of thought and how philosophical thought performs in and through writing.

In chapter 6, Cecilia Sjöholm discusses how Descartes's anatomical writings and anatomical images engage questions on images and drives explored in contemporary psychoanalysis. The key word here is *gaze*. The speculation on the inside of the human body inscribes a scopic drive articulated through the dissection of eyes and heart, laying open the nervous system and the tubes of transport that run between brains and limbs. A gaze of fascination transcends the sheer anatomical aims of visualization. Descartes's inquiries into "inner images" can be explored through the psychoanalytical theory of the gaze. The Cartesian studies of various states of consciousness—such as the sleeping dream, the state between dreaming and wakefulness—takes us well beyond an analysis of consciousness. The multifaceted investigations of forms of consciousness can also be attached to corporeal instigations of affects and desires—the points at which mind and body are not simply separated, or simply joined, but overlaid with conflicts. In his writings *Treatise on Man*, *The Formation of the Foetus*, and *Passions of the Soul*, Descartes shows, similar to Sigmund Freud, that the subject that thinks and feels is rooted in biological life. This, in turn, suggests the existence of a theory of the drive presaging psychoanalysis.

In chapter 7, Cecilia Sjöholm shows how a Cartesian notion of the unconscious emerges with *Passions of the Soul* and other writings that differ from how the common psychoanalytic readings of Descartes have mainly focused on the split cogito identified by Jacques Lacan. Exploring the fetal state and the life of the infant, Descartes develops a notion of psychic life that touches on theories of repression, affects, and object relations. In this way, Descartes can be seen as a precursor to psychoanalysis. In Cartesian scholarship, his writings on the infant are usually quoted to demonstrate that the challenge to dualism is to be found in his own writings. But the same writings can also be seen to foreshadow the radical theories of the drive formulated by Freud and Melanie Klein. Descartes conceives of the relation between thought and emotions in a conception of the "thinking fetus." He finds that the infant is not simply attached to the maternal body through its needs. The infant is a subject of affects and emotions that develops in and with the maternal body. Sjöholm argues that the Cartesian notion of subjectivity connects to early psychoanalytic theories of repression, fantasy, and incorporation.

In chapter 8, Marcia Sá Cavalcante Schuback reads Descartes's thoughts of love and proposes a theory of Cartesian love. She argues that in the Cartesian conception of love, the dualism of body and soul can be rephrased in terms of the love between body and soul. Descartes's thoughts of love appear in his letters, and some letters can also be read as love letters, even if disguised due to respect, as he himself confesses. The author proposes a discussion about letters, love letters as a "means" of love, and presents views on why love longs for writing love letters. Here, it emerges that the experience of love, Cartesian love, is a love of the between, between body and soul, image and thought, vigil and sleep.

1 Descartes's Visceral Aesthetics

The Violence of the Beautiful and the Ugly

Cecilia Sjöholm

The Beautiful, the Sound, and the Music

One of the most basic doctrines in philosophical aesthetics is that modern aesthetics is born with the discovery of *taste*. Taste makes beauty into a pleasurable, subjective experience, rather than the property of an object. From Immanuel Kant's *Critique of Judgement* to contemporary neuroaesthetics, aesthetic experience is considered in terms of pleasure, enjoyment, and gratification in this tradition. It is also considered in terms that make it universal and ahistorical.[1] To Kant, disinterestedness guides the basic definition of aesthetic judgment.[2] Pleasure and beauty, in turn, are qualities that explain how and why humans "fit" into the world.[3] Contemporary neuroaesthetics, also, for which the experience of beauty can be associated with certain features of the brain, assumes that beauty arouses a feeling of pleasure that is independent of its source. It may connect to cognitive functions and to the intellect.[4] Still, although it can be attached to capacities beyond aesthetic experience—such as a cognitive value, for instance[5]—aesthetic experience is best explained as a kind of harmonization of a state of consciousness: free and playful.

A Cartesian aesthetics, however, is at odds with such an idea of harmonization. Pleasure and beauty are at the forefront of aesthetic inquiries—together with the introduction of taste. However, in exploring experiences of poetry, images, and music, Descartes also shows how bodies are gripped by affects and desires that lie beyond rational control. Reading Descartes, we move in a pre-Kantian universe where relations between bodies create an order of nature that affects the mind (as in, e.g., G. W. Leibniz, Thomas Hobbes, and Baruch Spinoza).[6] But Descartes's writings are not only exploring affects; they are also exploring aesthetic experiences. They explore the subject of aesthetics as a baroque organism with many layers, as a thinking and sensing subject endowed with an enigmatic physicality that surpasses the certainty of reason. The open reflections on and of such an embodied subject of affects are layered "as in a picture" and "as a fable."[7]

Descartes was actively involved in the ordering, and sometimes the sketching, of images that followed his natural philosophy. Some sketches have been retained. Descartes's images of human anatomy, in text and sketches, are not formed to understand the body as an object. They are construed to understand human affects, emotions, and thoughts. The body, Descartes says in *De L'Homme*, is a "statue ou machine de terre," a statue or a machine of the earth.[8] But Descartes's man-machine is not a self-regulating organism—it is an aesthetic machine, energizing the interaction between bodies, objects, and phenomena, as well as between the senses, affects, and thought. In the explorations of such an aesthetic machine, Descartes shows how what we usually describe as aesthetic phenomena emerging from sound, vision, and touch may give rise to experiences that in turn are intrinsically related to imaginative explorations of anatomy and physical experiences. In works such as *The Passions of the Soul*, Descartes describes both a warm experience of beauty and a physical abhorrence of the ugly—and an ambiguous mixture of both. In Descartes's writings overall, such as the *Meditations*, experiences of this kind may become subject to reflection. In *Passions of the Soul*, however, they are reflected in thought and intrinsically intertwined with drives that originate in a corporeal inside, described through an anatomical imagery. They also determine the character of Descartes's aesthetic machine, which allows for the contour of a subject to emerge, but it is a subject to be understood as something wholly other than a subject of reflective judgment. Descartes construes an aesthetic subject otherwise than in eighteenth-century thought. Rather than focus on experiences of the beautiful, this "other" subject/aesthetic machine gives prominence to phenomena that appeal less to taste and judgment and more to drives and corporeal affects: evoking the fascinated gaze, corporeal attraction, and revulsion; undoing the limits between physics and metaphysics, inside and outside. These are the typical features of a baroque design of thought—the aesthetic machine is a "body-thought," which is not to say it allows for a coherent theory. It is rather the result of a dualism that sometimes grasps itself beyond the borders of separation, sometimes morphs into new categories. The aesthetic machine can be observed throughout many of Descartes's writings, in various guises. Traversing Descartes's mechanistic, rationalistic, and metaphysical universe in its various stages of development, it opens a visceral dimension of aesthetic experience where the encounter with sensual objects is colored by physical sensations. The visceral, in this context, can be understood in a literal sense: bearing on a gut-like sensation that appears as an instinctual apprehension of the world, through attraction and repulsion.

A philosophical history of aesthetics that sticks only to the discovery of taste and judgment and the philosophy of beauty and pleasure as its origin risks overwriting a long and powerful tradition that attaches aesthetic experiences to powerful, corporeal affects. Therefore, it is important to discuss Descartes's writings on the physical sensations that can be offered by the beautiful and the ugly, or by phenomena and artifacts that we consider as art, as exercises in a pre-Kantian aesthetics. This chapter endeavors to demonstrate that Descartes's writings, although they may well in certain places reflect on taste, pleasure, and beauty in a more contained manner, belong rather to a tradition that uses the body's whole capacity in order to explain the nature of perception and affect.

Descartes is the well-known progenitor of Maurice Merleau-Ponty's much commented struggle to understand the nature of modern painting as the undoing of "scientific" perspectives, bringing painting back to a body where the senses interact in an open intertwinement with the world. However, Merleau-Ponty's attention to Descartes's theory of perception has in many ways overshadowed the physical, visceral theory of the body of the latter. In the arts, Descartes can rather be counted into a corporeal tradition where embodiment and art are intrinsically enmeshed, an aesthetic tradition counting writers such as Charles Baudelaire and Georges Bataille, artists such as the surrealists, and psychoanalytic critics such as Julia Kristeva among its modern proponents. This is a tradition when the sheer corporality of aesthetic experiences overtakes what we talk about as judgment, when the abhorrence and fascination with corporeal phenomena such as ugliness, death, putrification, and so on is forwarded as the "other" side of pleasure and beauty, but equally relevant to art. Throughout history, this "other" aesthetics of the drives has been forwarded as major components in and of a history of the arts, talked about in terms of sublimity, the formless or abjection. In the case of Descartes, it comes to the fore as visceral components, through which a complex, corporeal "inside" with a hidden pattern of tubes, connections, and fluids connect with the sensual and emotional experiences that art gives rise to. In this way, the aesthetic machine of Descartes has given rise to a visceral aesthetics.

Descartes scholars have pointed to the fact that he may be considered a progenitor of a notion of the aesthetic.[9] But the extent to which such a visceral aesthetics develops as a baroque fantasy of hidden connections, between his early writings and the anatomy assumed in *Passions of the Soul*, remains to be explored. It manifests itself between imagery and writing, between different states of consciousness, between body and mind, even between the unborn fetus and the child. The numerous states of in-between are an intrinsic feature of Descartes's thought. Through a complex map where the internal is externalized and even metaphorized, Descartes's writings construe a body that is not only physical, sensual, and affective but also thinking and memorializing. The body is an object for empirical observation in studies such as *Optics* and *Description of the Human Body*. It is also used to understand the experiences offered with encounters of beauty and ugliness, pleasure, wonder, and shock. These experiences are situated in a domain in-between, or even turn dualisms inside and out: in these writings, we can detect a visceral aesthetics that surpasses any intellectual concept of judgment.

Affects and emotions are the key to Descartes's baroque aesthetics: belonging to the zone of the in-between, they are both body and mind, both outer and inner. They belong to the makeup of an internal world in the same way that memories, dreams, and fantasies do, but they also belong to the world of the senses and the apprehension of the body. Emotions are described as "internal sensations" that can be stored in corporeal memory. But they are also "confused thoughts."[10] Emotions, internal images, fantasies, and dreams are all forms of thought. In the exploration of this aesthetic universe, one can attend to one's own emotions as a corporeal form of thinking, both subjective and universal. Emotions and affects, after all, are an area in which everyone, and no one, is an expert. One does not need to be a philosopher to know what an affect feels like, and everyone may reflect on the quality of an emotional experience.

Therefore, rather than wishing to alleviate the burden of affects from the understanding of subjective life, Descartes welcomes the stirring of emotions. Affects may change our perceptions of the world and our thoughts about it. The agitation of the body is not detrimental to thought. The arts that produce emotions and affects do not so much teach us something specific as allow for new sensations and thoughts. In the so-called Olympian dreams of 1619, a recount of a dream that has been preserved as manuscript, Descartes praised poetry for being "full of sayings, more serious, more sensible, and better expressed than those found in the writings of the philosophers."[11] Poetry helps distill one's judgment, not by controlling emotions or preventing affects but by evoking them.[12] In this way, the universe of thought is also expanded through aesthetic convulsions.

The visceral dimensions in Descartes's writings assume the aesthetic domain to be very powerful—perhaps this is also what brings it beyond judgment. The encounter with the beautiful and the ugly in Descartes's writings can be highly conflictual, possibly even devastating. Described in terms of desire/love or devastation/repulsion, Descartes's visceral aesthetics has its origin in the desire of a subject exploring affects that lie beyond the control of the subject. Such desire derives from an unknown origin that can be traced back to an archaic prehistory of the body. This archaic prehistory has the potentiality of coloring all aesthetic experience with a certain ambiguity, even with a certain potentiality of violence. It can make the beautiful appear as miraculous, but also haunting. It can make the ugly be experienced not only as the opposite of the beautiful but also as a direct threat to mind and body.

Descartes's first philosophical treatise was, indeed, on an aesthetic topic—namely, on music: *Compendium Musicae, Abregé de Musique*, written in 1618. In many ways, the treatise offers a square and simple conception of aesthetics, such as it was picked up later in the field by thinkers such as Alexander Baumgarten and Immanuel Kant—it has to do with the judgment and understanding of sensory phenomena, producing a particular kind of knowledge. Descartes's treatise begins by establishing that "all senses are capable of producing pleasure." Music is the producer of sounds, made to "please and to arouse various emotions in us."[13] In a famous letter to Marin Mersenne from 1630, where he returns to the arguments of his old essay, concepts of judgment and taste are introduced even more clearly than in the essay itself: "What makes some people want to dance may make others want to cry." In other words, we do not experience aesthetic phenomena in the same way.[14] Concepts such as "beautiful" and "pleasing," Descartes writes, signify a relation between our judgment and an object. But because men's judgments are so various, there cannot be any definite standard of beauty or "pleasingness."[15] From this perspective, Descartes is forwarding an aesthetics of judgment, taste, and pleasure, such as was later developed by eighteenth-century philosophers.

However, what distinguishes Descartes from the tradition of aesthetics that developed later, and offers a vision of baroque complexity, is the way in which he describes the judgment of sensual phenomena to be situated in a body whose needs and drives are not always disclosed. In the early work of *Compendium Musicae*, this derives from the fact that the body is inscribed into a worldview that is seemingly both Pythagorean and mechanistic, where mathematic figures can be used to determine the outcome of sound and to predict the way in which bodies are affected by music. Unlike the ancient school of Pythagoreans, however, Descartes refers to arithmetic rather than geometrics as the tool of understanding when it comes to how sounds are produced and experienced: lines and numbers help us conceive of the spatial and temporal proportionality that determines the outcome of rhythms and chords. Through figures and lines, Descartes refers to aesthetic experiences not to confirm but rather to refute a mechanistic worldview, undoing, as in the famous letter to Mersenne, afforded ideas that the impact of sound and rhythm is automatic. The use of figures in the treatise may well throw light on the way in which aesthetic experience became an increasingly complex issue to Descartes. He repeatedly returned to the idea that the craft of art was crucial for the transmittance of his ideas. The experience of artists (artisans) and musicians, combined with a grasp of mathematics, he argues, provides us with better knowledge of cosmological shapes and "consonances" in music than the senses alone, or the "imagination of a hermit."[16] The particular combination of mathematics and imagery is superior to scholastic reasoning: it is better to insert nature in philosophy than philosophy in nature. This is done through the image: "I believe that nothing can be imagined that cannot be solved by a line," he writes to friend and mathematician Isaac Beeckman, to whom the treatise on music is also dedicated.[17] The lines of imaginative solutions are arithmetic images—used

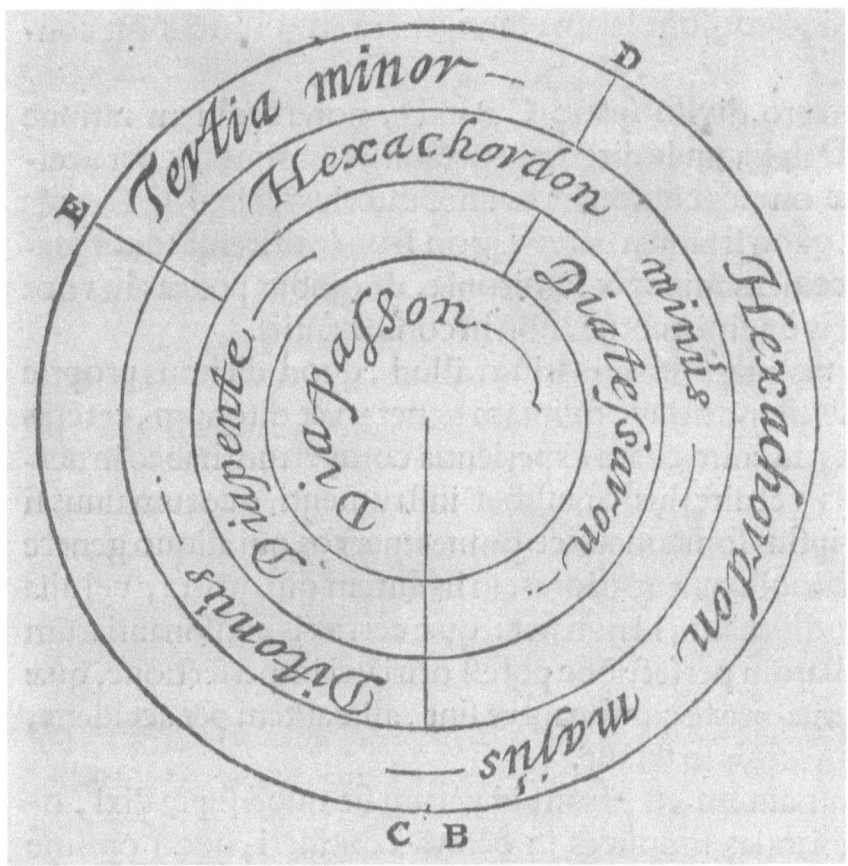

Figure 1.1. *Musicae compendium, Trajecti ad Renum*, 1650, Royal library Stockholm.

to explain phenomena of light, colors, atmospheric movements, natural formations, sound and music, and so on.[18] In this way, the analysis of string diversion, voices, bass sound, and more are the result of an analysis of proportion and difference that attempts to grasp the domain of the in-between through figures—music not only strikes the soul but also enwraps the body.

Already in his treatise on music, Descartes introduces figures as a key to understanding worldly phenomena: figures capture the physical identities of shape, size, and motion. The line of a figure can capture the motion of music, implicating music's impact on a body through invisible discretions. Distinct rhythms are used in dance, where the motion of our bodies is "naturally impelled by the music"—we are stricken by "sounds on all sides."[19] This immersion carries its own moods: a faster rhythm creates joy; a slower rhythm invokes fear, sadness, and so

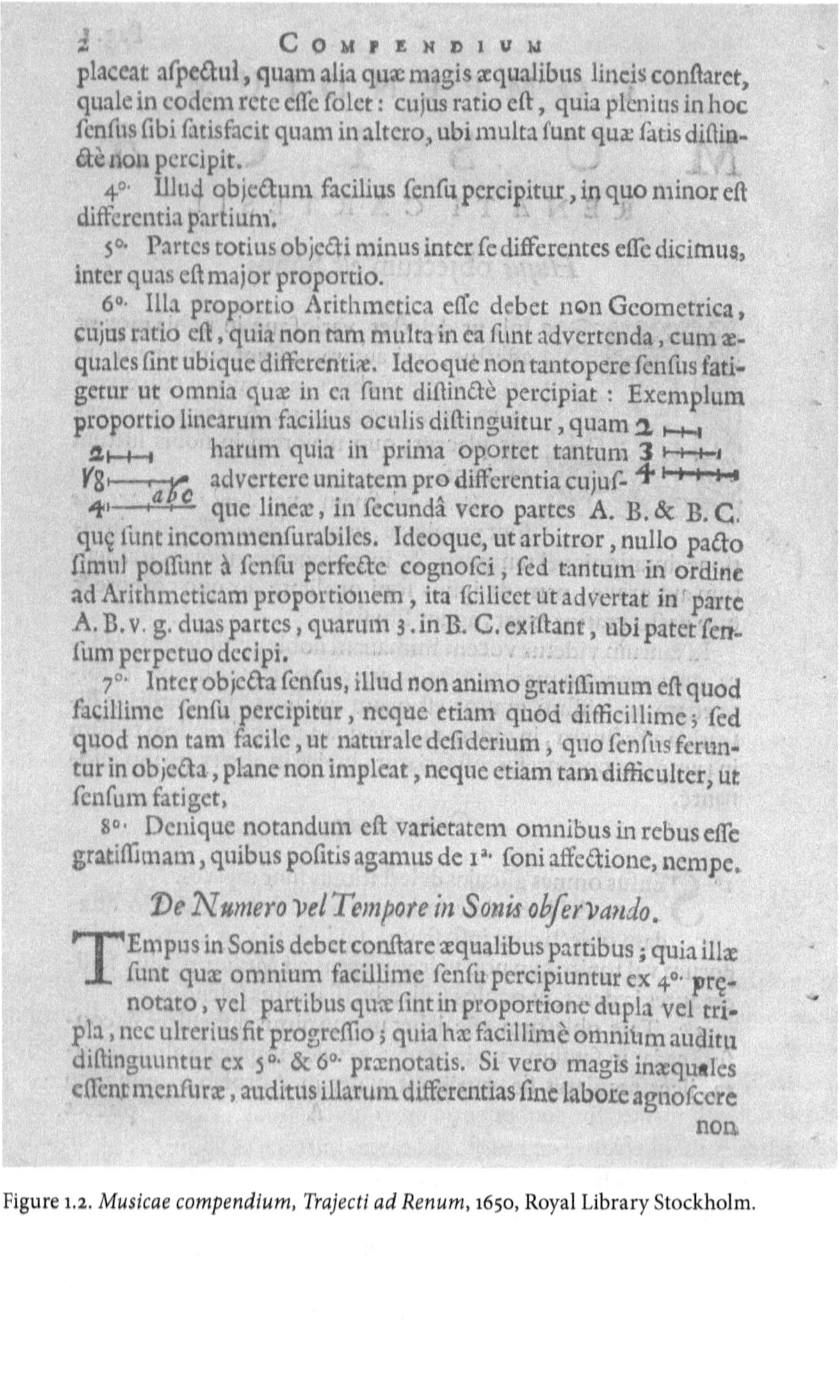

Compendium

placeat aspectui, quam alia quæ magis æqualibus lineis constaret, quale in eodem rete esse solet: cujus ratio est, quia plenius in hoc sensus sibi satisfacit quam in altero, ubi multa sunt quæ satis distincte non percipit.

4°· Illud objectum facilius sensu percipitur, in quo minor est differentia partium.

5°· Partes totius objecti minus inter se differentes esse dicimus, inter quas est major proportio.

6°· Illa proportio Arithmetica esse debet non Geometrica, cujus ratio est, quia non tam multa in ea sunt advertenda, cum æquales sint ubique differentiæ. Ideoque non tantopere sensus fatigetur ut omnia quæ in ea sunt distincte percipiat: Exemplum proportio linearum facilius oculis distinguitur, quam 2 ⊢⊣
harum quia in prima oportet tantum 3 ⊢⊢⊣
advertere unitatem pro differentia cujus- 4 ⊢⊢⊢⊣
que lineæ, in secundâ vero partes A. B. & B. C. quę sunt incommensurabiles. Ideoque, ut arbitror, nullo pacto simul possunt à sensu perfecte cognosci, sed tantum in ordine ad Arithmeticam proportionem, ita scilicet ut advertat in parte A. B. v. g. duas partes, quarum 3. in B. C. existant, ubi patet sensum perpetuo decipi.

7°· Inter objecta sensus, illud non animo gratissimum est quod facillime sensu percipitur, neque etiam quod difficillime; sed quod non tam facile, ut naturale desiderium, quo sensus feruntur in objecta, plane non impleat, neque etiam tam difficulter, ut sensum fatiget,

8°· Denique notandum est varietatem omnibus in rebus esse gratissimam, quibus positis agamus de 1ª· soni affectione, nempe.

De Numero vel Tempore in Sonis observando.

Tempus in Sonis debet constare æqualibus partibus; quia illæ sunt quæ omnium facillime sensu percipiuntur ex 4°· pręnotato, vel partibus quæ sint in proportione dupla vel tripla, nec ulterius fit progressio; quia hæ facillime omnium auditu distinguuntur ex 5°· & 6°· prænotatis. Si vero magis inæquales essent mensuræ, auditus illarum differentias sine labore agnoscere

non

Figure 1.2. *Musicae compendium, Trajecti ad Renum*, 1650, Royal Library Stockholm.

on. In addition, rhythm (time) creates a sense of pleasure in itself: a wish to dance, to enjoy. Music affects the body. This is also why music—particularly rhythmic music—can be used in military training.[20] The idea of how to use music to produce a certain corporeal affectation can be put to the test—Descartes himself likely wrote the *Ballet for the Birth of Peace* under the requisition of Queen Christina when he arrived in Stockholm in 1649. The intention was to glorify a powerful regime—the music was to encompass the immobile presence of Christina herself in the middle of the scene at its staging. In this way, the rhythm, movements, and sounds were to fuse a sense of passion and power.[21]

But whereas music can be used to evoke certain moods, its effects are also individual, as Descartes writes to Mersenne. The experience of pleasure that derives from music has to do with a complex interaction between ideas and sensibility. The way in which tones and rhythms are perceived is associated with ideas. This has most often been interpreted as having to do with taste. But whether we enjoy dancing depends not so much on a free-floating imagination as on traces inscribed in the body—memories evoked by music.[22] Music attaches to the visceral domain of the body, to its inside. The joy, pleasure, sublimity, or memory of music has nothing to do with any transcendental emotive sphere beyond language. The passions evoked by music are aroused through a complex system of tubes and traces that attaches body and brain to one another.

In other early texts, such as *Treatise on Man*, this is made visible through a model of the body as an aesthetic machine.[23] Descartes compares the body to musical instruments played near fountains or in the church. The machine of the body-instrument is made to facilitate the flow of spirits—which in Descartes's imagery corresponds to the sounding of the pipes. Three distinct entities are used in the consideration of the aesthetic machine: bodily organs, fluids, and animal spirits—the latter causing internal sensations in us through the way air is moved around in cavities and inner tubes by the pressure caused by internal "bellows" or "wind chests" and distributed in different pipes by the way in which an internal organist "moves his finger on the keyboards," distributing the air in different keys. This causes a mixture of affects, such as desire and diligence, but also malice and ruthlessness.[24] The internal activity of the aesthetic machine is always alive, through dreams and sleep as well as intense daytime pursuits. It is, however, distinguishing the states of sleep and wake, through the way in which these states affect the brain in different ways. The most important activity in the state of wake is "how ideas of objects are formed in the place assigned to the imagination and to the common sense, how these ideas are retained in the memory, and how they cause the movement of all the bodily parts."[25] The difference between the states of sleep and wake is also distinctly drawn as the difference between a machine with "open" pipes of perception and a closed system.

18 | Through the Eyes of Descartes

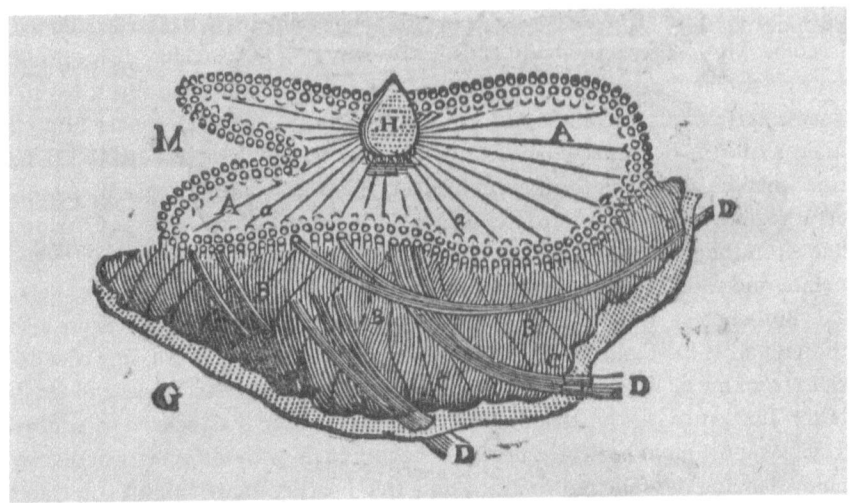

Figure 1.3. *L'Homme: Et un traitté de la formation du foetus*, Paris, 1664, Royal Library Stockholm.

The aesthetic machine is integrating the perception of objects with ideas so that the soul may experience movement, size, distance, colors, sounds, smells, and other aesthetic qualities, linking them to physical sensations as well as emotions. In this aesthetic machine, the sensation of colors is distributed through the same channels as physical sensations of the body, such as pleasure and pain. This is done primarily through the imagination, or the complex machinery of the apprehension of objects, and not through the direct imprint in the brain of traces of perception.[26] Objects, and our perception of objects in the world, may act in radically different ways: they may impinge on us and enwrap our beings entirely, or they may be perceived as distant and less important; they may cause rage or joy, sadness or laughter. Moods and affects are closely intertwined with perception. In this way, we are, as aesthetic machines, not self-enclosed systems. Instead, we are, through our emotions and affects, wholly with the world. The subject is never just perceiving or sensing in a neutral manner; it is perceiving and sensing through moods and affects, and through the capacities of imagination and memory. Our bodies are permeated by the "pipes" that play us with and through every perception, to the extent that we were affected even as infants in our mothers' wombs. It is in this way that Descartes's body is aesthetic: open to the world, even unshielded from its affective impacts. As it acts on us, we are brought to states of emotions and affects that may even play violently with us. This does not mean, however, that the machine can be described to act causally on sensations or perceptions—we are played also in our dreams, where the very

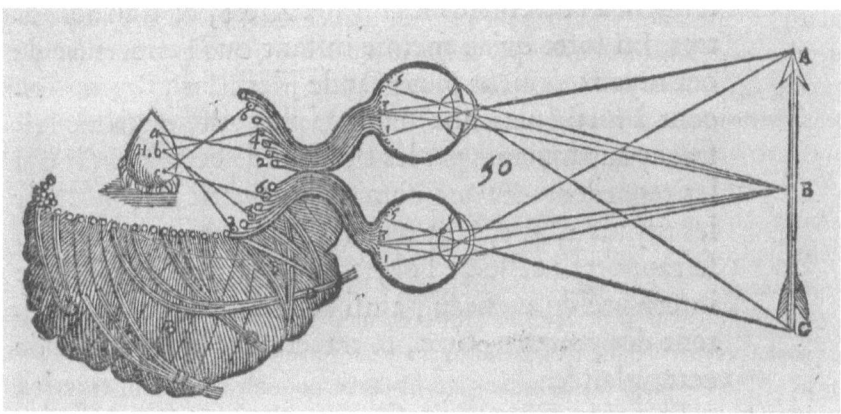

Figure 1.4. *L'Homme: Et un traitté de la formation du foetus*, Paris, 1664, Royal Library Stockholm.

ideas of objects may change, and the mood, the affect, and the physical impression are juxtaposed in a new way.

The Anatomy of Affects

The seventeenth century can be characterized as a visual culture.[27] Physiology's birth was copresent with its graphic description and the visual figuring of structures and processes inside the body. In the seventeenth century, there was no clear-cut distinction between a philosopher and a scientist—and in a way, an artist. The categorization of disciplines did not resemble those of today. But Descartes is the only philosopher to have explicitly philosophized not only with but through physical images. These are not for decoration: Descartes is producing a visceral aesthetic where the relation between affect and perception is a production of image as much as of thought. Descartes was himself involved in the production of graphic forms from the early 1630s, in works such as *Le Monde* (published posthumously in 1664) and *L'Homme* (published posthumously in 1662). Sketches and engravings were not typically made by Descartes but by artists in close collaboration with him and his editor. Many of the images pertained to the relation between perception and the inside of the human body: the brain, the eye globe, and nerves were revealed in detail. This pictorial imagination of inside/outside returns in *Passions*, even if the images there come as textual constructions rather than sketches by Descartes's hand.

As Merleau-Ponty has shown in his essay on Paul Cézanne's painting, modern art has helped capture the difference between the "prescientific" conditioning of our perception and the renaissance scientific perspective that opened with the use of geometry, for instance. Cézanne, as a pioneer of modern painting, did not try to use color to *suggest* the tactile sensations that would give shape and depth. These "distinctions between sight and touch are unknown in primordial perception. It is only as a result of a science of the human body that we finally learn to distinguish between our senses."[28] In this way, we may experience depth, surfaces, smoothness, or hardness through vision, vision contributing to a grasp of the world in which all the senses interact. Showing in his text on "Cézanne's Doubt" how modern art offers not only the suggestion of a world but also an actual opening of and into a world, Merleau-Ponty distinguishes such a world from reason's science. Modern painting, in this way, offers a world through a prescientific grasp of perception. However, in Descartes's anatomy, where perception is construed in pictorial manners in the form of a scientific imagination, as joined to the pipes inside organs, for instance, not only do the senses interact in the construction of this very picture but their affective capacity meets the eye of the reader and beholder. The visceral is seen, felt, and understood through this conjunction of sensual, affective, and imaginative experience, indicating that the scientific imagination of Descartes cannot do without its prescientific suggestion of corporeal anatomy and its suggestion of shapes, sizes, and motion.

Modern art's prescientific vision, as evoked by Merleau-Ponty, is colored by its opening toward a world in which nature demands to be thought through color, form, density, and depth, seen by and intertwined with the body and vision of the painter. From such a point of view, the pictorial universe of Cartesian anatomy can easily be discarded as reason's grappling with an objectified body. But Descartes's images of human anatomy, in text and pictorial outlays, are not construed to be understood merely as models of the sciences, observable and objectifiable. The inside of the body is, as we have shown, construed as an aesthetic machine. It orchestrates the intrinsic interaction between the shape and movement of the particles of the world and that of the sensorial and affective capacity of the human body. In opening the dwindling effects that emerge when the light and motion of vision meet the pressure of internal juices speeding through the "pipes" of our bodies' internal organs, the pictorial imagination is construing the shape and movement through which senses and affect intertwine. In the anatomical images, we encounter not reason so much as an opening to the world that Descartes's pictorial eyes, so poignantly shown to be sometimes open to the world and sometimes attentive to the body's own inside, attempt to capture. Phenomenology's transcendental understanding of what it means to "see" the world may be more sophisticated in explaining the way in which embodiment both limits and makes possible such a vision. But Descartes's pictorial imagination, though perhaps claiming a certain universal hypothesis of how the eye captures the object of vision, is still, through its metaphors, its descriptions, and its dwindling use of figures of motions and shapes, producing what phenomenology calls a lived body, experiencing the magic of its own inside.

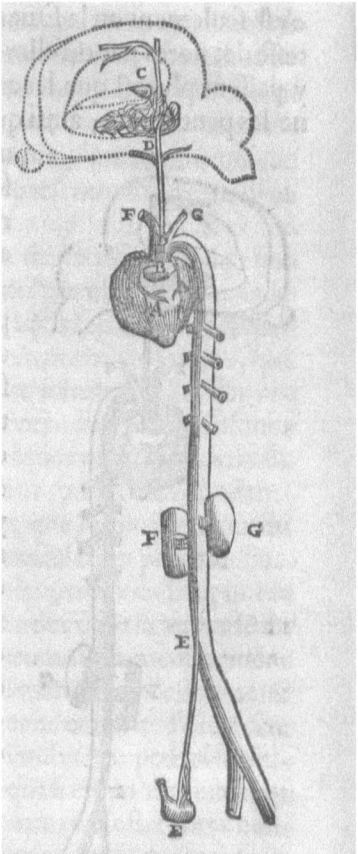

Figure 1.5. *L'Homme: Et un traitté de la formation du foetus*, Paris, 1664, Royal Library Stockholm.

In more recent developments of the phenomenological notion that art can produce a world in which the senses interact, affects are also introduced. Vivian Sobchack has shown how cinematic perception involves us in aesthetic forms of experience that are multisensorial. In film, affect becomes a thematizing tool of the narration; we are affected not just at the level of consciousness but at a sensorial level where the senses interact with the quality and nature of our affects.[29] In this way, the corporeal rootedness of perception is shown to be intrinsically intertwined with physical affects. Not only do we feel sad, happy, etcetera when we go to the movies: as our eyes "touch" the screen, the cinematic experience makes us fear and enjoy at a physical level.

Again, although not recognizing the limits of a subject's sensual experience or production of the world, it is precisely this corporeal intertwinement between figure, passion, and perception that Descartes is seeking to produce. His anatomical images offer the keyholes through which we may perceive the conjunction between perceptive and affective capacities, while producing these capacities through his pictorial imagination. The explanations of what occurs inside the body when external stimuli affect skin and nerves are long and detailed. With the visceral material and his detailed description and imagery of viscerality, we are given an account of how feelings are produced. As readers, we look and assess and are caught in a logic where the internal affects may also be felt in the reading process—in the early copies of Descartes's pictorial work with *The Treatise on Man*, for instance, the same image of a fire burning a human being could be repeated over several pages in order to amplify the physical sensation of pain. Fire is here a sign of pain that the reader turns to affect, a sign that becomes what Brian Massumi has described as a kind of command, a sign transformed into experience that bustles over into other affects: fear, a sense of threat, nervosity, and so on, a semiosis through which the subjective and the communal intertwine.[30]

Passions of the Soul, published in 1649, is pursuing the ambition to sketch the aesthetic machine of a sensing human body of affects. It does not itself hold images but is a direct consequence of the earlier anatomical work—and its aesthetic components. It is also a direct consequence of Descartes's own interest in and involvement with the arts. His theory of affects and emotions was widely used and interpreted by the musicians and performers of the Cartesian afterworld.

A copy of the book held in the Royal Library in Stockholm, the city where Descartes passed away in 1650, bears witness to his involvement in the arts. The copy is said to have been presented to a famous Dutch painter, David Beck, who also painted a portrait of Descartes. The copy bears witness to the kind of environment in which Descartes was situated, depicting a court of painters and scientists surrounding Queen Christina. Descartes was called to Christina's court to start an academy of the sciences, something he subtly refused by authoring statutes that forbade foreign members. Descartes had ideas that border on what would be considered artistic research today, wanting to educate artists in different mediums and techniques with professors who were knowledgeable not only in the arts but also mathematics and physics. In a treatise ascribed to Descartes depicting a possible project for a school of the arts, mixing artists and scientists, professors would be able "to answer all the artists' questions, to give them a reason for things" so that the artists could "give birth to new discoveries in the arts."[31] Even if Descartes may never have held a possible project for himself in that vein, his own writings clearly demonstrate that

Descartes's Visceral Aesthetics | 23

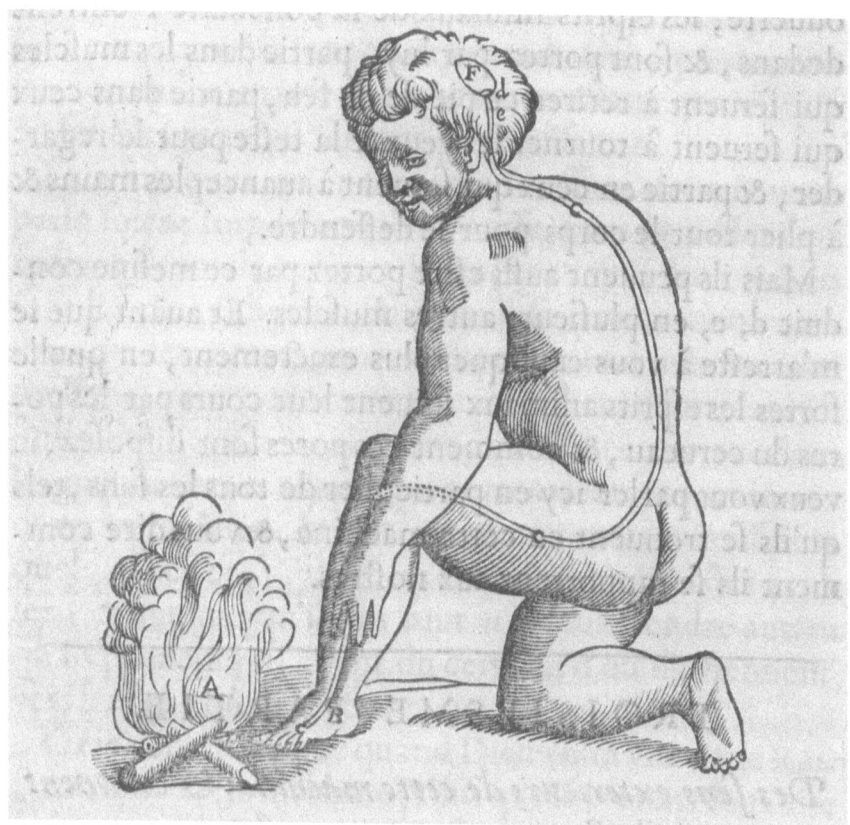

Figure 1.6. *L'Homme: Et un traitté de la formation du foetus*, Paris, 1664, Royal Library Stockholm.

the work of the artist is closely related to the work of the natural philosopher—the *physicien*.

In the original print of *Les Passions de l´âme*, as offered to the painter David Beck at Queen Christina's court by Descartes himself, the introduction is written as a fictive exchange of letters. Here Descartes declares that his book is intended for a wider audience—not expert philosophers. He is exploring the passions not "en orateur" or as "philosophe moral" but as a "physicien."[32] He is not writing as a rhetorician or a Stoic, which was the moral philosophy prevalent at the time. Detaching himself from the school of Stoicism, he wishes to ground the understanding of affects in natural philosophy. The self-definition of the *physicien*, or natural philosopher, must be read in conjunction with the gaze that permeates the whole book; Descartes "reads" affects from inside the body, through a pictorial imagination transmitted by the text, in terms of their visceral impact. In fact, one cannot underestimate the impact of anatomical drawings from other works. *Passions* is not a book of images—but older works such as *L'Homme* were, and the images of such works form a distinct background to the text of *Passions*. The body's inside, the relation between organs, is visualized to understand the affective relation of the human body to an outside.

The visceral aesthetics of *Treatise on Music* is, as we have seen, conceived through figures. The visceral aesthetics of *Passions of the Soul*, in turn, is primarily construed after such an anatomy. Mostly, Descartes adheres to the most typical motives in seventeenth-century medical imagery. His descriptions of organs and tubes belong to a visual literature based not only on evidence and observation but also on a tradition of imagination and aesthetic pedagogy. Descartes took inspiration from, most notably, William Harvey's work on the circulation of the blood, echoing precedents such as Harvey's *De Motu Cordis*, from 1628. Harvey's work, in turn, echoes that of slightly posterior publications of contemporaries, such as Olof Rudbeck's *Disputatio anatomica, de circulatione sangvinis*, from 1652.[33] In this way, images were an integrated aspect of what it meant for Descartes to work "like a physicien": the images of the human body wholly permeated his ideas of perception, emotions, and affects. When Descartes writes that he wants to examine the emotions like a physicien, his role as a physicien is already mediated by visual imagery.

This graphic intertwinement between images and thought also had repercussions in the heated debate on the relation between body and soul, or mind.[34] Famously, *Passions of the Soul* was written as the result of an exchange with Elisabeth of Bohemia, who was unsatisfied with Descartes's material dualism, asking for a clarification on how a possible union between the two could be conceived.[35] This was in itself a motive for exploring the human body and the mind, from the inside in graphic detail. In *Meditations*, Descartes presented the "I" of the *cogito* as a "thing that thinks: that is, a thing that doubts, affirms, denies, understands a few things, that is ignorant of many [that loves, that hates], is willing, is unwilling, and also which imagines and has sensory perceptions."[36] The subject of *Passions* does the same: it reflects on the relation between its sensibility and its emotions, and in doing so, its visceral language points to the kind of causality accounted for in the early images of the internal body.

Produced both in text and image in works such as *Treatise on Man, Optics*, and *Description of the Human Body*, the anatomical studies establish a link between the somatic and the psychic, between body and gaze. The speculation on the inside of the human body lays open the nervous system and the tubes of transport that run between brain and eyes, blood vessels and heart. In *Passions of the Soul*, the ideas and images of transport are iterated—but also further qualified. Speaking of emotions that are, so to speak, internally raised but still felt in the body, the book is distinguishing passions of the soul proper, or what we would perhaps rather call emotions—joy, love, sadness, and so on—and affects such as fear, that have a more physical side. For that reason, *Passions* may, ironically, appear to be even more caught in the very dualistic system that Descartes himself wishes to overcome. We must learn to distinguish, separate, and reflect on what feelings do to us through the nervous system and through the brain. And what Descartes presents us with is how such distinctions and reflections can be made. The aesthetic machine is a dual system that is reflective of itself; feelings have a passive side, as passions, and an active side, which makes us act on what they do to us.

The problem of how the reflective system can be formed, distinguishing emotions and affects and yet showing their production as aspects of the aesthetic machine, is not altogether new to Descartes. As early as 1642 in his *Principles of Philosophy*, Descartes proposes a link, although a conflictual one, between body and soul as we are hit by passions. Here he presents a difference between affects that are mere bodily affectations and passions of the soul, that are "the feelings of love, hate, fear, anger, etc." They are, he argues, "confused thoughts which the mind has not from itself alone, but from its being closely joined to the body, from which it receives impressions." These are very different from our knowledge of "what is to be embraced, or desired or shunned," or what we today would call affects that have a physical cause of stimulation.[37] In other words, affects have a cognitive side—we learn what to avoid and what to search for.

But in *Passions*, Descartes also describes how we may learn something from what we today would consider emotions, that have no obvious causal relation to a stimuli. This is also what may explain its tremendous impact over the centuries within the arts—emotions are what the arts produce. In times largely dominated by poetic regulations and rules—even in the performative arts, which was itself involved in exploring the passions—Descartes affirmed their emotional dimension. Its tremendous impact over the centuries was enforced with it being taken up by Charles Le Brun in *Méthode pour apprendre à dessiner les passions* (1698), produced with famous engravings of the expression of love, anger, wonder, and horror. Descartes's text and Le Brun's images were consequently much used in the visual and performing arts.

In its later editions, books II and III of *Passions of the Soul*, where we find the famous catalog of emotions, Le Brun's drawings established a much-used view of the relation between performativity and emotion. The idea that passions can be figured in and through the masks of the theater has a long history, originating with Xenophon. But *Passions of the Soul* formulated a "doctrine of emotions" that was at once philosophical, scientific, and aesthetic in its approach; therefore, it came to be widely used in baroque theater, music, and literature.[38] The translation between text (Descartes) and graphic work (Le Brun) contributed to the creation of a new point of reference in which affective and emotional physiology

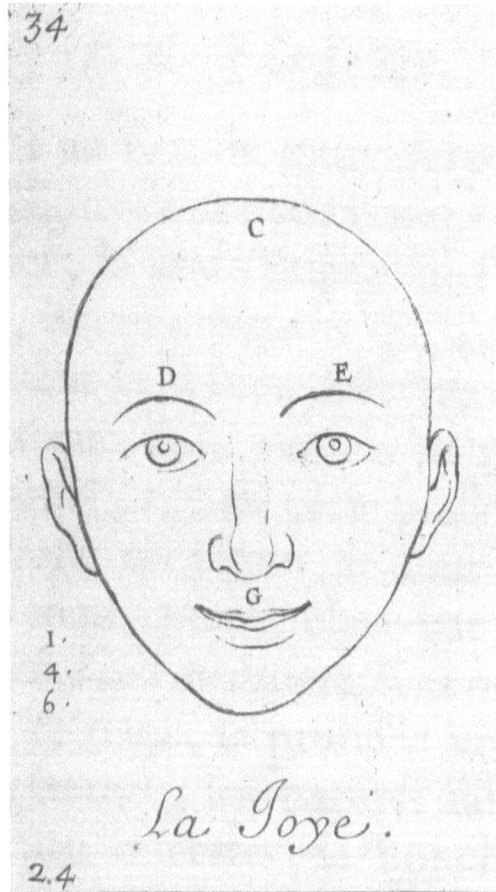

Figure 1.7. Charles Le Brun: *Conférence sur l'expréssion générale et particulière*, Paris, 1698, Royal Library Stockholm.

became aesthetic. What we see and experience in our mind is dependent on external forms of visualization of the soul: faces, movements, and gestures speak to us through sighs, tears, and laughter. Affects may be grounded in bodily movements, caused by stimuli, but it is the soul that speaks to the body proper. In the theater, body and mind are conjoined. This is also what makes the arts a venue for new forms of knowledge.

As Stephen Gobert has noted, Descartes's explorations of the passions allowed for emotions to be perceived not only as embodied but also as subjective and unique—in this capacity, they contributed to highlight the art of the actor, placing the spotlight on the capacity to create a physiology of the face that is revelatory of an actor's inside. Cartesian theater, in this way, contributed to an era of the passions in French theater, both tragedy and comedy.[39] But opera, also, integrated the Cartesian passions in its musical representations—composers from Jean-Philippe Rameau to Friedrich Händel scoring the representation of wonder through voices, faces, and stage effects. In this way, the passions became not auxiliaries of the performing arts but their focus.

Desire and Beauty

Descartes inscribed the passions in the performing arts, in the visual and poetic arts, and in the complexity of the mood of music. All belong to the experience we call aesthetic. In this way, what distinguishes Descartes's aesthetics from a phenomenological *aisthesis* is that it relies as much on the visceral drives of attraction as on the spark of the senses.

Desires and drives originate in a corporeal inside: the movement of bodily fluids, and the direct corporeal impact of experiences that attaches to traces of memories and to states of consciousness (the "soul"). Beauty attaches both to formal qualities—the beauty of a flower, for instance—and to desires and drives that originate in the body. Aesthetic experience is situated at the crossroads between body and mind. By consequence, the beauty of a loved person is not classified as something distinct from the beauty of an object. Both are experienced through a kind of desire, which Descartes describes both in spiritual and corporeal terms. Aesthetic experience—the joy of beauty, the grip of music experienced through a piece of music, and so on—may also link emotions, or what he calls passions of the soul, to corporeal forms of affects. As we have seen, it is also through this turning inside out between sensual experience and physiological impact that *Passions* was received by the visual and performing arts world of his own times. But it is the idea that aesthetic experience is situated at the crossroads between desires and drives, body and mind, the sensual and the physiological, that serves to reactualize and remobilize Descartes's baroque aesthetics today. Using Descartes as a source of the field that we call aesthetics, we can see that it is produced by a reflection, an involvement, an intertwinement of kinds of emotions and kinds of sensation that covers much more than an experience of beauty.

In *Passions of the Soul*, the physiological explorations of embodiment are not merely a prephenomenological point of reference for the way in which perceptions are made. They imply the experience of a limit between an inside and an outside. To Descartes, the experience of this limit is mobilized in the confrontation with the beautiful as well as the ugly. Affects are not simply hitting us from the external world but also from the soul proper, among them wonder, love, desire, joy, hatred, and sadness. These cannot be produced at will. In this context, the experience of the beautiful is interesting on two accounts. First, it gives evidence of an overlapping of body and soul, which at times even appears antagonistic. Second, it points to the visceral dimension of the body, which is also what truly signifies a baroque aesthetic. Descartes describes two forms of beauty, the first being one of contemplation of beautiful forms. We experience the attraction of such beauty through our senses, primarily through our vision: "the beauty of flowers / . . . / incites us to look at them."[40] We cannot know such beauty until we see it, and when we see it, our eyes do not want to turn away.

But Descartes also describes another kind of beauty that is directed not toward an object of contemplation but rather to an object of desire. In contrast to the object of beauty, which is luring and peaceful, the object of desire appears contingent, surprising, and sometimes even violent to the self. This beautiful object of desire may well be a person—there is not a qualitative distinction made by Descartes himself between a person and a flower. The fact that both are treated as beautiful objects gives rise to intricate problems formulated in terms that closely parallel contemporary psychoanalysis. How is it possible that I do not always desire—find beautiful—what is good for me? From this perspective, the desire of beauty gives witness to reason's shortcomings. The fact that feelings such as love are confused thoughts—that is, emotions that are not altogether aligned with the intellect of what ought to be loved—creates an interesting complication with regard to the experience of beauty.[41] There is a rich analysis of these phenomena in Descartes that applies not only to conscious reflection but also to the flow of the unconscious, in the form of memories unattained by consciousness, for instance. The beauty of music, as explained in *Passions of the Soul*, engages us not through its forms, but the desire it awakens in us has to do with the traces of memories.[42] Affects and emotions can also be passed on from mother to child in the womb.[43]

The contemplation of beauty and the contingent desire of the beautiful do not derive from the same origin. Whereas the pleasure taken in the contemplation of forms, whether in music or flowers, appears to derive from the soul, the desire of beauty is neither prepared in the soul nor contemplated by the senses; instead, it hits us in a moment split between recognition and devastation. What is perceived as beauty, by desire, derives from the impact on perception of visceral movements between memories, nerves, and affects, a baroque entanglement between inside and outside.

The complexity of such an experience of beauty by desire finds its physical counterpart in article 47 in *Passions*, where Descartes describes the way in which soul and body meet in the pineal gland. The pineal gland is a hypothesis of imagination, the invention of a bodily organ that Descartes needs in order to posit a mediation between the soul and the body. In the same article that poses this relationship, however, we encounter the kind of conflicts at the center of Descartes's queries. The arousal of inner conflicts is explained in terms of two distinct causations. On the one hand, we may want things due to the way external stimuli act on us (arousal of animal spirits acting on the soul through movements in the body). On the other hand, the mind has its own inclinations. The conflicts that occur in us are caused by the encounter between two separate systems: on the one hand, the will, which is unable to cause passions; on the other, the passions that accompany the sentient being and that act on the soul, through "nerves, heart and blood."[44] The passions of the soul, although they are fundamental to us, are thereby not "simple," and they often appear conflictual in us. Desire is continuously in struggle with itself. Often the soul feels driven, almost at the very same time, "to desire and not to desire one and the same thing."[45] This is desire: to be driven toward and yet to shun. Desire is not directed toward an object that is "good" for us, although that might be an imaginary expectation. Desire is a struggle, with itself and against itself, incapable of judgment. This is the nature of desire: it is both corporeal and mental, and the pineal gland is unable to stem the conflict.

It is this very detachment of desire from the reason, or intuition of what is "good" for us, that makes Descartes so interesting from a contemporary perspective; he produces a distinct boundary between moral knowledge and the experience of what we love and desire—which is often a beautiful object. There is, in other words, no moral dignity inherent in man that raises an intuition to desire the good and the beautiful. What we desire originates, instead, in a visceral form of embodiment. This notion is put forward in Descartes's discussion of desire and love, which will be treated at length in the chapter on the thinking fetus—desire is sexual. It is not provoked by beauty but by a defect. Descartes remembers the cross-eyed girl who was his first love. Her memory remained as physical traces; for a long time, Descartes would desire cross-eyed girls.[46] In *Passions of the Soul*, he returns to this feeling of fixation on a unique feature of a person: "The inclination or desire that arises in this way from attraction is commonly called 'love'; 'it is this inclination or desire that provides poets and writers of romances with their principal subject matter.'"[47] Descartes differentiates between the attraction of love and the attraction of beauty. Both objects of love and objects of beauty can be represented to the soul by external and internal senses. When we judge things by our internal senses, we call them "good" or "bad." When we speak of representations, we call things "beautiful" or "ugly." The experience of the "beautiful" and the "ugly" is much more powerful than any other: it gives rise to sensations that we can neither control nor influence.

There is a decisive disparity between the "good" and the "beautiful." To the beautiful, we feel an attraction—a desire—that is not a passion of the soul, and it is not good for us. Attraction is a base form of desire. This form of attraction or desire is, in the same way as revulsion, derivative.[48] We experience it through our senses, but we have no idea what its cause is.[49] We are exposed and vulnerable to the desire of the beautiful—there is, potentially, a force in what we see that threatens our beings.

Why and when does attraction hit us? It has nothing to do with perfection. It is something that simply hits us, such as the gaze of the squint eyes.[50] It seems to be contingent. But attraction as well as desire is connected to the gaze, and it is trapped in the eyes of the other. To Descartes, all emotions are revealed through the eyes. There is no passion that some particular action of the eyes does not reveal. This has to do with the "many changes taking place in the movement and shape of the eye."[51] Love is driven by a fascinated gaze. In love's apprehension of beauty, Descartes inscribes in *Passions* not dualism proper but a breaking point, between a scopic drive of fascination that is driven by desire and a warm experience of beauty as something good that approaches pleasure.

We feel much more love for something beautiful than for something good. The desire that arises from beauty is much more powerful than any inclination toward the good: whereas the good is on the side of moral inclination, beauty may touch us at the core of what we are ourselves. The most heightened sense of beauty "comes from the perfections one imagines in a person who one thinks can become another oneself."[52] The most powerful and possibly devastating attraction is caused by the sight of beauty. To Descartes, this is also why love is an aesthetic matter, something that poets and writers of "romance" deal with.[53] Love is here derivative of the visceral experiences of desire for the beautiful, which is also the primary motive of art.

Beauty does not awaken any notion of the good. The desire of beauty is not connected to any kind of "will" that directs us toward the good. As he argues in *Meditations*: "for even if the things that I may desire are wicked or even nonexistent, that does not make it any less true that I desire them."[54] The strongest and the most significant forms of desire are those that arise from attraction (agrément) and those that are opposed to revulsion (horreur)—and these are experiences that are inherently aesthetic. The objects we find attractive, and we desire, are not "good." Instead, they act upon the senses in ways that may run counter to our willpower. The beautiful hits us through a desire we did not know we had in us. Aesthetic experiences cut between the sensual and the visceral—although experienced by the senses, their source is to be found in the drives that may run counter to willpower.

The Violence of Aesthetic Experience

The same kind of divide that runs through the "good" and the "beautiful" runs through the "bad" and the "ugly." We feel revulsion when we encounter something ugly. But we do not judge that something is ugly through any inner inclination or through any judgment that we could make on moral grounds. If, in his letters on beauty and in the compendium on music, Descartes describes something that could be the equivalent of taste, he explains in *Passions of the Soul* that the ugly is wholly a product of repulsion. What is astonishing here is the truly violent nature that Descartes ascribes to certain aesthetic experiences. In fact, attraction and repulsion may be more violent than other passions and more violent than the good and the bad because "what comes to the soul represented by the senses affects it more forcibly than what is represented to it by its reason."[55]

In other words, we are much more violently repelled by something ugly than by something bad. This has to do with the way in which traces of abhorrence may be described in our bodies through associative paths. We are revulsed by the sight and smell of a certain food if we have been previously poisoned by it.[56] But the senses interact, also with the memory of phenomena. Moreover, imagination may create feelings or sensations as powerful as that of direct physical contact with things. Descartes provides this example: we feel revulsion when we are presented with "stories of death, the touch of an earthworm, the sound of a rustling leaf, or our own shadow"; in other words, by taking pains here to include a number of senses, as well as a number of forms of encounter with the ugly, Descartes describes aesthetic revulsion as an event outside of the ordinary. It truly hits us. We do not only feel revulsion as in "I really do not like the sound of that rustling leaf." What is at stake here is something that strikes at the very core of our being: "one immediately feels as much excitation as if a very plain threat of death were being offered to the senses."[57] Revulsion is wholly visceral; it strikes at our very sense of life. It destroys us.

The fearful sense of life's tenuity is a quintessential baroque feature of the aesthetic. It may strike us through revulsion, at the sight of a certain quality of the ugly, or formless. It lies at the core, also, of the art of the tragic, pity and fear striking at the sense of life. It is also found in the sense of apprehension, which can be mixed with wonder at the sight of nature: such as pagans found the sight of forests, springs, or mountains. If Cézanne painted the "prescientific" condition of perception in his many renderings of Mont Sainte-Victoire, Descartes declares the pagan vision of nature to be tinted with a mixture of reverence and apprehension—not simply a source of religious sentiment but of an aesthetic experience that mixes wonder and apprehension.[58]

This extraordinary and visceral power of baroque aesthetics returns in later-day modernism. To Kant, the flower was the least complicated example of "free" beauty. To Baudelaire, it was a symbol of decay and its beauty a vulnerable shield against the same kind of putrefaction and death that aroused such fascination in contemplating open animal cadavers (*Flowers of Evil*, 1857). To George Bataille, the flower's pointy pistils were, in turn, a sign of its inherent perversion, a reminder of the connection between sex, fecundity, and excess. In the surrealist journal

Documents, nature is rendered obscene in Bataille's "The language of flowers" (1929), where he explores the violent force in aesthetic experience in his writings as well as in his speculations on the birth of art. Bataille, struck in awe in front of the cave paintings in Lascaux, witnessed not only an exuberant joy of life in the lavish depiction of hunting scenes but a strong fascination with death. This fascination is invisible, sheltered behind an unspoken prohibition: "the dead, at least the faces of the dead, fascinated, overawed the living who made haste to forbid that they be approached."[59] Such enjoyment of art's hidden sacredness identifies a visceral aesthetic as a moment of transgression. One sees here a pulverization of the self in an enjoying experience where the difference between the beautiful and the ugly is all but obliterated; this is what Julia Kristeva, in turn, calls abjection.[60] The abject is, in Kristeva's analysis, a development of the "informe," to use Bataille's expression: an indeterminable phenomenon that is impossible to contain within categories of intentionality or understanding; it belongs to the field of the drives.[61] The abject is not simply something that is outside us, that disgusts us; it charges our physiognomy, disgusting us at a physical level through phenomena that appear to be situated at the border of our bodies, such as blood, puss, semen, or hair. Abject is human baroque anatomy turned inside out. Represented also in art by bodies without life—Kristeva refers to Holbein's paintings of the body of Christ—the abject is at the heart of baroque art through its capacity of striking at the limit between the sensual and the affective. In being neither "subject nor object": the abject threatens the self, it is a "fallen object, which pulls me to the point where meaning collapses."[62] This is the aesthetic explored by multiple artists of the twentieth and twenty-first centuries: from the surrealists to Andy Warhol, Andres Serrano, Cindy Sherman, or Teresa Margolles.

In a similar way, Descartes saw that the aesthetic experience has an extraordinary power over the self, to the point of its dislocation or even its devastation. Aesthetic experience has its cause almost literally inscribed in the traces connecting the eyes and brain, the body and the mind. The link between the somatic and the psychic in Descartes's physical schema shows why we are drawn toward a point of fascinum that is the physical reality of our own being, and the way in which this physical reality conditions our sensual and intellectual experience of the world—the point of fascinum is that of an inside whose flows and tubes we can only imagine. It is a point of fascination in which we may ourselves vanish.

Descartes inscribes in *Passions* not a dualism proper in his description of the aesthetic but rather a breaking point between a scopic drive that may push us to the limits of our beings and the joyful warmth of sensual experiences. When Descartes negotiates the good and the beautiful, and the bad and the ugly, he shows that encounters with objects of beauty or grimness are conflictual by their very nature. Breaking points, in general, are inscribed in all Descartes writings. We find them straddling the line between passivity and activity,[63] in the rays of light of refraction, between the I that doubts and the I that exists, signifying itself through a shifter through which the subject will always break. We also see a distinct breaking point between the I that sees—reason—and the "eye" that sees, hit by affects that it cannot control. The aesthetic experience is beset by the effect of a *trompe l'oeil*: what I look at is not what I think I am seeing. The gaze is captured at a vanishing point, where the scopic drive is retracted toward itself.

Many have said, in the vein of Mario Perniola, that "the modern history of the appropriation of feeling by thinking" begins with Descartes.[64] But it is more fair to claim that Descartes gives witness to the conflicting emotions and affects that objects may claim, a conflict that much contemporary art negotiates today.[65] Descartes's own interest in imagination and dreams, moreover, contributes to the creation of a complex, internal landscape of the subject. In this internal landscape, the arts also saw its own practice develop, by seizing the complex reality of the passions and the way in which the passions act on our sensual experience. Aesthetics is sensibility, inner or outer emotions, moods, humors, moral forms, and sometimes sheer physical sensation. The most important dualism in the schema of the aesthetic machine, then, is not established between body and mind—it derives from a mixture of somatic and psychic sources. The aesthetic machine, again, is not a self-enclosed system but a wide-open subject of perception.

It does not matter, then, if our desire to think and reflect on the world is awakened by a flower in the external world or in our imagination. In the same way, it does not matter if our abhorrence of the ugly comes from a repulsion that is internal—physical and incorporated—or from something in the external world. Aesthetics is not a simple response to sensible afflictions. It is also not what overcomes the mind-body dualism. It is quite distinctly what lies between mind and body, inner and outer, dream and wake. Through an understanding of this visceral model of baroque, aesthetic experience, Descartes can be brought into the twenty-first century.

2 Philosophical Emotion
Descartes and the Aesthetics of Thought
Marcia Sá Cavalcante Schuback

CARTESIAN THOUGHTS ON aesthetics and the aesthetic of Cartesian thoughts are primarily understood as the aesthetics of Descartes's philosophical writing. The literary qualities of his writing are the common way to address the question about the relation between Descartes's philosophy and aesthetics. But there is still another dimension, which perhaps only Paul Valéry, the most Cartesian of all French poets, has addressed. It is the question about the sensibility of the intellect, or to use Valéry's expression, the "emotion" that a thought produces and is produced from.[1] This question is unfamiliar and strange; thus, it presupposes that there is a kind of sensibility and emotion that belongs to thinking, not only to how the senses and the body affect the soul or the mind but also to how the mind or the soul relates to the body of senses and the senses of the body. In Paul Valéry's readings of Descartes, one discovers the possibility of an unknown portrait of Descartes, which is at the same time an unknown portrait of philosophy itself: the image of a *philosophical emotion*, of a specific *philosophical sensibility*. The present chapter aims to proceed from the inspiration by Valéry and extract from a reading of Descartes the features of this philosophical emotion and sensibility. To Descartes's visceral aesthetics presented and discussed by Cecilia Sjöholm in the former chapter, I will add a discussion about Descartes's philosophical emotion.

How to Conceive a Philosophical Emotion

Descartes gives us an indication to answer to this question. In *The Passions of the Soul*, he speaks about "emotions of the soul," "interior emotions of the soul," and "intellectual joy." In article 27, the passions of the soul, which differ from other affections, are defined as "emotions": "After having considered in what respects the passions of the soul differ from all its other thoughts, it seems to me that we may define them generally as those perceptions, sensations or emotions of the soul which we refer particularly to it, and which are caused, maintained and strengthened by some movement of the spirits."[2] Descartes's concerns here are about the "emotions of the soul," and he conceives of the soul as the thinking soul, not merely the living principle or the principle of movement in living beings. He believes he is presenting something completely novel in the treatment of emotions or passions insofar as his aim is not to conceive bodily emotions but to examine how the body acts on the soul rather than how the soul imprints life and movement in a body, as the ancients have discussed.[3] Descartes writes in *Passions* that "an action and a passion must always be a single thing which has these two names on account of the two different subjects to which it may be related."[4]

What Descartes proposes here is the need to investigate how the soul is acted upon by its actions, how it is affected by the way it affects, how it refers to itself in a way that it provokes an emotion, a passion that is entirely of the soul, albeit acting on the body, as he himself puts it: "I note that we are not aware of any subject which acts more directly upon our soul than the body to which it is joined."[5] Reading *Passions of the Soul* from the perspective of this being a thing of simultaneous or reflexive action and passion, and considering that the "emotions" of the soul are and arise from the being acted upon by its own actions, it is in relation to this "reflexivity" of action and passion that the meaning of a "philosophical emotion" and sensibility should be developed.[6]

The starting point for discovering the vestiges of a philosophical emotion and sensibility—the meaning of the baroque aesthetics of thought in Descartes's philosophy we are proposing here—is careful attention to the new foundation of philosophy he presents, departing from this "reflexivity" of being acted upon by the action. Thus, this "reflexivity" is at the core of the novelty of Descartes's philosophy.

What is the novelty of Descartes's philosophical foundation? How does Descartes describe this novelty? He was very aware not only of his novelty but also of the moment he seized upon this novelty, his *eureka* moment. He reflects on this in his notes about the famous dreams from November 10, 1619, when he was in Germany in the Neuburg neighborhood alongside the Danube. According to *Discourse on the Method*, it was at this moment that he made the decision to elaborate anew the whole system of human knowledge and conceived the foundations of his method.[7] Descartes wrote down these dreams and was very careful to preserve these notes insofar as they were part of the notebook containing various early writings, probably written during the years 1619–1622 while he was traveling in Europe. He lost the notebook, but the well-known philosopher Gottfried Wilhelm Leibniz had copied the notes, which were found and published in 1859 with the title *Cogitationes Privatae* (Private thoughts). Following the account of Descartes's biographer Adrien Baillet (1649–1706), the notebook was divided into sections that included the *Praembula* (Preliminaries), the *Experimenta* (Observations), and the *Olympica* (Olympian matters).[8] Descartes's dreams are part of the *Olympica*.[9]

It is worth reviewing some of the passages in the narrative of Descartes's dreams found in Adrien Baillet's biography *The Life of Descartes* from 1691,[10] but these passages cannot be found in the English translation of Descartes's Complete Philosophical works.[11] This narrative is Baillet's rendition of what is presumably Descartes's account:

On November 10, 1619, Descartes had three consecutive dreams "after going to bed full of inspiration and completely absorbed by the thought of having that very day discovered the foundations of marvelous knowledge."[12] In the first dream, he saw some phantoms who frightened him so much that he, walking in the dream, was forced to leave the left side of the street to get to the place where he wanted to go, even though he was feeling weak on the right side of his body. He tried to stand but felt "a windstorm" that, carrying him along in a sort of whirlwind, made him make three or four turns on his left foot. Trying to reach the college chapel, he realized that he had passed a man of his acquaintance without greeting him. He tried to return to address him properly but was violently hurled back by the wind. In the middle of the courtyard, someone else called him by name and asked him to give something to another person. Descartes thought it was a melon imported from some foreign country. "What surprised him more was to see that the people gathered around this man were erect and steady on their feet, while he remained bent and staggering." Descartes woke up, feeling a sharp pain, and thought it might be some evil spirit that wished to captivate him. "Immediately, he turned on his right side, for he had gone to sleep and had the dream on his left side." Descartes recalls that he then prayed to God to ask for protection "against the evil spirit of his dream and to be preserved from all the misfortunes that could threaten him as damnation for his sins." He went to sleep again "after an interval of nearly two hours of various thoughts on the blessings and evils of this world."

He then had another dream in which he believed he heard the strong noise of thunder. Frightened, he awoke and perceived sparkling lights scattered about the room. He wanted to be helped by explanations taken from philosophy, making observations by alternately opening and closing his eyes, about the quality of the sensible forms that appeared before him.

Shortly after, he had a third dream in which he found a book on his table. He opened it and felt delighted to see it was an encyclopedia (*Dictionnaire*). At the same instant, he felt under his hand another book, an anthology of poems by different authors called the *Corpus Poetarum*.[13] In one of the verses he read, *Quod vitae sectabor iter?* (What path of life shall I pursue?).[14] Then someone handed him a piece of poetry beginning with "Est et Non,"[15] which Descartes knew as one of Ausonius's poems. Still in the dream, Descartes came upon several small copperplate portrait engravings (*gravez en taille douce*), which made the book very beautiful.[16] In his account of Descartes's dreams, Baillet considered that "the remarkable thing to note here is that, while wondering if what he had just seen was a dream or a vision, he not only decided in his sleep that it was a dream, but he had interpreted it before he awoke." Descartes decided then that the encyclopedia symbolized all the branches of learning and that the anthology of poems symbolized philosophy and wisdom joined. "Indeed, he did not believe that one should be so very astonished to see that the poets, even those who write nothing but twaddle, were full of sayings more serious, more sensible, and better expressed than those found in the writings of the philosophers.[17] He attributed this marvel to the divinity of Inspiration and to the power of Imagination, which produce the seeds of wisdom (which are found in the spirit of all men, like sparks of fire in pieces of flint) with much greater ease and even much greater brilliance than Reason can produce in philosophers." Descartes continued to interpret his dream in his sleep and judged that the verse *Quod vitae sectabor iter?* was the good advice of a wise person or even moral theology. He then woke, and "with his eyes open continued the interpretation of his dream," wrote Baillet. "By the poets collected in the anthology he understood the Revelation and the Inspiration by which he did not despair of seeing himself favored. By the poem Est & Non, which is the Yes and the No of Pythagoras, he understood Truth and Falsity in human understanding and profane learning." He then concluded that "the Spirit of Truth had chosen to use this dream to reveal the treasures of all the disciplines of learning to him." All that remained for him to explain were the little engraved portraits that he had found in the second book, and he no longer sought their explanation after an Italian painter paid him a visit no later than the next day.[18]

According to Descartes's own interpretation, the last dream referred to his future, whereas the two earlier dreams were related to his past life. The melon he received in the first dream, he said, "signified the delights of solitude, though presented by purely human appeals." The wind was the evil spirit that tried to force him into a place that he wished to go by his own free will (a margin note by Descartes read, "*A malo Spiritu ad Templum propellebar*"—I was driven to the church by the Devil). The fear he felt in the second dream indicated, in his opinion, his "*synteresis*, that is, the prick of conscience concerning the sins which he could have committed up to that point in his life." He understood the thunder he heard as a sign of the spirit of truth taking possession of him. According to Baillet's account,

> the last imaginative interpretation surely smacks of Inspiration, and it would easily lead us to believe that M. Descartes might have been drinking the evening before he went to bed. It was, indeed, the eve of Martinmas, an evening when it was customary in the place where he was, as in France, to devote oneself to revelry. But he assures us that he had passed the whole day and the evening in complete sobriety, and that it had been three months since he had last drunk wine.[19] He adds that the spirit that excited in him the inspiration that

he had felt, which had affected his brain for several days, had predicted these dreams before he retired to bed, and that his human spirit had no part in it.

* * *

These dreams have been the topic of extensive discussion and interpretation.[20] Even Freud has written about them, confessing that he did not have a lot to say since, for him, Descartes's dreams could not be very much distinguished from a state of consciousness; thus, the most interesting thing in them was the fact that the dreamer interpreted the dreams during the dreams.[21] Apart from this "hermeneutical" central feature of the Cartesian dreams, there is a further astonishing aspect. According to Baillet, Descartes writes in these notes that these dreams happened on the night in which he was filled with enthusiasm for having found that day "the fundamental principles of a wonderful science," of a *mirabilis scientia fundamenta*.[22] The enthusiasm preceded the dreams; the dreams followed the enthusiasm of a discovery that had happened suddenly in a moment that very same day. What the "fundamental principles of a wonderful science" are is never described in these notes, even though Descartes establishes himself as the interpreter of his own dreams.[23] This will be "told" eventually, and the self-interpretation will be revisited in Descartes's later writings.

In the second part of *Discourse on the Method*, a text written originally in French and published 1637, eighteen years after the eureka moment and the dreams generated by the enthusiasm of his discovery, Descartes refers to this journey in Germany but does not mention the dreams. He mentions the situation in which he might have discovered the fundamental principles. He wrote, "Finding no conversation to divert me and fortunately having no cares or passions to trouble me, I stayed all day shut up alone in a stove-heated room, where I was completely free to converse with myself about my own thoughts."[24] Throughout this part of *Discourse*, Descartes claims there is a need to reform the intellect in such a way that it could come "so close to the truth as the simple reasoning which a man of good sense naturally makes concerning whatever he comes across."[25] His plan, as he continues, "has never gone beyond trying to reform my own thoughts and construct them upon a foundation which is all my own."[26] "Uprooting" (*déraciner*) old views, learned thoughts, the doctrine and dogmas of the schools and of tradition is the verb Descartes uses repeatedly in *Discourse*. He describes the method of this "foundation which is all my own" in four rules that he should never fail to observe:

> The first was never to accept anything as true if I did not have evident knowledge of its truth: that is, carefully to avoid precipitate conclusions and preconceptions, and to include nothing more in my judgments than what presented itself to my mind so clearly and so distinctly that I had no occasion to doubt it; the second, to divide each of the difficulties I examined into as many parts

as possible and as may be required in order to resolve them better; third, to direct my thoughts in an orderly manner, by beginning with the simplest and most easily known objects in order to ascend little by little, step by step, to knowledge of the most complex, and by supposing some order even among objects that have no natural order of precedence; and the last, throughout to make enumerations so complete, and reviews so comprehensive, that I could be sure of leaving nothing out.[27]

The decisive shift here is how the *I* can have evident knowledge of the truth of something and how to include what is presented to *my* own mind in my own judgments so clearly and distinctly that *I* have no occasion to doubt it. It is only then that thoughts can be directed in an orderly manner, that they can follow the path from the simplest to the most complex and can then make complete enumerations and comprehensive reviews without omissions. The evidence of the knowledge of the truth of something depends on how something is presented to one's own mind so clearly and distinctly that there can be no doubt about the truth. What kind of presentation must that be? What kind of vision is at play here? This presentation must be a direct and immediate one. It is as immediate as the knowledge of God and of the infinite.[28] Descartes is, after all, the philosopher who introduced the modern concept of immediacy and the immediate.[29] It cannot, however, be the immediacy of the perception of anything external to the mind insofar as the knowledge of its truth can always be doubted. To define this presentation that is so clear and distinct that no doubt can remain, Descartes proposes to "reject as if absolutely false everything in which I could imagine the least doubt, in order to see if I was left believing anything that was entirely indubitable."[30] He then rejects the immediacy of the senses, the immediacy of demonstrative reasoning, and even those of accomplished thoughts insofar as they can "occur" (*venir*) equally during wakefulness and sleep: "I resolved to pretend that all the things that had ever entered my mind were no more true than the illusions of my dreams."[31] Descartes describes this most clear and distinct presentation to the own mind as the one that cannot occur from abroad, either through the senses, syllogistic demonstration, or whatsoever way a thought can "enter" the own mind. But in doing so, he "immediately" noticed that "while I was trying thus to think everything false, it was necessary that I, who was thinking this, was something. And observing that this truth 'I am thinking, therefore I exist' was so firm and sure that all the most extravagant suppositions of the skeptics were incapable of shaking it, I decided that I could accept it without scruple as the first principle of the philosophy I was searching."[32] The immediacy that Descartes discovers is indeed the one of an action and a passion being the same thing: "I am thinking, therefore I am, I exist." It is what could be called the immediate reflexivity of thinking and being, one immediately reflected in the other. The philosophical emotion and sensibility are, somehow, connected to the immediate reflexivity of action and passion at stake in the Cartesian "identity" of thinking and being.

Dominant Views on the Immediate Reflexivity of Thinking and Being

Descartes's phrase has been considered a "proper name"[33] or a "magic formula,"[34] and has replaced, or perhaps served as a modern translation of the Delphic-Socratic γνῶθι σεαυτόν, know thyself.[35] In this "translation," the relation between thinking and being is considered the discovery of the firm ground provided by an identity only granted through reflection. What we call the reflexivity of thinking and being here has been understood in post-Cartesian tradition in terms of reflection. What does reflection mean? Reflection means literally bend back, turn back something to itself, hence thinking back to itself. It has currently two main significations. It has the "material" signification of a wavefront—either of light, sound, or water—that upon reaching a surface turns back into the medium from which it originated, but reflection also has the "spiritual" meaning of a deep meditation on some subject or matter. Descartes is considered the founder of the modern philosophical signification of reflection insofar as his *ego cogito ergo sum* ("I am thinking therefore I am, I exist") has been predominately interpreted as the thought that thinks that it thinks, meaning both a thought that turns away from any consideration of objects and the external world of experience and thereby turns back to itself, thematizing the subject of thought and rendering this turning back—reflection—the principle of philosophical thought. In reflection, the subject of thought turns away from the immediate experience of the world and turns back to itself, immediately becoming the object of thought. In this view, modern Cartesian philosophical reflection means self-relation, self-mirroring, and self-foundation.[36] Whatsoever sense the *sum* ("I am, I exist") might discover, it should then derive from the "I think that I think," which is condensed in the *cogito*—that is, in the "I think." It is from this main line of interpretation of the Cartesian cogito that Leibniz defines reflection in *Nouvelles Essais de l'entendement* as "*attention à ce qui est en nous*" (nothing but attention to what is within us),[37] an attention that Alexander Baumgarten further considers to be "*attentio in totis perceptionis partes successive directa*," an attention successively directed at the parts of a total perception.[38] Kant translates the Latin word *reflection* to the German *Überlegung*, defining it as that which does not have to do with objects but solely with the subjective conditions to reach concepts of the objects,[39] being the consciousness of the relation between representations. Reflection relates to an internal or interior movement of the mind, through which thought becomes object for thought, representation for representation, which allows Kant to discuss "transcendental reflection" (*die transzendentale Überlegung*). For Kant, this is a state of the spirit, *Zustand des* Gemütes.⁴⁰ As Martin Heidegger interprets Kant's account of the Cartesian cogito and his critique, the expression of this interior reflection, accomplished by the cogito, is a *cogito me cogitare*,⁴¹ literally "I think myself thinking," from which the knowledge of the world and of the things and bodies of the world should be deduced. For Kant, Descartes's biggest error was not in identifying the cogito with reflection—Kant believed this was, indeed, Descartes's greatest achievement—but in conceiving that from the simple proposition "I think" a whole new philosophical science could be deduced, which includes the deduction of the substantiality of the soul, its simplicity, its unity through time, and its relation with the bodies—that is, with all possible objects in space. According to Kant, the "I think," the *cogito*, comprehended as *cogito me cogitare*, can only assure a "formal unity" that follows all my representations, but it is not enough to serve as the foundation for a whole system of philosophical knowledge. With the "I think," I can only know my thoughts and representations but nothing about what I am or can be outside my representations.⁴² Kant's *Critique of Pure Reason* aimed to show that if this phrase laid the foundation for representation as such, it is not enough to serve as the foundation for the representational knowledge *of* things and *of* the world.

These very brief remarks indicate a main line of interpretation of the cogito, of the "I think," as immediate reflection that occurs when I think myself thinking, *cogito me cogitare*—indeed, when I think that I think. Moreover, it has been from this interpretation of the cogito, as reflection, that the substantiality of the cogito has also been defined. The capacity or ability of the cogito to think that it thinks reduces it to a thought of thoughts, which includes of thought things. But understood in this way, things become reduced to thoughts—that is, to representation—and thought to a "thing" that can be thought. Still, within the framework of an understanding of the cogito as reflection, the "I think" appears to enunciate a reification of thinking, through which the "I" that thinks appears as a thing that thinks in such a way that it turns everything it thinks into a "thing." Turning the subject of reflection into an object for reflection, the cogito as *cogito me cogitare* would therefore reduce the "I" into a thinking *thing, res cogitans*, and thinking to a pure act of objectification and reification. Some of the phenomenological critiques by Edmund Husserl and Heidegger directed against Descartes focus on this meaning of reflection, on the substantiality of the cogito and the reification of the subject, grounded on this immediate reflection.

The point of departure for Husserl's phenomenology and Heidegger's critical development of phenomenology is, indeed, the deconstruction of the Cartesian cogito. The central critical point is the distinction between subject and object, the separation between the interiority of consciousness and the exteriority of the world or reality, and the consequent isolation, encapsulation, and reification of the "ego." For a phenomenologist, consciousness is not a thing encapsulated in itself, a separated sphere from the world that has the capacity to know the world from outside or above. Consciousness, the thinking subject, is in fact not at all a thing but a life, a way of being, which is of the world in the world. Ideas can therefore not be innate, and the transcendental viewpoint is rather immanent for it is always situated in the world. The reification of the cogito, of the "I think"—namely its explanation as a "thing," *res*, whose substantiality is totally independent from the substance of the world and of the world of things—is, from the viewpoint of phenomenology, a principle mistake of Cartesian philosophy. But the central target of, for instance, Heidegger's critique is also the reification of the *sum*, of the "I am," "I exist," that leaves the *sum*, the "I am," the "I exist" totally undiscussed (*unerörtet*) and unclarified, even when positioning the *sum* as original as the cogito.[43] The principle should be inverted—and expressed rather in terms of "I am, I exist therefore I think": *ego sum ergo cogito*. As Heidegger says: "the first statement is '*sum*,' in the sense of I-am-in-a-world. As such a being, 'I am' in the possibility of being toward various modes of behavior (*cogitationes*) as ways of being together with innerwordly beings. In contrast, Descartes says that cogitations are indeed objectively present and an ego is also objectively present as worldless *res cogitans*."[44]

It is the isolation of the *sum*, of the "I am," "I exist," its wordlessness, that is for Heidegger the most critical point. Descartes's ontological ground, which is the understanding of being as thing—hence, as reification and objectivation—not only falsifies and misunderstands the meaning of Being qua being but also the meaning of a thing, what Heidegger will develop in his later essays about the thinghood of things (*das Dinghafte des Dinges*).[45] Leaving the *sum* undiscussed, reified, isolated, and worldless, Descartes can only behold a thought on thinking that thinks whatsoever from the model of introspective reflection, as I think that I think, a *cogito me cogitare*.

Husserl sees the problem of the Cartesian cogito mostly as an inaccurate understanding of reflection. According to Husserl, Descartes failed to account for how the I think that I think is a thinking myself thinking, and hence, what expresses rather the experience of thought than the contents of the cogito.[46] At stake are the experiences (*Erlebnisse*) of thought and their unity and continuity in the flow of consciousness, which renders the subject not merely conscious of him/herself thinking but a presence to him/herself. According to Husserl's critique, Descartes could not account for the experience of experience. Reflection is, for Husserl, the way consciousness gives itself as phenomenon to consciousness—that is, how it is experienced as consciousness by and through consciousness. This means that phenomenologically, consciousness is a realm of experience and not only of thoughts about experiences; it is attention to the experience of thoughts and not of things, and, indeed, the possibility to experience experience. In this Husserlian sense, reflection is rather reflexivity in a sense that is not much of a departure from immediate reflexivity as in Descartes, conceived as the being one of action and passion, of being acted upon by the action.

Following the phenomenological critical position in relation to Descartes, but departing from a critique of both Husserlian and Heideggerian critical standpoints, Maurice Merleau-Ponty proposed in the *Phenomenology of Perception* the notion of "true *cogito*," defined as follows: "The true Cogito does not define the subject's existence in terms of the thought he has of existing, and furthermore does not convert the indubitability of the world into the indubitability of thought about the world, nor finally does it replace the world itself by the world as meaning. On the contrary it recognizes my thought itself as an inalienable fact, and does away with any kind of idealism in revealing me as 'being-in-the-world.'"[47] Merleau-Ponty's intention was to restore what he called the "temporal thickness"[48] of the Cartesian cogito, and thereby to reveal "yet there is consciousness of something, something appears, there is a phenomenon—such is the true cogito."[49] The true cogito is the appearing of things from themselves and hence fundamentally prereflexive, immediate reflexivity.

Whether the sum should precede the cogito, or the cogito should be understood as the experience of thought, or further as the prereflexive appearing of things from themselves, the framework to understand the "identity" of thinking and being enunciated in Descartes's formula *ego cogito ergo sum* remains the reflexive structure of thinking as the capacity of self-reference, self-relation, self-foundation, and even self-revelation that is present even in the notion of a prereflexive true cogito. But does *ego cogito ergo sum* really mean *ego cogito me cogitare*? Is the relation of thinking and being expressed in this "magic formula" a reflection, a reflexive identity, or an immediate reflexivity understood as being acted upon by the action?

Ego Cogitans Existo

How would Descartes respond to these contemporary objections, he who developed his thoughts dialogically, either in the style of soliloquies or in letters and by presenting responses to objections? Indeed, Descartes never wrote the Latin phrase *"cogito me cogitare"* ("I think that I think") that Heidegger attributed to Descartes and in which he saw the main critical point of Cartesianism. This is actually Heidegger's formulation.[50] In a letter to the theologian and mathematician Antoine Arnauld from July 29, 1648, Descartes writes: "Being conscious of our thoughts at the time when we are thinking is not the same as remembering afterward. Thus, we do not have any thoughts in sleep without being conscious of them at the moment they occur, though commonly we forget them immediately."[51] The main response would be the "thickness" of this "at the same time," of thinking *while* thinking, indeed, of the I am thinking, and not the reflection operating in "I think *that* I think," a thickness that before being restored still needs to be stored. The core of his answer resides neither in the cogito (I think) nor in the sum (I am, I exist), and even less in the *res* (the thing). It lies in the *cogitans*, in thinking, used by Descartes in the gerundive mode, which is the mode to express an ongoing action. In fact, Descartes did not fail to write an even more precise formula for the experience he discovered to be the principle for his marvelous science: thus, instead of *ego cogito ergo sum*, he once also wrote *ego cogitans existo* (thinking I exist),[52] a formula that is to be read in its double meaning: thinking I exist, and, while thinking, I exist.

In French, Descartes's famous formula reads in the present tense: "*je pense, donc je suis.*" The English translation, "I am thinking, therefore I exist," renders the meaning of this present tense even clearer: thus, at stake here is nothing but the thinking act, being conscious "at the time" of thinking, thinking *while* thinking, indeed, the immediacy of this experience, which is the experience of a unique kind of immediacy.[53] This is what Descartes could accept, "without scruple," as "the first principle of the philosophy" he was seeking. The emphasis on the kind of immediacy of the experience of thinking *while* thinking shall give a "firm" direction to seize the meaning of philosophical emotion and sensibility we seek. Thus, it does not have to do with the pleasure that rational intellect may experience when arriving at a true conclusion, or with the beauty of a rational proof, or with the feeling of harmony and order rationality can produce. Indeed, very decisive here is to behold a crucial distinction between the thoughts produced by a rational intellect and the *act of thinking*; thus, it is the latter that Descartes accepts as the first principle of philosophy. And it is from this principle of the *act of thinking* that the meaning of the "I" and of the "subject" brought to philosophical language by Descartes might become more "clear" and "distinct."

Georg Wilhelm Friedrich Hegel envisioned this meaning, at least to a certain extent, in his *Lectures on the History of Philosophy*. Acknowledging Descartes as the founder of modern philosophy in these lectures, he observed: "We come now for the first time to what is properly the philosophy of the modern world, and we begin with Descartes. Here, we may say, we are at home and, like the sailor after a long-voyage, we can at last shout 'Land ho.' Descartes made a fresh start in every respect. The thinking or philosophizing, the thought and the formation [of reason] in modern times, begins with him. The principle in this new era is thinking, the thinking that proceeds from itself."[54]

Reading Hegel's words more carefully, one can observe that what Hegel recognizes as "the principle of the new modern era" is not properly the dominance of rationality and science upon reality, the encapsulating of the intellect and of the human in its subjectivity and egoism, but "thinking," "thinking that proceeds from itself." Nor does he speak about reason but rather about *Bildung*, "formation,"[55] pointing out the activity of thought and its autonomy. Hegel sees not only that the Cartesian novelty is the one of beginning with thinking, "*um erst vom Denken aus auf etwas Festes zu kommen*"⁵⁶ but also that it is "*das Denkende,*" the thinking that for Descartes is the "I." Hegel's reading is very attentive to the distinction between think and thinking, *das Denken* and *das Denkende*, and shows that what Descartes calls "I" is not a subject that is first in itself and then thinks or has as its main attribute the capacity to think, but the thinking act itself *is* the subject. The "I" *is* the thinking, he says. It opens the path to consider that it is while thinking that the "being" thinking becomes immediately clear and distinct in its inseparability of this act. In Hegel's words: "As subject, thinking [*das Denken*] is the being-thinking [*das Denkende*] and this is the 'I'; thinking is the inward being-in-myself, the immediacy in myself—this is proper simple knowing. Immediacy is however the same as what is called Being."⁵⁷

Therefore, it can be said that "*Ich ist gleich Denken,*" "I is equal to think." The subject, the "I," is nothing but the thinking, which shows the immediate identity of being and thinking. The "*donc,*" "*ergo,*" "therefore," "*also*" as Hegel points out is not the "Also des Schlusses," the "therefore of the syllogism"⁵⁸ but only the connection [*Zusammenhang*] of being and thinking. It expresses the immediacy of the belonging together or identity of being and thinking in the act of thinking. In his brief but insightful summary of Descartes's new foundation of philosophy, Hegel touches upon the core of the Cartesian *eureka*—namely, the seizing, in the instant, all of a sudden, of the being thinking while being thinking, a flash moment in which being and thinking are the same, presenting itself to the thinker in pure immediacy. Hegel does not develop his insight on Descartes's insight, but he understood quite clearly that the first principle of philosophy is the one of departing from the immediate awareness of the belonging together or identity of being and thinking that is given in the moment the *being thinking* presents itself in the act of thinking. This moment of seizing the being thinking in its own act might have been the source for Descartes's enthusiasm the night of November 10, 1619, an enthusiasm followed by dreams interpreting dreams and by a new foundation of philosophical wisdom. It is also from this immediate "identity" or belonging together, when thinking "sees" itself thinking while thinking that the meaning of a philosophical emotion and sensibility can gain more clarity. What is at play here is the attention to the *cogitans* and not to the *res cogitans*, to the thinking while thinking and not to the thing (the subject, the "I") that thinks. In so many centuries of responses and objections to Cartesian philosophy, a more thorough examination of Descartes's *ars cogitans*⁵⁹ is still lacking—to his way of thinking, to the way he seizes the act of thinking in its very action. It therefore seems legitimate to reread his *Meditations on First Philosophy*, using a focus on the *cogitans* as our point of departure, on the way he writes down the thinking while thinking, in short, on the act of thinking while it is taking place and time.

Rereading Passages from *Meditations*

Descartes had some clear ideas about how to read his texts. In the letter he wrote to the translator of *Principles of Philosophy*, his friend Abbé Claude Picot, he says that the truths he included among his principles "have been known all time by everyone" even if up to now "no one has recognized them as the principles of philosophy."[60] This explains why he still has to "prove that they do indeed qualify as principles of that sort."[61] But surprisingly, instead of proposing a doctrine that should be learned, he considers that "the best way of doing this is to get people to see by experience that this is so, that is to say, to invite my readers to read this book."[62] Descartes considers that the experience needed to follow his thoughts is the *reading experience*, not rational or intellectual skills or any sort of intellectual "experience." He adds some lines about how to read *Principles* that can be extended to his other books as well:

> I should like the reader first of all to go quickly through the whole book like a novel, without straining his attention too much or stopping at the difficulties, which may be encountered. The aim should be merely to ascertain in a general way which matters I have dealt with. After this, if he finds that these matters deserve to be examined and he has the curiosity to ascertain their causes, he may read the book a second time in order to observe how my arguments follow. But if he is not always able to see this fully, or if he does not understand all arguments, he should not give up at once. He should merely mark with a pen the places where he finds the difficulties and continue to read on to the end without a break. If he then takes up the book for the third time, I venture to think he will now find the solutions to most of the difficulties he marked before; and if any still remain, he will discover their solution on a final re-reading.[63]

What will be pursued here is certainly not a "final rereading" of the *Meditations*, but a rereading of certain passages that proceed from the attention to the *movement* of thinking in the text and not merely from the thoughts here expressed or from the rational chain of arguments. Descartes employs the term *Meditatio*, which was used before Descartes to translate Marcus Aurelius's Greek title Τὰ εἰς ἑαυτόν, "things to one's self," into Latin. The use of this term links Descartes with a tradition that runs through St. Augustine's *Confessions*, to Teresa of Avila,[64] Jean-Jacques Rousseau's *Confessions*, and more recently, to Jacques Derrida[65] and Jean-François Lyotard.[66] This tradition considered meditation to be writing down thoughts that are drawn away from the presence of any listener or exterior influence or contact and are thought inside oneself, in reflexive introspection. In *Discourse*, Descartes describes the insight he experienced on the "wonderful science" when he withdrew from the company of and conversation with other people and went into the solitude of his *poêle*, his stove-heated room, an image that

Figure 2.1. Rembrandt Harmensz. van Rijn, *Le Philosophe en contemplation, longtemps appelé aussi Philosophe en meditation*, 1632, Louvre Museum.

can be seen, for instance, in Rembrandt's well-known painting of the *Philosopher in Meditation*, also called *Interior with Tobit and Anna*, that hangs today at the Louvre Museum. Even if Descartes can be read in the lineage of ancient and medieval meditations and confessions, his aim was not so much to write down his thoughts but much more the movement and flow of thinking; indeed, he wanted to record the act of thinking taking place and time.

The first *Meditation* begins by revisiting a central motive from the early *Discourse on the Method*, which is the purpose of uprooting old ideas and beliefs, the need to accomplish the "general demolition" of current opinions and views. "I am here quite alone, and at last I will devote myself sincerely and without reservation to the general demolition of my opinions."[67] In order to perform this demolition, he must find in what he until now considered to be "most true" "at least some reason for doubt." Whatsoever reason to doubt of the truest is enough to throw the belief away until he finds what cannot be doubted. Descartes does not seek what is false in a judgment but what can be doubted in what is most true. Senses are the first source for what is "most true." But they also deceive. To show that the realm of sensual truths must be left behind for the sake of finding the first and undoubtable principle of this marvelous science, Descartes proceeds in an unusual way. He does not describe or discuss sensual-perceptive illusions as he does in other texts and contexts. He does not discuss optical illusions due to distance "when stars or other very distant bodies appear to us much smaller than they are"[68] or how "sometimes towers which had looked round from a distance appeared square from close up; and enormous on pediments did not seem large when observed from the ground."[69] Here he neither talks about physical deceptions provoked by physical harm or disease, such as the phantom limb,[70] or those who, because of "jaundice, see everything coloured yellow."[71] He departs quite unexpectedly from the truest perception, in a sense, namely that "I am here," which continues, "sitting by the fire, wearing a winter dressing-gown, holding this piece of paper in my hands," and so on.[72] The condition of all truth brought by or through the senses is the *being here*, and it is from this *being here* that the truest fact, that "these hands or this whole body are mine"—that is, the truest fact perceived in self-perception and self-sensation—relies upon. But even this truest fact—which is related to self-perception and self-sensation and not to the perception and sensation of something else, or exterior to the perceiver and "sensor"—can be doubted; thus, the self or subject of perception and sensation could be a madman, "whose brains are so damaged by the persistent vapors of melancholia that they firmly maintain they are kings when they are paupers, or say that they are dressed in purple when they are naked, or that their heads are made of earthenware, or that they are pumpkins, or made of glass"[73] (Descartes sketches so many fairy tales in just this sentence!). The whole discussion here is about the belief of being what one is not. The madman presents the possibility of doubting the most undoubtable, even in any deceptive sense perception—namely, the being here, indeed, being. How can we relate this specific mode of deception—namely, insanity—to the question about sense-perceptual illusions? Why does Descartes not discuss illusions produced by the senses but rather the insane that takes not being for being, "being king when they are paupers," "being dressed when they are naked," believing that their hands and body are not their own? These confusions are not at all common illusions produced by the senses. What renders these beliefs "mad" is that in them the senses doubt themselves—which they otherwise never do. It can be said that the argument of illusion or of insanity in the *Meditations*, as a matter of fact, is rather a *sensual doubt*, the way senses doubt themselves, the way senses do not trust themselves, or the way senses do not trust their overwhelming self-evidence that allows the insane not only to say but to feel that "his hand is not his."[74] This argument tries to bring to light how the sense of a "here" doubts itself, also indicating the possibility of a here that is not here, a now that is not now. This is, indeed, a very important aspect of the time-sense of thinking, insofar as the "I am thinking" is here and now, but nonetheless, not here and not now in the common spatial-time we are accustomed to using and experiencing for these terms. After the presentation of the argument of illusion and madness, the argument that presents the sensual doubt of the senses, a small leap occurs in the movement of thoughts. Recognizing how people who believe they are what they are not, who mix being and not-being, are insane, and that he, the thinker, would also be insane if he took anything from them as a model for himself, the thinker acknowledges ironically "what a brilliant piece of reasoning," and continues: "as if I were not a man who sleeps at night."[75]

Indeed, what a "brilliant" or rather strange piece of reasoning! What was being called into question was: from where the thinker should take the model for his scrutiny, if madness, meaning to believe that one is what one is not, cannot be a model. But why should it follow the observation, "*as if* I were not one that sleeps?" The figure of speech that calls attention here for the leap is "as if." Descartes does not connect the "as if" with the dreams but first with the sleep. In sleeping, one is "as if" awake. In sleep, one is dreaming "as if thinking"; hence, when thinking, it could also be said that one is "as if" dreaming. Thinking thinks things awaken, whereas dreams dream sleeping. How can this distinction between being awake and being asleep help distinguish these two actions in the present—thinking and dreaming? Descartes proceeds using the "as if" as a kind of method, one that, more than conjecture, is an index for all kinds of illusion and what could also be used in relation to an "idea." Thus, there is something in ideas that is "as if" a dream. This something has to do with the temporal and spatial features of both. My claim here is that the distinction between awake and asleep does not introduce only a "criterial problem," as the important Descartes scholar Martial Gueroult discussed it,[76] but a criteria to describe the strange sense of place and time in the act of thinking, of the taking place and time of thinking. To describe the way thinking is real and present, he introduces the "as if" as an index of illusion, meaning unreality, not being here and now. Therefore, Descartes reasons *as if* the I am thinking, the gerundive mode of thinking, *cogitans*, could be taken either for insanity or for a dream. And why could it be taken for one or another? Because the "reality" of thinking, its mode of presence, is enigmatic and intriguing, because it is the most present and real but in a totally different way than any reality. It could be taken for insanity insofar as the I am thinking is present here and now but not as things are present here and now; it could be taken for what it is not. And it could also be taken for a dream: "for how do we know that the thoughts which come to us in dreams are any more false than the others, seeing that they are often no less lively and distinct?"[77] Nevertheless, there is a difference that seems more intense: "Although sometimes our imaginings in sleep are as lively and distinct as in waking life . . . our reasonings are never so evident or complete in sleep as in waking life."[78] Indeed, the reality of "I am thinking" reveals another sense of reality that exceeds the real but is not confounded with the unreal. The chain of arguments circles around the being here in dreaming and thinking, believing I am here—that is, standing or sitting, when in fact I am lying down. And dreams, where do they take place? In sleep. Do we think while dreaming? Does one think *like* one dreams? Thinking shares with dreaming a here and a now that is and is not here and now and hence a place and a time so confusing to describe that the meditative thinker feels "dazed" (*obstupefeam*). Thus, how do we grasp the event or act of thinking and dreaming if both are here and now, not being here nor now? Descartes continues by analyzing what can be seized in dreaming, which is an act that is ungraspable as much as thinking. He knows that in dreaming, one can dream of dreaming. This is an important characteristic of his own dreams from 1619. But one also dreams of things and events that could be "here and now" in the way things do, although dislocated to the obscure here and now of the act of dreaming, of the taking place and time of dreaming.

Descartes moves then to a discussion about "dreams" and no longer about dreaming. But he does so in a surprising way; for him, "the visions which come in sleep are like paintings."[79] In the movements of thought that follow Descartes's famous dream argument, it is possible to find a theory of painting, something I will discuss later. In the different kinds of dreams, indeed of "paintings," Descartes discusses three different modes of relating to real existence: dreams that "have been fashioned in the likeness of things that are real"; dreams that show imaginary things, that "create sirens and satyrs with the most extraordinary bodies" but only "jumble up the limbs of different animals"; and last, dreams that "manage to think up something so new that nothing remotely similar has ever been seen before—something which is therefore completely fictitious and unreal."[80] But even so, there must be some connection to the real existence, "at least the colours used in the composition must be real." In the whole sequence of the arguments, it is the reality of existence, the very certainty of existence, that is under scrutiny. Even the "facts" that are furthest from real existence still are real, because the fact and act of madness, the fact and act of sleeping and dreaming, are real facts and acts. Indeed, they are all factual acts though they may produce unreality and fictions. Maybe Descartes would agree with the French writer Maurice Blanchot, that dreams are the work of resembling not merely things and realities but resemblance itself.[81] But what seems implicit in Descartes's dream argument is how these degrees of resemblance to reality accomplished in these three kinds of dreams can respond to the question about the specific place and time of dreaming as such, and hence as a gateway to responding to the main question, which is the kind of question that relates to real existence of the thinking while thinking, that the thinking act exposes.

Descartes continues his meditation, which flows from one move to another organically and always through unexpected moves. Arriving now in the realm of colors, of pure images—that is, of the shape of extended things, the quantity, or size and number, in short, the realm of ideas—he discusses their way of being real and present, the place they may exist, the time they may endure. He is now in the realm of abstract ideas, which naturally follow the senses and dreams. Here, the sense of here and now becomes even more dazzling, even more obscure and stupefying. He observes that even the most sure and certain abstract ideas and foundations can be put in doubt because ideal rational entities, such as extension, shape, size, and place, may not exist; thus, maybe "an omnipotent God who made me the kind of creature that I am . . . has brought it about that there is no earth, no sky, no extended thing, no size, no place." Maybe God is a deceiver, and in this case, the ideal existence of rational entities appears to be nothing but fictions, nonexistent. And moreover, God itself, maybe "God is a fiction," so that even the certainty one might have about metaphysical matters, about the necessary existence of a God, a cosmic order, a reason for the existence of existence itself, these metaphysical certainties can also be doubted. When in all these certainties—those provided by the senses, those by the state of consciousness, those by rational reasoning and presuppositions, and those by metaphysical views—all that seems "most true" can be doubted, what sense of reality can remain? Senses delude, reasoning can fail, God can deceive, and a malicious demon can employ all energy to misguide. Descartes—the thinking existence—can suppose that a malicious demon used its utmost power to deceive him; he can think "that the sky, the air, the earth, colours, shapes, sounds and all external things are merely the delusions of dreams which he has devised to ensnare my judgment"[82]; he may consider himself "not having hands or eyes, or flesh, or blood or senses, but as falsely believing that I have all these things."[83] But what is left? The rest is not silence for Descartes; rather, "I shall stubbornly and firmly persist in this meditation."[84] Even without having the power to know any truth, he should continue to meditate, to go along with thinking. And what remains true? In the second meditation, he asks this question and says, "Perhaps just the one fact that nothing is certain."[85] It is the doubting itself that remains true. Thus, if nothing exists for certain, not even the sky and the earth, not even the minds and the bodies, the doubting—rather than the doubts—exists, and in such an immediate way that it follows that I exist. If there is a deceiver of supreme power who is continuously deceiving me, "let him deceive me as much as he can, he will never bring it about that I am nothing so long as I think that I am something."[86] From all that, he can conclude that the proposition "I am, I exist" is necessarily true.

As Descartes affirms himself in his *Responses to the Second Set of Objections*, the second meditation accounts for the "abduction" (*abducere*) of the soul from the body and the senses. Only rarely, Descartes speaks of "separation" between the body and the soul,[87] more frequently using the Latin verb *abducere*, to abduct. The movement of the meditations has abducted the thinking existence from sensual perception, from rational truths, from metaphysical beliefs, from different levels and realms of immediate certainty about existence as planted in the here and now. The only certain existence that remains is the existence of the one who doubts—that is, of the one who is thinking. The only true and certain existence is that I am, I exist, not as a thing among other things and bodies, earthly or cosmic, but as a *thinking* thing: *res cogitans*. In the second Meditation, Descartes continues his thinking movement by revisiting how this "I" should be understood. He proceeds by following his method of demolishing and uprooting former opinions and beliefs by means of seeking the least reason to doubt the truest in these old ideas. The first one would be the certainty that this "I" should be understood as a "man," a "rational animal." What would urge him to answer questions of the kind? What is rationality? The attempts to understand the "I" reflecting upon its attributes, the shape of the body, its extension, the ways it can be perceived by the senses, the ideas about the body as what has the power of self-movement, of sensation, of thought—all these known attributes can be put in doubt the same way it was done in the first meditation, when the figure of a malicious demon was brought into play, and everything that one might say the "I" is, a body, a soul, the relation between body and soul, to everything that can be put in doubt for one reason or another, its most certain truths. If sensual, rational, and metaphysical meanings of existence can be put in doubt, what kind of existence is the I am, I exist? What remained from all these meditations was the fact of "I am doubting," "I am thinking," *ego dubitans, ego cogitans*. "Thinking? At last I have discovered it—thought: this alone is inseparable from me."[88] I am, I exist— he says, and asks "but for how long?" "For as long as I am thinking."[89] Here, the "I" acquires an explicit fundamental temporal aspect, not described in the usual terms of having a short life—that is, of a finitude defined in the realm of a chronological representation of time—but "as long as" (*nempe quandiu cogito*) I am thinking. How do we understand the meaning of an existence—the "I"—which exists "as long as thinking"? What kind of thing is it, "*res*"—that is, something that exists? Descartes insists in his answer—this kind is a "thinking thing," *res cogitans, dixi cogitans*. And what is a thing that thinks? His famous answer reads: "A thing that doubts, understands, affirms, denies, is willing, is unwilling, and also imagines and has sensory perceptions."[90] These lines serve as the opening to the third meditation, where they will also be extended: "I am a thing that thinks: that is, a thing that doubts, affirms, denies, understands a few things, is ignorant of many things, is willing, is unwilling, and also which imagines and has sensory perceptions."[91] The French version also adds a thing that "loves, hates."[92] The meaning of existence and being that emerges here is one determined not by bodily or rational attributes but by the *as long as*, a sense of "whileness," of duration, which is not temporal in the sense of something undergoing a chronological chain of events but rather expresses the strange existence of what is solely as long as it acts.[93] Even if this is a bit of a departure from the question and the vocabulary addressed in our discussions, it could be said that this aspect is not at all specific to thinking; thus, given both the French mathematician Pierre Gassendi's and the British philosopher Thomas Hobbes's objections to Descartes, I could say that I am walking and therefore I exist—that is, there is no causal relation between thinking and being, as Descartes had assumed. Descartes responded to these objections, claiming that if I say I am walking or going for a walk, this is already thinking. Hegel also commented on these objections, and in Descartes's response, "When I say 'I,' that *is* thinking,"[94] I say 'I am walking,'" what is already in the realm of thinking is related to a bodily function that refers to the current sense of factual existence as existence here and now. Only in thinking while thinking can another sense of being be experienced that enables me to say, "I am, I exist."

The mode of existence—the "I" that Descartes is trying to define—is "inseparable," as he says, from thinking. It is as inseparable, we could say, as the lightning is from its flash, as Nietzsche once pointed out; thus, as much as the lightning does not exist first, as something that then flashes, the I does not exist as we usually conceive of existence as something in itself that then thinks. The "I" *is* thinking; thinking is the "I," the "subject," as Hegel clearly saw.[95] In order to find a way to explain the mode of existence of this "puzzling 'I,'" which although being "mine" is the most obscure, Descartes considers the things that are most commonly taken for clear and distinct—namely, the bodies. The well-known description of the wax, praised through centuries for its literary qualities, culminated in the Cartesian definition of the body as "*rex extensa.*" It is also surprising that the substantiality and thinghood of the body is defined as *extension*, which is the fundamental attribute of a figure. Indeed, the path of argumentation involved in the discussions about the wax is anchored in the problem of imagination and of the distinction made by Descartes between what is perceived by imagination and what is perceived solely by the mind. If imagination is the faculty that produces images and figures, the mind is the faculty capable of perceiving figures without figures, what he calls "extension." As he says: "It is of course the same wax which I see, which I touch, which I picture in my imagination, in short the same wax which I thought it to be from the start. And yet, and here is the point, the perception I have of it is a case not of vision or touch or imagination—nor has it ever been, despite previous appearances—but of purely mental scrutiny."[96] Thus, what is being perceived here is no longer "the wax in itself," as one can be "tricked by ordinary ways of talking," but the act of perceiving. The wax is perceived as being perceived as wax. The copious literature about Descartes's skepticism, about his denial and refusal of the world, the restless debates about his extreme idealism and absolute rationalism, tend to omit how the main question in these read and reread pages of *Meditations* is how to seize this strange mode of existence that only exists in action, and which expresses correlatively as existing while thinking and existing while being, perceived the being perceived—that is, as perception coming "from the scrutiny of the mind alone."[97] Thus, Descartes observes insightfully that the difference between what the eyes see and what the mind perceives, between a realist or materialist and an idealistic point of view, resides in the fact that visual perception forgets that the eyes are seeing and hence are essentially involved in what is being seen, whereas the perception of the mind, achieved by Descartes, is the one of thinking the thinking while thinking, of perceiving the perceiving, of seeing the seeing. The act in its acting, this is what Descartes discovers as a totally different sense of existence, of being, the one that is inseparable from thinking—it is the puzzling, strange existence of what is solely as long as it is acting and performing. Neither corporeal nor intellectual existence, neither sensible nor intelligible, but a thinking sensibility: Descartes's cogito is the cogito of a performance.

3 Descartes's Performative *Cogito*

Marcia Sá Cavalcante Schuback

"I AM THINKING THEREFORE I am"—this magic formula appears only very few times in Descartes's writings. Nevertheless, it is among the most recognized philosophical quotes in history. It appears first in the *Discours de la méthode, pour bien conduire sa raison, et chercher la verité dans les sciences* (published in 1638 in French: *Je pense donc je suis*), and was soon after translated into Latin where the famous phrase *ego cogito ergo sum* was printed. The passage from *Discourse* is well known: "But immediately I noticed that while I was trying thus to think everything false, it was necessary that I, who was thinking this, was something, and observing that this truth 'I am thinking, therefore I exist' was so firm and sure that all the most extravagant suppositions of the sceptics were incapable of shaking it, I decided that I could accept it without scruple as the first principle of the philosophy I was seeking."[1]

The same "magic formula" appears in 1644 in *Principa Philosophiae*, written first in Latin and then translated into French. The passage is very close to the one of *Discourse*:

> In rejecting—and even imagining to be false—everything which we can in any way doubt, it is easy for us to suppose that there is no God and no heaven, and that there are no bodies, and even that we ourselves have no hands or feet, or indeed any body at all. But we cannot for all that suppose that we, who are having such thoughts, are nothing. For it is a contradiction to suppose that what thinks does not, at the very time when it is thinking, exist. Accordingly, this piece of knowledge—I am thinking, therefore I exist—is the first and most certain of all to occur to anyone who philosophizes in an orderly way.[2]

It is surprising that this phrase, which expresses the first principle of a whole new philosophical foundation, does not appear in the *Meditations*, where the step-by-step process of Descartes's discovery of this principle is more carefully described than in previous works. In the *Meditations*, the phrase, which is written in the style of a motto, instead reads: *ego sum, ego existo*, I am, I exist.[3] The absence of the motto from the *Meditations* could suggest that it is more "the name of a thought," "a singular intellectual operation," "a protocol of reflection,"[4] than a thought proper. Descartes himself poked fun at his intellectual operation in a dialogue written around 1647 and published posthumously, entitled *La Recherche de la Vérité par la Lumière Naturale* (*The Search for Truth by Natural Light*). In one passage, he puts in the mouth of Epistemon, one of the characters of the dialogue, the following ironic observation:

> But after two hours of discussion, I cannot see that he has made much progress. All Polyander [another character] has learnt with the aid of this marvelous method which you are making such a song about is the fact that he is doubting, that he is thinking, and that he is a thinking thing. Marvelous indeed! So many words for such a meager result. Four words could have done the trick, and we should all have agreed about it. As for myself, if I were required to spend so much time and engage in such a long discussion in order to learn such an insignificant fact, I would be very reluctant to make the effort.[5]

As the first principle of the wonderful science he discovered, "I am thinking therefore I am," the phrase that says all, easily becomes an empty formula, saying in fact nothing, but echoing in such a way that it becomes a phrase repeating itself, repeating itself, infinitely. In the dialogue, the "meager" result that it expresses—I am thinking—and therefore "I am"—is compared to an "acrobat who always lands on his feet, so constantly do you go back to your 'first principle.' But if you go on this way, your progress will be slow and limited."[6] The image of the acrobat always landing on his feet is perhaps the ideal image to show how this phrase expresses an action or act of thought that becomes the "principle" of thought. "I am thinking, therefore I am" is the formula for a movement of thought, the movement of an "acrobat who always lands on his feet." The character Epistemon, who, as the name suggests, is involved with science in Greek, takes the Cartesian motto ironically because the phrase does not fit in the general idea of a scientific philosophical argument developed through inference and structured in the form of a syllogism. For centuries Cartesian scholars have discussed the inferential character of this phrase, the syllogism upon which it could be formulated. However, in his responses to the second set of objections, Descartes clearly rejects this "scientific" or epistemic procedure for arriving at his phrase. He writes, "When someone says 'I am thinking, therefore I am, or exist' he does not deduce existence from thoughts by means of a syllogism but recognizes it as something self-evident by a simple intuition of the mind. This is clear from the fact that if he were deducing it by means of a syllogism, he would have to have had previous knowledge of the major premise 'Everything which thinks is, or exists'; yet in fact he learns it from experiencing his own case that it is impossible that he should think without existing."[7]

This phrase, he says, is not the expression of a thought deduced by means of a syllogism but apprehended as "something self-evident by a simple intuition of the mind," learned "from experiencing his own case." The opposition between an inferential thought and a thought seized as self-evident by a simple intuition of the mind is the opposition between a thought that arises from binding relations between conceptual thoughts and thoughts taking place—that is, the thinking movement appearing to itself in its own movement. It is the difference between thoughts and thinking, between inferences, deductions, and the act of thinking, as a performative act. But in what sense should we assume that the famous Cartesian *cogito*, the "I am thinking," from which follows as self-evident an intuition of the mind that "I am," is a performative utterance? Are these words doing something in the sense the British philosopher of language J. L. Austin gave to the "performative"?[8] Are they performing an action rather than saying something? Are they performative insofar as they are issued in the "doing of an action"? In Austin's discussions of "speech acts"—performative utterances and illocutionary acts or forces—the focus resides on the distinctions between "performing an act" and "saying something" and further between "the performance of an act *in* saying something," called an illocutionary act, and the "performance of an act *of* saying something."[9] His examples move within the dimension of speech Aristotle called *logos semantikos*, which is neither true nor false, the utterance of a wish or a prayer, in opposition to the *logos apofantikos*, which is an utterance to which the quality of being true or false can be ascribed. Austin discusses performative utterances in close connection to declarative utterances, to sentences that implicate nonexpressed but nevertheless very clear meanings due to the tight bonds to the context and circumstances in which they are uttered. Descartes's dictum could be understood as performative in the sense of being a kind of declarative sentence: *je pense, cogito*, "I am thinking," but it both performs an act and says that it performs an act: the "reference" of the statement is the very statement. It is similar not to a promise, a wish, or a prayer but to an utterance such as "I am saying that I am saying"; thus, the "I am thinking" means I am thinking I am thinking. That is why the Cartesian cogito has been understood through the centuries as self-reflexive, self-referring, and self-revealing. At the same time, it is also the performance of an act in saying and of an act of saying, indeed, of an act in writing and of an act of writing, understanding writing as a saying without sounds. Further, what immediately seems to confirm the performative feature of the Cartesian dictum "I am thinking, therefore I am" has to do with the "I," since the phrase would not be at all performative—that is, meaningful—without referring to anything outside itself, if one said: Descartes thinks therefore he is. In his famous article about Descartes's dictum as performative, Jaakko Hintikka considered that performative sentences are those that are "existentially consistent"[10]: "I am thinking, therefore I am" proves its performative force insofar as it is said by this "I." I can say that someone else who exists does not exist, but *I* cannot say that I do not exist insofar as I am saying it. If I said, "I don't exist," I would only prove that I exist by the very act of saying it. The "I" in Descartes's cogito—*ego sum*—always says, even without saying, that I am saying I am saying, I am thinking I am thinking.

What most discussions about speech acts and performative utterances let easily come to a second level is the dynamics of the act as such. Indeed, what happens *during* a happening? What happens *during* a performance? How does the performance perform? Hintikka compared the relation between *cogito* and *sum*, "I am thinking" and "I am," as one of a process to its product. He even makes use of a musical metaphor and argues that "the indubitability of my own existence results from my thinking of it almost as the sound of music results from playing it or (to use Descartes's own metaphor) light in the sense of illumination (*lux*) results from the presence of a source of light (*lumen*)."[11] In Descartes's performative phrase "I am thinking, therefore I am," the "therefore" can be understood as the index of the instant of emergence of a product from a process, the "light that results from the presence of a source of light." But Hintikka was also sensible enough to remark that the "therefore" marks, rather than any "because" or "in so far," an "as long as": as long as I think, I am, as much as the music is as long as it is being played. That is why Descartes speaks not only of cogito, I think, but above all, *cogitans*, thinking, and of *res cogitans*, a thinking thing; thus, it is as long as there is light that one sees. What remains undiscussed is how, during the act of thinking, the act of thinking itself is seized as such and apprehended during its act, how the happening is apprehended during its happening. It cannot be apprehended or seized by any cognitive act that implies a distance in space and time. In connection to this, Descartes speaks of an "intuition of the mind." Only this intuition can seize the happening while happening, the thinking while thinking, the perceiving while perceiving. In this intuitive apprehension, while I am thinking, I suddenly apprehend *that* I am thinking, and this in such a clear and distinct manner, in such a self-evident and intensive mode, that I experience that I am being. Indeed, what appears without any doubt is that to *be thinking* is what allows me to think being in such a way that the discrepancy between thinking and being is overcome: seizing that I am thinking while I am thinking means to experience the identity of thinking and being.

Central here is the character of suddenness, of an insight, "the role of the instant"[12] in Descartes's cogitation. Indeed, the way the act is seized as an act during the act: this is, in our view, the main question related to the performative. In every word said, the being said is necessarily always co-implied but rarely an object of awareness. If I say I am saying—"I am saying to you this or that" and even "I am saying that I am saying," this performative utterance can remain reflexive but still not really "experienced." Writing, however, "I am thinking therefore I am," Descartes brings something more to the question of "performative utterances" and "speech acts." He brings the *experience*, the experience of thinking, which the English translation stresses when saying "I *am* thinking," and that Descartes also stresses when writing in the seventh set of replies: "I begin to philosophize as follows: I am; I am thinking, I am, so long as I am thinking" (*sum, cogito; sum, dum cogito*),[13] *ego cogitans existo*,[14] and later in the same set, "noticing that there was nothing which I could know more certainly or more evidently than that I existed so long as I was thinking, I was right to make this my first assertion" (*deinde advertens nihil certius evidentiusque a me cognosci, quam quod ego cogitans existerem, non male etiam hoc primum afferui*).[15] It is the experience of thinking that is expressed by the "so long as," *dum*, and by the present participle, or more specifically, the gerund *thinking, cogitans*, that enables Descartes to say *I am*, in the very sense of "I am experiencing being while thinking, for I am experiencing the very experiencing"—and indeed the experiencing of a movement of thinking coming to words, coming to expression. In his *Confessions*, St. Augustine signals that the meaning of thinking derives from the Latin word *cogitate*, from bringing together, *cogo*, relating these words to *ago* (I do) and *agito* (agitate) or *facio* (I make) and *factito* (I make frequently).[16] It is an action that gathers, according to Saint Augustine, the very action of logos, which means language, thought, and gathering, the very action of bringing the coagitation of the soul, of the breath that animates the body, into words.[17] Thinking (i.e., coagitation), or in Jean-Luc Nancy's reading of Descartes, *chaogito*,[18] is an experience that experiences itself, of being surprising itself being. Again, how does thinking surprise itself thinking?

The Art of Thinking as the Art of Seeing the Seeing

In a letter to Antoine Arnauld from July 29, 1648, Descartes writes the following: "Being conscious of our thoughts at the time when we are thinking is not the same as remembering afterward. Thus, we do not have any thoughts in sleep without being conscious of them at the moment they occur, though commonly we forget them immediately."[19] Being conscious of our thoughts at the time we are thinking—this is the core of Descartes's cogito. The consciousness of the *cogitans dum cogitans*,[20] of this *while* thinking, is what Descartes considers the evidence expressed with "*donc*," *ergo*, "therefore," which surpasses any certitude derived either from the senses or from syllogisms and pure abstract reasoning proper of learned "philosophers who take no account of experience and think that truth will spring from their brains like Minerva from the head of Jupiter," as he wrote in Rule VI.[21] The *experience* to be accounted for here, Descartes claims, can be described as an attention that is neither a sense-perceptive attention nor an abstract ideal attention, being even more overwhelming than the formers. As previously mentioned, Descartes understood this thinking attention in terms of *intuition*, a mental or, more precisely, a thinking intuition that is not at all dissimilar to Husserlian accounts of intuition. In *Rules for the Direction of the Mind*, Descartes says: "By 'intuition' I do not mean the fluctuating testimony of the senses or the deceptive judgment of the imagination as it botches things together, but the conception of a clear and distinct mind, which is so easy and distinct that there can be no room for doubt about what we are understanding [. . .] That everyone can mentally intuit that he exists, that he is thinking" (vol. 1, 14). Be aware, conceive, pay attention—that is, "intuit" that one exists, that one is thinking—this is a mental intuition entirely distinct from sensuous intuition. It is another kind of intuition with even more intensity of certitude than bodily intuitions. As thinking *intuition*, it differs from sensuous intuition, but as *thinking*, this intuition should be differentiated "from certain deduction on the grounds that we are aware of a movement or a sort of sequence in the latter but not in the former, and also because immediate self-evidence is not required for deduction, as it is for intuition, deduction in a sense gets its certainty from memory."[22] It is from this stronger evidence brought by thinking intuition that the first principle for all possible knowledge shall be taken. This thinking intuition of being (thinking) while thinking provoked Descartes's *enthusiasm*, the dreams he dreamed and interpreted while dreaming, and further influenced the way he conducted his life. This thinking intuition is even more than an "intuition"; it is indeed an emotion: the way thinking moves thoughts in existence and existence in thoughts.

Modern philosophical conceptions of Descartes focus on the Cartesian cogito, extracting it, however, entirely from its temporal "thickness," from what is most central in it, which is the "as long as" and "while." They focus rather on the subjective capacity to render thought an object of thought, paying attention to the constitution of contents of thoughts rather than the experience of the flow and movement of thinking. Insofar as what is in question for Descartes in this thinking intuition is, above all, the seeing of seeing and not the seeing of something—indeed, the thinking of thinking and not the thinking of something even if itself, the laws of reflection are not very suitable. Descartes writes in his *Replies to the Six Set of Objections* that

> it is true that no one can be certain that he is thinking or that he exists unless he knows what thought is and what existence is. But this does not require reflective knowledge, or the kind of knowledge that is acquired by means of demonstrations; still less does it require knowledge of reflective knowledge, i.e., knowing that we know, and knowing that we know that we know, and so on *ad infinitum*. This kind of knowledge cannot possibly be obtained about anything. It is quite sufficient that we should know it by that internal awareness which always precedes reflective knowledge.[23]

How should we understand this "internal awareness which always precedes reflective knowledge?" In contrast to the infinite regress that follows the reflection and its knowing that we know that we know that we know, and so forth, this internal awareness is the enigmatic awareness of seizing the movement while moving, without any fixed point outside the movement, which would enable an observation of it, but the movement itself—I am thinking—becomes the only fixed point. This means that the I am thinking—the unfixed in chronological time and in geometrical space, becomes the only fixed point from which the infinity of time and space can be "seen" and thought. Descartes proposed here a very strange perspective, not the central perspective as in classical thought, art, and philosophy but a perspective in which the point of fugue is itself in movement, is itself in fugue, the perspective anchored in "I am so long as I am thinking," a perspective from within the in-between. The difficulty lies in the fact that—while moving, while happening—thinking and seeing withdraw while happening in such a way that what "remains" is not something or even an image but rather a kind of afterimage or, more accurately, an imageless image. Nevertheless, it is surprised in a certain moment as such—namely, as a moving movement—therefore acquiring some consistency even if inconsistent, we could say, showing a figure even if without contents.

* * *

The question is then how the "I am thinking," which is a sort of movement, is touched by its own movement in such a way that it is surprised by it and "seizes" it with thinking (mental) intuition as the own being. The I am thinking, the *cogitans*, is a verb mode, which is the present participle or continuous form in English, and that denotes an ongoing action, indeed the movement proper to an ongoing act. It is about a movement proper to a duration, a time-space in-between. It is neither movement nor rest; thus, it does not describe the change from one position to another that could be measured according to a previous and a posterior. It presents a proper and enigmatic physics of movement—indeed, the physics of a thinking movement. Although we do not find a clear treatise of the "physics" of the thinking movement while thinking in Descartes, there are passages in his works where the movement of thoughts are described. They present rather a "physiology of the thinking movement"; thus, they aim to present a clear figure of the movements of thoughts within the thinking body. Here, Descartes is also a "physician." In the *Treatise of Man*, *Traité de l'Homme*, written in French in 1664,[24] Descartes performs his proper study of the relation between body and soul, which is the one of studying carefully how external impressions and interior sentiments act upon the physical body and how the physical body produces sensations, sentiments, and senses; he analyzes the digestion of meats; the beating of the heart and of the arteries; the nourishing and growing of the organs; respiration; being awake and being asleep; the reception by the body of light, sounds, odors, tastes, and warmth; the external movements of the organs that follow both the actions of the objects presented to the senses as well as the passions; the impressions to be found in the memory; and the impression of ideas in the organ of common sense and of imagination.[25] The human body is presented as a machine, an automaton, a comparison that has been a source of fascination in the modern and postmodern eras from La Mettrie and Vaucanson, the materialist physicians from the eighteenth and nineteenth centuries, until our era of artificial intelligence and robots. But this human machine is compared to some specific machines—to those used in royal gardens to bring water to large extensions, to musical organs in the church—mostly machines that are featured with tubes conducting and distributing the elementary forces of air, water, sound, and light. In Descartes's physiological descriptions, we find close parallels to Leonardo da Vinci's scientific studies, his drawings of the human muscles and organs, where arteries, for instance, appear as tubes and irrigating canals, the body tissues and ligaments in their closest similitude to vegetal fibers. Descartes writes: "Again, regarding the brain, they will not be able to imagine anything more plausible than that it is composed of many tiny fibres variously interlaced; for, in view of the fact that every type of skin and flesh appears to be similarly composed of many fibers or threads, and that the same thing is observed in all plants, such fibrous composition is apparently a common property of all bodies that can grow and be nourished by the union and joining together of the minute parts of other bodies."[26]

The similarities between Descartes's view of the body as machine and Leonardo da Vinci's has been keenly observed and discussed by Paul Valéry.[27] A more detailed comparative study between both studies on optics, on light and shadow, on the laws of reflection and refraction, and above all, their anatomic views and studies of the tourbillon and winds, would be out of the scope of our present work, but nonetheless a very exciting task.[28] Nevertheless, what we can stress by this reference to the pictorial dimension of Descartes's descriptions of the human body-machine is how it is depicted as the drawing of built landscapes, with tubes and canals, almost resembling a Dutch landscape painting, which shows the similitude between the forms and functions of the body and the forms and functions of a cultivated nature.

In this comparison with built landscapes, with canals, ducts, tubes, threads, fibers, and ligaments, the movement of thoughts within the body are described by Descartes in sketching out a physiology of thinking. In the *Treatise of Man*, Descartes is interested in how the object and its figures, understood as what "can give the soul the occasion to perceive movement, size, distance, colours, sounds, smells and other such qualities,"[29] imprint not only on the brain but on the "spirits"—these winds produced along the circulation of the blood—upon the surface of the gland where imagination and the common sense are located. These impressions of the figures of the objects, taken in the sense used in the quote above, within the moving surface of the spirits upon the gland, Descartes calls "ideas"—that is, "the forms and or images which the rational soul united to this machine will consider directly when it imagines some object or perceives it by the senses."[30] Here, Descartes proposes a theory of thinking movement that is much closer to a theory of drawing than to a physical theory of movement. He speaks of traces and lines, of imprints of impressions upon volatile surfaces, the spirits, defined as "a very fine wind, or rather a very lively and pure flame, which is called the *animal spirits*,"[31] passing upon the gland, which is the place of imagination and common sense, the sense that, as early as the time of Aristotle, is the one that senses the senses. The whole issue of this "machine" that moves by itself, automatically, is the astonishing internal, subcutaneous landscape of fluids and flames, nerves and ligaments, fibers and tissues, so similar to subterranean floods and rivers, roots and sources, in which the internal movement of the blood in the body—for him, nothing but "continuous circulation"—emerges as the external movement of the water in the external world. Descartes is fascinated with the intensive life taking place inside the body, in this secret cave so similar to the "caves and fountains that can be found in the gardens of our king,"[32] that, though not being able to receive air and light directly, if not when wounded and thereby at the risk of death, can only live through the way the elements air, light, water, and food penetrate the body through an amazing net of perpetual communication and circulation, accomplished by the movement of the blood.

What is interesting to observe here is this strange art of imprint that Descartes connects to how ideas are formed within the body. It is an odd imprint in that it imprints impressions in winds upon the surface of this special gland found within the brain, a distinct kind of image when compared to the usual description of an imprint upon a wax surface or any solid surface. Descartes is much closer to the way lines are drawn in the "air," closer to a kind of aerography or even of drawings of lines upon the sky. Looking at how he wanted the drawings in his *Treatise* to appear, we can see, for instance, the gland inside the brain connected to the eye. Descartes could have had an engraving—we should not forget that these illustrations are engravings of drawings[33]—only with the brain and the gland, but he is interested in the connection between the eye and the gland, not only because he was attached to the common metaphor of the eyes of the soul but perhaps because he aimed to see how the eyes can see the movement of ideas being conceived within the body. (See fig. 6.1.)

To see the eyes seeing evokes the question of a point of blindness that renders every seeing possible. Indeed, the eyes cannot see the eyes if not using something other than the eyes, as a mirror. Since without the "prosthesis" such of a mirror the eyes cannot see the eyes, they experience a blindness precisely when seeing something. This is a departing point for Jacques Derrida's discussions on drawing blindness in his beautiful book on drawings, *Memoirs of the Blind, The Self-Portrait and Other Ruins*.[34] In his thoughts on the drawing's blindness, the blindness implicated in the painter's and drawer's seeing, Derrida, looking at works in the Louvre Museum that depict blindness, pays attention not only to the loss of view that renders vision possible but also to how blindness is the visual force of every self-portrait; thus, a self-portrait is indeed the portrait of an eye—the painter that cannot see the eye seeing—the painter. It is also from the blindness

64 | *Through the Eyes of Descartes*

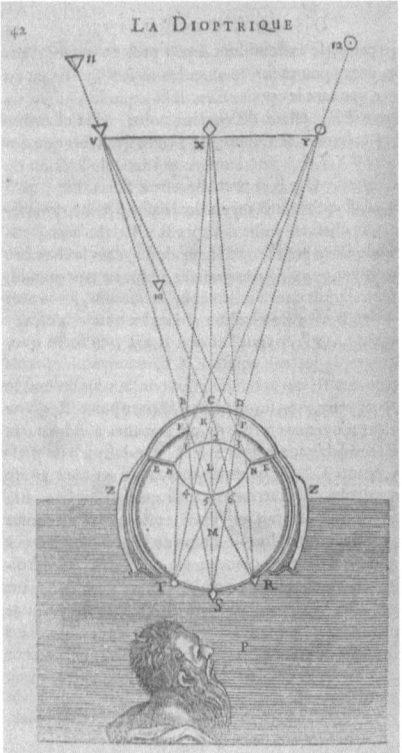

Figure 3.1. *Dioptrique*. In *Discours de la methode*, Leyden, 1637, Royal Library Stockholm.

of the drawing and painting eye that Derrida accounts for the distinction between drawing and writing. A further motive in his discussions in the book is on the focal point of the drawing pen, which cannot be seen while drawing. Point of fugue, blind spot, focal point, and the point in which the blinds tend to fall into the abyss of blindness, all these decisive instances and moments render sensible the blindness of seeing in the very seeing. Without being able to expose here the richness of Derrida's thoughts and how he relates this blindness to memory and ruins, the latter understood mainly as inceptive loss, few works have "seen" so deeply the touching and tactile vision of blindness as this book. However, there is still a "blind spot" in his reflections, which is the experience of seeing a moving line, a movement while moving, the experience of moving eyes, something that the performativity of Cartesian cogito discovers to a certain extent. This experience has to do with the strange vision of a line drawn by the hands, which is indeed what defines a drawing and which the English word expresses so clearly.

As mentioned before, the eyes cannot see the movement of ideas being conceived in the same way they see things, objects, figures, or images of things. To see these movements implies the same difficulty as to see the seeing *while* seeing—that is, to see the movement of seeing—not to see the eyes seeing what a mirror could provide but something even more difficult—namely, to see the movement of seeing while moving the seeing. This requires an entirely different perspective and laws of vision.

Questions related to this awkward "vision" of seeing while seeing, indeed of the thinking while thinking, appear in other works as well. In Rule VIII and in the eighth part of the *Meteors*, Descartes tries to solve the problem of finding the shape of a line *anaclasis*, a term derived from the ancient Greek ἀνακλάω, meaning refraction, the forced bend of a joint, used in physics and mathematics to describe the point where a line or a ray of radiation stops, is interrupted, focusing all parallel rays to a single point, that which formulates the phenomenon of refraction in distinction to reflection. This term has also been used in rhetoric and poetical treatises, meaning the replacement of a long syllable by a short in order to break the rhythm. The notion of an anaclastic line could be borrowed here from Descartes's more technical studies on physics and optics for the sake of indicating what kind of "image" is the one of the thinking while thinking, of seeing while seeing. Thus, this line is a line "traced" along with the view of the proportion or ratio between the angle of incidence and the angle of refraction.[35] This line is traced in the air, and considering Descartes's further discussions in *Meteors*, it can be described *qua line* as a kind of cloud-drawing in an aerial surface. In looking more closely at the drawing of this line in the air than the mathematical and physical problems that urged its formulation, we must look at the lines being drawn and hence with the vision of a line *while* being drawn in the air and not only with a drawn line. Scientifically and philosophically, Descartes's thinking is very close to that of an artist who depicts above all the drawing of lines itself. The "I am thinking," *ego cogito*, is not far from "I am drawing," meaning I am seeing lines being drawn. Descartes's cogito could therefore be described as a drawing *cogito, cogito designans*.

The Soul of Cartesian Eyes—A Critique of Merlau-Ponty's Critique of Dioptrics in the Eye and the Spirit

The drawing and painting dimension of the Cartesian cogito has already been examined by Paul Valéry and the way he approached Descartes's cogito from Leonardo da Vinci, situating Descartes among the painters and da Vinci among the philosophers. In his readings of Descartes, Paul Valéry focused on this figure of a man looking at the eye from inside the body, of the eye seeing the eye, the seeing seeing the seeing printed in the *Optics*, and he insisted that Descartes's obsession was with observing the observing, with imagining the imagining. For

Valéry, Descartes is the closest to Leonardo da Vinci, and his beautiful essay about the *Method of Leonard da Vinci* can and should be read as a translation of Descartes's thoughts on method to the language of painting. Da Vinci, as Valéry insists, is a painter who has taken painting for philosophy.[36] Making this connection from the ambitions of both men to a *mathesis universalis* based on order and measure, from the way science was seen by both as a way to scrutinize the interiority of matter, revealing how both were, in many ways, surgeons and anatomists of all existing bodies and how the mind and the spirit was placed in the body of matter, Valéry opens the possibility to reread Descartes's medical scientific investigations as an exercise of the observing and imagining vision, very close to a painter like Leonardo da Vinci. Thus, the larger discussion about Descartes's denial of the world, his skepticism and extreme idealism, can be read differently, indeed, as the seeing of seeing rather than the nonseeing of the world. Focused on the seeing of seeing, on observing observing, on thinking thinking taking place and time, Descartes's Archimedean point shows dimensions that bind the philosopher and the painter who aimed to see the seeing of things in the possible concepts and images of things. As much as da Vinci, Descartes's philosophy shares the enthusiasm that arises from the instant of a vision.

Few contemporary philosophers have been so influenced by the poetic thoughts and essays of Valéry and have written so insightfully on painting as Merleau-Ponty. His entire body of work is marked by a critique and deconstruction of the Cartesian cogito, for the search for prereflective and prelinguistic realms of experience in which body and mind could be surprised in their chiasmatic unity.[37] The *Eye and the Spirit* is a book about the seeing of the seeing as the fundamental gesture of painting. As Claude Lefort writes in his introduction, Merleau-Ponty aimed to show in this book that "painting does not celebrate any other enigma than the one of visibility."[38] The whole book is about showing that the act of painting is a wonder born from the fact of vision: from the fact *that* we see, *that* there is vision, rather than *on* what we see, *on* what can be seen. It is also an attempt to render philosophy capable of thinking this fact as painters paint it—that is, as they render visibility visible. Merleau-Ponty always keeps the famous quote by Paul Klee in mind, saying, "*Kunst gibt nicht das Sichtbare wieder, sondern Kunst macht sichtbar*" (art does not reproduce the visible; it makes visible). This demands from philosophy, as it does Merleau-Ponty, a learning from and with painting for the sake of unlearning centuries of philosophical habits of seeking the redemption of the soul in the abstraction and refusal of the sensible ("*chercher le salut de l'âme dans la deliverance du sensible*").[39] For centuries, perception and sensible awareness have been sacrificed. Therefore, according to Merleau-Ponty, all philosophical problems can only be solved through the examination of perception. For him, this perceptive solution stands in direct conflict with the philosophy of Descartes. If Descartes has a program to take leave from the senses, Merleau-Ponty aims to bring thoughts back to the senses, the mind back to the body as its unique source of creation. He aims to learn from the painter who *"pense en peinture,"* who thinks in painting. It is quite interesting to observe that despite the capacity that Valéry recognizes in da Vinci and the similar quality he sees in Descartes, Merleau-Ponty, himself a devoted reader of Valéry, considers this the strongest opposition in relation to Descartes. Merleau-Ponty's starting point is the phenomenological insight in the twofold sense perception, that the senses are sensed at the time they sense, that one is touched when touching as much as one is seen when seeing. For Merleau-Ponty, phrases like "My body simultaneously sees and is seen" (*"Mon corps est à la fois voyant et visible"*),[40] "the undividedness of the sensing and the sensed" (*"l'indivision du sentant-sensible"*),[41] "the inside of the outside and the outside of the inside" (*"le dedans du dehors et le dehors du dedans"*),[42] express the true enigma of the body. Painting renders visible this seeing that is seen when seeing. Painting "gives visible existence to what profane vision believes to be invisible" (*"donne existence visible à ce que la vision profane croit invisible"*).[43] Without using the same vocabulary we use here, he seizes the present tense as a source of understanding—or of thought—in this very particular way of thinking in/through painting. He writes that "the painter, whatever he is, *while he is painting* practices a magical theory of vision" (*"le peintre, quel qu'il soit, pendant qu'il peint, pratique une théorie magique de la vision"*).[44] The painter interrogates about the secret genesis of things in our bodies, painting therefore a kind of philosophy of vision, a vision of vision, indeed, this reflexivity of the sensible, of the visible. According to Merleau-Ponty, every painting shows that which also explains the passion of painters for self-portraits, mirrors, in which the seeing eye is seen while painting.

It is in the realm of a discussion about mirrors that a critical discussion of Descartes's *Optics* appears in Merleau-Ponty's text.[45] For Merleau-Ponty, the mirror is "the instrument of a universal magic that changes things into spectacles, spectacles into things, me into other and the other into me" (*"l'instrument d'une universelle magie qui change les choses en spectacles, les spectacles en choses, moi en autrui et autrui en moi"*).[46] He says that painters have often dreamed of mirrors because, through this mechanical trick and perspective, they have recognized "the metamorphosis of the viewer and the visible, which defines our flesh and its vocation" (*"la métamorphose du voyant et du visible, qui est la définition de notre chair et celle de leur vocation"*),[47] thoughts inspired by the French painter Robert Delaunay, the founder of the Orphism art movement.[48] He considers that this striving for seeing the being seen by the seeing corresponds to a drift to "total or absolute vision."[49]

Descartes appears in Merleau-Ponty's discussions as the extreme opposite of the painter's vision. Thus, for him, Descartes is one who "no longer aims to frequent the visible and who decides to reconstruct it according to a model from it."⁵⁰ To Merleau-Ponty, the only aim of Descartes is to investigate how vision is produced in order to invent, if this would be the case, "artificial organs" to replace and correct natural vision. Descartes searches the light as an action through contact, like things touched by the cane of a blind person. The blind person sees with the hands, which is what helps explain the Cartesian model for vision as being the hands. It is strange that Merleau-Ponty does not consider that painting is not only a "praise to the hands," borrowing the title of Henri Focillon's remarkable essay,⁵¹ but above all, a thinking *with* the hands. For Merleau-Ponty, Descartes cannot understand the poetics of a mirror insofar as a Cartesian cannot see himself in the mirror. "A Cartesian does not see *himself* in the mirror; he sees a dummy, an 'outside,' which he has every reason to believe other people see in the very same way but which, no more for himself than for others, is not a body in the flesh" (*"Un cartésien ne se voit pas dans le miroir: il voit un mannequin, un 'dehors' don't' il a toutes raisons de penser que les autres le voient pareillement, mais qui, pas plus pour lui-même que pour eux, n'est une chair"*).⁵² Following this line of thought, Merleau-Ponty adds, "The mirror image is nothing that belongs to him" (*"son image spéculaire n'est rien de lui"*).⁵³ These can be considered strange remarks if we recall how his contemporaries have portrayed Descartes, being the philosopher that most possesses portraits.⁵⁴ Instead of alluding to the question of portraits in painting, Merleau-Ponty discusses the icons. The textual basis for addressing these thoughts is Descartes's own observations about engravings in copper, the *tailles-douces*, which reads:

> The perfection of the image often depends on its not resembling its object as much as it might. You can see this in the case of engraving (*tailles-douces*): consisting simply of a little ink placed here and there on a piece of paper, they represent to us forests, towns, people, and even battles and storms; and although they make us think of countless different qualities in these objects, it is only in respect of shape that there is any real resemblance. And even this resemblance is very imperfect, since engravings represent to us bodies of varying relief and depth on a surface which is entirely flat. Moreover, in accordance with the rules of perspective they often represent circles by ovals better than by other circles, squares by rhombuses better than by other squares, and similarly for other shapes. Thus, it often happens that in order to be more perfect as an image and to represent an object better, an engraving ought not to resemble to it.⁵⁵

A similar position against resemblance can also be found in the first line of Descartes's treatise *The World*, where he argues that "although everyone is commonly convinced that the ideas we have in our mind are wholly similar to the objects from which they proceed, nevertheless I cannot see any reason which assures us that this is so."⁵⁶ His starting point is therefore that "there may be a difference between the sensation we have of light (i.e., the idea of light which is formed in our imagination by the mediation of our eyes) and what it is in the objects that produces this sensation within us (i.e., what it is in a flame or the sun that we call by the name 'light')."[57] Descartes dismisses resemblance as a source of truth, as many scholars have pointed out,[58] and many scholars inspired by Foucault's thoughts of Descartes dismiss the whole renaissance order of analogies and resemblances for the sake of founding the modern grounds of representation,[59] which is a transformation of the concept of *mimesis*. In Merleau-Ponty's readings of the passage cited above, Descartes is "clearly" refusing the reflexivity of the seeing and the seen that emerges strongly and in an obvious manner in the experience of a mirror. Descartes sees the image in the mirror, as does Merleau-Ponty, as something that excites and stimulates our mind as words and letters that do not resemble at all what they mean, as much as the engravings give us "sufficient indices to form an idea about the thing that does not come from the icon." In this sense, the engraving or painting acts for us as a book or text proposed for our reading. For Merleau-Ponty, in doing so, Descartes "liberates" us from the task of understanding how the painting of things in the body could make them be felt by the soul: "We need no longer understand how a painting of things in the body could make them felt in the soul" ("*Nous sommes dispensés de comprendre comment la peinture des choses dans le corps pourrait les faire sentir à l'âme*").[60] He concludes then that "there is nothing more going on between the things and the eyes, and the eyes and vision, than between the things and the blind man's hands, and between his hands and thoughts. Vision is not the metamorphosis of things themselves into the sight of them; it is not a matter of things belonging simultaneously to the huge, real world and the small, private world" ("*des choses aux yeux et des yeux à la vision il ne passe rien de plus que des choses aux mains de l'aveugle et de ses mains à sa pensée. La vision n'est pas la metamorphose des choses mêmes en leur vision, la double appartenance des choses au grand monde et à un petit monde privé*"),[61] what renders present the absent, what pierces the heart of being.[62] In Merleau-Ponty's view, painting is for Descartes a metaphysics but never a metamorphosis. Moreover, he also criticizes Descartes because he takes drawing as a kind of model for painting,[63] because he prefers the engraving, *tailles-douces*,[64] for presenting the object only through its exterior or its envelope.[65] Besides missing the reflexivity of vision, in taking drawing for a source for painting, Descartes also remains blind to painting insofar as, according to Merleau-Ponty, he did not examine the so-called second qualities (e.g., colors,[66])—that which rendered it impossible for him to meet the problem of a universality and an openness to things without concepts.[67] But the most important experience and notion that remains closed for the Cartesian eye is depth: from Merleau-Ponty's point of view, there is no depth in Descartes's visions; there is no eye for depth in Descartes.

But should Descartes's lines necessarily be read in this way? Do the *tailles-douces* and Descartes's appraisal of them and of drawings prove blindness for an openness to things without concepts? Maybe not without concepts, but intriguingly without images. Is Descartes such a superficial thinker, lacking any depth and profundity of vision? The question is whether what Descartes really aims for is "the limpidity of perceptions without objects in the margins of a world without equivocation," a "thought that no longer wants to haunt the visible and decides to reconstruct it according to the model it forges to it."[68]

Descartes's Unwritten Treatise on Painting

It is interesting that Merleau-Ponty could not recognize how Descartes's views on drawings allow not only a parallel between Descartes and the painters, such as da Vinci, as Valéry suggested, but also a strong connection to Valéry's views on drawing and its dancing essence. Descartes's aesthetical views are not only close to the aesthetics of drawings, which so strongly characterize the era in which he lived; they are also very close to abstract nonrepresentational art. Descartes is critical of representation, in language and in art. If representation is understood as resemblance, for Descartes "signs and words [. . .] in no way resemble the things they signify."[69] He has a similar conception of images: "In no case does an image have to resemble the object it represents in all respects, for otherwise there would be no distinction between the object and its image."[70] And the most "modernist" conception in relation to the unrepresentational feature of images is uttered in the same passage:

> Indeed the perfection of an image often depends on its not resembling its objects as much as it might. You can see this in the case of engravings: consisting simply of a little ink placed here and there on a piece of paper, they represent to us forest, towns, peoples, and even battles and storms; and although they make us think of countless different qualities in these objects, it is only in respect of shape that there is any real resemblance. And even this resemblance is imperfect, since engravings represent to us bodies of varying relief and depth on a surface which is entirely flat. Moreover, in accordance with the rules of perspective they often represent circles by ovals better than by other circles, squares by rhombuses better than by other squares, and similarly for other shapes. Thus it often happens that in order to be more perfect as an image and to represent an object better, an engraving ought not to resemble it.

Descartes proposes in these lines an aesthetic theory of the image as a regime of nonresemblance. It could be understood as an excess of representation rather than nonrepresentation.[71] It also leaves room for a thought about a thinking without images, or perhaps more precisely, about a thinking with figures that are without narrative contents—indeed, with abstract figures. The short unwritten treatise on visual arts that we find in Descartes's *Meditations*, and to which we have already alluded, is characterized mainly by a distinction between three kinds of painting and a very peculiar theory of colors. The first sort of painting

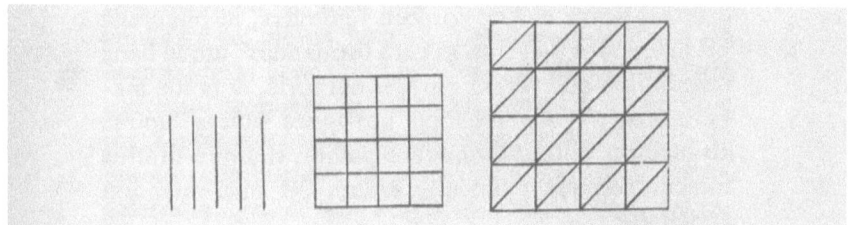

Figure 3.2. René Descartes, *Regulae ad directionem ingenii*; texte de l'édition Adam et Tannery; notice par Henri Gouhier, 413, Royal Library Stockholm.

one finds in this "unwritten treatise" can be called *realistic* or *figurative painting*, being "paintings, which must have been fashioned in the likeness of things that are real, and hence that at least these general kinds of things—eyes, head, hands and the body as a whole—are things which are not imaginary but are real and exist."[72] The second kind of paintings are those that although trying "to create sirens and satyrs with the most extraordinary bodies . . . cannot give them natures which are new in all respects; they simply jumble up the limbs of different animals."[73] This could be called *imaginative painting*. But there is still another kind of painting that "manage[s] to think up something so new that nothing remotely similar has ever been seen before—something which is therefore completely fictitious and unreal."[74] It could then be called *fictitious* or *unrealistic painting*. It is when discussing the third kind of painting, the fictitious and "unreal," that Descartes affirms that despite being totally fictitious and unreal, it still has something real—not only because it exists but because of its colors: "at least the colours used in the composition must be real."[75] The colors are the index of reality of the unreality of totally fictional things. Indeed, a discussion about "abstract" painting surprisingly emerges here, for Descartes states immediately after that "real colours (are) from which we form all the images of things."[76] Such an affirmation could have come from the mouth of Cézanne, above all, the Cézanne of Merleau-Ponty, the artist who recognized himself in Balzac's character of Frenhofer in *Le Chef d'oeuvre inconnu*, a painter who sought to express life through the use of color alone.[77] It could have been Mondrian as well, or any other abstract geometrist. And it is from this affirmation about colors that Descartes proceeds to a short discussion about "images" and shapes," *imago* and *figura*, and further to the "corporeal nature in general," to extension, quantity, size, number, place, and time—indeed, what we call abstract proprieties or qualities, that, if read from the viewpoint of modern abstract painting's practices and theories, renders Cartesian argumentation much more a painting argument than a dreaming one.

To these thoughts on colors found in the Meditations, we should add his discussions about colors in *Rules* twelve. Discussing how to conceive of shape in a clear and distinct way, Descartes takes color as a suitable example to explain

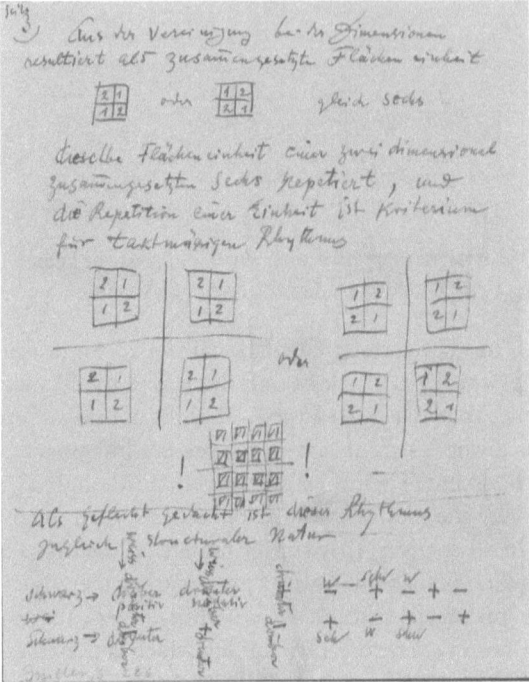

Figure 3.3. Paul Klee. *Bildnerische Gestaltungslehre: I.4. Gliederung*, Zentrum Paul Klee, Bern.

shape. He considers that no one can deny that a color is extended and consequently has shape. To show this he proposes an "abstraction," "setting aside every feature of colour apart from its possessing the character of shape, and conceive of the difference between white, blur, red, etc, as being like difference between the following figures or similar ones."

Even if Descartes does not develop these reflections on the relation between colors and lines, this translation of colors into lines opens a discussion about rhythm, or what Paul Klee called in his lessons at Bauhaus "structural rhythms" from which a doctrine of colors can be developed.

Finally, the theory of colors as shapes outlined by Descartes—"for it can be touched as well as seen"—is to be unfolded from his theory of light, which is for him the main concern that connects his physics and his metaphysics, the body and the soul. Regarding painting, Descartes considered that "a painter cannot represent all the different sides of a solid body equally well on his flat canvas, and so he chooses one of the principal ones, sets it facing the light, and shades

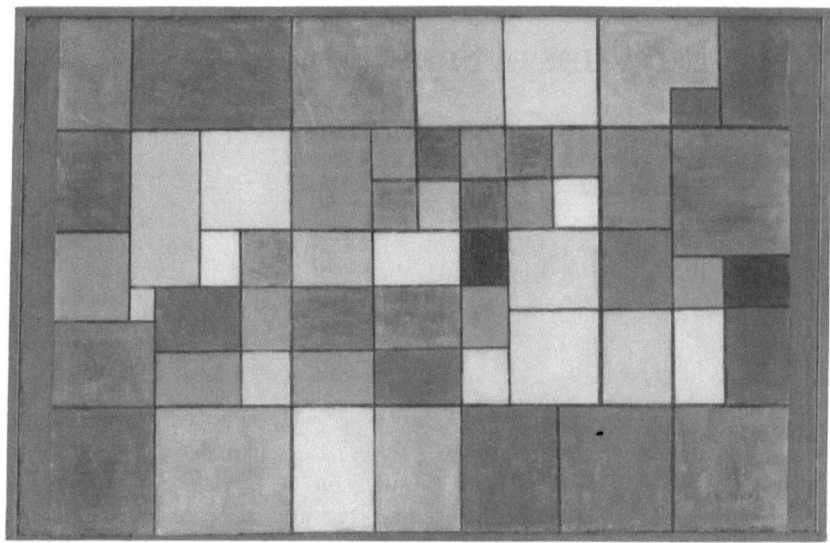

Figure 3.4. Paul Klee, *Bildnerische Gestaltungslehre: I.4. Gliederung*, Zentrum Paul Klee, Bern.

the others so as to make them stand out only when viewed from the perspective of the chosen side. In just the same way, fearing that I could not put everything I had in mind into my discourse, I undertook merely to expound quite fully what I understood about light."[78] Central to the reconstruction of Descartes's short treatise on visual arts is the thought that painting represents solid bodies—not images, not contents, not narratives—facing the light; hence, for him the act of painting is the double action of depicting the seeing of the seeing and the facing of how light hits the body.

4 Rhythms of Snow

Figures of Differentiation in Descartes's Meteorology

Cecilia Sjöholm

Shapes of an Ontology

On February 4, 1635, Descartes writes, I walked on the streets of Amsterdam and observed first the formation of the evening frost and then the fall of hail. The last particles had "six tiny teeth," like "wheels of clocks," "very white, like sugar, whereas the grains, which seemed to be of transparent ice, seemed to be nearly black."[1] He walks out again the next morning and observes, to his great astonishment, a kind of snow "of which I have never heard anyone speak": it is "composed of small blades . . . completely flat, highly polished and very transparent."[2] He spends days observing—and indulging in—a severe storm that shifts between snow and hail, marveling at the infinite variety of size, formation, and shape of the blizzard, speculating on its relation to clouds, winds, and temperature and on the origin and regularity of the patterns.

Meteorology (*Les Météores*) was published as one of three essays in *Discourse on Method* in 1637. It has received relatively little attention. But in times of climate change and dramatic shifts of weather, its grappling with atmospheric phenomena such as wind, rain, snow, light, and minerals, its mode of experimenting and writing is reactualized. It is not merely a testimony to Descartes's investment in and fascination with nature—accounted for in graphic details of landscapes and environments.[3] It is also a testimony to the limits of philosophy. Many have read the essays in *Discourse* as attempts to put the doctrines in the method of deduction to the test. But *Meteorology* belies the possibility of finding the cause behind phenomena that are as diverse in their expression as they are beguiling to the senses. Human subjects cannot master the elements or predict the weather, Descartes tells us.[4] It hits us, and we are subject to its vicissitudes. While offering a key to the composites of nature, it also impels the limits of reason.

In times of climate crisis and unpredictable variations in weather conditions, not least the climate of the North, Descartes's treatise, written during the Little Ice Age, has never been more significant. The kind of transformations that a northern climate materializes is given form through bodies of extension: small particles changing shape and movement, intertwining, interfering, and reorganizing. The treatise, which renews the Aristotelian tradition of writings on meteorology understood as the predilections of earth and water, does not only present us with hypotheses of nature's smallest building blocks. It offers a materialist vision of ontological dignity: the discourses on vapors, exhalations, winds, and clouds construe an aquatic world, consisting of water in different shapes, the particles of which are only partly visible. The discourses on snow, rain, and hail analyze drops in temperature dramatic enough to cause distinct shifts in size, movement, and organization. This universe is, by Descartes, considered as full: there are no gaps, although there are transformations: Cartesian ontology is concerned with the nature of these transformations, their cause, their variety, their physical dignity.

In the early prints of the book, the text is accompanied by images of the formations of snow and hail depicted in detail. The sensorial particularity of the formations, together with their figural transposition, is enough material for a heightened understanding of how the weather of the North is formed, exposing men to elements that they cannot control. The variation and transformation of frozen particles and the relation between all the elements that create them point to such a complexity that Descartes draws the conclusion that the weather cannot accurately be predicted by men. Not only the wondrous but also the violent character of phenomena of nature bring men to the brink of what they may even be able to imagine. Clouds may form materials that seem like milk or blood or flesh, and even engender "certain small animals"; therefore, we may have rains of iron, blood, or locusts.[5]

These images are not illustrations. They are thought-images, philosophical approximations of a preconceptual dimension of experience that abstract language fails to seize. In this way, they point to a dimension in Descartes's philosophy that has been little commented upon, the use of aesthetic means to capture a dimension that lies between the res extensa and the res cogitans. The use of aesthetic figures is a methodology explicitly appreciated by Descartes, as developed in *Rules for the Direction of the Mind*. Figures do more than illustrate the text; they are productive of the ontological notion of an infinite universe that is posited in the shape of minute particles. This offers a key to Descartes's *Meteorology*. Here, Descartes relies on rhythmic figurations in image and narrative that bring them to the limit of reason. Descartes posits a full universe of an infinite variety of aquatic shapes that move and transform in a way that we can never fully predict. The treatise does not construe rhythmic figurations as illustrations of what it says. Rather, it relies on a rhythmic conception of the "shapes, sizes and motions" of atmospheric phenomena.

This chapter is not concerned with situating *Meteorology* within Cartesian natural philosophy or an assessment of his method of deduction. The aim is rather to bring this work into a contemporary horizon of inquiries where shapes, or "figures," can be negotiated as philosophical thought-images of differentiation and production of differences. Descartes approaches the atmosphere as an aesthetic kind of organization, like music or painting. In this conception, rhythm is a descriptor transgressing the division between a metaphysical notion of the infinite and the sensual experience of atmospheric matter. This aesthetic dimension of the treatise, defined as a mode of encountering and reflecting on atmospheric phenomena through senses, emotions, and intellect, characterized by an open involvement with worldly experiences, is an integral aspect of the text. *Meteorology* is not only based on observation and experiment but also on narrative and figures.[6]

There is an affinity between the repetition of lines in Descartes and abstract painting and drawing: a visual experience of a rhythmicality in the extension of space, and of matter. It can be experienced, perhaps, through the body, but this does not mean that it refers to the body. Rather, it strives to move outside of it, to depict the very line between embodied experience and the physical movement that lies beyond. It carries us over to what we cannot perceive: the dimension of volume, of geometry, dimensions that are irreducible to anthropomorphic conceptions.

The reason why Cartesian natural philosophy has attracted newfound attention in recent years is perhaps that it flickers between the res cogitans and the res extensa, the subject of deduction and the fleeting character of matter and of bodies. Traditionally, it has been widely held that Descartes takes us to a point where we must choose between the certainty of reason and the flickering transformations of nature that are vaguely perceptible to the senses. As has been mentioned many times in this book, Cartesian dualism—or what is perceived as such—is routinely one of the most berated doctrines in contemporary thought.[7] But Descartes's natural philosophy is so varied and rich that it is hard to even identify a dualistic system.[8] Rather than exemplifying a doctrinal metaphysics, *Meteorology* can be situated between Descartes's metaphysical writings and his physics.[9] The standard criticisms of Descartes's dualism have now been supplemented with a new view on his natural philosophy and the varieties of antinomies that are being challenged there. Moreover, a complex philosophy of imagination is integral to the notion of understanding, putting the idea of certainty in a new light.[10]

Still, *Meteorology* is one of the least referenced texts. This is reason enough to read it anew. In this chapter, rather than treat *Meteorology* as a treatise that exemplifies a certain method of deduction developed in *Discourse on Method*, we will analyze its figurative approach to nature as a meaningful creation that does not translate into anthropomorphic ideas or concepts. Rather than engage in models of representation, Descartes's hypotheses are concerned with the action on and between bodies in modes that can be described in terms such as affects, flows, and rhythm.

The Historical Background of the Images in *Meteorology*

Meteorology tells of an involvement with cold weather that speaks of great fascination. The weather of the North is valorized as meaningful and wondrous. It is perhaps *Meteorology* that gave rise to rumors circulating in the Nordic countries that he did not die in Stockholm at all; instead, he traveled to a Sami village in the north of Sweden to learn to play ceremonial drums.[11] The most intriguing aspects of *Meteorology* is the visual force with which he depicts snow, wind, and ice, using not only abstract reason to work out the "shapes, sizes and motions" of nature's invisible components but also images.[12] Attempting to find "the causes of everything that is most admirable above the earth,"[13] *Meteorology* is one of the treatises that most forcibly uses images to, paradoxically, bring out what we cannot perceive and to develop an iconography.[14] Snow, wind, and other phenomena of nature are here transposed into complex particles rather than visualized as anthropomorphic reductions.

The treatise was supposed to have been included in a work of modern cosmology and technique: *Le Monde, The World* in 1633. However, for fear of being condemned as a heretic, Descartes withdrew the publication of *Le Monde*. Instead, *Meteorology*, together with his treatise on vision, optics, and geometry, appeared together with *Discourse on Method* in 1637. As mentioned, whether the essays are to be read together with *Discourse* is often debated, and not a line of questioning pursued in this chapter. What is at stake is rather the aesthetic vision, which has been kept between the earlier and the later project of publication. The aesthetic dimension, as a mode of encountering and reflecting on atmospheric phenomena through senses, emotions, and intellect, and characterized by an open engagement with worldly experiences, is an integral aspect of *Meteorology*. The treatise is based not only on observation and experiment but also on narrative and figures, a baroque aesthetics intertwined with scientific thought. The weather of the North, and the minerals and atmospheric phenomena that accompanies it, determines the hypotheses of nature's smallest building blocks.[15] Rhythmic figurations in image and narrative intersect with sensual experience; Descartes is positing a universe of an infinite variety of aquatic shapes that move and transform. This ontological version of a natural philosophy does not construe rhythmic figurations as illustrations of what it says. Rather, it relies on a rhythmic conception that is already inherent to the description of the experience of weather and other atmospheric phenomena that belong to it.

The figures, describing sensual appeal as well as the shock of sharp tastes, are not there solely to work out a possible model of a hypothesis. They must be seen in conjunction with the overall project described in *Principles of Philosophy*: How do we acquire knowledge of what we cannot see? Descartes's natural philosophy departs from the shapes, sizes, and motions he believes he can demonstrate by using mathematics.[16] But the letters also make clear that the images are not merely mathematically construed diagrams. Nor are they allegories or mimetic depictions of facts. They are not immediate translations of things.[17] Instead, the figures imply an infinite variety of differences in perceptible objects, giving an ontological status to the production of differences that challenges the subject of scientific knowledge through their unpredictability.

As Descartes conceives it, clouds and vapors are, in themselves, objects for poets and painters.[18] They are extraordinary phenomena to be explored by the senses as well as understood by the mind. Alternating between the hot and the cold, the hard and the soft, between the soft winds on the shoreline and the storm over the oceans, little snowflakes and thunderous avalanches, the weather, and its transformations is a source of wonder, often mediated through Descartes's own experiences—and sometimes through conjecture and scattered evidence.[19] The treatise is concerned with finding causes. But phenomena such as weather, which envelopes us, has a sense in itself. We may explore it by thought. But we cannot find it by thought; it enwraps us.[20]

Visualization was an explicit means to transmit the beauty that was not only the object of *Meteorology* but also at the origins of its conception: the colors of the rainbow, the perfectly proportioned stars of snow, and so on. In *Meteorology*, Descartes was closely involved in the making of the images. He engaged Frans van Schooten the younger, who was both a painter and a mathematician, a combination Descartes repeatedly advocated the importance of.[21] Before the publication of the three essays in the discourse, Descartes wrote to his friend Marin Mersenne in March 1936 and explained that he was particularly concerned that the book would be beautiful—the paper and the font should be appealing. Beauty is a quality in its own right. This also applies to the images. In a tone of mocking humility, he expresses hope that Mersenne can perhaps explain to the engraver how his own poorly drawn figures are to be interpreted.[22] Moreover, as he later writes to Mersenne, he has attempted to find the most beautiful examples of what he wants to demonstrate as the building blocks of nature. The book on *Discourse* and the three essays, Descartes explains to Mersenne, were to present a "universal science" addressing a lay audience, made in such a way that even novices could understand it.[23] It is the mind that sees and not the eye; an argument made in relation to painting both in *Optics* and in *Discourse on Method*, which were published together with *Meteorology*: the image of painting is used to figure how thought works, between light and shade, the visible and the invisible.[24]

The concept of figures can be seen in this vein. In seventeenth-century France, the word *figure* had many uses, ranging from aesthetic to mathematical.[25] *Figurae* (Latin) carry a dimension that stretches from image, implying the subjective capacity of imagination—one figures things—and the more linear deductions of mathematics and mechanics. Descartes refers to his own sketches as figures. His images are crucial for his philosophy of nature because shapes, sizes, and motions are also mathematical.[26] "Figure" is also the concept of the often-referenced rule twelve in the *Regulae Philosophicae, Rules for the Direction of the Mind*, which Descartes began writing in the 1620s. It was published in 1684, after his death. The concept of "shape," also, derives from *figurae*; it is "figure" in French.[27] But in *Rules*, it becomes clear that shape does not capture the meaning of figure. Nor does diagram, which some scholars have utilized.[28] Unlike geometrical lines, and the diagram, the figures in rule twelve have extension. They imply a spatial and embodied vision, a kind of flesh.

The question of how to interpret the notion of figure in the *Rules* has been an object of debate. This has often been construed through their uses in other writings. Dennis Sepper has placed Descartes figures in the realm between imagination and knowledge: they cannot be reduced to ideas or representations but refer both to some kind of sensible experience and beyond—"all figuration requires activity—the minimum of which is like conceiving figures mentally or sizing up an object in a glance."[29] As German philosopher Sybille Krämer has argued, Descartes transforms geometry into a figurative "language of the eye," which not only represents the objects but constitutes them; the objects arise through the operation.[30] In this way, the figure referred to in rule twelve, as has been shown by French philosopher Jean-Luc Marion, occupies a space between the res cogitans and the res extensa, if we are to read Descartes's work while retroactively applying his own terminology. This gives the hypothetic character of the figure a certain status that is irreducible to both geometry and "psychology"; the figure is not knowledge inscribing itself in the world, Marion writes, but the world expanding in a uniform way before and under knowledge.[31] Figures are ideas manifesting themselves as sensations, which may find their immediate support in the form of pain, cold, heat, and so on. These sensations are described through bodies. But what is particularly notable is the arbitrariness of the codification; things are figured that lack form in the outside world, such as colors.

Nothing is, as Descartes writes in the *Rules*, more readily perceptible by the senses than figure, for it can be touched as well as seen. By this, Descartes refers to the fact that figures are construed by a multiplicity of the senses. In the figure, we perceive not the real world but the phenomena. We perceive it not as an idea but as a thing in space and time, of proportions and dimensions that have weight and color, taste and the quality of touch, and so on. Figures are both sensual and intellectual; they arise between passive responses and intellectual elaboration and present themselves to the mind spontaneously, preconceptually but distinctly different from other things and phenomena. They are not "real" in the sense that they directly correspond to something manifest in the outside world. They are, however, caused by a sensual imprint; sense impressions are in themselves altered figures of their source, transmitted through rays of light or nerve endings in the body.[32] Figures may have a variety of sources. They may be passive impressions or active elaborations of the mind. A figure may arise as we concentrate "our mind's eye" on one thing in order to perceive the shapes of the world of extension.[33] A figure captures the extended body of the res cogitans: that which we reflect in our mind's eye while we perceive it through our senses. A figure is not a representation but rather an abbreviated suggestion: "the more compact these are, the handier they are."[34] For that reason, in an image, certain things can be exaggerated and other things left out. Responding to a critique, Descartes defends his choice to publish an image of a sheep's brain rather than a human brain in *Optics*: certain parts, such as the ventricles, were depicted much bigger than in a human brain. But to Descartes, such a figure served much better to "make visible" what he had to say.

In the end, knowledge is the perception of nature's composition in its simplicity.[35] In *Geometry*, the images are made up of lines.[36] The geometer knows well, Descartes writes, that lines have no breadth and surfaces no depth, yet he goes on to construct the one from the other. When figures are drawn and displayed, it is easier for us to understand surfaces and volumes, proportions and relations. Straight lines are also figures since they allow us to apprehend an extended object.[37] Mathematical figures, in this way, are mediated through a figural imagination of extension and forms—making Cartesian science not just an object of reason but also a baroque figural thought.[38] This method is used in *Meteorology* throughout. In *Optics*, geometrical and algebraic methods are applied that construe the hypotheses of vision, light, and atmosphere in the form of lines.

Meteorology deals "mainly with the nature of salt, the causes of wind and thunder, the figures of snow, the colors of the rainbow (where I also try to demonstrate the nature of each color) and the crowns, or halos, and suns or parhelia as those that were seen in Rome some six or seven years ago."[39] The latter indicated that Descartes in fact never experienced this; but it was a common theme in early modern visual culture and indicated an omen of significant events. The very function of "halo," the parhelia, was to Descartes immediately connected to "hyperbole"—that is, a geometrical figure, an example of how the transposition between *Meteorology* and *Geometry* was embedded in the notion of figure.[40] The final essay, *Geometry*, presents "a general method of solving all the problems that have never yet been solved"[41]—referencing the distinct use of figures as a source of deductive reasoning. However, the figures move beyond a consistent method of deduction.

The images in Descartes's work have a variety of sources: some are copied from Descartes's own manuscripts and are evidently drawn by Descartes himself. Some have been added in editions after Descartes's death and have no relation to any original (e.g., Charles Le Brun's famous faces in *Passions of the Soul*). Some images, and this includes the bulk of the images in *Meteorology*, are the result of Descartes's personal engagement with editors and artists. The address to a wider audience is crucial, but so too is the philosophical impact. The pedagogical and philosophical aspect of the images, in turn, cannot be distinguished from their aesthetic elaboration—using images in his books, Descartes also distanced himself from Aristotelian metaphysics and engaged in new theories of perception that were brought into his work on mathematics and physics. The work of "artisans" contributed to the amalgam between figure and reason. Together, they stimulated the senses while interpreting movements and proportions in the outside world. To Descartes, perception relates to objects in the world in the same way that images relate to perception. Image and object are not the same, just as the perception of an image and an image are not the same. In both cases, an apprehension of the outside world is created through the qualities inherent to images: lines, movement, and suggestions of extension.[42]

In *Optics*, Descartes describes the differentiation between perceptions and external objects. Perceptions are not identical to external objects; they are instead prepared in the brain as images. With this insight, Descartes ended the philosophical doctrine of simulacra (i.e., the idea that the world is planting images in us that resemble that which is outside, or that perception would be a natural mirror of the external world). It is the soul that sees and not the eye, a proposition that is made in accordance with the reflection on the perception of engraved images, pointing to the fact that we see more sides of an object in an image than are actually represented.[43]

Descartes also worked with his publishers concerning the layout of the book,[44] and with Huygens in particular, there was much discussion about the figures. Descartes provided sketches (figures), and he was particular about their placement, measurement, and repetition. The images were supposed to be worked up in *taille en bois* (wooden print) by a craftsman or artist.[45] Again, it was crucial that the artist was also well versed in mathematics.[46] As we have seen in the discussion of *Treatise on Music*, mathematical figures were seamlessly interwoven with his philosophy. To Descartes, this provided a modern dimension to philosophical thought, which extended beyond the aesthetic experience of music. He considered the particular combination of mathematics and imagery as superior to scholastic reasoning more broadly, not least when it came to the understanding of natural phenomena: it is better to insert nature in philosophy than philosophy in nature.[47] As we have seen, this is done through the image: I believe that nothing can be imagined that cannot be solved by a line, as he writes to

Beeckman.[48] Such lines belong to arithmetic and music, but also to the discourse on light and the atmosphere.[49] The wish for an artisan-mathematician applies not only to *Geometry* but to all three essays following *Discourse on Method*.

Descartes was particular with the choice of artist.[50] He mocks his attempts to be the "artisan" of his own books.[51] The artists are neither to provide arithmetic diagrams nor mimetic images but to convincingly represent the differences between particles that are entangled with one another: water, fog, rain, and hail.[52] This demand resonates both with the scientific hypotheses presented and the aquatic world produced by the text: to Descartes, the world is full of matter in different shapes and sizes, which is also what causes the transformations of atmosphere, weather, and climate.[53] The shape of a particle will determine the way in which it moves and how it is transformed, and its relation to other particles and their shape and the spaces between them. The notion that the universe is full, there is no vacuum, as well as the notion that the universe was without limits was subject to derision by Hobbes, because it could not be tested. Perhaps this would not have been a problem, had Descartes's *Principles* as well as the essays launched metaphysical doctrines rather than hypotheses of natural philosophy.[54] But Descartes was only interested in using observation, imagination, and demonstration of different aspects of the ontological differentiation that he was exploring.[55] Accordingly, after the essays, Descartes had the intention of proving the existence of even smaller particles, inconceivable to the eye, that filled the spaces that the other particles left open.[56] The differentiation between particles is infinite; thus, the factors of shape, size, and movement affect the weather in such infinite variety that we end up not knowing the extent to which they can transpose, alternate, and metamorphose.

In *Meteorology*, as well as *Optics*, the images are produced to induce a process of cognition situated between the abstract and the sensual. In *Optics*, the images often reference themselves: a hand making the drawing may be placed in the engraving, for instance. In the early editions of Descartes's natural philosophy, the same images would be repeated on several pages in a row in order to allow for the abstract apprehension of the text and the process of visualization simultaneously. This was done so that the reader would not, as Descartes's friend Constantijn Huygens put it, have to err in the search for an image in the same way that "a bird attempts to encircle the tree he has left."[57] In older editions of *Le Monde* (i.e., *Les Météores, Dioptrique*, and *L'Homme*, in the Shuyl edition from 1664 as well as the *Opera Filosofica* from 1656),[58] the same illustrations are used repeatedly, page after page. In this way, Descartes inserts the reflexive subject in the reading experience. The perception of images is intertwined with reflection of how perception is structured.[59] In the Shuyl edition of *L'Homme*, one can see the image of a person that has burned himself repeatedly. The person is "burning" from a fire that hits the nerve endings that run from the foot. Repetition is

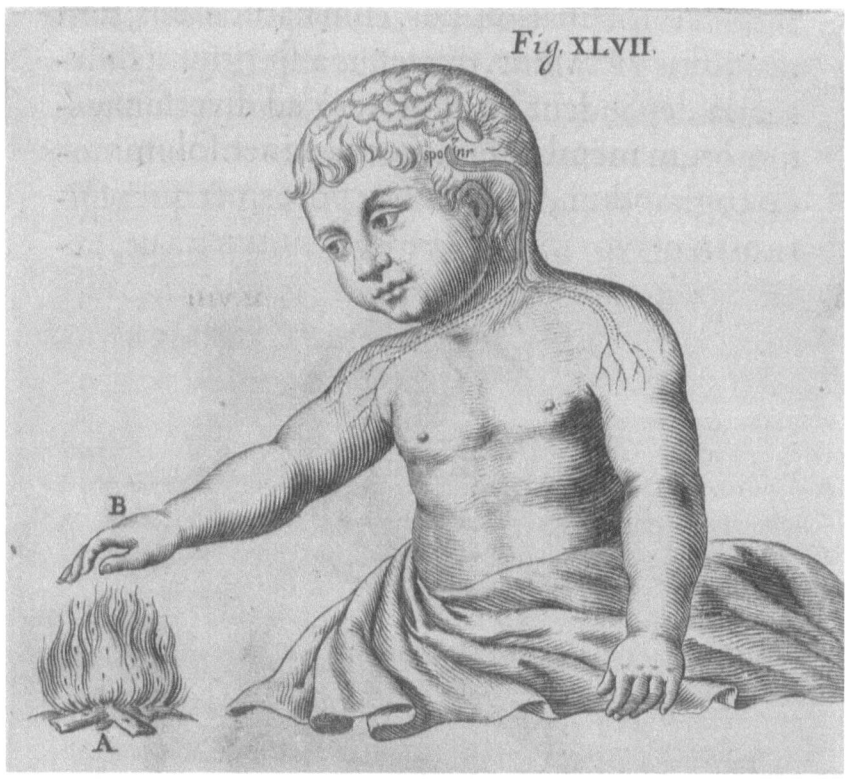

Figure 4.1. *L'Homme: Et un traitté de la formation du foetus*, Paris, 1664, Royal Library Stockholm.

in itself, as German philosopher Edmund Husserl has shown, inherent to the perception of images as such. The image always has a dimension of phantom to it: I posit each mode of the appearance of an image as a mode of appearance of something that already has been. The engraving, which is inherently repeating the same through being printed and distributed in a number of volumes, is a mode of repetition that carries a phantom at each page. It is the carrier not so much of a corporeal memory as of a figment: an idea, a fluctuant piece of fantasy. Through their very repetition, however, the engravings acquire a reference. They are not representing a natural object but serve as what Husserl calls a recollective representation.[60] In the engravings, the body is mimicked as a physical entity. It is rather made out as a phantom, whose mode of being, in space and time, lies in the repetitive recurrence of the same physical sensation over and over again—in this way, the pictorial mode of the engraving corresponds to the very idea of how corporeal affects work.

The image is repeated several pages in a row. In this way, the figures are not mere vehicles for the imagination, adding life to an abstract text. They construe a line between pain as "inner" corporeal experience and the perception of pain as an image of the mind. Descartes also worked with similar sketches in his letters; for instance, he addresses a friend explaining how experimenting with the flame of a candle made him meditate on the difference between inner and outer images. This is also what he attempted to achieve with the images of *Meteorology*—showing the difference between the structure of the weather and the way it is felt on a human body.[61]

The Senses of *Meteorology*

A multifaceted and flexible method of observation, including sensual experience and the capacity to be moved, is integral to *Meteorology*. It is this method that may be described as aesthetic; it is construed through the gathering of sensible information, which is then transposed into imagery. This method assumes that the experience of nature is meaningful in itself, sometimes made knowledgeable through arithmetic figures, but in the end irreducible to mathematics.

If we are to find the causes behind that which is the most "wondrous above the earth," as stated in the introduction to *Meteorology*, we must begin our inquiries in a state of wonder.[62] Wonder, in *Passions*, is defined as an affect that incites the production of new knowledge.[63] It is a passion of the soul, which means that it is not a physical reaction but rather intrinsically intertwined with intellectual elaboration. The knowledge produced by wonder takes place in a brain "where the organs of the senses are that contribute to this knowledge."[64]

Nature produces a marvel that sparks thought, we are told at the beginning of the treatise. Once we have understood the causes of weather, we no longer need to marvel at it.[65] Here, Descartes implies a separation between aesthetic experience, which sparks the emotion of wonder, and scientific knowledge, which provides answers to the questions that wonder helps raise. In every inquiry, there must be something unknown.[66] Once answers are provided, wonder is to be extinguished.[67] Critics have taken this to be a quaint goal of Cartesian *Meteorology*.[68] However, wonder is intrinsically interwoven with the Cartesian ontology of differentiation; it always comes anew. Observing and experimenting with the visible world, the weather, water, the rainbow, and the behavior of minerals in water, thought grapples with the expansion, contraction, agitation, and movement, the transformation and the intertwinements that take us from the visible to the invisible. Therefore, thought also engages with figures that lies between the sensual and the abstract, implicating an experience of "the sizes of the bodies we see, their shape, motion, position, duration, number and so on" as Descartes writes in *Principles*.[69] Thought can retract from sensual experience, but is also intertwined with it, through the passion of wonder. There is an intrinsic relation between the wonders of sensual experience—of the cold and the snow—and the wonders produced at the thought of the sublime cause of these experiences. The latter, however, is not to be found to the full: it is retracting from reason.

Shape is a primary category in *Meteorology*, which figures the world of water in the northern hemisphere: sea, rain, ice, salt, vapors, clouds, snow, hail. It is a full and infinite universe of differentiation and movement, intertwining, separating, and metamorphosing. The images are the result not only of observation but also of metaphor: the way in which a particle can be described in a rich pictorial language affects its geometrical figuration. Imagine, Descartes writes to his friend Henricus Reneri, "the air to be like wool" and the ether within to be like little whirlwinds."[70] Water is "like little eels."[71] Rain can appear like perfect rounded shapes, but also transform by air and weight. Rain can turn into vapor, and vapor, when it gets cold, transforms into various shapes of snow and ice. They can join like "slender fibres" or they can freeze like drops, forming "small knots or lumps of ice" with surfaces that are "velvety, or covered all around with hairs."[72] The particles are construed so that they can fit into different bodies, or shape-shift with one another.

The formation of clouds, the shift between winds, the formations of frosty landscapes, marshlands, and shorelines—all point toward the invisible dance of a full universe of differentiation. Its shape and movement and the size of its particles are brought forth in the images of the text as well as the wooden prints. The images are composed of a mix between particles and landscape, where the small, invisible particles are drawn above natural size, figuring components of volumes and proportions.[73] Some of the images gather several kinds of invisible components of different aspects of the atmosphere in different compartments of the image. Winds are figured in a certain way, vapor in another, water in a third manner. Its transformations, from water into vapor, comes from transitional effects of spinning and swirls, invisible energies creating movements that create an effect of inside-out; we are drawn into imperceptible centers of production. "I am following your advice on the figures," Descartes writes to Huygens, "and place them in relation to the text, made in wooden print."[74] The most difficult is, as you have seen, to "represent how the drops of water are disposed in the skies . . . and how they have extended into vapors that cause a wind as strong as a steam engine." Here Descartes inserts distinct marks for strong winds, making visible how they affect the volumes of the atmosphere. It is also difficult to explain how drops of water "twist around the parts of salt in the sea," which are, he explains, the latest images he has made. "I hope," Descartes says, that when it comes to the flakes of snow, "winter will help."[75]

Causality is deeply intertwined with shape, and shape can be demonstrated in figures. "To see a world in a grain of sand," William Blake wrote, and Descartes

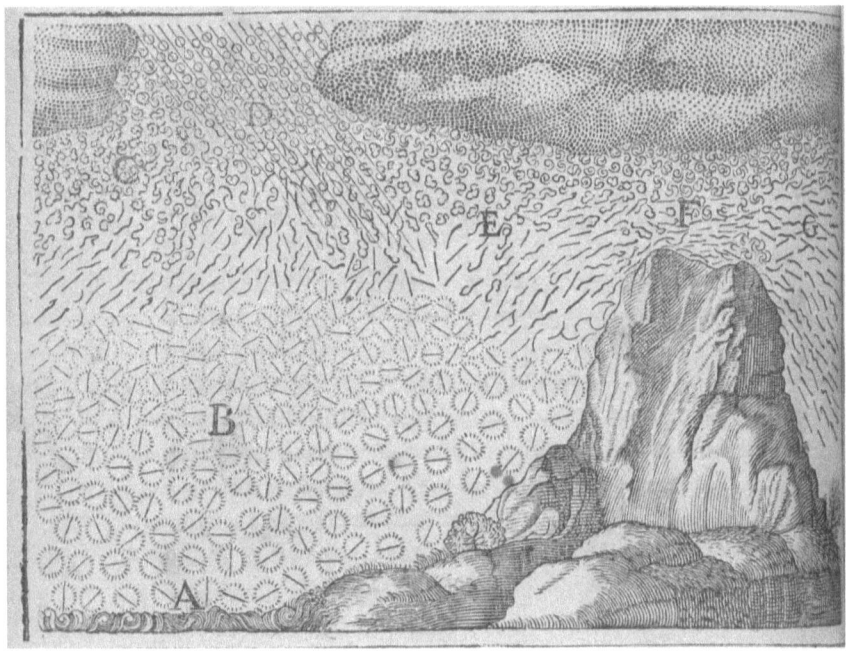

Figure 4.2. Vapors, *Les Météores*. In *Discours de la methode*, Leyden, 1637, Royal Library Stockholm.

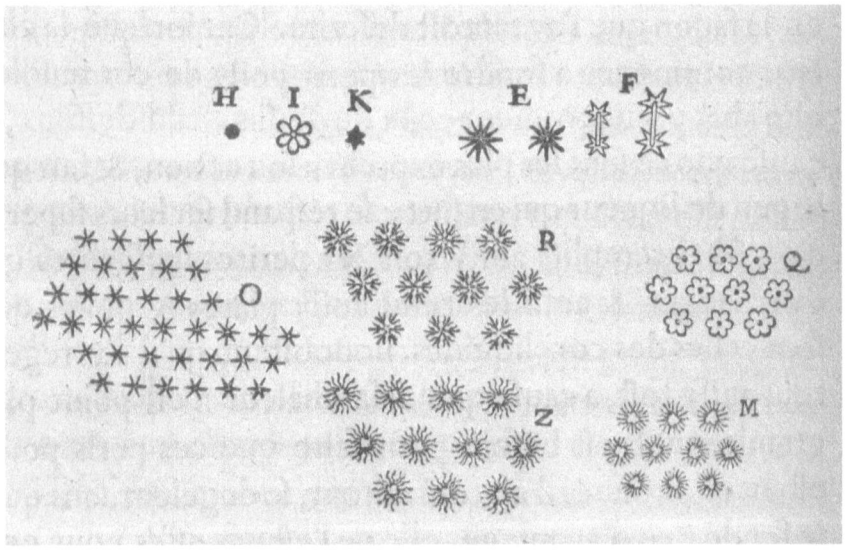

Figure 4.3. Snowflakes, *Les Météores*. In *Discours de la methode*, Leyden, 1637, Royal Library Stockholm.

does precisely this in his discourse on salt.[76] This is a text in which we still have access to images produced by Descartes's hand. It demonstrates that the senses, and a capacity to be astounded in front of natural phenomena, offer an access to the ontological differentiated universe. The world is meaningful in itself, and it is presented to us in aesthetic forms that we experience through our emotions, our senses, and our curiosity. The text does not isolate salt as a material substance; its spinning and swirling in the water puts to the test what the world is in terms of "rhythmic extension."

The discourse on salt is accompanied by five little figures, four of which are evidently drawn by Descartes as reported by de La Forge.[77] We see little particles, rounded cylinders by approximation, accrue in bigger shapes after each step. Particles of salt have their own shape, Descartes writes, different from water, which is also what makes salt behave the way it does in relation to other bodies, to wind, to fire, to fluids. Salt has a penetrating quality; it preserves meat by entering it through small pores. Through such penetrations, it also helps create the refraction of light on the sea and the miracle of ice in the middle of the summer.[78] It also creates the taste of salt on the tongue, sharp needles penetrating the pores.[79]

The miracle of crystallization becomes, in Descartes's text, a result of the movement of particles, their gatherings and their splits, their coming together in the flakes that we today may serve as table salt and their dissolution in hot water. Salt water and fresh water swirl and twirl in rivers, seas, mists, and rain, above the skies or under the earth, moved by fire and heat or other particles. The crystals of salt are formed by much tinier particles that they eye cannot perceive, but we can perceive the behavior of the flakes, from the moment they come together until the moment they break, by heat, into powder, when their "tiny prisons" are broken. The flexible behavior of salt can be explained by the particles of water hosted in the flakes. The shape of water particles and salt have developed over time, Descartes argues; water has become pliant, bendable, and flexible. This affects the salt particles, which are hard like "cylinders or rods."[80] These particles can also be corrupted and turn into acidic water, which has quite a different shape and agitates the nerves of the tongue differently.

"Sizes, shapes, positions and motions are my formal object (in philosophers' jargon), and the physical objects which I explain are my material object," Descartes explains in a letter to a friend. But as we can tell from the narrative above, empirical observations are ingrained by sensual data. From "the oblong and inflexible shape of the particles of salt, I deduced the square shape of its grains, and many other things which are obvious to the senses." Observation is not enough; Descartes wants to "demonstrate the cause by the effects a posteriori."[81] The effects produced in nature that we may perceive, Descartes writes in *Principles of Philosophy*, "almost always depend on structures which are so minute that they completely elude our senses."[82] Observable effects have imperceptible

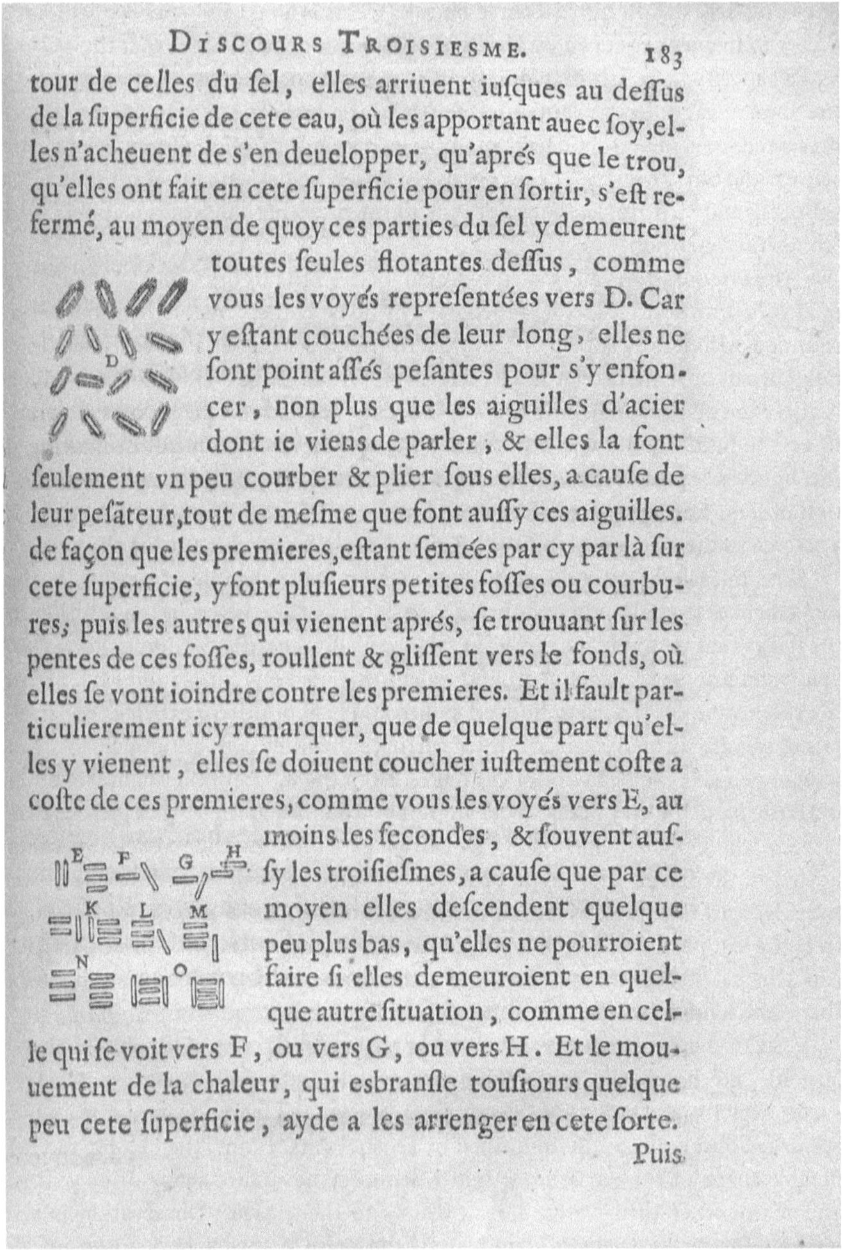

Discours Troisiesme. 183

tour de celles du sel, elles arriuent iusques au dessus de la superficie de cete eau, où les apportant auec soy, elles n'acheuent de s'en deuelopper, qu'aprés que le trou, qu'elles ont fait en cete superficie pour en sortir, s'est refermé, au moyen de quoy ces parties du sel y demeurent toutes seules flotantes dessus, comme vous les voyés representées vers D. Car y estant couchées de leur long, elles ne sont point assés pesantes pour s'y enfoncer, non plus que les aiguilles d'acier dont ie viens de parler, & elles la font seulement vn peu courber & plier sous elles, a cause de leur pesateur, tout de mesme que font aussy ces aiguilles. de façon que les premieres, estant semées par cy par là sur cete superficie, y font plusieurs petites fosses ou courbures; puis les autres qui vienent aprés, se trouuant sur les pentes de ces fosses, roullent & glissent vers le fonds, où elles se vont ioindre contre les premieres. Et il fault particulierement icy remarquer, que de quelque part qu'elles y vienent, elles se doiuent coucher iustement coste a coste de ces premieres, comme vous les voyés vers E, au moins les secondes, & souuent aussy les troisiesmes, a cause que par ce moyen elles descendent quelque peu plus bas, qu'elles ne pourroient faire si elles demeuroient en quelque autre situation, comme en celle qui se voit vers F, ou vers G, ou vers H. Et le mouuement de la chaleur, qui esbranfle tousiours quelque peu cete superficie, ayde a les arranger en cete sorte.

Puis

Figure 4.4. Salt, *Les Météores*. In *Discours de la methode*, Leyden, 1637, Royal Library Stockholm.

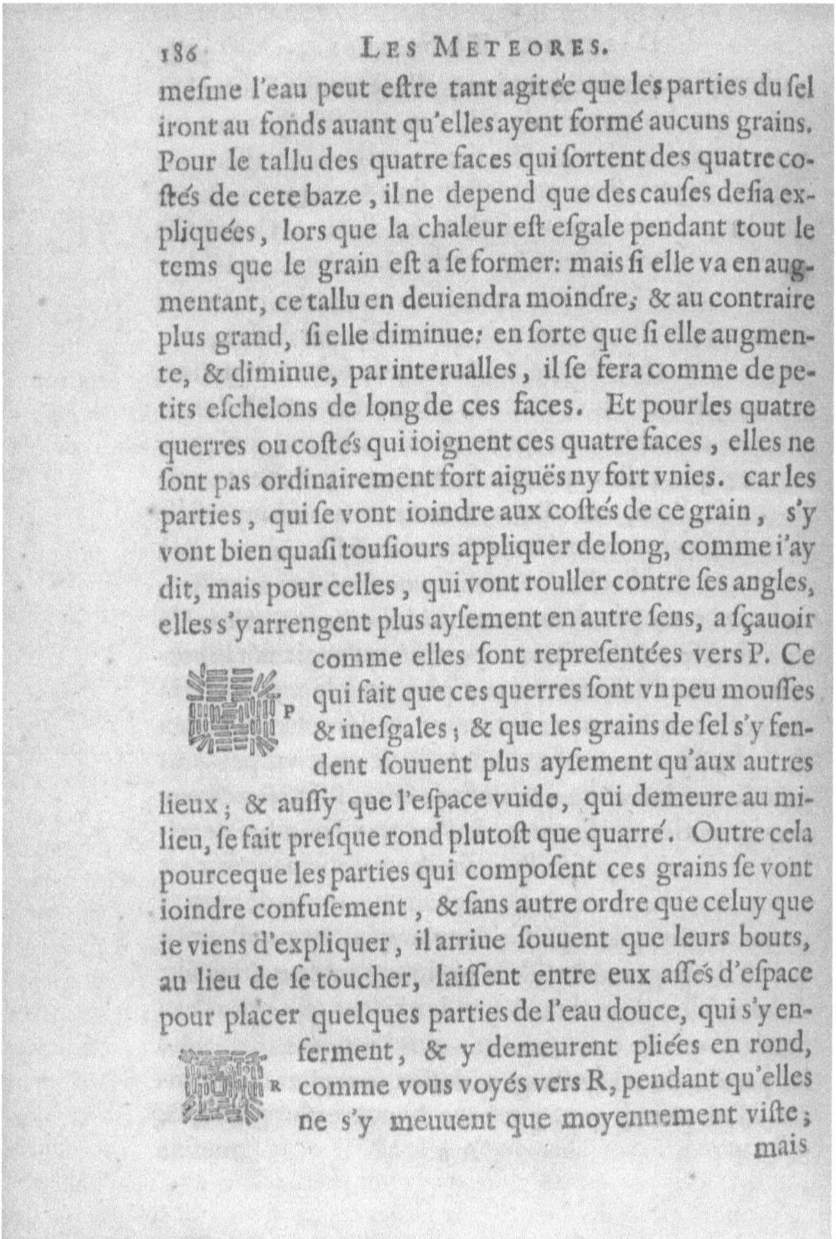

186   LES METEORES.

mesme l'eau peut eftre tant agitée que les parties du sel iront au fonds auant qu'elles ayent formé aucuns grains. Pour le tallu des quatre faces qui sortent des quatre costés de cete baze, il ne depend que des causes desia expliquées, lors que la chaleur est esgale pendant tout le tems que le grain est a se former: mais si elle va en augmentant, ce tallu en deuiendra moindre; & au contraire plus grand, si elle diminue: en sorte que si elle augmente, & diminue, par interualles, il se fera comme de petits eschelons de long de ces faces. Et pour les quatre querres ou costés qui ioignent ces quatre faces, elles ne sont pas ordinairement fort aiguës ny fort vnies. car les parties, qui se vont ioindre aux costés de ce grain, s'y vont bien quasi tousiours appliquer de long, comme i'ay dit, mais pour celles, qui vont rouller contre ses angles, elles s'y arrengent plus ayfement en autre sens, a sçauoir comme elles sont representées vers P. Ce qui fait que ces querres sont vn peu mousses & inesgales; & que les grains de sel s'y fendent souuent plus ayfement qu'aux autres lieux; & aussy que l'espace vuide, qui demeure au milieu, se fait presque rond plutost que quarré. Outre cela pource que les parties qui composent ces grains se vont ioindre confusement, & sans autre ordre que celuy que ie viens d'expliquer, il arriue souuent que leurs bouts, au lieu de se toucher, laissent entre eux assés d'espace pour placer quelques parties de l'eau douce, qui s'y enferment, & y demeurent pliées en rond, comme vous voyés vers R, pendant qu'elles ne s'y meuuent que moyennement viste;
mais

Figure 4.5. Salt, *Les Météores*. In *Discours de la methode*, Leyden, 1637, Royal Library Stockholm.

causes, but shapes and formations construe preconceptual hypotheses of nature's consistency.

The first figure of Descartes points to the line in which salt particles will move in hot water, the second to their loose floating around on the surface of the water, the third shows their gathering in regular patterns, and the fourth and fifth the consolidation and then loosening of that pattern. The patterns are made up of little cylinders properly counted in symmetry. The images have an obvious arithmetic and geometric dimension to them: they are in part figured through calculation. But the senses intertwine with the figural; water against the tongue gives a sense of fluidity like "little eels," whereas the sharpness we experience on our tongue through the taste of salt leads to the hypothesis of hard cylinders. The particles are figured as an equal result of narrative and visual imagination, the pattern of crystallization and separation is conceived as an aesthetic experimentation involving sight, touch, and taste. In this way a full universe is posited where bodies are offered extension and movement.

Figures of Rhythm

Descartes's "shape" does not mimic nature. But its status is not contingent. The images serve as scientific evidence in times of "cognitive pluralism."[83] *Meteorology* and *Optics* provide thought-images that are a conglomerate of reason and imagination.[84] This means that are produced both out of reason and imagination—not one or the other, but both at the same time. They have, of course, some kind of illuminating function, but they are not illustrations.[85] This is not without its problems. Using images in this way has been called a form of "visual reductionism."[86] But it is not certain that the figures of weather and salt are objects of deduction. They imply the existence of an infinite variety of movements and transformations, pushing beyond the limits of reason: the complex variety of particles supersedes the capacity to make futural predictions about their behavior.[87] Rather than being products of reason, the images and figures are conjectural images of understanding, of how the production of small particles behaves.

The weather, as well as atmospheric phenomena, is governed by formations that Descartes explicitly tells us we cannot control. Whereas *Optics* placed more emphasis on the relation between consciousness and perception, *Meteorology* puts the production of differences into focus. This can be seen in his account of the aquatic world of formations of snow, rain, hail, salt, and so on, but also in his account of colors. In *Rules*, Descartes makes the claim that colors, also, can be figured.[88] In his discourse on the rainbow in *Meteorology*, he does just that. Descartes picks up his pen to calculate, but also draws angles through which light is reflected in water.[89] Colors are produced by movement in the matter that hits the eye, interacting with light.[90] This hypothesis can be compared to the figures in *Rules*, where Descartes seeks to demonstrate the difference that makes colors, also, into figures or shapes. The abstract figures drawn there are not to be seen as geometrical translations of color but as a hypothetical demonstration of the difference between colors, suggesting that their variety is endless: "the infinite multiplicity of Figures is sufficient for the expression of all differences in perceptible things."[91] (See fig. 3.2.)

Figures, then, do not mimic objects, but neither are they abstractions or models. In rule twelve, they are presented as preconceptual gatherings in a universe of infinite possibilities. They actualize several senses, producing multidimensional forms in space and time: "we must think of the external shape of the sentient body as being really changed by the object in exactly the same way as the shape of the surface of the wax is altered by the seal."[92] Bodies have shapes that we may touch, and all our senses participate in their apprehension as figures; figures are, then, inherently aesthetic.[93]

Figures are suggestions of formations and movements. Descartes combines speculation on the makeup of invisible particles with a sensual approach to their composition. The key to figurability in Descartes's writings can, indeed, be seen in his treatise on music. The ground of figures is based on a kind of rhythmic seriality of duplicity and change. Rhythm shapes the particles so as to suggest endless combinations. Just like the atmosphere, through wind, snow, and so on, gives witness to the spinning of invisible structures, so does musical experience imply movements in the atmosphere that the eye cannot perceive.

Descartes the natural philosopher or "physicien" examines music in the same way as the atmosphere.[94] This means working by a form of reasoning that only superficially resembles deduction; it builds more on sense experience and figuration, and the attempt to understand what connects atmospheric movements to passions. The notation of tones expresses the same kind of movement as tones that we hear, Descartes argues.[95] The invisible vibrations of the atmosphere in music are subject to algebraic calculation as well as sensual shaping, just like the invisible realm of particles in physics. Figures seize the variables of regularity as well as of distinction. This is also the key to aesthetic experience. The pleasure that we may experience in music is produced through the differentiation of tones. I cannot tell you which musical octave I find the most beautiful, Mersenne responds to a question posed by Descartes, because the senses cannot distinguish their repercussions in the atmosphere.[96]

The notion that the figures can be seen as preconceptual gatherings in a universe of infinite varieties, of proportions and space, can be seen in relation to contemporary philosophy's theorization of rhythm as a descriptor. Rhythm has passed, in the phenomenological tradition, from being described in the constitution of consciousness, to acquire the status as a descriptor in posthuman philosophy of nature. In the work of Husserl, rhythm is not only repetition or

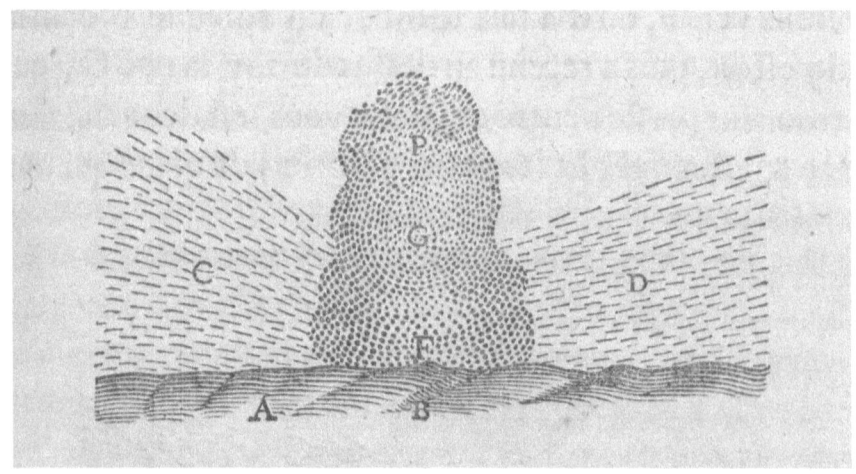

Figure 4.6. Clouds, *Les Météores*. In *Discours de la methode*, Leyden: 1637, Royal Library Stockholm.

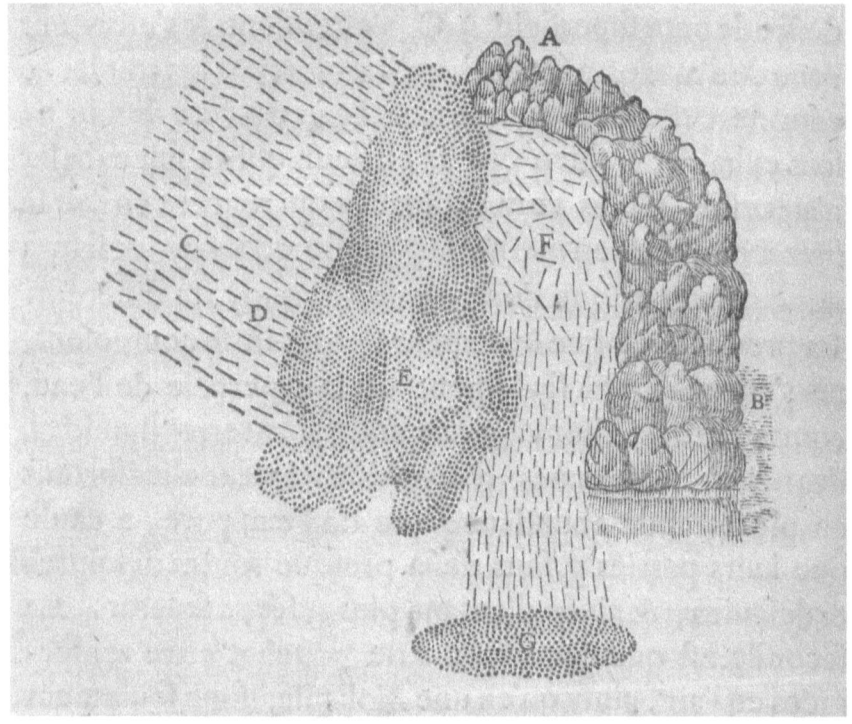

Figure 4.7. Wind, *Les Météores*. In *Discours de la methode*, Leyden: 1637, Royal Library Stockholm.

sequence but also the constitution of an inner consciousness that crosses the line between self and world, affect and perception.[97] This is made clear also in the world of extension identified by Descartes: colors appear in a form of "numeric identity" in the thing-bodies that appear visually.[98] What we perceive through our senses is offered to us through forms of regularity and repetition; this is, in Husserl's aesthetic reflections, often aligned with the understanding of aesthetic forms themselves, such as images and painting and music.[99] However, after Husserl, in the work of Maurice Merleau-Ponty, rhythm is not seen as constitutive of consciousness but rather as an aspect of the way in which the world of extension is inhabited by other beings. Rhythm is life beyond the human; it can be identified in the "crawling" offered to us through a line of light or in a painting where rhythm can be perceived as an atmosphere, a sense of space, a new dimension of perception.[100] In this way, rhythm is an aspect of aesthetic perception as such: although nonhuman as descriptor, it implies that we see the world as inhabited and that our perception is intertwined with that of other living beings.[101] Merleau-Ponty also suggests that forms we tend to perceive of as wholly abstract may still be enveloped in a sense of rhythm. We may experience even a line of light as the rhythm of living movement. Through its "crawling," it becomes a "virtual substance."[102]

In music or painting, rhythm deploys depth of expression, as Jessica Wiskus has shown. Rhythm emanates from a line that is "freed"; it becomes a membrane through which "a certain depth or volume radiates."[103] The different lines of blue that are used in Cézanne's *Four Bathers*, for instance, indicate living tissue, intertwining the world of living beings and space.[104] This implies that rhythm, irreducible to anthropomorphic shapes, gives depth and space to perception without being inherent to consciousness as such; there are, so to speak, shapes of rhythm "out there."

Rhythm is also a category used in theories of the posthuman, a term employed to point to forms of meaningful creation that do not translate into anthropomorphic ideas or concepts. Famously, the art exhibition *Documenta* XIII in Kassel in 2012, with its focus on ecological systems, brought this into attention. It engaged a shift from representation to the action on and between bodies in modes that can be described in terms such as affects, flows, and rhythm. Exchanging signs of representation for "abstract descriptors," such as emotions, instincts, rhythms, and flows, a landscape or weather can be as much of an aesthetic experience as music or painting.[105] In this conception, rhythm is not so much a depiction of life, as it tends to be in Merleau-Ponty's phenomenology, where it gives witness to the interconnection between bodies and human life. It is rather something that happens in the intertwinement between the seriality of the designator and the qualities of extended bodies inherent to the experience. One can compare with the rhythmic drawings of Cy Twombly, where the

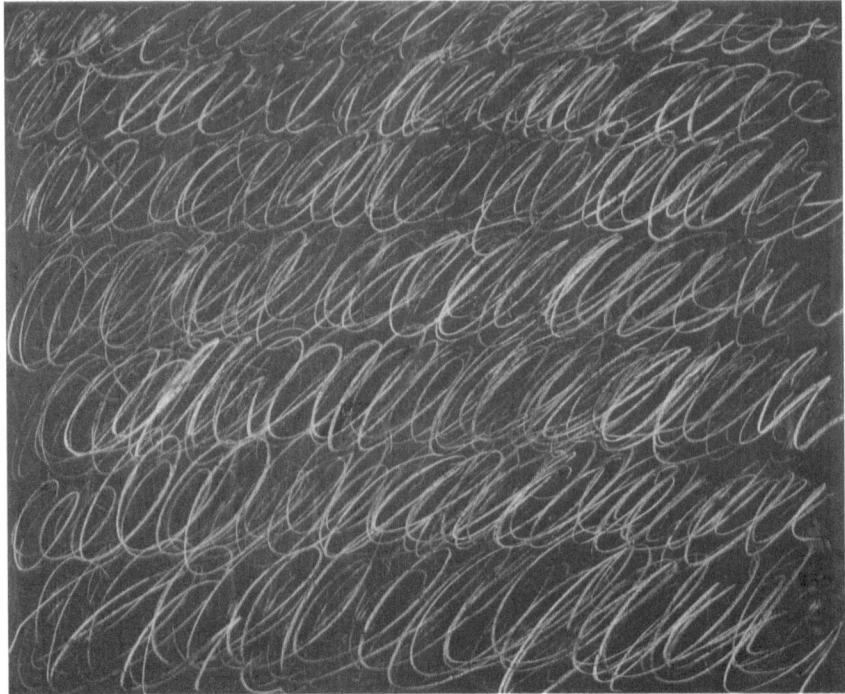

Figure 4.8. Cy Twombly, *Untitled*, 1969. Oil paint, wax crayon.
© Cy Twombly Foundation.

rhythmicality is produced by the techniques, materialities, and modes of work. What transpires is a rhythmic movement that stands as itself. It is not a thing, and it is not a matter. Neither is it a body. It comes across as a figuration in and through the lines themselves. Although the figural rhythm seen in Twombly can perhaps be conceived as time, the extension in space matters even more perhaps; the lines are curved as a result of a certain timing. What makes a rhythm protrude is not the repetition of the same but rather the differentiation, the way in which a sequence differs against another sequence. But most importantly: the rhythmicality lies in the open-endedness of the figure. The lines of Twombly's drawings are uncontained. They move on, outside of the image. This move, beyond, implies some kind of infinity, a metaphysics perhaps.

For Descartes as well, lines are not just abstract shapes; they are also flowing motions.[106] In this way, the rhythmicality of the images implies an infinity, a cosmic dimension. This dimension is irreducible to mathematics, or reason. Lines belong not only to the world of geometry. They designate formations of emotions, instincts, rhythms, transformations, and flows that affect bodies. Descartes's fondness for rhythmically composed figures may be seen in this light. Lines capture movement in rhythmic formations and become thought. Lines cross the limits between imagination, embodied experience, and the physical movement that lies beyond. They carry us over to what we cannot perceive: spinning beyond the composition of the figures—nothing can be imagined that cannot be solved by a line, as he writes to Beeckman.

The relation between the figures of Descartes's *Meteorology* and *Compendium on Music* can be seen in this light. His analysis of tonal value is figured not only through musical notation but with a variety of figures that explain the differences between harmonies, rhythms, and other kind of musical expressions. In this way, the figures in *Meteorology* and *Compendium on Music* serve similar purposes: they may "fail" to ascertain knowledge, but they seize a dimension between the abstract and the sensual. *Compendium on Music* suggests that rhythm is more important than harmony: through rhythm, "sound strikes all bodies on all sides." It is a physical motion, like "bells and thunder," that will induce passions like "languor, sadness, fear, pride," and so on.[107] Through rhythm, the senses enwrap the whole body. Even animals can learn to dance. Rhythm is also what produces the passions that music shares with poetry.[108] Descartes then notes that rhythm may also appear when it is not produced as music: as ordinary sounds that take on a certain regularity, such as creaking windmills. Rhythm is produced, then, through the very appearance of patterns. It appears also as threads. In rule ten in *Rules*, Descartes perceives aesthetic qualities as the patterns of ordering in the every day. Such patterns are particularly adapted to human cognitive capacities. In fact, ordering is often an aspect of the products of everyday life, for instance, weaving or carpetmaking. Regularity and differentiation cooperate in "the more feminine arts of embroidery, in which threads are interwoven in an infinity of varied patterns."[109] This is what differentiates rhythmic form from mere algebraic composition: like in the discourse on salt, rhythm catches not only the patterns of the particles but also the spinning of differentiation.

Rhythm, in the figures of Descartes, is produced by lines. They figure movements and transformations of the universe that lie beyond our reach. Descartes's drawings are strikingly articulate in rhythm, line, and allusions. At once economical and expressive, they contain a language. What makes rhythm protrude, and what makes the figure cohere with the treatises, is not simply the repetition of lines, of snowflakes, eels of water or tables of salt, and so on, it is the spinning of differences and the modes of penetration by which bodies intertwine with other bodies. Rhythms are produced by lines in a repetitive mode of shapes, using stress, timing, shades, and nuances to create the open-endedness of figures, between sensual expression and suggestion of abstraction.

Indeed, the images challenge the dualism between res cogitans, the subject, and res extensa, material bodies.[110] We feel the weather and the matters that create it as hot and cold, hard or soft, slippery or metallic; these properties guide the imagery of invisible particles. In *Principles of Philosophy*, Descartes refers to this as some kind of practice: we are prone to use our experience of large bodies to understand what lies beyond the senses. We need to apply mathematical and mechanical rules to understand the shapes, sizes, and motions of the small bodies that elude the eye.[111] But we still need to use the senses to grasp the presence of invisible, penetrable particles. This is what figures help us do: we grasp what we cannot see through what we can see. For this, the figures of the observations need not be exact. The visualizations may be exaggerated.

Many have questioned the relation between *Discourse on Method* and the treatises *Optics*, *Meteorology*, and *Geometry* that followed. To Descartes, it appears to have been perfectly coherent, because *Discourse* was applied as offering the rules for what was to provide a knowledge of certainty.[112] It was rather the case that relation between the mind and its grasp of the world of extension demanded sensual deliberation through drawings and sketches—that were able to provide images of the invisible. In this way, the dualism in Descartes is both erected and shattered at the same time: the senses cannot perceive the small particles, but they are nevertheless posited from a position where a combination of sensual experience and mathematical formula are necessary to grasp them. As Merleau-Ponty described in his notes on *Nature*, Descartes's philosophy of nature is in search of an "ontological midpoint" in order to resolve the problematic duality between object and mind, order of causality and order of meaning.[113] Such a midpoint produces a viewpoint that straddles two different aspects at the same time; as Renaud Barbaras puts it: the "abstract object" offered by Descartes is, to Merleau-Ponty, the result of a strife to find an original meaning that looks at both its singularity and its place in a causal chain.[114] Seen from this perspective, the images are an integral part of the struggles not to reduce nature's own expression. They are descriptors transgressing the dualism between the mind's abstraction and corporeal, sensual experience.

The aesthetic dimensions of scientific hypotheses in *Meteorology* are indeed putting several dualisms in motion: between passion and knowledge, image and text, rhythm and geometry. Weather does not need thought, but thought needs aesthetic means to seize the depictions of a multitude. This is not the only example where Descartes both raises and challenges dualisms within his own writings. The charges against Descartes as an abstract humanist appear to lack a distinct target; Descartes's version of seventeenth-century humanism was never a rigid model of reason's sovereignty.[115] In this context, the aesthetic elaboration of *Meteorology*, embodied in its figures, can be inserted. The weather gives witness to the limits of reason: the varieties of its composites are infinite.[116] This insight is integral to *Meteorology* overall.

Cartesian engravings are not intended to illustrate what the text says about the particles of nature, as a secondary source of imitation of what lies "out there." They are rather the result of experimental imagination. Rhythm is not repetition or sequencing; it is differentiation in and through figures. One can see this not only in the natural philosophy but also in the treatise on music.[117] Only the intellect "is capable of perceiving the truth." But we must sometimes use imagination and sense perception to acquire knowledge.[118] Only the senses can seize the imperceptible forms of differentiation that make up the Cartesian. This inquiry into the relation between the intellect's capacity for abstraction, and the figures as conglomerates of sensation and experience, permeates *Meteorology*. The images in *Meteorology* are not primarily a pedagogical feat; they are not mimetic interpretations of phenomena. They are an aspect of the knowledge produced.

5 Thinking through Lines with Descartes

Marcia Sá Cavalcante Schuback

The "image" of thinking while thinking, of seeing while seeing, is not the image of something but rather of a line in movement. A drawing *cogito* is the one that aims to seize in an instant the line of a movement while moving as clouds in the sky. A spur of Descartes's drawing cogito—even if not "consciously" observed by himself—can be found, for example, in his attention to the formation of clouds, which are intimately connected to the drawing of lines in the sky, or in his observations of the orbits of moon and sky in *Principia Philosophiae*.

Descartes's interest in studying how to seize in a vision a line in movement, how to "see" the moving while moving, is also evident in his special enthusiasm about the "miraculous" perspective called anamorphic perspective.[1] Descartes's fascination with the works of Jean François Nicéron on anamorphosis, particularly his book *Thaumaturgus opticus*, published in 1638,[2] and on the so-called secret and magic perspectives, and the realm of visual enchantments, is well-known.[3] The intricate and effortful calculi in this perspective has to do with how to calculate the point or instant for viewing the whole painting or image while passing through it—that is, while the eyes are moving along it.[4] Thus, to see a line in movement, one has to see with moving eyes. In a text by the French bishop and theologian Jacques-Bénigne Lignel Bossuet (1627–1704), there is a description of this point found suddenly along the movement of seeing that provides a vision of the whole movement, that renders the anamorphic perspective clearer:

> Quand je considère en moi-même la disposition des choses humaines, confuse, inégale, iregulière, je la compare souvent à certians tableaux que l'on trouve assez ordinairement dans les bibliothèques des curieux comme un jeu de perspective. La première vue ne montre que des traits informes et un mélange confus des couleurs qui semblent être ou essai de quelque apprenti ou le jeu de quelque enfant plutôt que l'ouvrage d'une main savant. Mais aussitôt que celui qui sait le secret vous le fait regarder par un certain endroit, aussitôt toutes les lignes inégales venant à se ramasser d'une certaine façon dans notre vue, toute la confusion se démêle, et vous voyez apparaître un visage avec ses lineaments et proportions, où il n'ay avait auparavant aucune apparence de forme humaine. C'est

Thinking through Lines with Descartes | 99

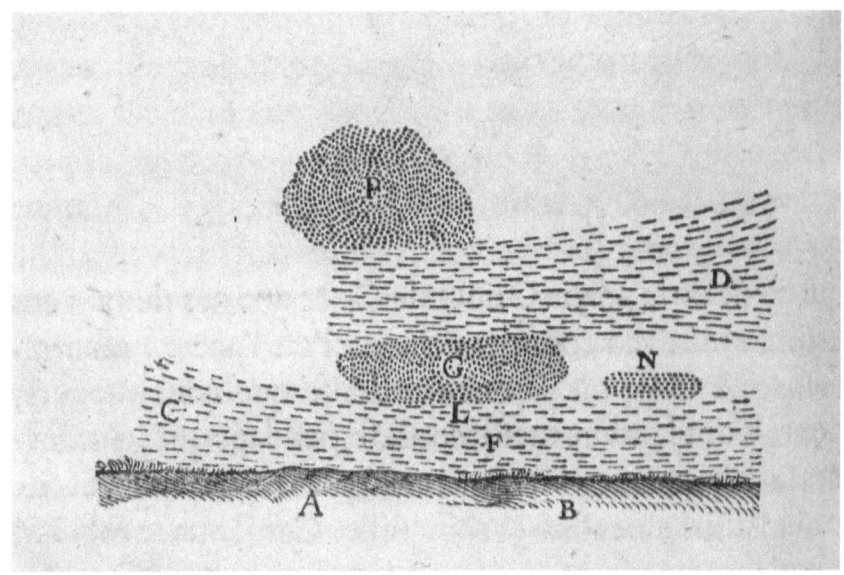

Figure 5.1. Clouds, *Les Météores*. In *Discours de la méthode*, 1637, Royal Library Stockholm.

ce me semble, Messieurs, une image assez naturelle du monde, de sa confusion apparente et de sa justesse cache, que nous ne pouvons jamais remarquer qu'en le regardant par un certain point que la foi en Jesus-Christ nou découvre.[5]

Anamorphic perspective, used with mastery by Hans Holbein in his very famous painting *The Ambassadors*, was conceived for the first time from a perspective of scientific aesthetics by Leonardo da Vinci, precisely to show the eye seeing.

In this anamorphic drawing by da Vinci, the eye can only see the eye in the image while passing along the drawing or when finding the unique point where the whole eye appears to vision, as a unique point where an egg can stand. It is about reaching a sort of point-instant that is neither an image nor a figure, a point-instant in which the whole appears at the time it is swaying away. This perspective is quite different from any view of figures, images, things, and entities. It is a kind of image happening in the profundity of the eye, an internal vision or view of the eye seeing the eye, the seeing seeing the seeing, that Descartes also pursues in his optical studies and even tries to depict as clear as possible through the engravings he orders and chooses to illustrate his work, such as the following engraving found in his *Dioptrics*.[6]

100 | *Through the Eyes of Descartes*

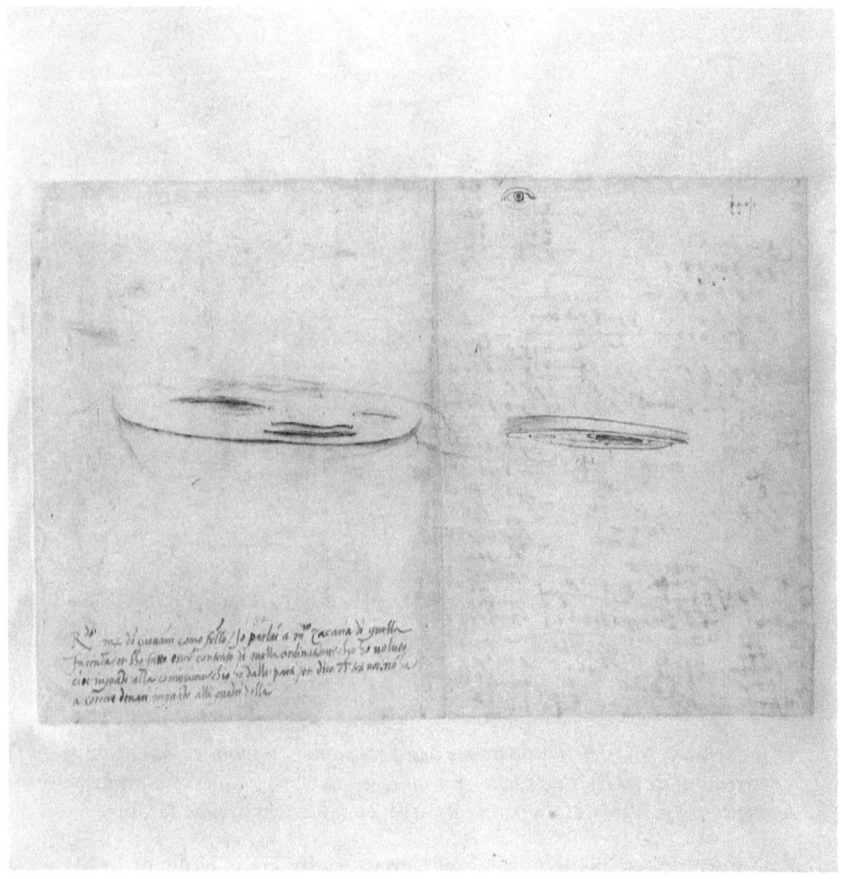

Figure 5.2. Leonardo da Vinci, *Anamorphosis: Study of the Eye*; on the left, *Juvenile Face*, in *Codex Atlanticus*, ca. 1478–1518; Milan, Biblioteca Ambrosiana; fol. 98r.; (artwork in the public domain; photo © Biblioteca Ambrosiana, Milan, Italy/De Agostini Picture Library/Bridgeman Images).

If anaclasis, as discussed before, can indicate the search of the shape of the line of thinking while thinking when seized in a point-instant, and anamorphosis provides the features of a perspective to see the whole while moving, these physical, optical, and mathematical concepts indicate Descartes's attention to the moment in which the movement while moving is seized. Thus, the question is how to seize a movement while moving. Considering the optical concepts of anaclasis and anamorphosis and the notions of "internal awareness" to be in opposition to reflection and reflective knowledge, as mentioned, and of "mind intuition," which we are here calling thinking intuition, Descartes discovers that thinking sees the thinking "at the time," "as long as," "while thinking" suddenly, in an

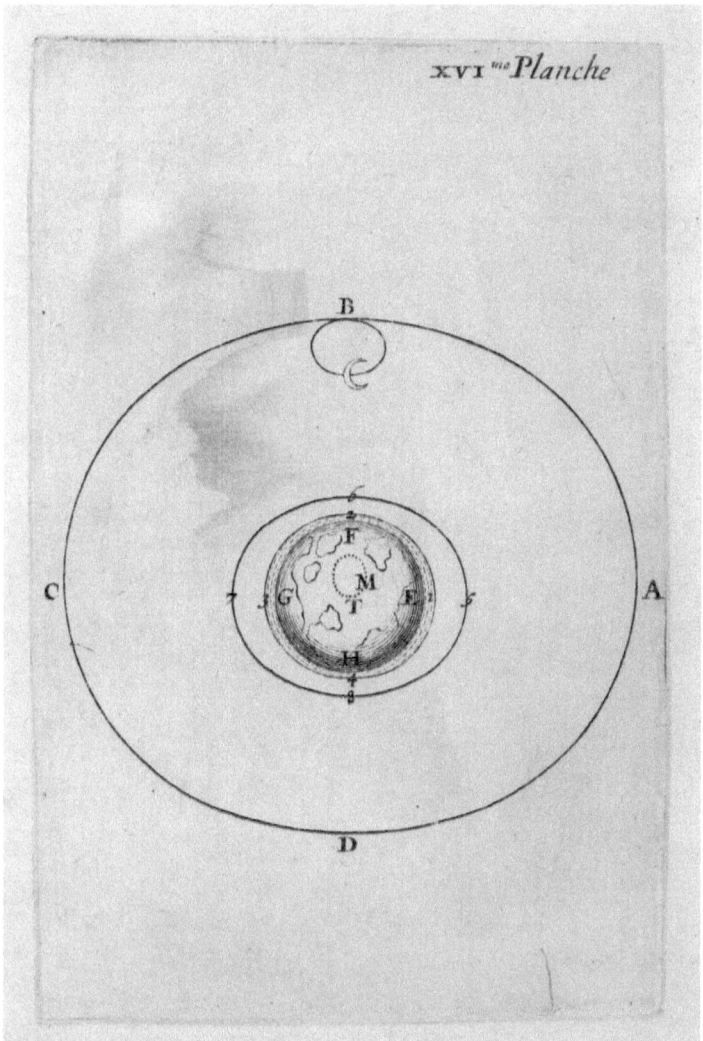

Figure 5.3. *Principia philosophiæ*, 1664, Royal Library Stockholm.

instant, which he expressed in the adverb "*donc*," ergo, "therefore," the adverb of the attention to the surprise of suddenly seeing the I am thinking while thinking.

This attention to lines being seized suddenly, in an instant, simultaneously, by which the moving can be seized as a unity, is what enables the "pleasure of the senses" when in music different lines of a chant are heard as one and the chant is conceived as a whole, as Descartes observes in his earliest writing, the *Musical Companion*.[7] Descartes's cogito, the I am thinking that suddenly, in an

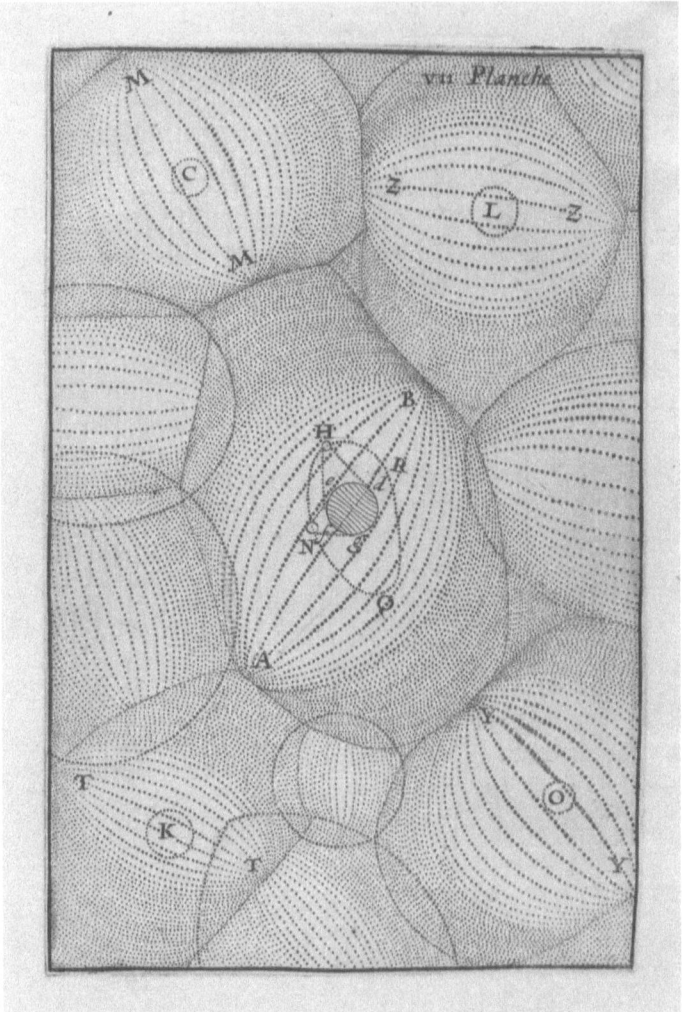

Figure 5.4. *Principia philosophiæ*, 1664, Royal Library Stockholm.

instant, "sees" the I is thinking while thinking, can be described, as Jean Wahl once proposed, as the actualism of Descartes's philosophy. His idealism is rather an actualism insofar as it affirms not an ideal realm of abstract ideas and concepts acquired solely by reason and rational inquiry but the fact that "only by an instantaneous act of thinking, the soul can get rid of its doubt."[8] The "actualism" of the cogito has to do with an attention that surprises at the instant the I am thinking, an overwhelming attention to what is happening, to the event of thinking in which thinking no longer needs to rely on memory, on the already

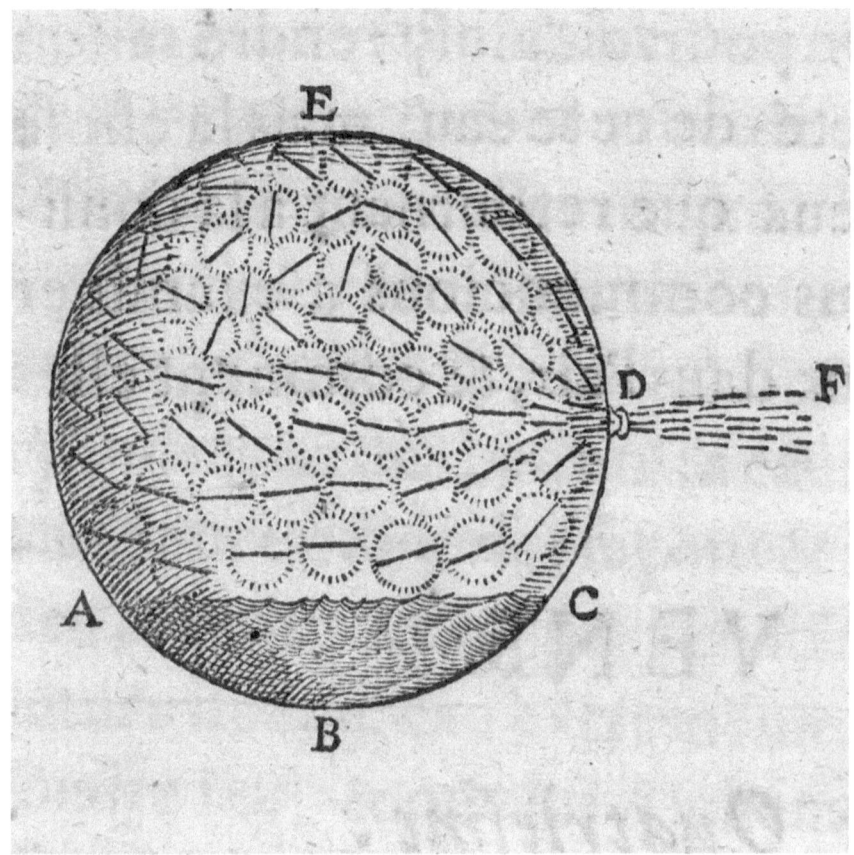

Figure 5.5. Winds, *Les Météores*. In *Discours de la méthode*, 1637, Royal Library Stockholm.

said and thought before. Here there cannot be a question of seeing something—a truth—by means of a syllogism, but only by thinking intuition. In a conversation with the Dutch theologian Frans Burman, who argues that Descartes contradicts himself when denying that the cogito results from a syllogism, Descartes answers by saying "I am thinking therefore I am," "I am attending only to what I experience within myself." And further: "I do not pay attention in the same way to the general notion "whatever thinks exists." As I have explained before, the authors do not separate out these general propositions from the particular instances; rather, it is in the particular instances that we think of them. This,

Figure 5.6. *L'Homme: Et un traitté de la formation du foetus*, Paris, 1664, Royal Library Stockholm.

then, is the sense in which the words cited here should be taken.[9] In question is the seizing in the instant, in the "particular instance," the movement of thinking itself, "the experience within myself," something that brings Descartes very close to Plato's concept of the instant as *eksaiphnes*. Some additional lines in the same exchange with Burman could be interpreted as contradictory to the role of the instant; thus, Descartes considers that it is false to affirm that "thought occurs instantaneously."[10] He claims, on the contrary, that "all my acts take up time, and I can be said to be continuing and carrying on with the same thought during a period of time."[11] Far from a contradiction, what Descartes says here is that the I am thinking takes up time, is happening, enduring, entirely immersed in the "as longs as," *dum*, and therefore "does not occur instantaneously." However, its seizing, the insight of it, its *eureka* or admiration and wonder—what Plato and Aristotle called *thaumatzein*—occurs instantaneously, something the discussions about the anaclastic line and the anamorphic perspective can help account for. The instant, quoting Jean-Luc Nancy, "is not a chronological measure; it is quite

Figure 5.7. Maerten van Heemskreck, *St Luke painting the Virgin's Portrait* (1532), Museum of Fine Arts, Boston.

evidently the achronic limits of such measure."[12] It is more of the proper temporality of an overwhelming attention, an attention to what cannot be grasped as things are grasped (i.e., in their solidity or fixity), but an attention that seizes the unfixable—I am thinking while I am thinking, the duration of the event of thinking.

As we have insisted in previous chapters, Descartes's cogito—I am thinking while I am thinking—although not occurring instantaneously since it "takes up time," is "seized" instantaneously in its wholeness, in its "taking up time." It is "viewed" as an artist sees a line being drawn while drawing. The motif of a hand drawing the drawing of lines has frequently appeared since the sixteenth century as well as in Descartes's time. Descartes himself speaks about it in the *Optics*.[13] There, he presents what Victor I. Stoichita called "automimesis," the mimesis of mimesis, showing of the showing, the drawing of the drawing and the painting of the painting, what is depicted as a shadow of the own body, as the shadow of the drawing and painting hands in a portrait.[14] One of the most famous

Figure 5.8. El Greco, *St Luke painting the Virgin and Child* (1567), Benaki Museum, Athens.

representations of this "automimesis" in painting is the canvas by the Dutch artist Maerten van Heemskreck depicting *St. Luke Painting the Virgin's Portrait* (fig. 5.7). It is indeed a large motif in the history of painting and iconography (see also El Greco's canvas, fig. 5.8), which confirms that the cogito of a drawer and painter is the one entirely dedicated to draw not things but the drawing of things, to paint not objects or narratives but to paint the painting of objects and narratives—indeed, to see the seeing turning the face of things to the light.

Cogito as *Mise en Abyme* and Its Perspective

But the most central aspect in the drawing cogito and its "automimetic" structure is how to depict the I am thinking I am thinking, the seeing I am seeing, without reducing it to a mere reflection—to I am thinking *that* I am thinking, to simple self-consciousness where the "I am thinking" becomes an object for the thinking subject, and hence what loses what it is—namely, duration, its happening. Thus, the I am thinking, the cogito, is neither a thing nor an object but a continuous passing "thing," a "trace" (also a Cartesian word), a vestige, or, to use a more contemporary term, an "after-image," as the one of a line drawing the drawing of a line. The anamorphic perspective gives some hints of how the "as long as," *dum*, the meanwhile or duration can be depicted. But we could also bring into our discussion the resource of a *"mise en abyme,"* which complements and develops the concept of "automimesis," to which we have already alluded.

The term *mise en abyme* was coined by André Gide in his *Journals* from 1893, where he explains his literary project as the writing of the action of writing, comparing it to Dutch painters such as Memling and Quentin Metzys, and to Velasquez's *Las Meninas* and the theater within the theater that Shakespeare presents in *Hamlet*. Nonetheless, he also says that this comparison is still not entirely accurate: "None of these examples is absolutely accurate. What would be more accurate, and what would explain better what I'd wanted to do in my *Cahiers*, in *Narcisse* and in *La Tentative*, would be a comparison with the device from heraldry that involves putting a second representation of the original shield 'en abyme' within it."[15] It was, however, when the French literary critic, essayist, and novelist Émile Henriot used this expression to characterize the proper character of the so-called *nouveau roman* in a popular article at *Le Monde* from 1957 that the term entered the theoretical literary and philosophical discourse in the 1960s, first through an essay by Alain Robbe-Grillet, *Pour un nouveau roman*.[16] In contrast to the drawing and painting automimesis, where the action of painting is painted and thereby the instant of an action is reproduced in the act of painting itself, as in Velazquez's *Las Meninas*, the concept of *mise en abyme* coined by Gide was taken theoretically to explain "any aspect enclosed within a work that shows a similarity with the work that contains it,"[17] hence as a conceptual key to read and decode the structure and formal aspects of the work addressed within the work.[18]

To seize the I am thinking while I am thinking is not the same as seeing an image of something in a mirror. As we have stressed above, it is rather the vision of an afterimage, in the sense of seeing lines at the moment they are being drawn. Here, it is not really a question of mirrors in the sense of an image outside the inside. In question is rather an intensive being in the action, an extreme act of attention in which it is not possible to differentiate the subject and the object, the action and the passion in which the fact that I am being becomes clearly and distinctly experienced. If this entire attention, which restricts attention to everything else and thereby fixes it in the unfixed and unfixable *ongoing* rather than primally in *what* is going, should be described as a *mise en abyme*, it is above all because it presents an action taking place *within* an action. I am thinking (I am thinking)—what expresses the awareness about the fact that existence itself is existing (I am)—exposes an action within an action and not an action seeing itself in a mirror. The heraldic *"en abyme,"* in Gide's considerations, differs from pictorial mirroring because it puts something (a second representation of the original shield) *within* it. The expression turns the theoretical attention from self-representation in a mirror to an action *within* an action, what is closer to the phenomenon of an echo, a sounding within the sounding that is nevertheless heard as one singular sound. I am thinking—a performative utterance that is the closest to a constative one—implies I am thinking I am thinking; I am seeing I am seeing. The way it "imitates" the very duration of the act is to write in such a way that it repeats itself through the very act of writing. Thus, to write renders a saying repeatable in itself infinitely insofar as, in the writing, infinity itself is in action. The intensive awareness of being, I am, when I am thinking is seized within I am thinking—that is, while I am thinking is itself the experience of an idea of infinity that negates the idea of an infinite in potency and of an infinite in progress—for Descartes, as Jean Wahl insightfully observed, infinity is in act.[19] I am thinking (I am thinking), I am seeing (I am seeing). The fact that the act of thinking, the I am thinking, is performed as writing, is performed precisely in the drawing of lines; thus, to write is indeed to draw lines. Descartes's cogito—I am thinking within/while I am thinking, and therefore I am—puts *en abyme* writing within thinking as its echo. In other words: Descartes's cogito is the performative utterance of I am thinking that surprises itself as thinking in writing. Descartes is the writing philosopher not only because he almost exclusively writes (differently from Socrates, who never wrote) but because with him, thinking and writing are as one, *instar unius*, experienced or seen as one, *uno intuitu*. Descartes is a philosophical writer.

Cartesian Philosophy of the Writing Hand

Descartes is well recognized as an adept philosophical writer. He inaugurates a new philosophical style, praised for its clarity and simplicity, for its "order and measure." Descartes is not only a philosopher who writes but also a philosopher who is a writer.[20] In this sense, it could be said that his thought has its own aesthetics. Essays have been written on Descartes's literary qualities, such as Durs Grünbein's recent *Der Cartesische Taucher* (*The Cartesian Diver*).[21] Descartes's disavowal of old philosophy relates to the shortcomings he saw in ancient and medieval metaphysical views and logic, and it has much to do with a rejection of the style of philosophizing, the classical aesthetics of thought,[22] eminently oratory.[23] He inaugurated not only modern philosophical prose and the French language of theory and philosophy but also the practice of translation in philosophy.[24] Descartes wrote in both French and Latin, though he preferred, however, to write in French, the "native language" (*langue de mon pays*), whereas Latin reminded

In E= maius erit quam D in A quadr. — Aq in E adaequentur igitur juxta superiorem methodum. Sumptis itaque coibus D in Eq — D in A in E adaequabitur — Aq in E, aut quod idem est D in Eq + Aq in E adaequabitur D in A in E. Omnia diuidantur per E. Ergo D in E + Aq adaequabitur D in A. Elidatur D in E. Ergo Aq aequabitur D in A, ideoque A aequabitur D bis. Ergo CD probabuntur duplam ipsius CD, quod quidem ita se habet. Nec fallit unquam methodus	iuxta superiorem methodum. Sumptis itaque coibus D in Eq — D in A in E= adaequabit — Aq in E, aut quod idem est, D in Eq + Aq in E. adaequabit D in A in E. Omnia diuidantur per E. Ergo D in Eq + Aq. adaequabitur D in A. Elidatur D in E. Ergo Aq aequabitur D in A. ideoq A aequabitur D bis. Ergo CD probabimus duplam ipsius CD, quod nullo modo ita se habet. sed semper fallit ista methodus.	Adaequabitur A in E, aut quod idem est A in E adaequabitur D in E. Omnia diuidantur per E. Ergo A adaequabitur D. Hic est elidendum. Sed aequatur D quod nullo modo ita se habet &c.

Si on aduouë que ce raysonnement soit bon pour la parabole on doit aduoüer aussy qu'il est bon pour l'Ellipse et l'hyperbole et toutes les autres lignes courbes qui sont au monde, or toutefois on voit clairement qu'il ne conclud pas la verité. Quant aux autres choses que ces m{ss}rs disent auoir esté inuentées par m{r} de fermat ie veux croire tout ce qu'il leur plaira, mais n'ayant jamais rien veu de luy que cet escrit de maximis et minimis et la copie d'une lettre dans laquelle il pretendoit de refuter le 2 discours de ma

him mainly of the "language of my teachers" (*langue de mes précepteurs*).[25] But in what sense is he a "philosophical writer"?

In the passage we cited from the fifth part of *Discourse*, Descartes compares his thinking procedure to a painter who, unable to represent all the different sides of a solid body equally well on his flat canvas, chooses one of the principal ones, and sets it facing the light and shades the others, "in just the same way . . . I undertook merely to expound quite fully what I understood about light."[26] Descartes writes in "just in the same way" a painter paints;[27] thus, both "let that be seen which allows to see."[28] The "same way" of writing like one paints can be observed in several aspects of Descartes's way of thinking. In Jean-Luc Nancy's inspiring readings of Descartes from the 1970s, he showed that Descartes's autobiographical "style" can be not only "read" but also "seen"—thus, to read is, indeed, first of all to see—as a self-portrait in the pictorial practice of it. It would not be out of context to instead compare Descartes's autobiographical *Discourse* with the art of self-portraits, such as can be observed when looking at one of his contemporaries Nicolas Poussin's self-portrait.[29]

Without making any comparison between Poussin's and Weenix's (see fig. Intro.4) art, we wish only to indicate that Descartes's autobiographical "style" is more a pictorial than a literary one that can be traced back to Marcus Aurelius, St. Augustine, and the tradition of *Meditations*. Or it could be more accurate to say that proceeding "just in the same way" as a painter, Descartes inaugurates another style of autobiography; thus, the focus is no longer the "subject" but the awareness of existence existing while I am thinking, an awareness that "takes place" in writing, while writing.

Dum scribo, intelligo—while I am writing, I understand: these words also belong to rule twelve, where Descartes presents his theory of colors as shapes and as such as (rhythmic) structures of lines. He compares this understanding that occurs while I am writing with senses, being stimulated by an object, receiving the object as a (nonfigurative) figure impressing the "common sense." Descartes describes this understanding that happens while writing in the following way:

> In exactly the same way I understand that while I am writing [*dum scribo*], at the very moment when individual letters are traced on the paper, not only does the point of the pen move, but the slightest motion of this part cannot but be transmitted simultaneously to the whole pen. All these various motions are traced out in the air by the tip of the quill, even though I do not conceive of anything real passing from one end to the other. Who then would think that the connection between the parts of the human body is less close than that between the parts of the pen? What simpler way of portraying [*excogitare*] the matter can be imagined?[30]

In his readings of this passage, Nancy calls attention to how Descartes aims to describe "within my writing gesture the mode of instantaneous transmission,

Figure 5.10. Nicholas Poussin, *Portrait de l'artiste*, 1650, Musée du Louvre, Paris.

without transit, which grants me in truth knowledge of the world."[31] He also observes in this passage of the *Rule* how Descartes recounts this instantaneous understanding that occurs while writing, of how the body and soul, though abyssally separated, are as intimately connected as "the parts of the pen." The pen—through which the I am thinking is written down, putting "en abyme," the thinking understanding, while writing—is the "simpler way of portraying [*excogitare*] the matter," the relation between body and soul, pen and writing, writing and thinking. In Nancy's own words: "The human body, in its exterior exteriors and its interior, in its multiplicity and its unity, holds itself like a pen, and no doubt more than a pen—formidable calamus."[32]

This passage from *Rules* therefore opens the possibility to reread the problem of Descartes's dualism, of the disconnection between the body and the soul, in a quite distinct way, if this relation is "read" and "seen" as the one between the thinking and the writing, hence from the connection between the thinking soul and the writing hand. This passage suggests something of an enigmatic "instantaneity" of thinking while writing, of thinking in writing and how writing is a privileged act of the hand that shows *en abyme*, a handling in act. It is amazing to follow Descartes's reflections on the "two-side" movements of a hand, writing with a pen; thus, he instructs us that while tracing on a sheet of paper individual letters, at the same time, the tip of the quill draws in the air invisible lines. While letters are been drawn on a paper (what is called writing), invisible lines are drawn in the air, "cartography" and "areography" coincide, something that Nancy did not overlook in his remarks, also underlining Des-cartes own name, the Sir of *Cartes*, of Paper and Letters. As such, corporeal and aerial lines are drawn simultaneously, one being the other without being an image of the other. This mysterious graphology, which should rather be called graphomancy, that writing is, exhibits the way the "whileness," the "as long as," indeed, the act can be seen in its "invisibility" and touched in its "untouchability," so to speak. This passage presents the scene of what Paul Valéry once called "*la main de l'oeil*," the hand of the eye,[33] the hand in act—drawing, writing, as the "image" of the handling as such, of the present participle thinking, writing, seeing, moving, acting, of the tense of a performative practice in which one *is* being, is existing in such a way that the existence of existence—I am—emerges for oneself as thoughts and emotions arise from letters on the paper. As Descartes says in *Principles*:

> It can also be proved that the nature of our mind is such that the mere occurrence of certain motions in the body can stimulate it to have all manner of thoughts which have no likeness to the movements in question. This is especially true of the confused thoughts we call sensations or feelings. For we see that spoken or written words excite all sorts of thoughts and emotions in our minds. With the same paper, pen and ink, if the tip of the pen is pushed across the paper in a certain way it will form letters which excite in the mind or the reader thoughts of battles, storms and violence, and emotions of indignation or sorrow; but if the movements of the pen are just slightly different they will produce quite different thoughts of tranquility, peace and pleasure, and quite opposite emotions of love and joy.[34]

The passage does not speak explicitly about the writing down of the movement of thinking but stresses how written letters, the very materiality of the paper, the pen and the ink, the movements done while writing (the engraving of lines, traits, and signs) provoke thoughts and emotions. Descartes does not speak of senses and meanings related to conventional signs but rather attributes to letters qualities that are proper to draw, to painted lines the thoughts and emotions they may evoke. Descartes reads letters in a visual artistic manner, letting lines "talk," so to speak. He thereby reminds us that a main characteristic of writing is that it comprehends the act of reading: writing is to read at the same time, but read the being written, the act of writing. He is less interested in the content of meaning and more attentive to what could be called the "physics of writing," for he seems to discover in it the actuality of thinking—that is, how the I am thinking appears to itself not as an image but as an action within this action, where being and thinking really become as one, *instar unius*. Writing is reading not only between the lines, as Nancy insisted, but the being written of lines, the movement of writing as such, which is figureless but nonetheless extreme figuration, the act of drawing lines of figures of and for thought. Descartes inaugurates the most modern style of writing that has been conceived in modernity: the writing down of the experience of thinking while writing.

There are many passages in Descartes's work where he accounts for his way of writing and even for the need to care about writing. Descartes was a writer that was not only always writing but was intentionally always rewriting. In a letter to Father Mersenne, we can read:

> You will be appalled at the amount of time it is taking me to complete what is supposed to be a very short Treatise which people could probably read straight through after dinner. . . . In case you find it strange that I have started writing several Treatises, . . . only to abandon each of them, the reason is quite simple: I kept gaining new knowledge as I worked, and in order to make room for it I always had to start afresh on a new plan. . . . But now at last I am sure that I shall not change course again, since my present design will be serviceable, whatever new knowledge I may acquire in the future.[35]

Hence, to write down the thinking means first to be continuously beginning to write, not only rewriting the same treatise but "writing several Treatises," to "start afresh"; thus, thinking never rests. For the common interpretation of Descartes's process and project, it could be understood that this continuous writing marks his early philosophical attempts until the moment he "shall not change course again, since my present design will still be serviceable, whatever new knowledge I may acquire in the future." How should we understand this "present design"; will be serviceable whatever new knowledge may be acquired? It can be easily argued that this "present design" is literature, or, more precisely, that the present design is the one that rendered philosophy literature. Descartes can be considered not only the father of modern philosophy but the father of modern French literature. Descartes himself compels his reader to read his *Principles of Philosophy* as a *roman*, a novel: "I should like the reader first of all to go quickly through the whole book like a novel, without straining his attention too much or stopping at the difficulties which may be encountered."[36] He can be considered the inventor of the "philosophical novel," *le roman philosophique*, if we assume Jacques Derrida's view.[37]

Discussions about Descartes's style, about his use of autobiography, about Descartes as a literary author and writer are many.[38] Essays on the relationship between Descartes and Marcel Proust[39] as well as Descartes and Beckett[40] arouse many interesting considerations about Descartes's literary skills and the role of his "philosophical or theoretical novel" for modern literature. For some,

Descartes can be defined as a theoretical novelist insofar as he proceeds in *Discourse* as a storyteller,[41] for introducing the narrative "I" in almost every paragraph of his works, with a few exceptions, such as the *Rules*. Autobiography is the form of *Discourse* in the sense it tells the story of the narrator. But it is also performative, thus the narrative I says that it says. *Discourse* was published first anonymously, though it deviates in style from the autobiography *strictu sensu*, since the "self" here is unknown; it presents a "self" that could be a fictional character about whom a biography is told. But what shall not be forgotten is that philosophical novel is a written novel, and hence the novel of writing itself. This is what emerges clearly in the Cartesian device of writing the biography of an anonymous "I," at least when conceived, and even if the secret about the narrative "I" was revealed some years later. Thus, through this device, an effect is produced that can only be done through writing—namely, the effect of instantaneous identification. Written, the "I" is read as everyone's own I. Indeed, written, the "I" is at once the most universal and the most singular: it is the I of each one (reader) and of everyone, and each one, the singular, is this I that comprehends everyone, the universal. Spoken, the "I" becomes, on the contrary, unmistakable; thus, the voice that says "I am" can only be this very one. The philosophical or theoretical novel inaugurated by Descartes differs from common fiction since it does not produce the mediate layers of identification between the reader and the characters of a novel; it is quite differently the performance of the writing's own performativity, the one of rendering the most singular the most universal, the here and now whatsoever here and now. Descartes explains his purpose in *Discourse*, saying the following:

> My present aim, then, is not to teach the method which everyone must follow in order to direct his reason correctly, but only to reveal how I have tried to direct my own. One who presumes to give precepts must think himself more skillful than those to whom he gives them; and if he makes the slightest mistake, he may be blamed. But I am presenting this work only as a history or, if you prefer, a fable in which, among certain examples worthy of imitation, you will perhaps also find many others that it would be right not to follow; and so I hope it will be useful for some without being harmful to any, and that everyone will be grateful to me for my frankness.[42]

Discussing the meaning of the Cartesian fable, Nancy stressed Descartes's "frankness" when saying that he writes not a fable but *as a* fable. He does not disguise his procedure but always makes it transparent when stating, for instance, in *The World* that he will clothe part of his discourse as a fable for the sake of making "this long discourse less boring for you."[43] He does not write in a fabulous manner but *as* a fable. Using the term *fabula* in such a clear way, such that he was even portrayed holding a book in which "*mundus est fabula*" is written and readable, he also makes clear, as Nancy showed so well, that differently from a fable that wants to teach precepts, he does not want to direct anyone, only give an account of how he had directed his mind himself in the search for truth.[44] Descartes's philosophical fable is a discourse that follows the course of his thinking *in actu*, which tells the story of the event of his thinking rather of his mind, something that cannot be repeated, that is inimitable, and hence what allows him to state "I am." It is therefore an inimitable example, an original that cannot be copied and that tells that in its way of telling. What Descartes's philosophical fable, his discourse, accounts for, is the course of the I am thinking being seized while I am thinking, the uniqueness of this event. The whole *Discourse* is performative. It is a performative discourse in the sense that Émile Benveniste described it and that Nancy explicitly recalls in his discussions:

> The performative utterance [*énoncé*], being in act, has the property of being *unique*. It cannot be produced except in special circumstances, at one and only one time, at a definite date and place. It does not have the value of description or prescription but, once again, of performance. This is why it is often accompanied by indications of date, of place, of names of people, of witnesses, etc.; in short, it is an event because it creates the event. Being an individual and historical act, a performative utterance cannot be repeated. Each reproduction is a new act performed by someone who is qualified.[45]

However, despite the clarifying aspects Benveniste offers about performative utterances, what the Cartesian philosophical tale performs is another kind of performative discourse since the uniqueness, the "here and now" of the event of thinking, is a here and now that *is and is not* here and now—for it is happening. The proper character of the "present participle," the "*cogitans*" through which Descartes describes the reality of the cogito, of the I think, and the uncountable uses of this form in this "fable" indicates the uniqueness of this performative uniqueness—namely, the one of being the most universally singular, of a here and now that are everywhere and at any time. Thus, *cogitans*, thinking, can be said in whatsoever tense: I was thinking, I will be thinking. But the most decisive thing here is to consider that thinking is a duration, a whileness, "*dum*," an "as long as," an in-between experienced from inside, that cannot be measured by a sequence of nows, insofar as it is the instancing of the instant, its all-comprehensive movement that confers the overwhelming sense that being is being, that existence is existing: therefore I am.

There is, however, a discrepancy between the I am thinking and I am writing I am thinking. This discrepancy is what Descartes's philosophical writing aims to write, indeed, the discrepancy between I am thinking and I am accounting not for my thoughts but for the experience of thinking and the emotions it provokes, indeed the e-motion, the moving this movement provokes. Descartes does not want to recall through memory the course of thinking, even if he cannot not do it. His intention is to write down the thinking while it is happening, what appears clearly in rule twelve in his discussions about the pen and the hand writing letters and lines. But there is always a gap between the experience of thinking and writing the event of thinking being experienced, a gap that is perhaps closest to Kafka's short tale about someone trying to set his watch by looking at the Prague astronomical clock: he will always be a second late. It is indeed the "second" of delay, the *aprés-coup* or afterimage between the thinking and the writing.

The fable of the "I" that is at once the most singular and the most universal is also renewed—for instance, in Descartes's decision to write *Discourse* in French. He also utters performatively saying, "And if I am writing in French, my native language, rather than Latin, the language of my teachers, it is because I expect that those who use only their natural reason in all its purity will be better judges of my opinion than those who give credence only to the writings of the ancients."[46] Derrida remarked insightfully on the incoherence between writing in "my native language, rather than Latin" for the sake of being more universally read by those "who use only their natural reason."[47] It is the incoherence of a national language being taken as the means for universality, a view that could be connected with Abbé Gregoire's linguistic project proposed to the French Commune during the revolution, which in fact was proposing the "annihilation of the dialects [patois]" and the instauration of a national language.[48] Descartes wanted to be read, however, rather in the sense that the reader would undertake his own "way"; the universality of his "method" was precisely the universality of each individual undertaking the search for truth and not absorbing the truth proclaimed and acclaimed by others or even imitating the "Philosopher's" method. Following the Philosopher's method means not following someone else's way or method. By choosing to write in French, Descartes also wanted to be read by women, "*j'ai voulu que les femmes mêmes pussent entendre quelque chose, et cependant que les plus subtills trouvassent aussi assez de matière pour occuper leur attention.*"[49] Incoherencies that might be attributed to Descartes, such as the decision to not write in Latin—still the "universal" erudite language of his time—for the sake of a universality even more universal, give rise to interesting discussions about Descartes's thoughts on language.[50] However, the point that must be stressed here is the literary "index" of Descartes's method, the narrative figure of the "I," the narrator that appears here as the most singular and the most universal at once. The question of who is the Cartesian "I" (the Cartesian subject), has, on the one hand, been affirmed and reaffirmed continuously and, on the other hand, consistently destroyed and deconstructed, its written status, "*Je*," "*ego*," "I," which renders it at one time mine (Heidegger's "*Je*" and "*Jemeinigkeit*")[51] and simultaneously everyone's, each one is not the last answer, when observing that the "I" is thinking. Or to render the ambiguity of this expression "I is thinking" clearer, when underlining that the I is the thinking. That means that I am thinking, the *cogitans* is the subject of this philosophical tale, the one who tells about itself. It is a cogitography or, to use a more common term, a psychography.

Descartes is the writer of the writing down the experience of thinking rather than thoughts. In this sense, it can be said that he writes a psychography or cogitography rather than an autobiography. The I am thinking writes and tells about itself, both *that* it is thinking and *how* it is thinking. The I am thinking, like all present participles, is in this way "present" in the here and now, that in the here and now, is brought everywhere and at every instant. This is what provides the certitude—meaning the overwhelming experience—that I am, indeed, that I am being. It is precisely this "uniqueness" that follows every instant while thinking that also renders this experience the experience of everyone as well, what is performed when putting *en abyme*, this event, in the very writing of this sentence. The unique experience of being thinking here and now, a here and now that exceeds every here and now, is uttered performatively, addressing everyone not in a dialogue but in a way that everyone is compelled to undertake the search for truth in each one, as each one, in the frankness of the own way.

A performative utterance is unique and proper. Nevertheless, it shows itself; it shows its own action. It exhibits the act of saying in saying as the writing exhibits its action I am writing and thinking when writing I am thinking. The sight involved in all performativity addresses the other in a certain way that is different from addressing another in a dialogue. Descartes was not a solipsist, although he withdrew from society and academia, preferring to be in a warm "room of his own." Nor was he, however, a Platonist in the sense of conducting a dialogue of the soul with itself. He wrote the *Meditations*, which have been considered a form of philosophical "retreat," in the manner of St. Ignatius, a kind of philosophical diary,[52] but even in these "meditative," intimist diaries called *Meditations*, he defines them in relation to the reader, this other always present for the writer, beginning with the writer himself who reads the writing while being written. As he says: "Analysis shows the true way in which the point in question was discovered . . . so that if the reader is willing to follow it, and pay sufficient attention to every point, he will make the thing his own, and understand it just as thoroughly as if he had discovered it for himself. . . . Analysis is the best and truest method of education, and it was this method alone which I used in my Meditations."[53]

If Descartes's method is to be considered analytical, it is not so in the sense of analytical philosophy and its compulsion to adjust philosophical method to the scientific idea of method. Descartes defines this scientific method rather as synthetic in the same passage. His own method he prefers to call "analytical" insofar as it renders it possible for the reader to follow "every point," the "flow" of thinking so that he can "make the thing his own, and understand it just as thoroughly as if he had discovered it for himself" because the reader must think while reading. I am thinking also appears suddenly when I experience "I am reading" while reading, *dum lego*.

What is important to keep in mind here is the way in which the other is addressed through Descartes's performative utterances. The other is addressed insofar as one also experiences I am thinking in such way that one may also say "I am," I *am* thinking—neither solipsism nor dialogue; neither dialogue with himself nor dialogue with others. Descartes proceeds in a manner more reminiscent of Shakespeare—they are indeed contemporaneous and also with Cervantes for a few years.[54] His cogitography is closer to a soliloquy. A soliloquy, such as those spoken by Hamlet and Julius Cesar in Shakespeare's tragedies, performs thinking in act. It is, first, not about talking with oneself but rather the utterance or exhibition of the happening of thinking before a spectator, before a reader. It has an essential dramatic feature to which Descartes was quite attuned.[55] It invites the other to be another by its own—being in this sense more for the other than with the other, as the writer is for his reader not being with the reader, while the reader is with the writing for being the reader one is.

But in Descartes, there are still other forms of being in his cogitographics (psychographics) and soliloquies. Descartes writes responses to objections. He does not engage in dialogue but responds, referring to former formulations, quoting himself in a certain way, retaking the movement of thinking in which thoughts have arisen. He responds in the form of letters and wrote many letters that are not merely responses to objections. Undoubtedly, writing letters and the act of correspondence inherently has the expectation of response. Descartes's letters are an important part of his body of work, and every critique of his "subjectivist," "solipsist," and "intimist" philosophical style should first be countered with the acknowledgment that Descartes's work was also epistolograhic. Descartes's letters correspond to the what that moves him altogether—namely, the experience of thinking, the experience of experiencing thinking, and therefore that "I am." Thus letters, which also means the letters on the paper, move the reader to write back; they demand a certain kind of response, which is the writing. In letters, the act of reading the writing is in itself writing. In their exchange and exchangeable character, letters perform what the philosophical discourse and meditation set out to do: that everyone undertakes the search for truth by oneself, that each one that reads, writes a response to what has been written, and this response remains both the most private—"my letter to you"—and the most public—a *written* letter that as written can, and would, be published.

Among the vast number of letters Descartes wrote, there are the famous letters to Elisabeth, Princess Palatine of Bohemia, written between 1643 and 1649, in which the question about the unity of body and soul are treated in a less (or even non-) dualistic manner. And the letters to Christina, Queen of Sweden, should not be left out of this discussion. In these letters addressed to noble and royal women, important aspects of Descartes's thought are presented in his own way of thinking in and through writing, and where his experience of thinking can be experienced by others in a way that makes their own experience of thinking while reading. These letters move the reader to write down the event of thinking. In this sense, it can be said that they e-move and e-motion the reader.

According to Descartes, in an earlier quoted passage from *Principles of Philosophy*, this work should be read as a novel and then read and reread until the reader himself could solve by himself all difficulties and problems he eventually could have found in his readings. As much as Descartes, the writer, always writes new treatises, his readers should read and reread until they feel themselves satisfied with their understanding. The work opens with a dedicatory letter to Princess Elisabeth. The dedication is a letter, and the letter, a dedication. Already, the intimate connection implied by a letter to a female reader and a dedication reveals much about the nature of his writing. The letter begins by stating, "Your Serene Highness, The greatest reward which I have received from the writings I have previously published is that you have designed to read them."[56] This special reader, Princess Elisabeth, is a special and privileged reader insofar as she, as Descartes affirms, in her "generous and modest nature will welcome the simple and unadorned judgment of a philosopher more than the polished compliments of those with smoother tongues."[57] He knows that this reader, Elisabeth, prefers to read and listen to philosophical judgment more than flattering words; he knows that philosophical judgments—that is, thinking thoughts—are more seductive than seduction. This is why he writes, "I shall therefore write only what I know to be true either from reason or by experience, and in this introduction. I propose to philosophize just as I do throughout the rest of the book."[58] The letter, the dedicatory letter to this special woman in Descartes's life, is a philosophical letter that philosophizes just as he does throughout the remainder of the book.

The dialogical character of philosophical thought is well-known since Plato introduced dramatic dialogue as a philosophical genre par excellence. It was also Plato who declared that philosophy is "the talk that the soul has with itself."[59] But Plato also wrote philosophical letters, among which the famous *Seventh Letter* contains the core of the Platonic understanding of philosophy, which also ushered in a long tradition of philosophizing through letters. Descartes—who could be considered the modern non-Socratic philosopher, who *only* wrote while Socrates *never* wrote, who voluntary preferred the solitude of his *poêle* to the company of his fellows, who wrote soliloquies and only very rarely dialogues— indeed philosophized through letters. Five volumes of the eleven that constitute the corpus of his philosophy, edited by Adam and Tannery, contain his letters. Letters can be understood as writing's proper form of dialogue, since in letters, the soul talks not to itself but to another, to an addressee, another that is present in its absence. Letters operate, so to speak, between the public and the private,

Figure 5.11. Elisabeth of Boehmia; Elisabeth at the age of twelve, from a portrait by Casparus Barlaeus, Herford Museum.

between the solitude of the self and the community with another. In letters, the writing is for someone, is dedicatory. This perhaps allows us to make an adventurous claim: that Descartes's philosophical novel and fable doubles as or is to a large extent a dedicatory letter.

A dedicatory letter is a letter moved by emotions. It is not difficult to "prove" that for Descartes, thoughts are not only rational, abstract, and conceptual thoughts. In article 9 of *Principles*, he asserts what is mean by "thought": "By the term 'thought,' I understand everything which we are aware of as happening within us, in so far as we have awareness of it. Hence, thinking is to be identified here not merely with understanding, willing and imagining, but also with sensory awareness" (*Cogitationis nomine, intelligo illa omnia, quae nobis confciis in nobis sunt, quatenùs eorum in nobis conscientia est. Atque ita non modo intelligere, velle, imaginari, fed etiam fentire, idem eſt hîc quod cogitare*).⁶⁰ Moreover, he also insists that very simple and self-evident matters become only more obscure when philosophers try to render through logical definitions. In *Principles*, Descartes also alludes to how "spoken or written words excite all sorts of thoughts and emotions in our minds."⁶¹ Revisiting a passage we have already quoted here, we can again read that: "With the same paper, pen and ink, if the tip of the pen is pushed across the paper in a certain way it will form letters which excite in the mind of the reader thoughts of battles, storms and violence, and emotions of indignation and sorrow; but if the movements of the pen are just slightly different they will produce quite different thoughts of tranquility, peace and pleasure, and quite opposite emotions of love and joy."⁶²

This passage follows a sentence in which Descartes discusses how the nature of the mind is such that various sensations can be produced in it simply by motions of the body. He observes immediately that "certain motions in the body can stimulate it to have a manner of thoughts which have no likeness to the movements in questions."⁶³ The emotions provoked by certain movements of the hand while writing letters—indeed, dedicatory letters and the responses of the one to whom the letters are dedicated and written—provoke, in turn, manners of thoughts that have no likeness to the movements that give rise to them. This sentence could also be read in the sense that Descartes's frank thoughts that arise in and through his thinking experience correspond to emotions provoked by certain bodily movements when writing, and indeed, in dedication to someone, here to Princess Elisabeth. Descartes is describing how the passions of his soul are disguised in thoughts that apparently have no likeness to what provoked them when reading a hand writing. Could it be possible that some thoughts that apparently have nothing to do with, for instance, love emerge when reading the hand writing of a beloved, when listening to words said by the beloved? Is philosophy then rather a disguised wisdom of love? Would it be so that his letters to Elisabeth are disguised love letters, in which philosophical emotion, the emotion that arises when, while thinking, thinking surprises itself thinking to the degree of intensity that it experiences that being is being, existence is existing, that "I am"? It is indeed a matter of wonder, this instant of sudden attention to the fact that I am thinking, that becomes apparent while thinking. "Wonder" says Descartes in *Passions of the Soul*,

> is a sudden surprise of the soul which brings it to consider with attention the objects that look unusual and extraordinary. It has two causes, first an impression in the brain, which represents the object as something unusual and consequently worthy of special consideration; and secondly, a movement of the spirits, which the impression disposes both to flow with great force to the place in the brain where it is located so as to strengthen and preserve it there, and also to pass into the muscles which serve to keep the sense organs fixed in

the same orientation so that they will continue to maintain the impression in the way in which they formed it.⁶⁴

In fact, it is what is caused by "a movement of the spirits, which impels the soul to join itself willingly to objects that appear to be agreeable to it" that Descartes defines love in *Passions of the Soul*.⁶⁵ Love, in the various forms Descartes accounts for, such as benevolent and concupiscent love, the first that "prompts us to wish for the well-being of what we love, and the other . . . which makes us desire the things we love,"⁶⁶ and things such as simple affection, friendship, and devotion, names a movement of the spirits provoked by several movements in the body in such a way that the body becomes aware of this moving movement along its event in the experience of wonder. Philosophical emotion, since the time of Plato and Aristotle, had been described as "wonder" and named *philia tes sofias*, *philo-sophia*, as love of wisdom discovers other dimensions with Descartes. It is the emotion of surprising oneself thinking while thinking, such an intensive presence at the instant, to the actuality of the instant—that is, to the acting while acting—that equals being in love and the love of being at this very instant.

6 The Gaze, Images, and Drives

Cecilia Sjöholm

Cartesian Theater and Inner Images

The Cartesian question of mind in *Meditations* is linked to perception; how do we perceive things in the outside world, and how is perception related to mental activities such as imagination and memory? These questions extend well beyond metaphysics. Anthropological and psychological issues of affect and physical entrapment are equally at stake—opening for theories of the drive that presage psychoanalytic theory. In *Treatise on Man*, Descartes inscribes a relation between physical affect and perception. In *Formation of the Foetus*, which is the final part of *Description of the Human Body*, the visceral origin of this relation is sought through a method of dissection. The way in which this method complements and exceeds the metaphysical writings concerned with inner images in *Meditations* is not often made an object in Cartesian scholarship—the writings in natural philosophy, to which the anatomy belongs, is almost always kept apart from the metaphysical work. However, as so many times with Descartes's work, things can be seen from multiple points of view: perception is a phenomenon of plural implications.

This search for some kind of origin, connection or ending is drawn toward a fleeting point of fascination—situated in a dissected eye, brain, or heart. In the Cartesian medical arts, in text and image, the gaze is particularly apostrophized: as the gaze of curiosity perhaps, or as the gaze of learning—but at the same time, in the splitting open of organs, it becomes trapped at its own vanishing point. In works such as *Optics*, but also in those on anatomy, emotions, and passions, Descartes takes us beyond the question of perception, toward the origin of the gaze—a point at which drives deriving beyond the reflective *cogito* intersect with the intellectual elaboration of mental images. In speculating on the inside of the human body, its streams and flows, temperatures and textures, laying open the nervous system and the tubes of transport that run between brains and limbs, Descartes inscribes a gaze of fascination that transcends the sheer anatomical aims of visualization—a scopic drive of dissection.

The Cartesian studies of various states of consciousness, such as the sleeping dream, the in-between of dream and state of wakefulness, or the very moment

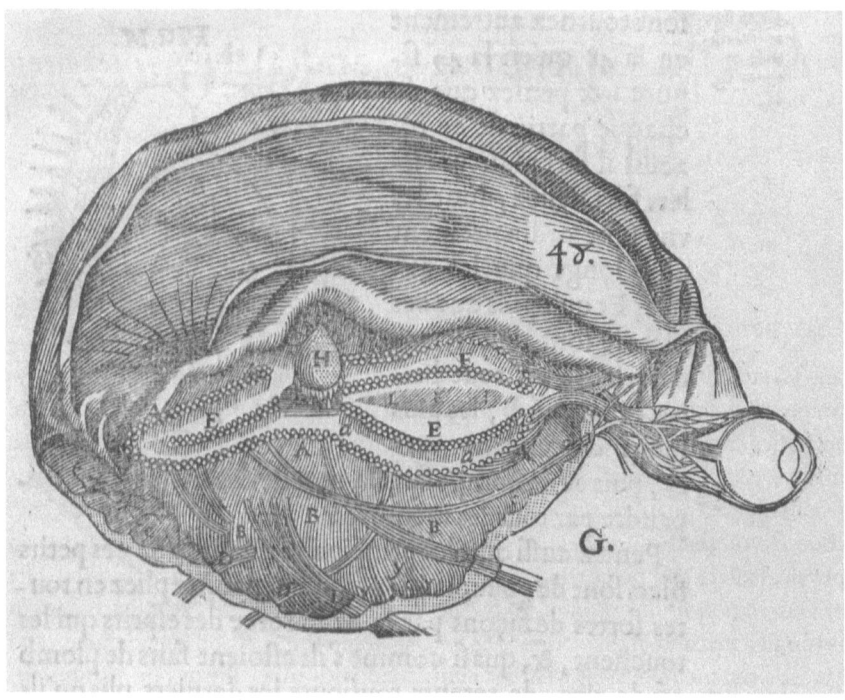

Figure 6.1. *L'Homme: Et un traitté de la formation du foetus*, Paris, 1664, Royal Library Stockholm.

of waking up, are particularly occupied with the quality and meaning of inner images. The scholarly inquiries on this theme are most often made with regard to the metaphysical inquiries of *Meditations*, as inquiries into the philosophy of mind. But in Descartes's own writings, the distinction between physics and metaphysics is not always so clear-cut, as we have demonstrated in the chapter on his visceral aesthetics. A similar argument can be made about the Cartesian inquiries into inner images—although they often have metaphysical implications, they can be seen in conjunction with the visceral impact on the inside of the body, which is connected to perception. The multifaceted investigations into various forms of consciousness can be seen regarding corporeal instigations and effects. Just as in psychoanalysis, mind and body are not simply separated or simply joined but overlaid with conflicts. In his writings *Treatise on Man*, *The Formation of the Foetus*, and *Passions of the Soul*, Descartes shows, just like Sigmund Freud, that the subject that thinks and feels is rooted in biological life. This, in turn, suggests the existence of a theory of the drive, the gaze of which is its primary mode of existence.

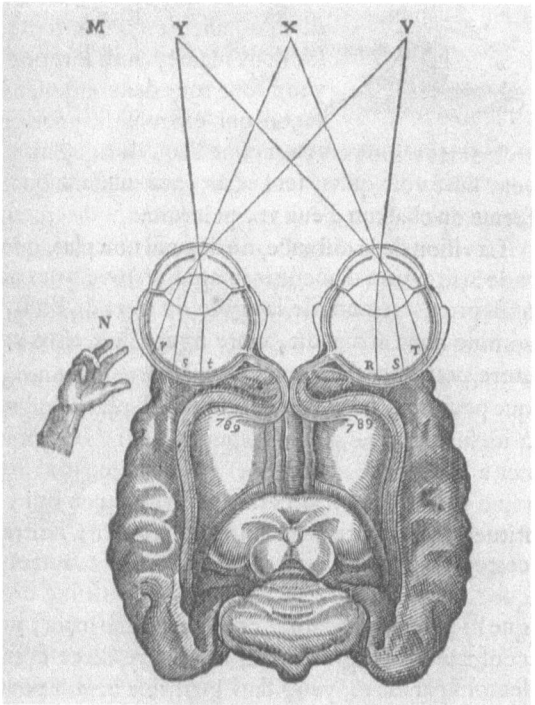

Figure 6.2. *Dioptrique*. In *Discours de la méthode*, Leyden, 1637, Royal Library Stockholm.

In *Optics*, Descartes inscribes a distinct breaking point between the I that sees—which is not only a subject of perception but also of reason—and the "eye" that sees, the eye of dissection. Breaking points, in general, are inscribed in all of Descartes writings. We find them between passivity and activity, inside and outside, dream and wakefulness. In *Meditations* we find a breaking point, between the I that doubts and the I that exists; signifying itself through a shifter through which the subject will forever become split to itself. Here, Descartes assumes the biggest challenge of the skeptic, to think without relying on sense perception. The sky, the air, the earth, colors, shapes, sounds are merely the constructs of a malicious demon, "delusions of dreams which he devised to ensnare my judgment."[1] This famous passage introduces not only a subject split between *res cogitans* and *res extensa* but also a subject scrutinizing its own inner images.

The separation between the inner images of dreams of fantasy—and the metaphysically secured knowledge of the cogito—is made possible through a distinct break performed with an older, Aristotelian worldview.[2] But Descartes's discussion of imagination and his reflections on inner images in general are not only there to posit a distinction vis-à-vis the cogito. It could well be the case that one cannot know the cogito unless one passes through the images. But this entails analyzing how inner images are produced.

We may doubt all our senses, says the first chapter of *Meditations*, but some things seem more certain than others: "I am here, sitting by the fire, wearing a winter dressing-gown, holding this piece of paper in my hands, and so on. Again, how could it be denied that these hands or this whole body are mine?[3] Descartes visualizes himself in different states of consciousness, as if seen from a third eye, from the outside. A variant of the same occurs in the third meditation, which reflects on what it means to think without images. All mental images will be regarded as "vacuous, false and worthless." The objects of sensory experience and imagination are thought not to exist, although sensory perception and imagination are very much in existence as inner images."[4] In denegating "mental images" of all things that belong to the extended world, *Meditations* describes not only the difference between the conscious self that has a conception of itself and the world outside of it but also the self thinking itself thinking without images. Such a consciousness, a cogito that thinks without images, can only be postulated through a radical negation. But consciousness cannot actually remove what is experienced as a world of inner images; it can only postulate its removal "as if."

Daniel Dennett has described the problem with this split in and of consciousness. In *Meditations*, Descartes observes experience to be shaped as a series of inner images. In these observations, he establishes a limit between inner and outer, between arrival and registration, "which is the necessary and sufficient condition for conscious experience."[5] Even if Descartes makes clear that consciousness is not the same thing as a representation of the outside world, there is an idea that inner images and sensual experience correspond. If we assume, Dennett argues, that our consciousness is equal to the inner images that we have of our experiences, we need to postulate that there is a part of us that registers these inner images, that, so to speak, watches the inner screen of our mental activity. Descartes postulates a little spectator, or a little homunculus or a small man studying everything that happens inside the brain. To explain the function of this homunculus, however, you need another one. And then another one—the idea of consciousness acquires the form of a reflexive unity where thought reflects on inner images. Consciousness ends up being construed as "Cartesian theater."

The critique of the Cartesian theater is, in turn, also widely criticized, but still a point of reference in the philosophy of mind. But the homunculus—that is, the figure of a split mind watching itself analyzing its own state of consciousness—does not necessarily give witness to an inconsistency of argument. What Descartes does, rather, is to demonstrate that subjectivity is inherently split. In doing that, he is positing a kind of split between conscious layers and the unconscious workings of desire and drives that have become a standard conception in contemporary psychoanalysis.[6] In figuring how we relate to ourselves through memories, fantasies, and other layers of inner images, he is not giving any psychological account of the self. He places us in front of an unknown point of production, an alterity or point zero. Inner images are active formations rather than imprints of an exterior on things and object.[7] The subject of thought points to the existence of something that does not think *of* the self so much as it thinks *in* the self. We encounter an unknown point of reference that captures the cogito, without being the cogito.

In his seminal work *The Four Concepts of Psychoanalysis*, Jacques Lacan shows the psychoanalytic subject to be a consequence of the Cartesian insight that the "I," which enounces its own being, points to the conditions for its own enunciation. The density of those conditions are imaginal—the cogito can pronounce its existence, but has difficulties grasping itself beyond its inner images. In Lacan's subject, the unconscious is situated in a language that, as Freud has shown, is prone to condensation and displacement. These are linguistic mechanisms. But they are also pictorial—the dream language is always displaced with the view of being as rich as possible in terms of inner images. Whereas Descartes introduced the subject, it was Freud who used the dream to demonstrate what subjectivity means: "In the field of dream you are at home. *Wo es war, soll ich werden.*"[8] This does not mean that the ego comes to rise, victorious over the unconscious, but rather that it cannot be seen as distinct from the unconscious. To psychoanalysis, the subject cannot be thought beyond the weave of inner images through which the subject reflects and affects itself—it is to be thought as a point of desire and drives rather than certainty or knowledge. Thus, psychoanalysis has demonstrated that the cogito is a point of radical negativity, negating not just the realness of things in the outside world but also itself, when it appears as nothing but an inner theater.[9] The Cartesian reduction of the subject to pure cogito implies that the very thing that goes under the notion of Cartesian theater covers the subject as pure void or negativity. It serves as a kind of shield over an empty space, an imaginary cover—filled with fantasies and dreams.

Inner Images and Mnemonic Traces

At the same time, the cogito is not all there is. If the cogito is the metaphysical endpoint of consciousness, the anchor of skeptical subjectivity asserted as negativity, there is also a subject of a phenomenal physicality, of corporeality and of sexuality, to be explored. If one looks at the Cartesian examination of "inner images" such as fantasies and dreams, it becomes clear that Descartes himself posits multifaceted layers of consciousness. Inner images such as fantasies, memories, and dreams belong not to a single form of consciousness but to topologies and layers that deserve not one explanation but several.

In the fragments that were left after Descartes death, called *Les Olympiques*, which were repeated in Baillet's biography forty years after his death and were also copied by Leibniz, Descartes writes about a dream. This scene has often been repeated in the literature on Descartes and given a symbolic status. In the dream, he makes his way toward a Jesuit cloister, and his path is crossed by strong winds and unlikely events as well as corporeal lameness. At the same time, a phrase comes to him, where the genius of poetry is described through the idea of "enthusiasm": "One could find it surprising that the most profound thoughts are to be found in the writings of poets rather than philosophers. That is because the poets have written under the dominance of enthusiasm and the force of imagination; the seeds of science are in us as the sparks of flint; the philosophers extract these seeds by reason, and the poets make them spurt out with their imagination: therefore they shine even stronger."[10]

Sketching what might be figured as a model of production of inner images, Descartes points to the intertwinement between writing, thinking, and dreaming. He knows that what appears to be the most intimate in the self, a flow of dreams and fantasies, gives witness to a fundamental split between the ego, which seeks to designate itself—by language and reason—and the subject that is the location of thought, which comes in multiple forms.

Descartes's problem of thought, then, although focused on the certainty of the cogito, explores a much wider notion of consciousness that precedes Freudian studies of the unconscious. Freud was aware of this himself: the dreams of *Olympica* became subject to analysis. To the psychoanalyst, they do not lack an obvious sexual symbolism: Descartes dreaming that he would be presented with a big melon from a far-off land. The maternal breast is displayed with all its insignia. But Freud does not see any content of interest for interpretation for the psychoanalyst. To him, the dreams are too intellectual, too put in place: they are dreams "from above" that are more like philosophical constructions than streams of consciousness.[11] In addition to the sexual symbolism of the maternal body, Freud misses out also on typical visceral conflicts that haunt the dreamer in his own work. Descartes has a dream of stickiness—he is flung to a wall by strong winds, unable to move, all the while others seem to pass him by. This corresponds to what Freud talks about as a "typical dream": movement being impeded. That this occurs in dreams in general, he says, can only partly be explained by organic stimulation occurring in one's sleep. Organic causes cannot do away with "the apparent freedom of the determination of the dream-picture."[12] This is what Freud will also apply to his own dream of impeded movement; the analysis of typical dreams is situated between organic input and the production of the dream-work. It is precisely this divide, and conflict, between corporeality and inner image that Descartes explores, and which is figured in the *Olympica*. The movement of the mind does not correspond to the paralysis of the body.

The inner film of consciousness gives witness to a variety of forms of production of which dreams are one kind. There are many others. From a Cartesian point of view, it is not a problem that what I know about myself appears in the form of an inner theater: this is congruent with the multifaceted way in which consciousness appears. In Descartes we find the preamble to the psychoanalytic idea of the layers of consciousness as forms of images created out of a flow of inscriptions of memories, dreams, and experiences, but also of physical imprints.

Freud posits that perception and consciousness are not simultaneous. Perceptions are construed as traces before they pass into consciousness or are brought up as memories. The psychic apparatus that gathers these traces consists of different layers of inscriptions. Perceptions leave in the psychic apparatus a trace, which we may call a memory-trace, Freud writes.[13] Perceptions first hit a system which retains nothing of sensory impressions. Behind this there is a second system "which transforms the momentary excitation of the first into permanent traces."[14] It is the second system of lasting traces that forms the basis of association. Traces can be remnants of emotions, images, or language. In the psychic apparatus, they are associated with each other, displaced and condensed, without us being aware. Here, inner imagery becomes possible because of the cut between remnants of perceptions and actual perceptions.

Descartes repeatedly stresses the way in which the traces of the mind allow for a circulation and association of inner images and words. In *Passions of the Soul*, he uses traces as a concept to describe the conditions for such an associative stream of thought. A trace, to Descartes, is a kind of inscription in the mind that paves the way for other perceptions to actualize themselves.[15] Like Freud, Descartes assumes traces to attach to each other through qualities of intensities and excitations. Unlike Freud, he does not posit any resistances to be present in the psychic apparatus. Descartes likened the scene of internal vision to that of memory; memories, like imagination, can be willfully produced. For this to happen, however, they need to be gathered as memory traces in the brain; just like Freud uses the idea of the trace to construe a psychic apparatus of association at the end of *Interpretation of Dreams*, Descartes uses the idea of traces that facilitate perceptions of the same idea to enter the mind.[16] Inner images may serve as a link between a variety of traces. Perceptions are internalized as memory traces and take part in an associative flow between traces. Perceptions are mediated by traces in the brain and moved around by the agitation of the spirits, so that we "feel" what we see; it is this sensual and visceral quality to perception that moves inner images in dreams, fantasies, and works of art.[17]

The associative stream of dreams, fantasies, and memories are linked to traces in the mind—"the spirit, agitated in various ways and coming upon traces of various impressions which have preceded them in the brain, haphazardly take their course through certain of its pores rather than others."[18] Whether construed by dreams or wakeful imagination, internal images are less vivid than live perceptions; they are more a "shadow" or a "picture."[19] It is precisely this secondary character of trace, as a shadow or picture, that makes a sensory impression part of an associative stream, evoked in dreams, imagination, and works of art. But the traces evoke not only inner images. The traces are internal also to the evocation and circulation of affects. These are explored in their own terms and as aspects of the imaginative faculties of the soul. They are produced by external or internal physical causes and by imagination and internal imagery, such as writing, dreams, and memories. What Descartes describes, then, is not only a multifaceted notion of consciousness but also an associative flow that links different layers of consciousness to each other, also through imprints that are not just ideas of the mind but are very much inscribed in the body—through affects, muscles, and physical needs.

Imagination and Perception

In Maurice Merleau-Ponty's lengthy critique of Descartes, in "Eye and Mind," he argues that the perspective in which Descartes remains caught is one of center-periphery, where images and colors are imprints of a world that is posited as "real." In a way similar to Dennett's critique of *Meditations*, Merleau-Ponty sees *Optics* present not a subject of seeing but rather a third party observing the seeing. The Cartesian theorization of images excludes the kind of immersion "from the inside" from which a painter construes a world.[20]

However, Descartes does not separate the painter from the subject—the subject *is* a painter in its production of inner images. In *Optics*, Descartes explains how perceptions are created through lines of light that transpose into inner images. The light that hits the eye forms traces that are interpreted by the mind, though perception is not a natural mirror of the external world. Perception in general is like the perception of a painting, or engravings, not depending at all on resemblances—on the contrary, the less alike, the more developed the perception. Engravings consist in "a little ink placed here and there on a piece of paper," and it is precisely this scarcity of signs that allows people, landscapes, and horizons to develop before our eyes.[21] As Husserl has shown, images do not represent an object in its actuality—we are, as Husserl explains, conscious of the "as if" mode of the representation. This is also a temporal suggestion: artworks have a hovering quality with regard to perception; they refer to a presence that is not quite a presence.[22] The hovering of the "as if" in time—as if the object is present, or perhaps has been present, or could be present—perhaps takes on a particular quality with engravings, given the repetition of their very form, the object of representation being withdrawn through the repetitive act itself.

Perceptions are created as light reaches the inner side of the eyes. These perceptions then become inner images that are related to other images, memories, and imaginations (fantasies). Between sleep and wakefulness, our perception is more conditioned by physical states and neurological traces than things in the outer world.[23] The same goes for visual impressions in states of dream: dreams "are like paintings," in which one can only trust the realness of colors.[24] It is not merely visual images that flow by; corporeal memories and emotions also find their way into the stream of consciousness.

Inner images result as much from the mind and from a visceral, physical inside as from appearances. This occurs in states of wakefulness as well as in dreams. Images stimulate our thought without being simulacra, or little copies of the representations printed into or minds. And the mind can be stimulated by "many other things other than images—by signs and words, for example, which in no way resemble the things they signify," Descartes writes in *Optics*.[25] Engravings—which are precisely what Descartes used in his books—do not need to be exact copies of what they represent: we will still forestall us humans, storms, woods . . . a hint of likeness is enough. As Merleau-Ponty has argued, perception in Descartes is a kind of decipherment.[26] This is well in line with Descartes's own idea that inner images and dreams are subject to decipherment—as they are in the Freudian analysis of inner images.

Feelings and ideas, inner images and corporeal movement may all have a variety of sources. Some inner images are woven together in a flow or weave between states of consciousness, where the "illusions of our dreams and likewise the waking reveries we often have" are created not by the will but by a consciousness that "wanders carelessly."[27] Some wakeful imaginations are like dreams.[28] These inner images are extra mysterious to Descartes, since they are neither perceptions created by stimuli from the outside nor creations brought forward by the will. They are not complete perceptions but "shadows" and "pictures,"—that is, they belong to an inner world that Descartes, even in trying to literally dissect it, never fully accessed.[29]

Art and writing, also, are produced by various forms of production that may belong to various states of consciousness. The capacity to release associative chains of thought is intrinsically linked to poetry. The images of poets come to them; they have minds stored with all possible pleasures of imagination. The enjoyment of poetry cannot be taught through theories.[30] It is a distinctly subjective process. It has to do with associations between objects, but also with stored memories and emotions. Associations are not merely figural; traces bind perceptions as visual imprints and emotions. In *Principles of Philosophy*, Descartes suggests that "spoken or written words excite all sorts of thoughts and emotions in our minds."[31] Literature affects us not only on an intellectual level. Writing is an associative stream and poetic language that stimulates a flow of images. "If the tip of the pen is pushed across the paper in a certain way it will form letters that excite in the mind of the reader the thoughts of battles, storms and violence, and emotions of indignation and sorrow; but if the movements of the pen are just slightly different they will produce quite different thoughts of tranquility, peace and pleasure, and quite opposite emotions of love and joy."[32] The inner images produced by writings are linked through a kind of après-coup logic; it is the movement of the pen that produces the emotions, as if the signs are the result of a flow and not of intentions. Writing is produced in a zone where signs orient us between imagination, perceptions, memories, and other kinds of thought, but not necessarily at will. Descartes understood writing as a free flow or exchange between words, images, and other remnants of the mind, including emotions. But poetry is not a willed expression of emotions: emotions erupt in and with the flow. Affects and emotions may come to us in states of sleep or wakefulness, unattached to any external cause. These emotions are no less real when we experience them; in the haze of being half-asleep, half-awake, we may still sense with our bodies and with our minds as if we were wide awake.[33] The cause of such emotions lies not in the external world but within us. Emotions take part of the trail of associations, the constant flow of thoughts that circulate between the mind and the body.

Imagination, in turn, is not just an unregulated activity of the mind. Instead, imagination *makes* us perceive things that have no correspondence in the world outside of us. It is a conscious act of creation that allows us to create worlds beyond the reach of the physical one.[34] Even the body itself may, for instance, be a source of imagination, so-called corporeal imagination. In *Rules for the Direction of the Mind* (1628), Descartes uses the concept to point to a sixth sense, which in modern language could be called kinesthesis; we can apprehend the movements of other living bodies through the movements of our own. Such a corporeal apprehension does not depend on clear perceptions; we may apprehend and sense the movement of other bodies also if we only have a vague perception of them.[35] We may imagine movement, our own and others, and as we do, we may sense it in our own bodies. Movement is linked to inner images, feelings, and ideas. Both imagination and dreams are joined to a production of emotions that are part of a circuit that may be only semiconscious.

Gaze and Scopic Drive in *Treatise on Man*

The introduction to *Treatise on Man* introduces the assumption that man is constituted both of body and soul, and its jointure: "These two natures would have to be joined and united so as to constitute men resembling us."[36] The first two editions of the treatise, published after Descartes death, used sumptuous images that followed Descartes's intentions in their description of the inside of the body. The images are more than illustrations—they are hypotheses. But they speak not only of a connection between body and soul. They speak of a connection between the gaze and the body that has archaic origins. It goes all the way to the moment of conception. The gaze, the emotions, and the fantasy of the mother, to Descartes, makes its imprint on the fetus—this will be discussed in the chapter of "The Thinking Fetus."

The question of the gaze is inscribed in the overall project of natural philosophy: How do we acquire a knowledge of what we cannot see? Descartes used images to make visible what does not present itself to the eyes, such as the particles in *Meteorology* and streams of light in *Optics*. The inside of the body, and its jointure of body and soul, which is the focus of *Treatise on Man*, is also a space that we cannot see without dissection.

One cannot underestimate the importance of the anatomical sketches, which mostly had no original to copy, but which were certainly made in fidelity with Descartes's intentions and style. Here, one thing stands out in contemporary research: the overall fixation on the eyes and their supposed connectedness to a corporeal inside. Descartes sketched the function of perception, as in the perception of things in an outside world, which was the primary aim with *Optics*. He also sketched the relation between the eyes and the inside of a body of affects, pains, flows, and memories, marked since its inception by its origination in the maternal womb. In this genealogy, which actualizes psychoanalytic theory, corporeal instincts are attached to the gaze. The gaze, in turn, is fixated on organs that are otherwise covered or unavailable to the human eye, such as the inside of the body.

Descartes first wrote *Treatise on Man*, which was to be included in *Le Monde*, in 1632. But for fear of punishment for its scientific standpoints, he delayed publication. In the end, the first edition was produced in 1662 by Florentio Schuyl after Descartes's death. Published in Latin, *De homine Figuris* leads us to understand that the purpose of the book is to figure the essential physical and anatomical makeup of a human being. The text of this edition was based on two copies, one by Van Zurck, a friend of Descartes, and the other by Pollot. The second contained two drawings copied by Schuyl, while the others were drawn by Schuyl himself.

The edition has a preface that designates two of the drawings to a manuscript made by Alphonsus Palotti. The originals have been found in Descartes's own work—that is, they were made by Descartes himself.[37]

The edition, which introduces sumptuous anatomical images and folds, includes skeletal constructions, blood vessels, nervous systems, and muscles. Descartes's aim is to figure the relation between perception and sensual stimuli, nervous system and corporal movement. This is accomplished through the detail in which the tubes, as Descartes calls the inner system of the bloodstream and nervous system, are connected. Some images figure whole humans in situations where stimuli and movement are introduced. But the bulk of the images, modeled after Descartes's own original drawings, figure visual perception and the

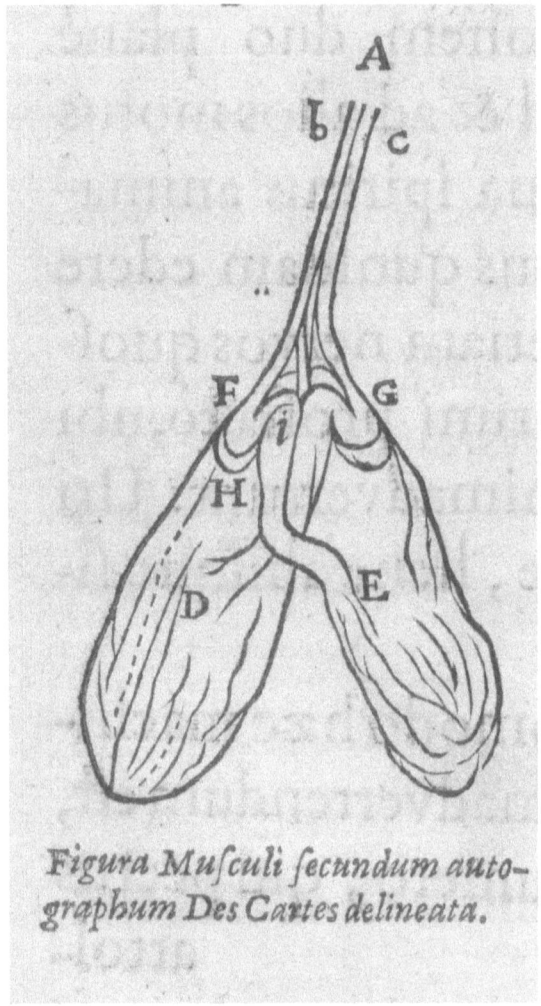

Figure 6.3. *De l'Homine Figuris* 1662, Leyden, Royal Library Stockholm.

relation between gaze and ocular construction—that is, eye, muscle, brain, and nervous system.

The second, competing edition of *L'Homme* is the 1664 edition illustrated by Claude Clerselier, which was translated into French.[38] In this edition, Clerselier introduces a manuscript that was not completed, "Description of the Human Body," to which he adds the title *The Formation of the Foetus*. Descartes originally intended the title to apply only to the final, fourth section of the text, but

Clerselier apparently considered the title suitable to convey the main purpose of the text.[39]

Clerselier wrote a preface to the edition where he describes the figures used by the artists Gérard von Gutschoven and Louis de La Forge. The aim was to explain the intentions of the text, illuminating the passage of the spirits to the movement of the muscles.[40] This passes through the eyes, as is made clear in an image that, according to Clerselier, is retained from a Cartesian manuscript.[41] Just like in the manuscript by Schuyl, the focus on the eyes and the gaze is maintained throughout. Many see the images as interpretations of the philosophical problem of the distinction between mind and body.[42] Perhaps Clerselier did: he then engaged de La Forge for the illustrations to demonstrate the existence of a possible union. As a result, de La Forge identifies a relation between an invisible and a visible sphere in Descartes's works and makes the transition between those two spheres the focus of his figures.[43]

But to Descartes, the mind-body issue was not only a question of speculation; his desire was visceral and graphic. He described a feeling of discontent with the limits of metaphysics when it comes to examining the relation between mind and body, inner images and reality. Overcoming these limits by a scalpel, he writes to his Mersenne with great enthusiasm: "Now I am dissecting the heads of different animals in order to explain what imagination, memory etc., consist of."[44] In *Optics*, published a few years later (1637), Descartes describes the refraction of light in conjunction with the dissection of eyes. The aim of this work was not so much to present the role of the physical eye as it was to discuss the nature of perception from a viewpoint that we would today consider more as brain research than as anatomical finds. We cannot assume that perceptions are identical to external objects; the sensory impressions that pass through the eyes are always prepared in the brain to become adequate occasions of what we call perception. It is the mind, not the body, that senses; this pertains also to vision. It is not the eye that sees, but the mind.[45] With this insight, to which the dissection of eyes contributed no small part, Descartes made the philosophical doctrine of simulacra come to an end (i.e., the idea that the world is planting images in us that resemble that which is outside, or that perception would be a natural mirror of the external world). Instead, perception is prepared in the brain. In Descartes's drawn figures of perception in *Optics*, the gaze is joined to the light of the outside world and refracted in the dissected eye. Perception, as described in the text and made out as figures—is not produced by a second little eye inside the brain; it is produced by movements in which mind and body are joined. This is not primarily a prephenomenological analysis of a body moving in the world—although it can be interpreted that way—what joins mind and body is rather the kind of movements that we find in nerve endings in the eyes, ears, and tongue, responding to stimuli.[46]

Descartes is as interested in what eludes vision as he is sensual experience itself—in the small, invisible parts of nature that we cannot seize. In his natural philosophy, Descartes thinks like a painter. Unable to represent depth and volume of something that he does not fully fathom through sense experience, he expounds on what comes to the fore in the form of materiality or sense perception, and he begins to add volume and depth from there. In the case of perception, the main thing is light.[47] Identifying light as the main element of perception, Descartes's notion of the image, outer and inner, develops toward a theory of the gaze.

Natural philosophy in general, and the analysis of perception more specifically, passes through works of art. Scattered signs on a paper may still make us experience a full landscape, battlegrounds, storms, and so on—if we are to grasp what perception is, this is where we need to begin.[48] It is the same with inner images. They cannot be understood as the decoding of outer signs, as Merleau-Ponty notes; they are rather the decoding of "signs given within the body."[49] One may take these "inner" signs to consist of emotions and memories. But the Cartesian propositions on perception depended on the anatomical practices of dissection as much as on prephenomenological descriptions of images and painting. And come to that: dissection, and the very specific gaze of fascination that came with it, was a recurrent theme in paintings of his own times.

At the table of dissection, Descartes's theory of perception becomes intertwined with what contemporary psychoanalysis calls "the gaze." The gaze is a central concept in the psychoanalytic theory of Jacques Lacan; it points to that in perception which eludes conscious elaboration of the intellect. It eludes, also, our sense of the real; the gaze is a phenomena that transcends the gap between consciousness and the unconscious, occurring in sleep as well as in wake reality. Whereas perception may be construed as the subject's elaboration of reality, its colors, sounds, and things, the gaze is rather the impingement in the subject of those things. It shows itself as the involuntary attraction or fascination with things, as the unwilled directedness of perception through details in an image. After having read Merleau-Ponty's *The Visible and the Invisible*, Lacan formulates the gaze as something that transcends the limits of the situatedness of the body, its muscular capacity, and its involvement in movements and actions. The gaze does not speak to the eye of the viewer; it preexists the perception of the world of the embodied subject. It is experienced not as perception of an image but as that which in the field of vision presents itself as contingency, fortitude, but also as a haunting, a quality of stickiness to the real. The gaze is a haunting of what Lacan calls castration anxiety; as such it presents itself through gaps and wounds, but also as immeasurable experiences of fascination and beauty. In the gaze, the world sees us watching; it may allow or not for a sense of the real to unfold, or it may retreat to a state of dream, or illusion. This uncanny directedness in the subject that sees itself seeing, and then is forced to retreat to its own sense of uncertainty, is the gaze functioning as what Lacan calls *objet a*. It is a concept that on the one hand designates the inexorable lack that follows with castration, on which the structure of the subject is construed. On the other, however, it is also a concept that transcends the limits between inside and outside, and the limits between eye and I. Given that it is driven by fascination and beauty, while stretching also to know the secrets of its own evanescent origins in images and pictures, Lacan's notion of the gaze as *objet a* can also be placed within the sphere of a visceral aesthetics.

The gaze, to Lacan, is to be understood through what Freud discusses as the scopic drive: the somatic entrapment in the wish to examine, through the eyes, the limits between what can be seen and what cannot be seen. The image in general, and the baroque painting in particular in its attempt to perspectivize the infinite, is a trap for the gaze in its capturing of the scopic drive. It can appear, such as Lacan has demonstrated, for instance through a vanitas motive, such as a skull almost invisibly inserted in a scene. It can also appear through the many illusions that are at work in baroque painting—through the sticky illusion produced by a *trompe l'oeil*, for instance, such as a painting in a painting, or a portrait in a portrait. Through doubling, luring, or creating illusions, painting points at the stickiness of the gaze.

Rembrandt painted *The Anatomy Lesson of Dr Nicolaes Tulp* was painted in 1632, the same year Descartes wrote *Description of the Human Body*. In this painting, a group of students gather around a surgeon opening a cadaver. The students are all leaning toward the open incision in the body, attempting to see the inside. Through the incision, a glowing light seems to emanate due to Rembrandt's distinct use of white and red coloring. What the painting captures is the gaze into the incision, through the embodiment of light.

The very capturing of the gaze is situated at the intersection between the inner and the outer—at the very limit that Descartes himself wanted to explore through the dissection of eyes. These images derive from the anatomy lessons in which Descartes himself took part, as a *physicien*. In the analysis of the living body, we perceive a dead body, a corpse split open. The *fascinum* engaging the scopic drive is captured in a body that cannot return the gaze. The gaze becomes a vanishing point, so that the scopic drive is retracted onto itself. What we find here is an *anamorphosis*, an inverted use of perspective, which, as Lacan has pointed out, shows "an original subjectifying relation."[50] Rembrandt's painting incorporates the same split as Descartes in his dissection of the eyes—he not only points to an ego seeing the world but to a gaze returning the vision. This is how the scopic drive becomes inscribed in the Cartesian explorations of the anatomy of perception—not only do I see the world but my gaze is also directed by a pulsating drive that directs my gaze. Such a drive is in the field of the other,

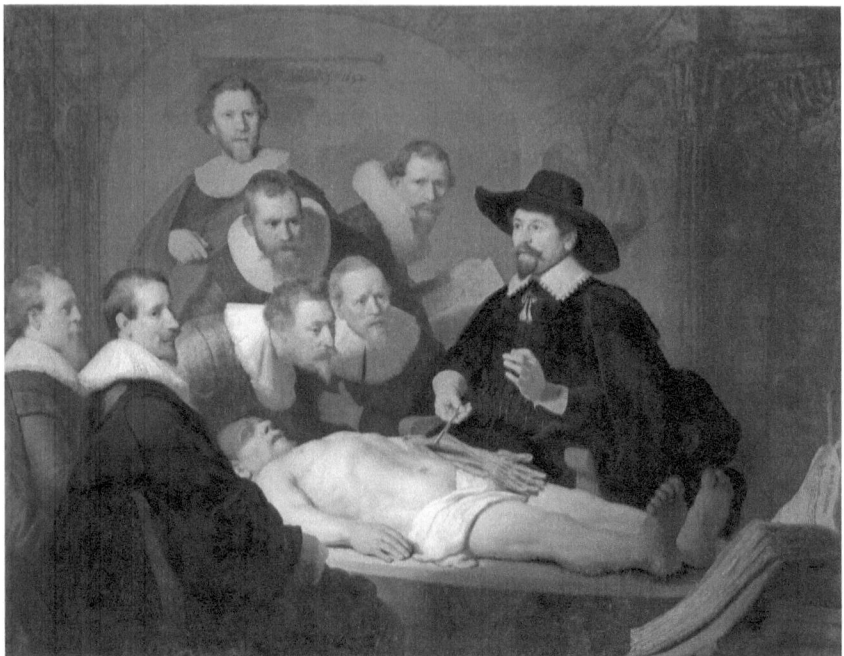

Figure 6.4. Rembrandt, *The Anatomy Lesson of Dr. Nicolaes Tulp* (1632) © Mauritshuis.

in the Lacanian analysis. This field is itself inhabited by a vanishing point—the evanescent point of vision that unlocks the stickiness of the real.

Freud identified the point in his analysis of Leonardo da Vinci's practices of dissection. The modern anatomical practice of sketching dissected corpses traces its origin to Leonardo da Vinci. It is also in the study of da Vinci that the psychoanalytic speculation of the gaze begins—through Freud's text on "Leonardo da Vinci and a memory of his childhood." In da Vinci's own words, his motivations are sparked by his ambition as a painter; he wants to understand the way muscles and joints are conjoined in order to better render the movement of living bodies. Complying neither with the legal nor the ethical framework that surrounded such practices in his time, da Vinci, just like Descartes, went to great lengths to pursue this understanding of the human body. Only medical doctors had the right to dissect. Da Vinci lacked such recognition and so pursued his studies outside of the legal frameworks.[51]

Cartesian Conception

This desire for knowledge, according to the legend promoted by renaissance art historian and critic Giorgio Vasari, is also what interfered with da Vinci's artistic ambition and ability.[52] Freud reinforces this legend, in turn, in relaying that da Vinci increasingly became a riddle to his contemporaries due to his turn away from art to science, in the end engaging in the "black art" of the alchemists in his treatment of the dead.[53] In Freud's analysis, da Vinci's fascination with knowledge as dissection is intertwined with a certain asexuality and frigidity. Above all, it can be seen as a symptom of fear of the female organ of procreation.[54] To Freud, each child carries fantasies about their own origin. The phase of infantine sexual investigation involves an indistinct conception of aggressive sexual relations. Da Vinci, who made drawings of an infant in the uterus as well as a drawing of the female sexual organ, sublimated these infantile desires into a quest of scientific curiosity. Freud retells an early childhood memory of da Vinci in which a vulture strikes the child's lips with his tail. To Freud, this memory is equally to be associated with homosexual desires and fantasies of suckling a breast. Ultimately, the desire of the male organ is only a negation of a fear of castration: in da Vinci's proud celebrations of masculinity, Freud sees depiction for "the unhappy creatures on whom the cruel punishment has, as he supposes, already fallen." To Freud, the perforation of the female body, depicted as images of the fetus, is then associated not just with the inside of the body in general but with the female organ of procreation, which is associated with an "uncanny and intolerable idea."[55]

Descartes's treatise, in both editions, omits all figuration of the womb or sexual organs, although they are discussed in the text. But in the Latin edition by Schuyl, there are other details that are worth pointing out in this context: as was sometimes the practice in early modern anatomical literature, several folds are introduced so that the reader can lift the lids and look inside the body. The human body is figured, in this way, both from the inside and the outside. This also applies to a sumptuous figure of the heart, which is a figural transposition, with lids, of Descartes's description of how the valves are shut and open with small lids. There is also an image of the human brain comprising a whole page. Given that the organ is cut into two distinct sides, with a smaller organ in the middle and a part resembling hair in the upper part of the brain, the image carries the distinct semblance of a female sexual organ. Given that the sexual organs are left out of the treatise—the process by which the Cartesian treatise makes visible what cannot be seen in human anatomy, makes the semblance fitting.

The idea behind *Treatise on Man* is to describe a mechanical system of the body that proves that certain movements withdraw from the soul and the will—which is also how Clerselier, who published the treatise, understood the intentions of Descartes.[56] In the beginning of his treatise, Descartes explains that his pedagogy relies on his readers having "at one time or another, seen various animals opened up, and gazed on the shape and arrangement of their interior parts,

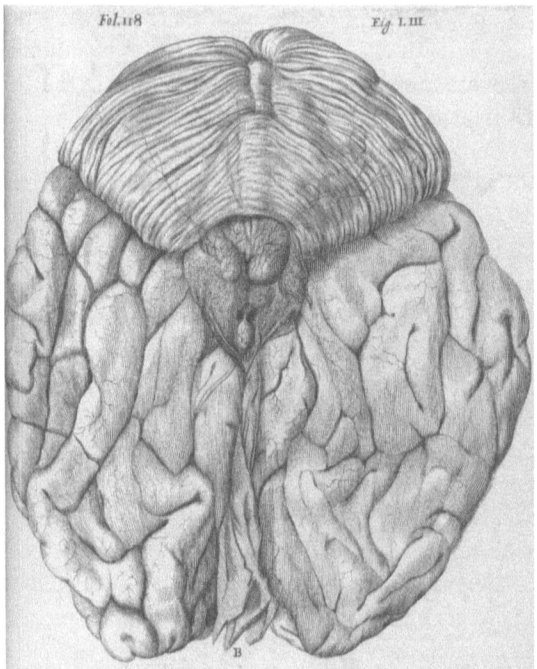

Figure 6.5. *De l'Homine Figuris* 1662, Leyden, Royal Library Stockholm.

which are very much like our own." The most important component of this image is that of the blood, which nourishes a heart that is fueled by heat, and the "animal spirits," which form a system within the bloodstream that is propelled by a fine wind. The animal spirits "dilate the brain" so as to receive impressions from thoughts as well as sense impressions.[57] Descartes then goes to great lengths to describe, in graphic detail, the internal veins of the heart, which he has not only looked at but also explored with his hands in animals. Descartes distinguished between "fluids," which are blood, humors, and spirits, and "solids," which are bone, flesh, nerves, and membranes.

Descartes then proposes his theory of conception: what differentiates humans from plants, he argues, is that the seeds of plants disseminate in ways that depend on the very hardness and immobility of the plant. But this is not the case with humans. Infant humans are soft; in the womb, its pores are wide open, which will shape its formation.[58] The seed of human beings is produced through

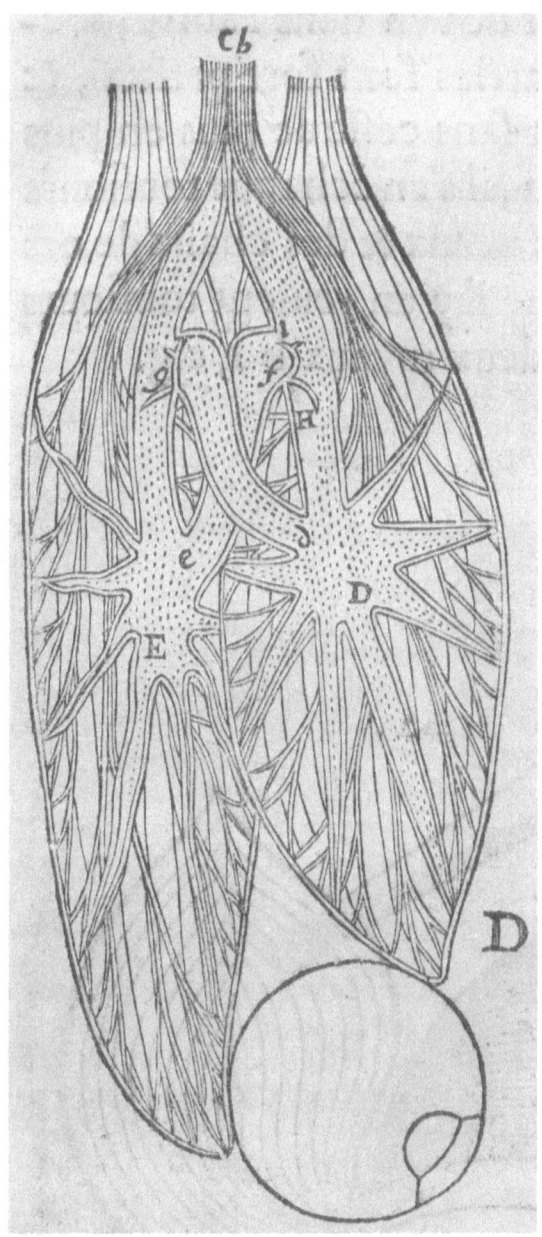

Figure 6.6. *L'Homme: Et un traitté de la formation du foetus*, Paris, 1664, Royal Library Stockholm.

the copulation between the two sexes, as "an unorganized mixture of two liquids, which act on each other like a kind of yeast." These liquids are ordered as particles that act and press on each other, some of the particles even becoming as agitated as fire. These movements and pressures are "putting them gradually into the state required for the formation of parts of the body."[59] The description of the movements in this monoliquid, which he calls seed and may consist of two parts, but which still disregards any female element in itself, resembles the conception of particles in *Meteorology*. The finest particles of weather, as well as that of the human body of procreation, withdraw from the eye, but the way in which human life is conceived is precisely the shape, size, and motion through which they form. Seed, in Cartesian anatomy, is formed in a variety of ways. It is imprinted upon and it carries imprints, which then shapes both the inside and the outside of the womb before the birth of an individual.

The seed, to Descartes, is formed in the maternal body, imprinted by a variety of limbs and organs through its spread by the blood flow and animal spirits—for instance, through two distinct "spermatic veins." The seed is a "mass," and the first organ to be formed is the heart.[60] In the graphic description of how the fetus is informed, the internal of the body is made up of small particles in different shapes that are more or less active, some of them shaping the inside of the womb through a seed marked by the qualities of the nerves—for instance, others pressing against the outside of the womb so as to create other limbs and other organs. Descartes goes to great lengths to explain the formation of the heart, the arteries, and the aorta.

To the heart belongs the valvules, lids of skin that close the pulmonary vein and the vena cava—these are depicted in the 1662 edition of *L'Homme* with images by Schuyl, created as cartoons of trompe l'oeil with tiny flaps of paper as lids of skin, which can be lifted on the page and looked into. The heart, as it is explained, is the most complex formation of the particle of the seed. It is also crucial for maintaining the relation to the child in the womb.[61]

In images such as these, where we find an intertwinement between a dissecting eye—which figures the dissection of the gaze—and what contemporary psychoanalysis would interpret as the scopic drive: what we see is a female sexual organ, figuring as a brain, and a heart erected as a penis, or clitoris. Using the Freudian analysis, which points to the female organ as a figure of castration in da Vinci, we may conceive of the sexual organ as a kind of vanishing point—it is both nowhere and everywhere to be seen. The brain-vulva and the clitoris-heart become, to use a figure of interpretation deriving from Lacan, images of anamorphosis. Anamorphosis is an inverted use of perspective, which, in Descartes own analysis of the gaze, points to "an original subjectifying relation."[62] In his anatomical description of the gaze, Descartes not only points to a subject apprehending the world but also to the limits of its perceptive capacities: an origin of the

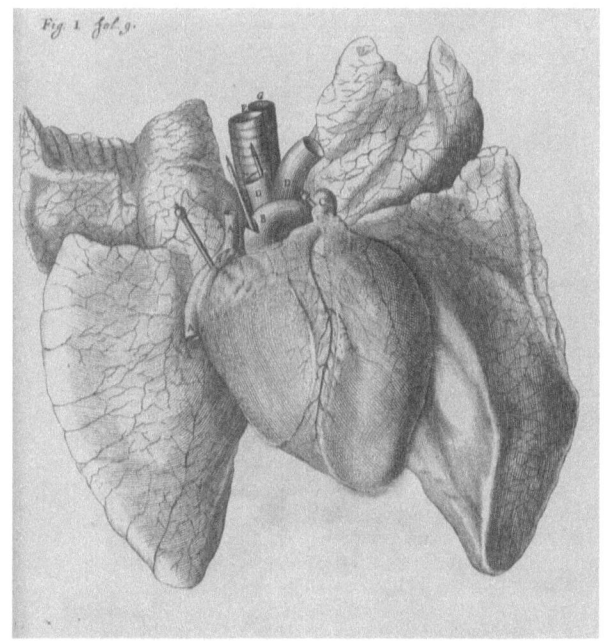

Figure 6.7. *De l'Homine Figuris* 1662, Leyden, Royal Library Stockholm.

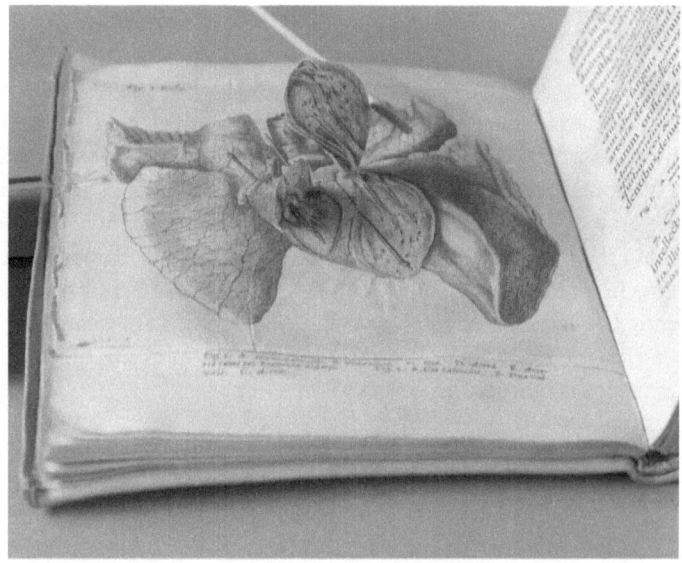

Figure 6.8. *De l'Homine Figuris* 1662, Leyden, Royal Library Stockholm.

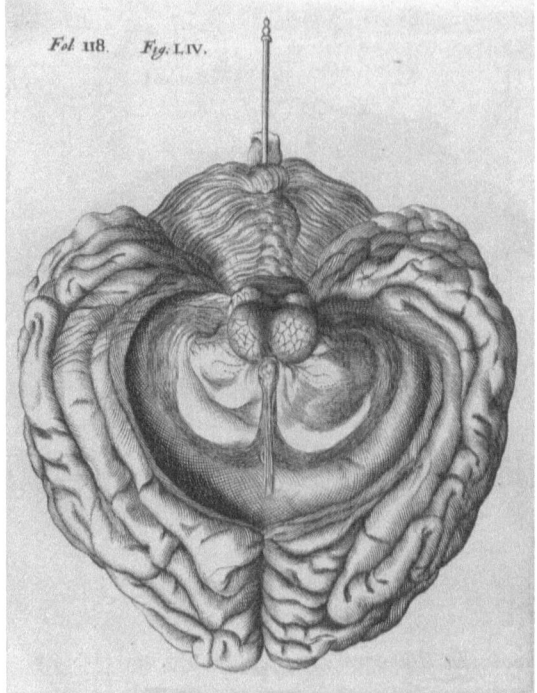

Figure 6.9. *De l'Homine Figuris* 1662, Leyden, Royal Library Stockholm.

gaze that the subject cannot make appear. The brain-vulva and the clitoris-heart line the limits of what we cannot see: the origin of the gaze, the origin of life, the origin of the formation of the fetus, and so on. The brain, which is supposed to figure the point at which perception is completed, becomes a trompe l'oeil vanishing point. The point of attachment of the scopic drive becomes more or less explicit. But it is already present as a vanishing point in Descartes's own text. The dialectic between the "eye" of and the "I," the physical eye and the subject of metaphysics, are both caught in that vanishing point of the gaze, the female sexual organ that is nowhere and everywhere to be seen.

7   The Thinking Fetus

Cecilia Sjöholm

Rethinking the Unconscious in Cartesian Writings

René Descartes's extraordinary autobiographic writings on his dreams, states between wakefulness and sleep, associations, desires, and needs have inspired and enticed psychoanalysis ever since Sigmund Freud.[1] After the work of French psychoanalyst Jacques Lacan, the psychoanalytic readings of Descartes's philosophy have primarily focused on a split *cogito*—the question of how "it" thinks in subjectivity.[2] But instincts, drives, object relations, and the mystery of infantile life, so relevant to psychoanalysis, is still largely uncharted territory in Cartesian studies. And yet, Descartes spends quite some effort to explain that the infant has a psychic life that will form the emotions, thoughts, memories, and fantasies of the adult. Sensations, passions, and appetites are with us already from birth, even from a fetal state of maternal symbiosis. How do the ideas on infantile life—developed in letters, anatomical writings, and images and *The Passions of the Soul* (1649)—connect to psychoanalytic theories of instinct, fantasy, and incorporation and Descartes's ideas of infancy indicate the presence of drives and unconscious motivations? Not only do his theories of the infant pave the way for psychoanalysis, they offer a new way of thinking about the unconscious in the Cartesian notion of subjectivity, beyond the structure of the cogito.

The fact that Descartes gives attention to infantile life has been interpreted as an expression of personal trauma—as an infant Descartes lost his mother. Given the strong biographical feature of his writings in general, such interpretations may seem compelling: when Descartes speaks of the infant's love and hatred, he seems to conduct a form of autoanalysis.[3] Older schools of psychoanalysis saw no problem in seeing philosophers as patients. Most would abstain from writing reductive psychobiographies today. But it is unquestionable that in an early modern universe of humors and fluids, Descartes's natural philosophy and anthropology stands out for the way in which it rethinks the attachments of the infant. This is not only relevant for the reassessment of Cartesian dualism, which has been attempted by many in philosophy and the history of ideas. The more pressing question is how the speculation on the life of the infant and its attachment to the maternal body opens new avenues for thinking about the relation between

Descartes and psychoanalysis, and perhaps new perspectives in the thinking of Cartesian subjectivity at large.

Two distinct lines of questioning open studies in this direction. Both are concerned with the "thinking fetus": a concept designating the Cartesian infant. The "thinking fetus" is immediately linked to "confused thought," a concept often evoked in Descartes's writings that points to the blurring of the line between body and mind. The first line of questioning concerns Descartes's idea that affects are rooted in infantile life. Can we trace a theory of object relations like that formulated by Freud and Melanie Klein? If so, how is it articulated? Is it conjoined to fantasy and drives? This can be examined in textual material that distinctly holds up the specific relation between mother and child to scrutiny—both before and after birth. The second line of questioning follows up on the first: Is there a prepsychoanalytic theory of repression in Descartes's writings? What does that do with our view of what Descartes meant by the notion of confused thought?

The Thinking Fetus and Confused Thoughts

Descartes's idea of the thinking fetus is in part contained within a theological and philosophical proposal. But just as importantly: in early writings such as *Treatise on Man* and *Description of the Human Body*, Descartes demonstrates the biological rootedness of the human subject. Here, he returns not just to childhood but to the very origins of the fetus in the maternal womb. *Treatise on Man* also goes by the name "The Formation of the Fetus" in the edition published by Claude Clerselier (published posthumously in 1664), although the title was meant to encompass only the final part of the treatise on human anatomy (in the following, I will use the title "The Formation of the Fetus" for the final part of *Description of the Human Body*).[4] Through the method of dissection, Descartes targets the invisible secrets of how internal organs help produce affects and perceptions. The actual, physical dissections were likely performed on a sheep. But they were used to demonstrate the beginning of life in the maternal womb, to throw light on what is most distinctly human—the capacity to think and feel.

In early modern thought, the human body was often considered to draw its life from the soul, as in the model of Latin philosopher Galen. But Descartes points out that the inner organs are not influenced by what we want or what we think. We cannot control reflexes sparked by hunger or pain through sheer willpower. This is to some extent a reason for dualism and for inferring the existence of a decisive split between anatomy and mind. The introduction to *Description of the Human Body* argues that there is a distinct difference between thought and the mere mechanics of the body that does not involve reflection. When we are children, we are not aware of this: we think that we can master our bodies.[5] But there is a split between the mind and the body of reflexes—which is quite a different thing from the body of the senses. But as Descartes traces thought to

Figure 7.1. *De l'Homine Figuris* 1662, Leyden, Royal Library Stockholm.

the formation of the fetus, the distinction between the body's "inside" and the senses blurs.

"Formation of the Fetus" tells the story of how humans are formed from conception to birth, invisible traces joining mind and body. These traces, which could be interpreted as a form of impression that distinctly cross the mind-body divide, may pass from mother to child. The body of a fetus, as well as that of a young child, is more permeable than that of an adult body. In utero, infant and maternal body are in symbiosis through "the external surface of the skin called the 'after-birth,' which envelops the child before it is born."[6] This may even take physical form as external marks on the body. But such traces may also transcend the divide between the physical and the psychological: a mother's perceptions can become imprinted on the limbs of the fetus as they form in the womb, something like a tattoo.[7] This idea also occurs in *Optics*: what the mother perceives when pregnant can imprint on the body of the child in the form of a birthmark. Even her fantasies may have the same effect.[8] In this way, Descartes posits a symbiotic relation between mother and child. The thoughts, imaginations, and perceptions of the mother will mark the mind and body of the fetus and remain in the life of the adult. The psychic life of the infant, then, is not determined by either body or mind but by a symbiosis that cuts across such a divide. What is challenged with such a conception is not just body-mind dualism but also the notion of the infantile subject as a "little cogito."

Descartes brings this up himself. "Formation of the Fetus" is not simply an anatomical treatise—it has a distinct bearing on metaphysical discussions on the cogito in *Meditations*, which recurs throughout when infantile life is brought up. In a famous letter to Elisabeth of Bohemia, Descartes describes three different faculties of knowledge: the first pertains to the pure, metaphysical understanding that uses concepts; the second joins intellect and imagination; and the third apprehends a kind of union between body and soul, producing a kind of bodily awareness in everyday life without us reflecting on it in our mind.[9] In everyday life, we do not usually think that we are thinking or reflect on the relation between body and mind. We simply go about our business. This is Descartes overcoming his own dualism from an anthropological point of view. But it does not solve any metaphysical problems—the fact that we experience our mind and body as one does not entail that there is ontological unity.

In an exchange between the theologian Antoine Arnauld and Descartes (whose responses were mediated by Mersenne) this problem is brought up. To Arnauld, the logic of the cogito infers that the subject cannot conceive of itself as not thinking. This, however, is an absurd assumption. The infant in the mother's womb has a mind, Arnauld argues, but it does not reflect over it. It is not conscious of itself.[10] But Descartes objects to the idea that the infant, or even the fetus, would be an unconscious form of mind: "I don't doubt that the mind begins to think as soon as it is implanted in the body of an infant, and that it is immediately aware of its thoughts, even though it does not remember this afterward because the impressions of these thoughts do not remain in the memory."[11] In other words, the fetus is thinking. But it is not thinking as a cogito able to retain its reflections. The next question to conceive of, then, is what the thoughts of the fetus are really like. And this is where Descartes enters into unknown territories.

The idea of a thinking fetus different from the cogito developed in exchanges with Pierre Gassendi. Here it was taken more distinctly beyond metaphysical or theological argumentation, and it was brought to light that thought does not look the same in an infant and an adult.[12] Gassendi's contention was that the moment in which the mind is infused in the body is undecidable. Do we think "while still in the womb. Or at birth?" The reflective powers of the mind of an infant in the womb must be meager, virtually nonexistent, he insists.[13] We are not always thinking, not as we are asleep and not as we are small children.

To this, Descartes responds that the mind, even in the mother's womb, "is always thinking."[14] And yet Descartes agrees with Gassendi that the moment in which "thought" begins—before or after birth—is undecidable, since we simply cannot recall our own birth. Sometimes the fetus is thinking in the womb; sometimes the mind appears to be "newly united" to the body at birth.[15] This undecidability follows Descartes in his writings throughout—when he talks about the infant, it is not always certain if he is talking about the unborn child or the young child. This fluid nature of the "infant" stresses its belonging in a maternal sphere.

If the fetus is thinking, what is it thinking? Of course, a fetus cannot, Descartes says, not without humor, "meditate[s] on metaphysics in its mother's womb, not at all."[16] This is because it is so invested in its own body that it cannot be detached from it. Sensations, affects, emotions, and instincts are with us already from birth, even from a fetal state of maternal symbiosis. The infant may not reflect on the extension of being or the difference between being and extension. But it thinks precisely because it is a mind connected to a body, even in the womb. Thus, our first thoughts come in the form of primary needs and physical afflictions: "a mind newly united to an infant's body is wholly occupied in conceiving in a confused way or feeling the ideas of pain, pleasure, heat, cold and other such ideas which arise from its union and, as it were, intermingling with the body."[17] In this passage, taken from the famous so-called letter to Hyperaspistes, which can be read as a response to Gassendi, we encounter the notion of confused thoughts—when the mind is impinged on by the body. Descartes said in the beginning of *Treatise on Man*: children cannot distinguish between will and corporeal reflexes. The mind of the child conceives of its needs, and this is infantile "thought." As explained in the conversations with Burman: "the mind is so swamped inside the body that the only thoughts it has are those which result from the way in which the body is affected."[18] Responding to its needs, the body "has an obstructive effect on the soul" and is "a hindrance to the mind in its thinking."[19] In early childhood, the mind is so closely tied to the body that the only thoughts that reach it are those of corporeal sensory awareness.[20] These are not connected to the comprehension of outside objects. Instead, what is felt is pleasure or pain, associated with things that are either harmful or enjoyable to the body in a direct manner.

It is not only the child that has confused thoughts—the body impinges also on the mind of adults.[21] In infancy, and in a state of half sleep, affects and needs impinge on the mind. But they are not produced by the mind.[22] The thoughts of the infant are close to that of someone who is half-asleep, or sick—the mind is wrapped in an acute corporeal and sensory awareness that pertains to the fixation on a single sensation. Not only the child but also the sleeping and sick individual is simply too much body. Confused thoughts are typical for, but by no means restricted to, the infant. This is also a metaphysical problem—which is how it has been reflected in the literature on Descartes in general. Gassendi asks, Is the child's mind less perfect than that of an adult? To this Descartes responds no.

Philosophers, in general, cannot distinguish between mind and body either. Our "earliest childhood judgments" reflect the conflation between body and soul in philosophy at large.[23] It may well be the case that the mind of the infant "does not work so well." But that is not because the body impedes the mind. It is because the mind, to a certain extent, depends on the body.[24] Descartes gives a double definition of the relation between mind and body; they are both joined, and not. It depends on how you can conceive of "thought," as free and distinct from the body, or as a wider range of perceptions, which in itself is a metaphysical problem.[25] One may take the notion of confused thought to point to the need for a new metaphysics—and the cogito as a solution to that. But these reflections on the infant also point to the fact that "thought" in Descartes must be seen as a much more generous concept than we tend to believe. It pertains to cognition, but also to emotions, and their relation.[26] In the following, we will see how this open notion of thought pertains to the passions—which is a word that refers both to emotions and affects, both internal modes of feelings and more physical affectations. A distinction will not be made in this context. Ultimately, it pertains also to the unconscious and to the drives.

The Maternal Body

Many have commented on Descartes's own attempt to overcome the dualism between mind and body in *Passions of the Soul*.[27] It has been read as a treatise that tries to solve the problem of dualism raised in *Meditations* and *Discourse on Method*, which is indeed one of the ambitions mentioned by Descartes himself.[28] It has often been read as a Stoic treatise, occupied with the deliberate "therapy" of emotions and affects.[29] Only few have commented on the fact that it is also an archaeology of emotions, with distinct threads of thought pointing toward contemporary psychoanalysis. To the exceptions belongs John Cottingham, who has seen the poignancy of the Cartesian notion of emotions and affects and early life. Drawing a comparison to Freud regarding the way in which the drive is present in the formation of affects in Descartes, Cottingham's philosophical lens, however, points to the "therapy" of emotions and affects rather than going further into the analysis of the drives and the unconscious.[30]

So in what way may the Cartesian notion of emotions touch the unconscious? Freud, in his first model of the ego, *Project for a Scientific Psychology* (1895), *Entwurf einer Psychologie* (1895), describes the self as the result of a development from instincts in infantile life, produced in relation to excitations from inside and outside. The ego develops as a kind of protection against strong corporeal experiences of pleasure and displeasure. Unsatisfied corporeal needs such as hunger cause tension and displeasure. Enjoyment, in turn, is explained as a discharge of tension. The original mode of this is breastfeeding: an infant seeks the breast for satisfaction. When it fails, a fantasy of the breast is produced in hallucinations or dreams. This is an early form of reality testing; the ego is construed as a shield, countering forceful stimuli through fantasies. The infant might be invaded by hallucinatory fantasies to the extent that it may threaten the development of the ego.[31] What is crucial with this account, regarding the model of the self, is the immediate connection it makes between fantasy and the capacity to construe a self. It proposes a radical cut between corporeal needs and the fantasmatic inner formations of gratification that are construed in the face of unredeeming harsh realities where the self is nothing but a vulnerable and fragile construct. It is in a similar cut, where the child is a fragile and vulnerable being of confused thought, that Descartes situates the origin of a subject that eventually will reach its capacity of thinking like a cogito proper.

Emotions, to Descartes, are "thoughts"—although perhaps confused thoughts. We might speak about them as emotions, affects, moods, humors, moral forms of sensibility, and sometimes sheer physical sensation. They are "internal sensations" and physical phenomena, broadly speaking, "all sorts of cases of perception or knowledge to be found in us."[32] What connects these "thoughts" is the way in which they simply seem to hit us, beyond our willpower. In *Principles of Philosophy* (1644), he deployed the word *affectus* to designate the function of emotions and affects that have certain qualitative differences but are close in their way of existing. Emotions and affects "affect" us. They come to us, regardless of our will. We cannot make emotions.

In treating emotions and affects as a "physician" or natural philosopher, Descartes is also demonstrating the somatic nature of emotions—they are literally in our bodies.[33] Like Freud, Descartes finds their root in early experiences of pleasure and satisfaction, relying on the gastric and nutritional systems. Bodies cannot use reason, only produce sensations and affects.[34] They are a bundle of unpredictable emotional experiences. Affects are perceptions in the most general sense—they are imposed on us.[35] What is of concern to Descartes is not just the relation between body and mind, or the way in which we may treat emotions. It is the source of emotions and affects, unavailable to reason.[36] Searching for that source, Descartes's inquiries move into the same territories as Freud.

Small children have a supersensitivity that stands in contrast to the free rationality of the adult; their minds are "swamped by affects."[37] But this is not because their minds are less developed. The affective inundation derives from the conditions of infantile life. Certain affects, Descartes explains, are with us "before birth."[38] Others, however, develop with primary needs—and this is where we may begin to search for a pre-psychoanalytical genealogy of object attachment. The infantile body, to Descartes, is dominated by needs that only the maternal body can respond to. Therefore, love is the most original emotion.

Descartes discusses the archaic roots of emotions in a famous exchange with Pierre Chanut, who was the French ambassador to Sweden. This exchange responds to a question indirectly posed to Descartes by Queen Christina: Which affect is "worse if immoderate and abused, love or hatred?"[39] The so-called letter of love is often evoked by philosophers and theologians for the way in which it distinguishes intellectual love and confused thoughts: the impingement on the mind of corporeal and instinctual love.[40] But not enough attention has been offered to the physical child and the "thinking fetus," which are to be found at the origins of the explanations of love in the letter. The original affect is fetal enjoyment, receiving its nourishment through the maternal body and then developing as maternal love.[41] It is in the nature of love to arise as confused thought, since love is "aroused by some motion of the nerves," which goes back to the moment of birth: "in love a mysterious heat is felt around the heart, and a great abundance of blood in the lungs, which makes us open our arms as if to embrace something, and this inclines the soul to join to itself willingly the object presented to it."[42] Descartes traces the origin of emotions and affects to distinct scenes of infantile life: as we come into this world—and even before we are born—and to a distinct affect: we experience immediate enjoyment, which derives from immediate nourishment; "it is scarcely likely that the body would have been in a good condition unless there were nearby some matter suitable for food."[43] Love is then the first emotion that the soul feels, and if there is no "food," sadness or hatred. This could, of course, be read as metaphysical or allegorical "food," but in a letter to Elisabeth this is clearly not the case: "For some people the first thing that upset them as babies was not getting enough food, while for others it was getting food that was bad for them." This experience of deprivation will forever be connected to "the passion of sadness."[44] This is an extraordinary observation, explaining the way in which love, or deprivation of love, is intimately connected to breastfeeding.

In *Passions*, also, this is how Descartes explains the origin of emotions and affects that are regarded as fundamental and as the source of all others: love, joy, hate, and sadness. The experience of pleasure, or enjoyment ("joy"), goes back to the time when we were newborns, or precedes birth, through veins nourishing and maintaining "the heat of the heart," which is enjoyment.[45] *Passions* also posits a distinct origin of the emotions in the symbiotic relation to the maternal body. But these recurring explanations of the passions do not figure prepsychoanalytic theories of attachment primarily for the way in which they depict love and enjoyment but rather for the way in which they conceive of deprivation at the roots of human psychic life. The maternal breast is not only an object of satisfaction. When the child is deprived of enjoyment, sadness follows—and then hate. These archaic emotions—with us already before birth—result from shifts between satisfaction and deprivation.[46] To Descartes, these emotions can only appear in the guise of corporeal instincts, or as confused thoughts. As long as the body depends on basic needs, no other emotions can develop. It means that in childhood, these emotions do not derive from judgments that deem objects to be good or bad—which adults are capable of.[47] Love follows enjoyment; hate and melancholy are the result of deprivation.

Early psychoanalytic theories of object relations offer similar genealogies. Object relations theory takes its cue in Freud. In *Three Essays on Sexuality*, the most archaic experience of pleasure comes with the suckling of the maternal breast: "no doubt stimulation by the warm flow of milk is the cause of the pleasurable sensation." To Melanie Klein, also, love is the most complex human emotion. It originates in the "mental life of the baby"—for whom the mother is the first object of love.[48] To Klein, like Descartes, psychic life is present already from the time of delivery. The maternal breast establishes the first relation of love.[49] The other side of infantile dependency is aggression, directed toward the body of the life-giving mother. When the breast is not there, Klein notes, the child feels as if it is lost forever. This is also where the contact with the breast extends to the mother—"the feelings of having lost the breast lead to the fear of having lost the loved mother entirely."[50] It is at this point that psychic life becomes ridden with a fear, sadness, and aggression that may turn to depression. Depression, however, is not devastation—what appears to be a simple thwarting of nourishment is the origin of a psychic life. The Kleinian description of infantile life shows that affects derive from an archaic model of attachments. Just like Descartes, Klein finds love to be fundamental; but Klein also finds deprivation to cause a conversion to hatred and depression, which shows the attachment to the breast to be the beginning of psychic life.

But this is not so because affects are free-floating between bodies; it is because they are attached to objects that may differ in forms of substance and representation. To Freud, breastfeeding is the origin of fantasy. An infant seeks the breast for satisfaction. When it fails, a fantasy of the breast is produced in hallucinations or dreams. To Klein, this early form of fantasmatic life is ridden with a fragility that may threaten the development of the ego.[51] There is no causal link between deprivation and fantasy; it is rather the case that the production of fantasms is the archaic life of the subject—it lives in the universe of persecutory or sadistic objects, mixing maternal breasts and paternal penises. The child is frustrated and sad at the loss of the breast. But it is aggression that is "of highest value" to the child's mental development.[52] Love is already from the start "disturbed by destructive impulses," struggling with hate in a way that will persist through life and become "a source of danger in human relationships."[53] Melancholy, in turn, is a product of splits and dissociations, where the separation between self and other is disavowed and aggression turned toward the internalized object, and consequently the self. Fearing the loss of the object as other, as well as loss of the self, the psychic universe of the melancholic is dominated by a constant fear of annihilation.[54] A depressive position may follow: "at that stage the child progressively integrates his feelings of love and hatred, synthesizes the good and the bad aspects of the mother, and goes through states of mourning bound up with feelings of guilt."[55]

What differentiates Descartes from both Freud and Klein is the immediate somatic nature, and subsequent effect, of the object. Objects, to Descartes, may be substances, but they are also "thoughts." Love, in the life of the Cartesian as well as the Freudian subject, is aroused not just by physical encounters but also by the "object of love" presenting itself to the mind (i.e., as a representation to consciousness).[56] Objects of this kind are neither the origin of fantasy nor the development of inner life. They have direct physical effects that are conceived as thoughts. Simply representing a loved object is enough to stimulate that flow of "alimentary juice" that is experienced as enjoyment. In this way, love is a self-enhancing circuit where enjoyment will lead the mind to dwell on that object—it becomes a thought. This dwelling is immediately rooted in an infantile form of incorporation. A representation of the breast might suffice for the flow of enjoyment: "a single thought of joy or love or the like is sufficient to send the animal spirits through the nerves into all the muscles needed to cause the different movements of the blood which, as I said, accompany the passions."[57] Love inscribes an original dynamic of blood flows and causes a sense of well-being, "the same bodily conditions . . . have ever since naturally accompanied the corresponding thoughts."[58] Hate, in turn, is the instinct of discarding an object that may or not be real, or appear as thought. It is the immediate denegation of an object at a corporeal level.[59]

Dominated by affective impulses, then, the "thinking fetus" is determined by attachments and refusals in a rhythmic flow that intertwines the somatic and the psychic. Love is more original than hate, but the Cartesian infant of "confused thought" is always wavering between love and hate. This Cartesian notion of a thought that at the same time is an object with a physical quality turns the relation between world and body inside out—the body acts on the fantasy of the breast as if it is "real." This suggests mind and body are interrelated. There is no longer a meaningful distinction to be made between inside and outside. Psychic representations have been placed in the body, and the maternal body incorporated in experiences wavering between pleasure and displeasure. We are brought beyond the everydayness of embodiment, to a body of instincts where primary objects are incorporated and the relation mind and body turned inside out.

Like Freud and Klein, what Descartes describes is not only an infant attached to the maternal body through its needs but also the development of psychic life in and through the object. In fact, there is no basic passion defined by Descartes that is not fundamentally directed toward an object, or which does not have its origin in an archaic relation to the maternal body. Like Klein, Descartes describes a relation to the world defined in a pre-Oedipal phase, where the breasts are a fountain of milk, "coveted as organs of receptivity and bounty from the time when the libidinal position is purely oral."[60] This is an extraordinary fact in itself. But it also shows a subject that may be altogether dominated by objects in a way more distinctly physical than either Freud or Klein accounted for.

The Animal Spirits of the Drive

In "The Formation of the Fetus," infants are shaped by an original fetal enclosure. This symbiotic relation to the maternal body gives a floating status to the beginning of life, childhood being a continuation of the fetal state, dominated by the search for enjoyment. Freud thought that breastfeeding awakens autoerogenous zones: "No one who has seen a baby sinking back satiated from the breast and falling asleep with flushed cheeks and a blissful smile can escape the reflection that this picture persists as a prototype of the expression of sexual satisfaction in later life."[61] Freud, like Descartes, speaks about the child as a body of supersensitivity; it is essentially autoerotic and finds its objects in its own body: "Its individual component instincts are upon the whole disconnected and independent of one another in their search for pleasure."[62] This polymorphous perversity makes the whole body of the child into a pleasure-seeking erogenous zone; what Lacan has called a montage of partial drives, originating in the polymorph-perverse body.[63]

To Descartes, also, children seek a pleasure that hinges on sexuality: when the lips of a sleeping child are tickled by a feather, he says, the ticklish enjoyment is direct—a scene bringing Freud's recounting of the dream of da Vinci's childhood to mind—da Vinci opening his mouth to a bird's tail. To Freud, this is a fantasy of suckling, embracing, and kissing the mother.[64] To Descartes, enjoyment entangled with love excites the instinct to "open our arms as if to embrace something."[65] There is a difference between desire as a "concupiscent love" or lust and love as what Descartes calls benevolent, a form of transferential love. But the transferential love of the child is never without lust. In the "confused sensations of our childhood," the dignified nature of love becomes intermingled with joy, sadness, desire, fear, and hate.[66]

In "Instincts and Their Vicissitudes," Freud affirms the all-encompassing domination of the pleasure principle of the psyche in what will become a first theory of the drive proper; an "instinct" is "a concept on the frontier between the mental and the somatic, as the psychic representative of the stimuli originating from within the organism and reaching the mind, as a measure of the demand made upon the mind for work in consequence of its connection with the body."[67] Pleasure, in this logic, is associated with the preservation of the ego, so that archaic impulses of love propel the satisfaction of needs. But Freud, also, offers a theory of conversion: it is the fate of instincts to be reversed, so that love becomes hate.

Descartes, like Freud, affirms the instinctual nature of love. But he does so with a model that even more distinctly holds on to the somatic nature of instincts, or what we may call drives. If the problem of Descartes is the nature of confused thought and its origination in the life of the infants, with the "thinking fetus" swamped in emotions at the roots of the Cartesian genealogy of affects, then he needs to find not just mental images for the zone in-between subject and object, body and mind, but also more distinctly somatic zones. In Descartes, the autoerotic infantile body—which seeks the heat and flows of enjoyment—works through the introjection and expulsion of objects through the corporeal mechanisms of pleasure and displeasure where the somatic goes all the way back to the fetal state.

In "Formation of the Fetus," the womb connecting mother and child is an organ not only of blood but also of spirits. The last organ of the fetus to be formed, by semen, is the navel. Blood flows through it and forms the heart, which is the original site of the passions.[68] The navel is a line of connection for the "spirits," which forms emotions in the fetal joining of body and blood.[69] The stronger the emotion, the more movement: "love depends upon an abundance of spirits."[70]

As we come out into the world, some "juice" enters the veins of the heart and gives it the flow of life. The soul, Descartes argues further, loves this. It joins itself to the body *de volonté*, a term that does not designate conscious will. It derives as much from the body as it derives from the mind. The instinct to join another soul "in volition" can be read against the background of early modern theology. "It is the nature of love to make one consider oneself and the loved one as a single whole of which one is a part; and to transfer the care one previously took of oneself to the preservation of this whole."[71] This is by no means a mere spiritual experience; the soul learns to join this nourishment to itself from the body "in volition, that is, to love it."[72] The spirits flow from the brain to the muscles, shaking the body so that the heart is fueled, "to make them send it more."[73] We love to feel the inside flow, which has its origin in the archaic maternal interconnection.

The concept de volonté, in volition, designates an instinctual move toward a split, not between body and mind but between the subject of separation and the object of love. The subject experiences an excitation, which impels it to join itself in volition to objects of pleasure.[74] I am not using the phrase de volonté to talk about desire, Descartes explains; it refers to the instinct to join with the objects we love.[75] At this point, the drive becomes sexual. Finding its origin in an archaic object, it is transposed into adult sexuality—the warmth of blood raising desires in the most energetic, strongest, and finest organs (apart from the brain), the "vessels destined for reproduction."[76] A prepsychoanalytic notion of the drive—that has a distinct sexual character—is propelled by the "animal spirits," a flow internal to the body that connects juices, moods, and ideas.[77] The body becomes a hypersensitive organ of desires.

Repression

The thought of the infant is not just an activity of the *res cogitans*, the subject conceiving of itself thinking. In the letter to Hyperaspistes and in the conversations with Burman, we see that the question of thought pertains also to the development of the child. Its mind is no less perfect than that of the adult, and yet the body impinges on it—it is a bundle of confused thought. This is so because the mind is set in motion "when the mind joined to a body thinks of a corporeal thing."[78] Such things can be affects, emotions, objects, or names with corporeal implications. These things create traces in the mind that remain in the life of the adult.[79]

So how does consciousness operate regarding these confused thoughts? Here, Descartes introduces the idea of childhood amnesia. We are, as children, marked by needs that we tend to forget as adults; our bodies are enveloped by pain and pleasure. As adults, we have difficulties remembering this exposure: "no traces of these thoughts have been imprinted on the brain" we hear in the conversation with Burman.[80] But in the letter to Hyperaspistes, mind and body are joined in such a way that "when the mind joined to a body thinks of a corporeal thing, certain particles in the brain are set in motion." This may be produced by the sense organs and outside objects, but also by the so-called animal spirits and by our own thoughts: "the motion of these brain particles leaves behind the traces on which memory depends."[81]

In other words, the fetus carries the seed of the cogito. But the corporeal needs of the fetus will also remain in the life of an adult. The traces and memories of infant life will remain unconscious, in the sense that they will cement "the impossibility of self-knowledge," which, in the words of John Sutton, characterized both the Cartesian and the Freudian project.[82] The most archaic emotions will always mark the life of the subject. But the body of an adult will carry them, unknowingly.

In Freud's *Three Essays on Sexuality*, for the breastfeeding child, the oral sensations of suckling form the "prototype of the expression of sexual satisfaction in later life."[83] Freud identifies the separation between the enjoyment of lactation and sexual stimulation as a split preceding child amnesia and repression.[84] Although childhood is a period in life of extraordinary sensual and emotive force, people tend to have no memories of it. This childhood amnesia, Freud explains, is because the strong affects become associated with the sexual impulses of childhood, which have been repressed.[85]

To Descartes, like Freud, the sexual instinct is rooted in traces that are lost to memory. Descartes traces the origins of the passions to the unborn child.[86] This unborn, bestowed with the capacity to love, is the "thinking fetus." An archaic symbiosis plays a pivotal role in the formation of passions. But the love that envelops the "thinking fetus" and the infant, as well as its ticklishness, its readiness for pleasures and satisfactions, its hate and anger—"do not remain in the memory,"[87] Descartes explains to Arnauld. "Infantile life remains unobtainable to consciousness."[88] Childhood amnesia—from "Formation of the Fetus" to *Passions*—plays an important role in the Cartesian conception of subjectivity. In treating the passions "as a physician" or natural philosopher, Descartes is also interested in their unconscious origins. Considered as forms of perception that create physicopsychological imprints on mind and body, they are identified as "traces" or "folds" that form a link to representations. In this way, Descartes formulates a theory of repression. It is as if memories hide in the body, its connections, tubes, and flows, only to erupt in the mind at a given signal.

Love goes back to the moment when infants are newborn. Descartes writes of this in the letter to Elisabeth that is usually quoted as establishing a connection between body and mind, thus overcoming dualism.[89] But another purpose, less explored by scholars, is to describe the way in which archaic needs influence adult life. Descartes speaks about these needs as thoughts. The thoughts, he argues, "that have accompanied some movements of our body since our life began still accompany them today."[90] These reactions, or thoughts, stay with us and are actualized by external causes that may "arouse the same thoughts," whereas thoughts arouse the same movements. Emotional memories are incorporated since childhood; and as we have seen, we cannot tell where emotions come from—they hit us without us knowing why.

Confused thoughts are a bundle of ideas and corporeal impulses that cannot be dissociated. Intellectual love cannot be disconnected from sensual desires and appetites. The confusion, however, does not only pertain to the fact that we cannot dissociate body and mind. It pertains also to the fact that we cannot use our will to love, or control our desire. We feel desire toward objects against our wishes, and we are unable to love objects we would like to love. The object, at the origins of desire, remains lost. Descartes, like Freud, notes that affective memories are associated with representation. In *Passions*, Descartes describes how the brain, as we are affected by something, acts on traces that have already been set before.[91] The brain creates folds as it is struck by the nerves stimulated by the senses—these folds have a tendency to be stimulated by the same objects.[92] Emotions always attach to archaic traces, not made in our minds but received "from things represented by them."[93] Traces of a childhood prehistory may then become reactivated.

In this way, Descartes identifies inscriptions in the mind that pave the way for other perceptions.[94] Dreams, fantasies, memories, and emotions are all part of this circuit. The cause of emotions lies not in the external world but within us, in the traces producing a flow between mind and body.[95] The associative stream of dreams, fantasies, and memories are linked to such traces. These in turn are associated with emotions and affects, just like the dynamic of mnemonic traces that Freud inscribes in the final chapter of the *Interpretation of Dreams*. The similarity stretches also to this: Freud explains the paths of association through traces marked by affects. The mnemonic traces can be remnants of images or language, but also of emotions.[96] In the psychic apparatus, they are associated, displaced, and condensed. Descartes argues in a similar manner: once a corporeal affect is established in connection with a representation, they will always be connected, but "the same actions are not always joined to the same thoughts."[97] In other words, the relation between traces of perceptions and emotions are continuously deferred, so that representations and emotions will shift.

Cartesian traces of the mind are to be understood in the literal sense, as neurological markers. Not only will the child react on traces from its own experiences but also the mother's experience. A mother's emotions and affective states will pass on directly to her child, although they will remain repressed. But strong affects suffered by a mother will be transposed to the child in the womb: "what is adverse to the one is harmful to the other." The experience will remain "imprinted in his brain to the end of his life."[98] The idea that the relation between mother and child is permeable is in many ways medieval—but in this context, it has another meaning. It is an example of how bodies, in Cartesian speculation, can be incorporated as traces, as memories. What distinguishes the Cartesian conception from contemporary neuroscience and approaches it to psychoanalysis is the temporal character of the flow between traces—their retroactive capacities and their distinct relation to desires and aberrations.

The Return of the Object

Through the unconscious imprints of affects and traces, objects dominate the life of the subject. Why does one love one particular person rather than another?[99] This seemingly rather precious question was posed by the French ambassador to Sweden, Chanut, in an exchange with Queen Christina. And so, the question was posed to Descartes himself, who gave a surprising response to Chanut: love is not provoked by beauty, it may just as well be provoked by a defect. Such was the case of Descartes's first love. When I was a child, I loved a girl of my own age who had slightly crossed eyes, he writes. This aroused the passion of love in me in every other instance that I saw a similar squint, "yet I had no idea myself that this was why it was." The affect remained with the object—"when we are inclined to love someone without knowing the reason, we may believe that this is because they have some similarity to something in an earlier object of love, though we may not be able to identify it."[100] Their memory remains as physical traces. For a long time, Descartes would feel tenderness at the sight of crossed eyes.

In *Passions*, he returns to this feeling of fixation on a unique feature in a person. The inclination or desire that arises in this way from attraction is commonly called "love" . . . "it is this inclination or desire that provides poets and writers of romances with their principal subject matter."[101] Here Descartes explains love in terms that are more neurological than theological. The attraction directed toward a lost object consists in the disposition of the parts of our brain.

Our desire is refound: directed as it is toward a trace or shadow of an object. Klein put it in a similar way: infantile dependency will later transfer love to other objects—"replacing the first loved person by other objects and things."[102] Freud, in a famous passage from the second of *Three Essays on Sexuality*, spoke of sexualization of the object forming *après-coup*: "At a time when the first beginnings of sexual satisfaction are still linked with the taking of nourishment . . . the sexual instinct has a sexual object outside the infant's own body in the shape of his mother's breast." This is then transferred onto the mother. But "not until the period of latency has been passed is the original relation restored. There are thus good reasons why a child suckling at his mother's breast has become the prototype of every relation of love. The finding of an object is thus in fact a re-finding of it."[103]

To Descartes, also, the basis of our sentiments is a form of repetition, a recurrence of affects that will always be connected to infantile nourishment, and the movements and functions that go with them. It is this secret imprint on our system that will haunt all emotions that come after and continue to withdraw from intellectual elaboration. It bestows emotions and affects with a "confused nature," which makes them difficult to understand. The nature of love, also, escapes from conscious understanding since it remains caught in the confused sensations of our childhood.[104] There is, then, in Descartes, no disruption of what Freud calls the latency period, or any distinction between the polymorphous-perverse body of the child and the sexual love of the adult. And there is not even any clear distinction between the love of benevolence and that of lust. This is precisely what haunts Descartes's writings on the infant: the question of confused thought is concerned with much more than the cogito or the relation between body and mind. It has to do with the fundamental imprints on body and mind that derive from childhood life. Descartes forms a theory of the unconscious that stresses the corporeal imprints on the mind and remains with the polymorphous body of the infant as a vestige of the thinking fetus in the life of the adult; a childhood amnesia still leaves imprints in the body that will remain in the form of confused thoughts and reactivate with the object: of love, hate, melancholia, and so on.

These prepsychoanalytic observations and speculations of the psychic life of the infant, and its repercussions in adult life, may also impact the way we read works such as *Meditations*. Remainders of the objectal notion of the unconscious will also appear in the metaphysics, where Descartes sees the free flight of the mind as fundamental to the adult cogito. Only in relation to an object will the cogito sense the opacity of its own origin. As Descartes demonstrates in *Meditations*: thought begins with a thing between body and mind, self and other, inside and outside. In this way, it also searches for what psychoanalysis has pointed to as a vestige of the cogito, an "it" that thinks, impelled through an unknown and untraceable origin.[105]

The Voice

The "it" that thinks, impelled through an unknown and untraceable origin, points to a remainder that has extension, but is still excessive to the cogito. Jean-Luc Marion has identified this remainder in Cartesian metaphysics as voice: in *Meditations*, we find the trace of an original alterity, posited before the cogito. That which thinks in me is an originary interlocution; "the ego, first being, has its existence from the call of another, whoever that may be, even if anonymous."[106] Here we sense the impact of that body to another, at the crossing between need and desire, the object of instinct, which comes close to a Lacanian *objet petit a*. The presence of an originary alterity in the "thinking fetus," the traces of which will remain in the cogito, is the voice: an object that is not an object but the remnant or excess of or an alterity that harks back to the individual prehistory of the dependency of the maternal body. In seminar 11, Lacan defines the *objet petit a* as the junction between desire and demand: it stands for the lack in the other with which the subject comes to identify and ultimately for a signifier that will define the subject beyond its own knowledge.[107] The voice, in Cartesian metaphysics, is a call that is more than metaphysics; it is also a signifier of desire, responding to the inscription of the split that is inherent in Cartesian subjectivity. The voice is that which calls, which allows for desire to be awakened, in the form of love, sadness, or wonder.

Descartes points to the premodern mystical notion of the voice as a foundation of the subject. The cogito and the method of doubt have mystical roots, for instance, in readings of Teresa d'Avila.[108] But Descartes's construction of the cogito also points to the subject as divided and as prone to decenteredness. There are a lot of references to voice in Descartes: inner voices, the voices of deceit, the voice of the self. For instance, Descartes advises Princess Elisabeth to follow the example of Socrates and listen to "the inner voice."[109] This anecdotal reference to the "inner voice" can be looked at as a trace of that excess of the voice that haunts the Cartesian meditations on the ego. I am able to grasp my limbs and my body both through sense perception and my body, Descartes writes in the second meditation, but I can use neither my sense perception nor my imagination to grasp myself: "it is surely surprising that I should have a more distinct grasp of things which I realize are doubtful, unknown and foreign to me, than I have of that which is true and known—my own self."[110]

It is at this point that the voice is introduced in the reading of Marion. Thoughts give evidence of there being something that thinks, but thoughts are in themselves not proof of there being a subject that is the origin of these thoughts. This is also how the problem of subjectivity is conceived in psychoanalysis. To Marion, the cogito in Descartes carries with it the problem of alterity, an an-otherness of the ego, a "yawning chasm," Marion says, quoting Husserl.[111] This is the voice of an originary interlocution; "the ego, first being, has its existence from the call of another, whoever that may be, even if anonymous."[112] The second meditation anticipates a subject that is split and a subject that is not congruent with the production of its thought. This is more than a problem of self-deception, or ideology or the possibility of reason. It is about an originary alterity inherent in the very possibility of the cogito, which psychoanalysis has identified. What Descartes points to is that it is not language that is the primary means of thought; it is the voice beyond language, which may also be a silent voice. This voice is the *objet petit a*, raised in me as a desire that I cannot respond to, only sense as a call.

In her diary, Hannah Arendt writes of Descartes, "*Die Ent-zweiung ist der Zweifel*" ("*dubitare*"—*zwischen zwei Seiten hin- und herschwanken*).[113] The chasm is the doubt; to doubt means to go back and forth between two sides, with no given direction. "The doubt of reality is the outstanding experience of thinking," she writes. The voice as *objet petit a* is caught in a chasm—between a stern sense of the real and its denial. The voice, however, cannot be the object of radical doubt. It cannot doubt itself. It is rather the trace of a physical object, a remnant of the confused thought of infantile life, a subject coming into being attempting to get hold of itself. If the thinking fetus is capable of grasping itself, it is precisely through the voice, through the presence of a thought that is embodied, rather than a reflection on existence. The voice does not belong to the body of extension, but it is not fully congruent with the cogito as sheer existence either. In this way, there is a trace of regression present also in *Meditations*, as it envelops a corporeal thought that is not yet thinking and not yet memorizing. The first sound of the voice in the life of a subject belongs to that of need: a calling to be nourished, to be soothed. It is that sound that remains in the life of the cogito, which makes of thought a chasm, something that can never be wholly detached from the remnants of a physical presence of maternal proximity.

8 The Love between Body and Soul

Marcia Sá Cavalcante Schuback

PLATONIC LOVE: THIS is perhaps the epithet one is most likely to hear in a discussion about Descartes and love. Descartes defines and discusses love in his *Passions of the Soul*. However, most of his thoughts on love are found in letters to his friend Pierre Chanut. Moreover, there are also his letters to Princess Elisabeth, letters of affection, dedicatory letters of devotion, the modes of love he describes in *Passions*. Descartes's letters to Elisabeth are love letters, letters that represent a philosophical emotion. For the sake of sketching out Descartes's conception of love, we should look at Descartes's love letters and letters on love.

The correspondence with Princess Elisabeth is regarded as exemplar correspondence since it "has been accomplished as specific genre."[1] Descartes met Elisabeth in The Hague and became impressed with her beauty, grace, sensibility, philosophical intelligence, and "admirable mind." In his letters to her, Descartes always confesses his admiration, affection, and devotion. No explicit declaration of love can be found in these letters, and as commonly claimed, these letters should be read above all as testimony of Descartes's view of philosophy as an activity for everyone, including women, an expression of his revolt against scholars and erudition.[2] But there are passages on "love" in these letters, and it is difficult to deny that these letters are moved by love, even if very much unconfessed.

In the first of the two letters on love that Descartes wrote to Chanut, Descartes reveals a certain strategy. He says:

> It is true that the custom of our speech and the courtesy of good manners does not allow us to tell those whose condition is far above ours that we love them; we may say that we respect, honour, esteem them, and that we have zeal and devotion for their service. I think that the reason for this is that friendship between human beings makes those in whom it is reciprocated in some way equal to each other, and so if, while trying to make oneself loved by some great person, one said that one loved him, he might think that one was treating him as an equal and so doing him wrong. But philosophers are not used to give different names to things which share the same definition, and I know no other definition of love save that it is a passion which makes us join ourselves willingly to some object, no matter whether the object is equal or greater or less than us.[3]

The strategy he uses when the beloved has a "condition far above ours" is to speak about devotion, admiration, wonder, and affection instead of confessing love and the desire of being together. One of the main threads in Descartes's correspondence to Elisabeth is about the unity of body and soul, indeed, about their togetherness. It can be said that the main subject of these letters is love, and indeed the love between body and soul, what makes one join willingly the other. Maybe there is a coded fable in Descartes's writings about the love of body and soul.

Cartesian love as the love between body and soul: this fable can be read to a certain extent in the letters on love that Descartes wrote to Pierre Chanut, his diplomat friend who served in Stockholm and through whom Descartes was brought to Sweden in 1649 to teach Christina, the queen of the "land of bears and ice," and where Descartes would meet his death. Chanut wrote to Descartes on December 1, 1646, in request of Christina who was wondering about some subjects and desired to receive the philosopher's answer. Her wanderings were formulated in three questions: What is love? Does the natural light by itself teach us to love God? Which is worse if immoderate and abused, love or hatred? Descartes responds to these questions in two letters, dated February 1, 1647, and May 11 of the same year. In these letters, which consist primarily of thoughts that will be published in *Passions*, Descartes begins by answering the first question by means of a distinction between rational and sensuous love. Rational love is exemplified by love to knowledge and love of knowledge. It consists in the joining willingly what the soul perceives as good, either present or absent; if present, then the "movement of the will" that accompanies the knowledge is joy; if absent, then this movement is sadness. What concedes rationality to this love of and on knowledge is the transparency of the movements of its will, of its joy and sadness, for nothing "could fail to be perfectly aware, provided it reflected on its own thoughts."[4] Although distinct from rational love, sensuous love is not its opposite. Thus, "since our soul is joined to the body, this rational love is commonly accompanied by the other kind of love, which can be called sensual or sensuous."[5] Sensuous or sensual love is a "confused thought, aroused in the soul by some motions of the nerves,"[6] but it is from this confusion (which we shall not forget is for Descartes a "thought") that "makes it disposed to have the other, clearer, thought which constitutes rational love." As much as a chaos must be invented for the sake of reaching Cartesian order, which Jean-Luc Nancy, based on his attentive reading of the Cartesian text, inspiringly called a *chaogito*,[7] sensuous love or confused thought is what disposes one to have the clearer thought called "rational love." Descartes described sensuous or sensual love as a "mysterious heat" felt around the heart that, combined with the feeling of a great abundance of blood in the lungs, "makes us open our arms as if to embrace something and this inclines the soul to join itself willingly the object presented to it."[8] Even if

Descartes considers the possibility of having a "feeling of love" without any object and of joining willingly something without feeling love, he connects very clearly sensuous or sensual love to rational love and to the feeling of a "mysterious heat around the heart." He says very explicitly that "these two loves occur together; for the two are so linked that when the soul judges an object to be worthy of it, this immediately makes the heart disposed to the motions which excite the passion of love."[9] Precisely when acknowledging this intimate link between the two kinds of love, Descartes revisits his recurrent thought that, because of the "soul's natural capacity for union with a body," there is an association between thoughts and certain motions or conditions of the body, so that when the same conditions occur in the body, the soul tends to have the same thought as much as the same thought occurring in the soul may provoke the same conditions in the body. With this thought, Descartes describes the e-motion, the moving that characterizes the act of thinking, connecting it to the link between rational and sensual love. He also compares this reciprocal relation of thoughts provoking emotions in the body and the body provoking thoughts to how we, learning a language, connect letters or the pronunciation of certain words, the material side of language, with their meanings, with thoughts, and this connection is such that when we later hear the same words, we conceive the same things.[10]

Descartes pursues his thoughts on love as the love of body and soul, proposing a theory of the birth of love from the first moment of life. Astonishingly, the first moment of life for Descartes is not the moment of "birth" but the embryonic moment of life in pregnancy. Descartes proceeds from this first moment of life before birth, unborn life. It is in this embryonic stage that he encounters the first moment of the union of body and soul, which is according to him a moment of joy.[11] The first—embryonic and pregnant—passion of this union is joy, and love arises from joy, what does not exclude that from this first joy, also hatred and sadness arise. "I think that the soul's first passion was joy, because it is not credible that the soul was put into the body at a time when the body was not in a good condition; and a good condition of the body naturally gives us joy."[12] These four passions: joy, love, hatred, and sadness are the only passions "we had before our birth."[13] It is quite interesting to follow how Descartes describes the "birth of love," so to speak, in unborn or pregnant life. He reveals his thinking, "I say that love followed because the matter of our body is in a perpetual flux like water in a stream, and there is always need for new matter to take its place."[14] Because in pregnant embryonic life (i.e., in the invisibility of the inner body) life is first of all nourishing, where the soul unites itself willingly to a new matter, Descartes identifies love already in the most elementary stage of life as confused sensations provoking heats in the body: "sensations of our childhood, which remain joined with the rational thoughts by which we love what we judge worthy of love." In these letters, love is connected to an extension of life that goes beyond life, currently experienced as the interval between birth and death. As Cecilia Sjöholm discussed in the previous chapter, Descartes connects love to the pregnancy of life but also to how probable it is that there is life on other planets, as soon as the indefinite extension of the world is accepted.[15] Love extends the unity of body and soul to before birth and to life beyond the earth. But what is important to keep in mind here for the sake of our discussion, is how love is linked to a perpetual flux "like the water in a stream," to a movement in motion that stretches back and forth, before and beyond oneself. This explains how Descartes finds an answer to the second question posed by Christina—namely, if natural light by itself can teach us to love God. Love of God poses the problem of how to argue for the intimate connection between the rational and sensuous, or sensual, in relation to God, if God cannot be an object or something that can be encountered as we encounter things and beings to love. Thus, to say that one loves God as one loves someone is to make of God an idolatry, an action akin to Ixion in the passage from the Satires by Horace,[16] as Descartes recalls, who embraced a cloud mistaking it for the Queen of the Gods.[17] Descartes considers that "the way to reach the love of God is to consider that he is a mind or a thing that thinks."[18] Instead of trying to imagine or figure God as something, the absolute spiritual essence of God must be accepted, and, indeed, that God is a thing that thinks, "*une chose qui pense*," the thinking act in its infinite movement and force. To love God is to love he who cannot be imagined and thereby sensuously experienced, but who, to be loved, must be sensed or experienced—thus love, as Descartes insists, is the connection between rational and sensuous love—"we can imagine our love itself, which consists in our wanting to unite ourselves to some object."[19] Love of God is a certain love of love in which we experience ourselves as a "minute part of all the immensity of the created universe,"[20] as "earth is smaller than the whole sky and a grain of sand in regard to a mountain."[21] It is in the experience of the infinity of God and the immensity of the created universe, and further, in the corresponding experience of the human being as a "minute part of all immensity," that love as desire to joining willingly to another, indeed to the other, using a more contemporaneous expression, shows its rational-sensuous nature. Thus, the rational dimension of love becomes itself sensuous as much as the sensuous becomes rational—that is, insofar as the confused thought that sensual love becomes clear and transparent of its own confusion. The question about loving God is therefore not a question of loving what is invisible or unimaginable but of loving what is much bigger than us, what is unequal in relation to who is in love since love makes everything equal, for love is reciprocity, an action that is acted by its action, hence at once action and passion, indeed, the very meaning of passion for Descartes.

The third question, whether love or hatred is worse if immoderate, Descartes answers more conclusively, admitting that "if I am asked which of the two passions carries us to greater excesses, and makes us capable of doing more harm to other people, I think I must say that it is love."[22] Because love, for Descartes, has more force and strength than hatred. Relating again to the "origin" of both love and hatred from pregnant life, which discovers love when the purest blood flows in the veins toward the heart and sends a great quantity of animal spirits to the brain, love gives then much more force, strength, and courage, whereas hatred produces bitterness of the gall and sourness of the spleen.[23] But the main argument for considering love more dangerous than hatred is the degree of attachment to its object, for it can give rise to hatred for many others.[24] For it seems that the greatest evils of love are produced or permitted "by the sole pleasure of the loved object or for oneself,"[25] something Descartes finds exemplified in Paris's love for Helen, and he continues to quote several lines of verse from the contemporaneous French baroque poet and dramaturge Théophile de Viau, who wrote in his Stances pour Mademoiselle de M. the following:

> How fine, ye Gods, the deed of his desire,
>   How fair his victim's fame,
> When noble Paris put all Troy to fire
>   To quench his own heart's flame.[26]

Despite these serious dangers of love, Descartes does not fail to recognize that "the greatest and most tragic disasters can be . . . seasoning for an immoderate love [it] makes it more delicious the more they raise its price."[27]

Finally, it is important to reemphasize that in Descartes's thoughts on love, he always connects love to a heat felt in the heart. In *Passions*, Descartes accounts for how thoughts are embodied, how they are connected to physical, bodily sensations and movements. It is a treatise on how the soul and the body act on each other, how one moves the other, how they are in love with each other. Descartes reverses a series of beliefs on this relation. He asserts that it is not the soul that gives movement and heat to the body, but the body that can give movement and heat to the soul, so that when the body dies and becomes incapable of movement and heat, the soul moves to leave the body.[28] He also denies the common belief that the heart is the seat of passions, showing what really happens—namely, that the passions make us feel some change in the heart[29]—indeed, a heat in the heart. However, love is always described as connected to the heart, to a certain strong movement of the blood and the spirits, which warms the heart in such an intensity that "the spirits sent by the heart to the brain have parts that are coarser and more agitated than usual; and as they strengthen the impressions formed by the first thought of the loved object, these spirits compel the soul to dwell upon this thought. This is what the passion of love consists in."[30]

Love is not something that happens in the heart, but it burns the heart. Though Descartes spoke rarely on love and mostly did so in his letters, the heart is for him a subject of passionate interest and intellectual inquiry in several works. From the most physiological to the most metaphysical inquiries, *Treatise of Man* and *Passions*, we see evidence of Descartes's wonder for the heart. It is through the beating of the heart that Descartes becomes aware both of the circulating winds he called "animal spirits" and of the blood's circulation. He is, moreover, surprised and moved to inquire how the heartbeat is an involuntary movement, something close to what today is called "reflex," distinct from other bodily movements produced voluntarily.[31] The heart beats when it "wants," so to speak, revealing a self-motion within the moving body, a very strange "thing" between the animal and the machine. The physiology of the body astonishes Descartes, and he remains convinced that if the heart is "*le grand resort*,"[32] upon which the movement of the muscles depend, its movement is of another sort than the movements that can be described as displacement; the movement of the heart is a heat. In *Treatise of Man*, the Cartesian heart is treated as the "seat of a continuous fire." The Cartesian heart is moreover described as a "fire without light."[33]

In a careful reading of Descartes, it is possible to discover what Cartesian love would mean—namely, the love between the body and the soul, that warms the heart, which is itself a seat of continuous fire, a fire without light, a heat-warming fire. It is also possible to discover that the separation of body and soul, of that which is an extensive and external thing and what is an interior and intensive thing, indeed shows what Nancy's reading of Descartes showed with such clarity—that the Cartesian body is an extension of the soul, pure exposition, an inside that is entirely outside.[34] However, Descartes was, without question, Monsieur Descartes, a man of *écarts*, and the Cartesian philosophical gesture is a gesture of *écartements*, of distancing. He does not leave the world behind or deny it; but he is constantly departing from his worlds: traveling, moving ever forward to Germany, Holland, Sweden. He also distances himself existentially, going into a room by himself, his oven-heated room, his *poêle*. Rather than a philosopher denying the world, Descartes's distancing, or *écartement*, is that of a writer. His solitude is that of a writer, a writer alone in a room. For some writers, such as Descartes and Proust, the room is a bed. For others, such as Marguerite Duras, the room is something of a window.[35] But in both cases, the room is also, without question, a pen and ink. Descartes's distancing is the solitude required for a writer, "a way of thinking, of reasoning."[36] Descartes is the "father" of modern philosophy, the inventor of the modern philosophical novel or fable, for he is the philosopher who scrutinized what it means to think through writing, the relation between thinking and writing, the love of thinking and writing, the love of body and soul. He thinks as one writes. He must cast away the books, ancient opinions, and quotes; thus, as a writer who sits in a room of his own, he must begin with the "blank sheet." A brief poem by Paul Valéry could have been written by Descartes as well, when saying,

> In truth, a blank sheet
> Declares by the void
> That there is nothing as beautiful
> As that which does not exist.
> On the magic mirror of its white space,
> The soul sees before her the place of the miracles
> That we would bring to life with signs and lines.
> This presence of absence over-excites
> And at the same time paralyses the definitive act of the pen.
> There is in all beauty a forbiddance to touch,
> From which emanates I don't know what of sacred
> That stops the movement and puts the man
> On the point of acting in fear of himself.[37]

To distance from the world as a writer means to come as close to the world as the one who creates a world: *mundus est fabula*, "read this book as a fable." In the French spoken during Descartes's time, *carte* was the word used for "page." Descartes was his name: *écartes des cartes*, the distancing of a thinking that thinks in and through writing.

This brief digression may complement our discussion about Descartes's love letters and letters on love. For there is also a certain love—that also links rational and sensuous love—which is the love of letters, the love of literature. Not literature as the collection of written texts but as the action of hands writing the event of thinking with pen and ink. There is a profound connection between the heat of love and love epistolography. Should we say that this "fire without light," which Descartes called heart, is the primal scene of writing? Is that scene what the old Greek narrative about the birth of drawing aims to rend visible? Boutade, the ceramist, suffering when seeing his daughter's suffering after bidding farewell to her beloved, fixed in the wall of his working room the shadow of her beloved while departing. These lines drawn upon a blank wall tell of the birth of a love letter as the graphic mark of the shadow of a departing movement. One could recognize in this narrative the graphic mark of an anamorphic drawing, the drawing of a line in movement, the departing lines of a body. Indeed, why do lovers write love letters so passionately? Why does love want to write itself, to say itself in words, if love is the most intensive experience of an act that has no need for words to enact, if love raptures the words and language from words and language? This old narrative is perhaps indicative that lovers write, and writing is so tightly linked to love, not because the lovers cannot stand a separation but because they want to keep, in the "fire without light" of the heart, the loving as such: its presence and absence, the becoming absent and becoming present that follows every time the beloved arrives and departs. Indeed, what love wants to hold onto is the loving—"I love you" indeed says I am loving, what in Latin languages is calling the beloved both the "loving," *l'aimant*, and the loved, *l'aimé*, reserving the meaning of the beloved in a sensuous way, the first one, the loving, *l'aimant*. Love aims more to preserve the loving, the act of being in love than the (be)loved. It aims to maintain the loving, which is *between* the lover and the beloved, which shows itself as a comma uttering itself in loud voice, through whisperings, screams, murmurings, loud breath movements, respirations. And as sounds escape from the mouth, writing escapes from the body through the hands. As Descartes writes to Elisabeth,[38]

> The honour your Highness does me in sending her commandments in writing is greater than I ever dared hope; and it is more consoling to my unworthiness than the other favour which I had hoped for passionately, which was to receive them by word of mouth, had I been permitted to pay homage to you and offer you my very humble services when I was last at the Hague. For then I would have had too many wonders to admire at the same time; and seeing superhuman sentiments flowing from a body such as painters give to angels, I would have been overwhelmed with delights like those I think a man coming fresh from earth to heaven must feel. Thus, I would hardly have been able to reply to your Highness as she doubtless noticed when once before I had the honour of speaking with her. In your kindness you have tried to redress this fault of mine by committing the traces of your thoughts to paper, so that I can read them many times, and grow accustomed to considering them. Thus, I am less overwhelmed, but no less full of wonder, observing that it is not only at first sight that they seem perceptive, but that the more they are examined, the more judicious and solid they appear.[39]

Considering that the "*cartes*," love letters, flow from the body of the lovers as sounds come from their mouths, as painters let flow as angels superhuman sentiments from a body, and that these letters and sounds are addressed to the loving—*aimants*—rather to the beloved, it may be possible to see more clearly why in love there is a profound need to write and speak of love *while* loving, and thereby to think the loving while loving. It seems that the entire reality has been embraced by the open arms of the loving, of being in loving. In this way, everything detours from itself to turn toward the loving. Love letters aim to preserve this detour, they aim to fix the unfixable being in love, the loving in its continuous present participle form, its moving e-moving and overwhelming everything. Love letters know that no word or letter, no image or expression would be capable of fixing this "fire without light," this heat that warms the heat of the heart, this breath and vertiginous wind. But they write, they draw traits and lines on a blank sheet. And in the velocity of its traits and lines—love letters are written quickly for the sake of coming to the hands of the beloved as quickly as possible—love apostrophizes itself. It does not get tired of saying "my love." But the apostrophe is not only the call that makes a detour from the addressee in order to turn to a third when writing "my love"; thus, in this turn, it speaks to the loving itself. It is not only the interpellation to someone or something that expresses an experienced emotion. The apostrophe is a diacritic sign, a typographic mark, a "high" comma, *hochkomma*, as it is called in German, the physical sign of an experienced emotion. It marks a respiration, a breath that accomplishes a contraction by means of an interruption, revealing thereby the action in the act of the loving while loving in the very act of writing—the apostrophe obliges readers a detour from its own reading that renders them attentive that what they are reading is being written while they are reading. The apostrophe realizes in the letter what the heart does in loving. It is the beating of the writing. Descartes makes a wonderful use of the apostrophe of the heart, so to speak, when, in the letters to Chanut, he employs the verb *"s'entr'aimer*," literally between-love or interlove, an unusual verb likely only used before Descartes by Corneille.[40] Cartesian love is neither catastrophic nor epistrophic, the latter meaning a love through conversion. It is not even strophic—that is, poetic. Cartesian love is apostrophic. In the letters to Chanut, as we have seen, Descartes meditates about the distinction between rational and sensuous love, as well as about friendly love and concupiscent or erotic love; he meditates about love of a flower, a bird, a building, and God. But not exclusively. He also meditates on the love between two men. It is a reflection about the love of two men, having in mind Virgil's narrative in the Aeneid (song IX, verse 427), the love between Nisus and Euryale, that Descartes describes with the verb *"s'entr'aimer"*: "*Mais quand deux hommes s'entr'aiment.*"[41] The French orthography of this reflexive verb is marked by two apostrophes *s'entre* et *entr'aimer*. Marked by this apostrophe, the verb *entr'aimer* that Descartes uses here puts the between-two in exergue, also reminiscent for French speaking ears of the verb *entrainer*, to carry along, to go on, and the present participle *en train d'aimer*, to be loving, the overwhelming presence that is more of a nerve, a pulsion in gerund. Descartes observes that in the act of *s'entr'aimer*, of between- or inter-loving, it is revealed that each of the lovers loves the other more than himself and affirms that "*leur amities n'est point parfait, s'ils ne sont prêts de dire, en faveur l'un de l'autre: Meme adsum qui fecci, in me convertite ferrum.*" The *s'entr'aimer* is only perfect if they are ready to say a word of love. These words written by Virgil say that the one who loves, who has done everything for the beloved, is not in the center but on the side, *adsum*, and compels *l'ami aimant*, the loving beloved to turn the iron against him. Here it is possible to find the direction of the detour made by the Cartesian *cogito*—I am thinking, therefore I am. When the cogito makes a detour from itself, it may encounter a loving cogito, the cogito of Cartesian love. Indeed, the loving Cartesian cogito that his friend, the poet and artist Constantjin Huygens, also a close friend of Princess Elisabeth, formulated in Latin in the verse, "*At sic, Amice, ego cogito, ergo sum Tuus*": "But in this way, my friend, I am thinking therefore I am yours."

Notes

Introduction

1. Erec Koch has made this description, although he uses it differently than we do in this book—to Koch it designates the image of a body/instrument. See *The Aesthetic Body: Passion, Sensibility and Corporeality in 17th Century France* (Newark: University of Delaware Press, 2008), 24.

2. Descartes, "Rules for the Direction of the Mind," in *The Philosophical Writings of Descartes*, vol. I, trans. Johan Cottingham, Robert Stoothoff, and Dugald Murdoch (Cambridge: Cambridge University Press, 1985), 19.

3. Hannah Arendt, *Human Condition* (Chicago: University of Chicago Press, 1958), 2–3.

4. Alexandre Koyré, *From the Closed World to the Infinite Universe* (Baltimore, MD: John Hopkins Press, 1957), 1–3.

5. Descartes, "Meditations on First Philosophy," in *The Philosophical Writings of Descartes*, vol. II, trans. Johan Cottingham, Robert Stoothoff, and Dugald Murdoch (Cambridge: Cambridge University Press, 1985), 16.

6. "He found the Archimedean point, but he used it against himself; it seems that he was permitted to find it only under this condition." (*Er hat den archimedischen Punkt gefunden, hat ihn aber gegen sich ausgenutzt, offenbar hat er ihn nur unter dieser Bedingung finden dürfen.*) Franz Kafka, *Aphorisms*, quoted in Arendt, *Human Condition*, 248.

7. Jean-Paul Sartre. "La liberté cartésienne," in *Descartes 1596–1650*. Introduction et choix par J.-P. Sartre (Genève-Paris: Trois Collines, coll. "Les Classiques de la Liberté," 1946), 10–11, trans. Annette Michelson, "Cartesian Freedom," in *Literary Philosophical and Essays* (New York: Collier, 1962), 180–198.

8. See, for instance, from the analytical point of view, Lilli Alanen, *Descartes's Concept of the Mind* (Cambridge, MA: Harvard University Press, 2003), and from the continental tradition, works by Jean-Luc Marion such as *On the Ego and on God: Further Cartesian Questions*, trans. Christina M. Gschwandtner (New York: Fordham University Press, 2007); *On Descartes' Passive Thought: The Myth of Cartesian Dualism*, trans. Christina M. Gschwandtner (Chicago: University of Chicago Press, 2018); and *Cartesian Questions: Method and Metaphysics* (Chicago: University of Chicago Press, 1999); and by Jean-Luc Nancy, *Ego sum: corpus, anima, fabula*, trans. Marie-Eve Morin (New York: Fordham University Press, 2016), *Corpus I*. trans. Richard A. Rand (New York: Fordham University Press, 2008).

9. Lilli Alanen, *Descartes's Concept of the Mind*; Sara Heinämaa and Timo Kaitaro, "Descartes's Notion of the Mind-Body Union and Its Phenomenological Expositions," in *The Oxford Handbook of the History of Phenomenology*, ed. Dan Zahavi (Oxford: Oxford University Press, 2018); Sabina Ebbersmeyer, ed. *Emotional Minds: The Passions and the Limits of Pure Inquiry in Early Modern Philosophy* (Berlin: De Gruyter, 2012).

10. Maurice Merleau-Ponty, *Phenomenology of Perception*, trans. Taylor Carman (London: Routledge, 2002).

11. See, for instance, Lilla Alanen, *Descartes's Concept of Mind*; Sara Heinämaa and Timo Kaitaro, "Descartes' Notion of the Mind–Body Union and Its Phenomenological Expositions."

12. See, for instance, Erik Larsen, "Le baroque et l'esthétique de Descartes" in *Baroque* [En ligne], 6 (1973), http://journals.openedition.org/baroque/416; DOI: 10.4000/baroque.416; R. Darren Gobert, *The Mind-Body Stage: Passion and Interaction in the Cartesian Theater* (Stanford, CA: Stanford University Press, 2013); E. Gilby, *Descartes' Fictions: Reading Philosophy with Poetics* (Oxford: Oxford University Press, 2019).

13. Pascal Dumont, *Descartes et l'esthétique. L'art d'emerveiller* (Paris: PUF, 2017), 236.

14. Dumont, *Descartes et l'esthétique*, 235.

1. Descartes's Visceral Aesthetics

1. Richard Shusterman, "The End of Aesthetic Experience," *Journal of Aesthetics and Art Criticism* 55, no. 1 (1997): 29–41; and Richard Shusterman, "Aesthetic Experience: From Analysis to Eros," *Journal of Aesthetics and Art Criticism* 64, no. 2 (2006): 217–229.

2. Jacques Rancière, *The Politics of Aesthetics* (London: Bloomsbury, 2002), 7–15.

3. Cf. the analysis of Kant's notion of beauty in Fiona Hughes, *Kant's Aesthetic Epistemology: Form and World* (Edinburgh: Edinburgh University Press, 2007).

4. Tomohiro Ishizu and Semir Zeki, "Toward a Brain-Based Theory of Beauty," *PLoS ONE* 6, no. 7 (2011): e21852, https://doi:10.1371/journal.pone.0021852.

5. Gianluca Consoli, "A Cognitive Theory of the Aesthetic Experience," *Contemporary Aesthetics* 10 (2012).

6. Sabrina Ebbersmeyer, *Emotional Minds: The Passions and the Limits of Pure Inquiry in Early Modern Philosophy* (Berlin: De Gruyter, 2012).

7. Descartes, *Discourse on Method* in *The Philosophical Writings of Descartes*, vols. I–III, trans. John Cottingham, Robert Stoothoff, and Dugald Murdoch (Cambridge: Cambridge University Press, 1985), vol. I 112, AT IV, 4.

8. Descartes, *Treatise on Man*, *The Philosophical Writings of Descartes* I, 99, AT XI, 120.

9. Pascal Dumont, *Descartes et l'esthétique: l'art d'émerveiller* (Paris: PUF, 1998); Erik Larsen, "Le baroque et l'esthétique de Descartes," *Baroque* 6 (1973). http://journals.openedition.org/baroque/416; DOI: 10.4000/baroque.416; Brigitte Van Wymeersch, "L'esthétique musicale de Descartes et le cartésianisme," *Revue Philosophique de Louvain* 94, no. 2 (1996): 271–293, 283.

10. Descartes, *Principles of Philosophy*, *The Philosophical Writings of Descartes* I, 279–280, AT IXB, 315–317.

11. Fernand Hallyn, *Les Olympiques de Descartes* (Genève: Librairie Droz S. A, 1995).

12. Descartes, *Discourse on the Method*, *The Philosophical Writings of Descartes* I, 114, AT VI, 7.

13. Descartes, *Compendium on Music*, trans. Walter Robert (Rome: American Institute of Musicology, 1961), 11, AT X, 89.

14. Descartes to Mersenne, March 18, 1630, *The Philosophical Writings of Descartes* III, 20, AT, 132–134.

15. "Un rapport de nostre iugement à l'objet; & pource que les iugemens des hommes sont si differens, on ne peut dire que le beau, ny l'agreable, ayent aucune mesure determinée [. . .]

ce qui plaira à plus de gens, pourra estre nommé simplement le plus beau, ce qui ne sçauroit estre determiné." Descartes to Mersenne, March 8, 1630, AT I.

16. Descartes to Huygens, November 1, 1635, *The Philosophical Writings of Descartes* III, 50, AT I, 331.

17. Descartes to Beeckman, April 23, 1619, *The Philosophical Writings of Descartes* III, 3, AT X, 157.

18. See note 38. One may, as Dennis Sepper has done, confer the intelligibility of the universe to "analogies" of a divine source, which is also what makes algebra meaningful despite its lack of objects. "Figuring Things Out: Figurate Problem-Solving in the Early Descartes," in *Descartes' Natural Philosophy*, ed. Stephen Gaukroger, John Andrew Schuster, and John Sutton, 245 (Cambridge: Cambridge University Press, 2002).

19. Descartes, *Treatise on Music*, 14–15, AT X, 95.

20. As exemplified by Kate van Orden: "The senses were instruments of control—receptors to be packed with edifying stimuli and tools of external domination." Both dance and drill "train the body to react automatically to regular stimuli." "Descartes of Musical Training and the Body," in *Music Sensation and Sensuality*, ed. Linda Phyllis Austern (London: Routledge, 2002), 31, 33.

21. Richard A. Watson, *Descartes's Ballet, His Doctrine of the Will and His Political Philosophy* (with a transcript and English translation of *La Naissance de la Paix*) (South Bend, IN: St. Augustine's, 2007).

22. Descartes to Mersenne, March 18, 1630, *The Philosophical Writings of Descartes* III, 19–20, AT I, 117–123.

23. Cf. Koch, *Aesthetic Body*, 24.

24. Descartes, *The Philosophical Writings of Descartes* I, 100–104, AT II, 41–44, 144–146, 164–166.

25. Descartes, *The Treatise on Man, The World and Other Writings*, 146, AT II, 174.

26. Descartes, *The Treatise on Man, The World and Other Writings*, 150, AT II, 177.

27. The term *natural philosophy* can be used to cover "the sciences"—optics, astronomy, and so on—whereas the idea of "science" is a nineteenth-century invention. Stephen Gaukroger, John Schuster, and John Sutton, eds., *Descartes' Natural Philosophy* (London: Routledge, 2000). See also the work of Horst Bredekamp—for instance, "Thomas Hobbes's Visual Strategies," in *The Cambridge Companion to Hobbes's Leviathan* (Cambridge: Cambridge University Press, 2007); Chiara Bottici, *Imaginal Politics: Images beyond Imagination and the Imaginary* (New York: Columbia University Press, 2014); Sybille Krämer and Christina Ljungberg, eds., *Thinking with Diagrams* (Berlin: De Gruyter Mouton, 2016).

28. Maurice Merleau-Ponty, "Cézanne's Doubt," in *Sense and Non-sense*, 14.

29. See, for instance, Vivian Sobchack, *The Address of the Eye: A Phenomenology of Film Experience* (Princeton, NJ: Princeton University Press, 1992), 57–97; and Vivian Sobchack, *Carnal Thoughts: Embodiment and Moving Image Culture* (Berkeley: University of California Press, 2004), 53–83.

30. Brian Massumi, "The Future Birth of the Affective Fact," in *The Affect Theory Reader*, ed. Melissa Gregg and Gregory Seigworth (Durham, NC: Duke University Press, 2009), 64–65.

31. Charles Adam and Paul Tannery, *Oeuvres de Descartes*, Tome XI (Paris: Leopold Cerf, 1909), 659. See also Alain Baillet, *La Vie de Monsieur Descartes*, Tome II (Paris: 1691), 433–434.

32. Descartes, *Passions of the Soul*, trans. Stephen Voss (Cambridge: Hackett, 1995), 17. In the English translation, *physicien* is translated as *physicist*, which does not quite capture the philosophical connotation.

33. See, for instance, Descartes, *Passions of the Soul*, 22, AT XI, 332.

34. The mind is the thinking soul, to Descartes. *The Philosophical Writings of Descartes* vol. I, 246.

35. Descartes, *Passions of the Soul*, xv.

36. Descartes, *Meditations*, *The Philosophical Writings of Descartes* II, 2, AT VII, 34.

37. Descartes, *Principles of Philosophy*, *The Philosophical Writings of Descartes*, 281, AT VIIIA, 320–321.

38. As Darren Gobert has shown, theater became "Cartesian" not only in terms of the plots, the stage, and the acting but also of the passions explored, of which wonder was privileged. *The Mind-Body Stage: Passion and Interaction in the Cartesian Theatre* (Stanford, CA: Stanford University Press, 2013), 41–45.

39. Gobert, *Mind-Body Stage*, 86–87.

40. Descartes, *Passions of the Soul*, 67, AT XI, 391–392, 395.

41. Cf. Dominik Perler, *Feelings Transformed: Philosophical Theories of the Emotions, 1270–1670*, trans. Tony Crawford (New York: Oxford University Press, 2018); or perception, as in Walter Ott, *Descartes, Malebranche, and the Crisis of Perception* (Oxford: Oxford University Press, 2017). As Walter Ott shows, Descartes's theories of perception responded to the question of how we are to conceive of sensible qualities such as color, sound, and so on, if they are neither an aspect of the objective world of cognition nor an inherent aspect of subjectivity. One may argue that aspects of the soul such as desire and love respond to the need to account for experiences of the outside world that cannot be accounted for in objective terms (i.e., geometrical, for instance).

42. Descartes, *Passions of the Soul*, 119–122, AT XI, 469–472.

43. Descartes, *Treatise on Man*, 150, AT II, 177.

44. Descartes, *Passions of the Soul*, 46, AT XI, 366.

45. Descartes, *Passions of the Soul*, 53, AT XI, 374–375.

46. Descartes to Chanut, June 6, 1647, *The Philosophical Writings of Descartes*, 322–323, AT V, 57.

47. Descartes, *Passions of the Soul*, 69, AT XI, 396.

48. Translated by Stephen Voss as abhorrence throughout *The Passions of the Soul*.

49. Descartes, *Passions of the Soul*, 65, AT 391–392.

50. See the discussion on object relations in the chapter "The Thinking Fetus."

51. Descartes, *Passions of the Soul*, 79, AT XI, 412.

52. Descartes, *Passions of the Soul*, 68, AT XI, 395.

53. Descartes, *Passions of the Soul*, 69, AT XI, 396.

54. René Descartes, *Meditations on First Philosophy*, trans. John Cottingham, *The Philosophical Writings of Descartes* vol. II, (Cambridge: Cambridge University Press 1984), 26 [37].

55. Descartes, *Passions of the Soul*, 65, AT XI, 392.

56. Descartes, *Passions of the Soul*, AT XI, 369.

57. Descartes, *Passions of the Soul*, 67, AT XI, 395.

58. Descartes, *Passions of the* Soul, 109, AT XI, 454–455.

59. Georges Bataille, *Prehistoric Painting or the Birth of Art* (London: MacMillan, 1920), 31.

60. Julia Kristeva, *Powers of Horror*, trans. Leon Roudiez (Columbia: Columbia University Press), 1982.
61. Georges Bataille, "Formless," *Documents #1* (Paris, 1929), 382, trans. Allan Stoekl, Carl R. Lovitt, and Donald M. Leslie Jr., *Georges Bataille: Vision of Excess: Selected Writings, 1927–1939* (Minneapolis: University of Minnesota Press, 1985), 31.
62. Kristeva, *Powers of Horror*, 198.
63. Paul Hoffman, *Essays on Descartes* (Oxford: Oxford University Press, 2009), 108–113.
64. Mario Perniola, *The Sex Appeal of the Inorganic*, trans. Massimo Verdicchio (London: Continuum, 2004), 8.
65. Cf. John Cottingham, *Philosophy and the Good Life: Reason and the Passions in Greek, Cartesian and Psychoanalytic Ethics* (Cambridge: Cambridge University Press), 1998.

2. Philosophical Emotion

1. "Je dis ému, car il est possible de l'être par des causes purement 'intellectuelles.' Il y a chez quelques-uns, vous en êtes bien sûrs, une manière de sensibilité intellectuelle [. . .] L'émotion intellectuelle est évidement plus rare que les autres. L'art qui la fixe et la restitue ne peut avoir qu'une résonance restreinte." La creation artistique in Paul Valéry, *Vues* (Paris: La table ronde, 1948), 287–288.
2. Descartes, "The Passions of the Soul," in *The Philosophical Writings of Descartes*, vol. I, trans. John Cottingham, Robert Stoothoff, and Dugald Murdoch (Cambridge: Cambridge University Press, 1985), 338–339.
3. For a discussion of "intellectual emotions" in Descartes that, however, does not search to develop a notion of "philosophical emotion," see Gábor Boros, *Sur les émotions intellectuelles chez Descartes*, http://filozofiaiszemle.net/wp-content/uploads/2016/10/G%C3%A1bor-Boros-Sur-les-%C3%A9motions-intellectuelles-chez-Descartes.pdf; and also Pierre Guenancia, *L'intelligence du sensible: Essai sur le dualisme cartésien* (Paris: Gallimard, 1998).
4. Descartes, "The Passions of the Soul," in *The Philosophical Writings of Descartes*, vol. I, 328.
5. Descartes, "The Passions of the Soul," in *The Philosophical Writings of Descartes*, vol. I, 328.
6. In his discussions on the passivity and the passion of thought in Descartes, Jean-Luc Marion comes close to what I am calling here reflexivity when discussing, for instance, Descartes's affirmation that "it is certain that we cannot will anything without thereby perceiving that we are willing it," hence, that active thought is only possible being at the same time passive. However, he does not address the question of the emotion provoked and experienced by this "reflexivity." See Jean-Luc Marion, *Sur la pensée passive de Descartes* (Paris: PUF, 2013), *On Descartes' Passive Thought: The Myth of Cartesian Dualism*, trans. Christina M. Gschwandtner (Chicago and London: University of Chicago Press, 2018), 209.
7. "At that time I was in Germany, where I had been called by the wars that are not yet ended there. While I was returning to the army from the coronation of the Emperor, the onset of winter detained me in quarters where, finding no conversation to divert med and fortunately having no cares or passions to trouble me, I stayed all day shut up alone in a stove-heated room, where I was completely free to converse with myself about my own thoughts." Descartes, "Discourse on the Method," in *The Philosophical Writings of Descartes*, vol. I, 116.

8. For a close study of Descartes's early writings, see Henri Gouhier, *Les premières pensées de Descartes* (Paris: Vrin, 1958).

9. Fernand Hallyn, *Les Olympiques de Descartes* (Genève: Librairie Droz S. A., 1995).

10. Adrien Baillet, *La Vie de M. Des-Cartes*, Premiere partie. A Paris, chez Daniel Horthemels, Rue saint Jacques, au Mécénas. M. DC. XCI. Avec privilege du roi.: 1691, quoted in AT X, 180f, Eng. trans. already 1693, *The Life of Monsieur Des Cartes*, containing the history of his philosophy and works: as also the most remarkable things that befell him during the whole course of his life. London: Printed for R. Simpson, 1693, vol. I, 80–86.

11. To read the whole narrative, see the appendix in which W. T. Jones's translation is reproduced. Jone's translation was originally published in "Somnio ergo sum: Descartes three dreams" in *Philosophy and Literature* 4, no. 2 (Fall 1980): 145–162.

12. The Latin text of the opening sentence was transcribed, "X. Novembris 1619, cum plenus forem Enthousiasmo, et mirabilis scientiae fundamenta reperirem." A marginal note at the beginning of the work read, "XL Novembris, coepi intelligere fundamentum inventi mirabilis—11 November I began to understand the basis of the marvelous discovery." This is the form given in the inventory of Descartes's papers published in René Descartes, 1596–1650. *Oeuvres*. 10 publ. par, ed. Charles Adam and Paul Tannery (Paris: Vrin, 1969), 7. The sentence quoted in Baillet's Vie, as printed in Oeuvres 10, s. 179, adds the year 1620. Is this an error, or did Descartes take a year to begin his understanding? (This note follows in Benton's translation.)

13. A marginal note reads: "Divided in five books, printed at Lyon and Geneva, etc." This information helps to identify the work as the *Corpus omnium veierum poetarum latinorum*, edited by Pierre de Brosses, which appeared in two editions before 1619, the first at Lyon in 1603, the second at Geneva in 1611. The Corpus was "big," being composed of two volumes in quarto, the first of 1,426 pages and the second of 888 pages (895 in the 1611 edition).

14. The poem, entitled *Ex Graeco Pythagoricum, de ambiguitate eligendae vitae*, Edyllium XV, was printed in vol. I of the Corpus, 655 (first edition) or 658 (second edition). It is printed with an English translation as Eclogue 2 in Ausonius, ed. H. G. E. White, Loeb Library (2 vols., London, 1919), vol. I, 162–169. On Ausonius's Eclogue and the crossroads of Pythagoras, see S. K. Heninger Jr., *Touches of Sweet Harmony* (San Marino, CA: Huntington Library, 1974), 269–271 (note from Benton's translation). For a digital version, see http://www.perseus.tufts.edu/hopper/text?doc=Perseus%3Atext%3A2008.01.0609%3Asection%3D2.

15. The poem "Est et Non" is the fourth Eclogue of Ausonius, ed. White, ibid., 170–173. The poem vigorously attacks empty dialectic debate. According to Norman K. Smith, *New Studies in the Philosophy of Descartes* (London: Russell & Russell, 1952), 35, the two poems of Ausonius appear on the same page of the 1603 edition of the *Corpus poetarum*, the edition that Descartes surely used at the Jesuit College of La Fleche, and on facing pages of the edition of 1611 (note from Benton's translation). Ausonius's poem The Pythagorean "Yea" and "Nay" reads as following in the refered English translation:

> "yes" and "no": all the world constantly uses these familiar monosyllables. Take these away and you leave nothing for the tongue of man to discuss. In them is all, and all from them; be it a matter of business or pleasure, of bustle or repose. Sometimes two parties both use one word or the other at the same time, but often they are opposed, according as men easy or contentions in character and temperament are engaged in discussion. If both agree, forth with "Yea, yea" breaks in; but if they dispute, then disagreement will throw in a "Nay." From these arises the uproar which splits the air of the courts, from these the feuds of the maddened Circus and the wide-spread

partisanship which fills the tiers of the theatre, from these the debates which occupy the Senate. Wives, children, fathers, bandy these two words in peaceful debate without unnatural quarrelling. They are the instruments with which the schools fit for peaceful learning wage their harmless war of philosophical strife. On them the whole throng of rhetoricians depends in its wordy contests: "You grant that it is light?" Yes? Then it is day!" "No, the point is not granted; for whenever many torches or lightening-flashes gives light by night, yes, it is light; but it is not the light of the day." It is a case of "yes" and "no" then; for we are bound to say: "Yes, it is light," and "No, it is not day." There you have the source of countless squabbles: that is why some—nay, many—pondering on such things, smother their gruff protests and bite their lips in raging silence.

What a thing is the life of man which two monosyllables toss about!

16. Neither of the editions of the Corpus printed before 1619 contained copperplate engravings.

17. This passage is very close to the Latin of the *Cogitationes privatae*, printed in Descartes, Oeuvres 10, publ. par, ed. Charles Adam and Paul Tannery (Paris: Vrin, 1996), 217: "Mirum videri possit, quare graves sententiae in scriptis poetarum, magis quam philosophorum. Ratio est quod poetae per enthusiasmum et vim imaginationis scripsere: sunt in nobis semina scientiae, ut in silice, quae per rationem a philosophis educuntur per imaginationem a poetis excutiuntur magisque elucent."

18. This passage is the only indication that Descartes considered a detail of the dream predictive.

19. Descartes was with the imperial army at Neuberg on the Danube when he had this dream. Three months before (when he had last drunk wine), he attended the coronation of Emperor Ferdinand II at Frankfurt.

20. See, for example, Jean-Luc Marion, "Does Thought Dream? The Three Dreams, or the Awkening of the Philosopher," in *Cartesian Questions: Method and Metaphysics* (Chicago: University of Chicago Press, 1999).

21. Sigmund Freud, "Some Dreams of Descartes: A Letter to Maxime Leroy," in *Complete Psychological Works of Sigmund Freud*, vol. XXI (1927–1931): The Future of an Illusion, Civilization and its Discontents, and Other Works, (Unspecified, 1961), 197–204.

22. Baillet in Descartes, *Oeuvres. 10*, publ. par, ed. Charles Adam and Paul Tannery (Paris: Vrin, 1996) 179, 1. 18; 181, 1. 12.

23. See Jean-Luc Marion. "Does Thought Dream? The Three Dreams, or the Awkening of the Philosopher," in *Cartesian Questions: Method and Metaphysics* (Chicago: University of Chicago Press, 1999).

24. Descartes, "Discourse on the Method," in *The Philosophical Writings of Descartes*, vol. I, 116.

25. Descartes, "Discourse on the Method," in *The Philosophical Writings of Descartes*, vol. I, 117.

26. Descartes, "Discourse on the Method," in *The Philosophical Writings of Descartes*, vol. I, 117.

27. Descartes, "Discourse on the Method," in *The Philosophical Writings of Descartes*, vol. 1, 120.

28. Descartes, "First Set of Replies," in *The Philosophical Writings of Descartes*, vol. II, 81. The French original reads: "De la même manière que la connaissance de Dieu en tant que cause supérieur est immédiate et non per progressum in infinitum" in (Réponses aux

premières Objections *Oeuvres. 9*, publ. par, ed. Charles Adam and Paul Tannery (Paris: Vrin, 1996), 88.

29. Ferdinand Alquié, "Descartes et l'immédiat," *Revue de Métaphysique et de Morale*, 1950, 370–375.

30. Descartes, "Discourse on the Method," in *The Philosophical Writings of Descartes*, vol. I, 127.

31. Descartes, "Discourse on the Method," in *The Philosophical Writings of Descartes*, vol. I, 127.

32. Descartes, "Discourse on the Method," in *The Philosophical Writings of Descartes*, vol. I, 127.

33. As Denis Kambouchner has suggested in his book *Descartes n'a pas dit* (Paris: Les Belles Lettres, 2015), 63.

34. Paul Valéry, Comments on Descartes from the Notebooks in *Collected Works of Paul Valéry, Masters and Friends*, vol. 9, trans. Martin Turnell (New York: Princeton University Press, 1968), 311.

35. It is the motto that according to Pausanias was inscribed in the forecourt of the Temple of Apollo in Delphi.

36. For a presentation of this dominant view and a discussion about the modern philosophical concept of reflection in Descartes and post-Cartesian philosophy, see Rodolphe Gasché, *The Tain of the Mirror: Derrida and the Philosophy of Reflection* (Cambridge, MA: Harvard University Press, 1986).

37. Leibniz, *New Essays on Human Understanding*, trans. Peter Remnant and Jonathan Bennett (Cambridge: Cambridge University Press, 1996), 52.

38. Alexander Baumgarten, *Metaphysics: A Critical Translation with Kant's Elucidations, Selected Notes and Related Materials*, trans. Courtney D. Fugate and John Hymers (London: Bloomsbury, 2013), § 626, 229.

39. "*Die Überlegung (reflexio) hat es nicht mit den Gegenstände selbst zu tun, um gerade von ihnen Begriffe zu bekommen, sondern ist der Zustand des Gemüts, in welchem wir uns zuerts dazu anskicken, um die subjektiven Bedingungen ausfinden zu machen, unter denen wir zu Begriffen gelangen können. Sie ist das Bewußtsein des Verhältnisses gegebener Vortsellungen zu unseren verschiedenen Erkenntnisquellen, durch welchs allein ihr Verhältnis untereinander richtig bestimmen warden kann*" (Immanuel Kant, Werkausgabe: in 12 Bänden. Bd 4 Kritik der reinen Vernunft. 2. Frankfurt am Main: Suhrkamp; 1976.) V, Amphibolie der Reflexionsbegriffe I, 290, f. Rc 354). Eng. trans. "Reflection (*reflexio*) does not have to do with objects themselves, in order to acquire concepts directly from them, but is rather the state of mind in which we first prepare ourselves to find out the subjective conditions under which we can arrive at concepts. It is the consciousness of the relation of given representations to our various sources of cognition, through which alone their relation among themselves can be correctly determined," *Critique of Pure Reason*, trans. Paul Guyer and Allen W. Wood (Cambridge: Cambridge University Press, 1998), 366.

40. Kant, I, ibid.

41. Heidegger, *Die Grundprobleme der* Phänomenologie, GA 24 (Frankfurt am Main: Vittorio Klostermann, 1997), 177.

42. Kambouchner, *Descartes n'a pas dit*, 72.

43. Heidegger, *Being and Time*, trans. Joan Stambaugh (Albany: State University of New York Press, 1996), §.

44. Heidegger, *Being and Time*, § 43, 195. Jean-François Courtine is not incorrect in pointing out that Heidegger is not simply denying the "sum," the "subject," but radicalizing the Cartesian sum in its worldliness and existentiality. See Jean-François Courtine, "Les méditations cartésiennes de Martin Heidegger," *Les Études Philosophiques* 1 no. 88 (2009): 103–115.

45. Tobias Keiling, "Ars Cogitans: Überlegungen mit descartes und Husserl zum Ursprung des Kunstwerks," *Kalliope, Zeitschrift für Literatur und Kunst*, Heft I (2009): 72.

46. For an account on Husserl's critique of Descartes, see Jean-Marc Laporte, S. J. "Husserl's Critique of Descartes," *Philosophy and Phenomenological Research* 23, no. 3 (March 1963): 335–352.

47. Maurice Merleau-Ponty, *Phenomenology of Perception*, trans. Taylor Carman (London: Routledge, 2002 [1962]).

48. Merleau-Ponty, *Phenomenology of Perception*, 464.

49. Merleau-Ponty, *Phenomenology of Perception*, 310.

50. For an account and critique of Heidegger's invented formula, see Jean-Marie Beyssade, *Descartes au fil de l'ordre* (Paris: PUF, 2001), 181; and Christophe Perrin, "Cogito me cogitare." Note pour servir la généalogie et la téléologie d'une formule clé de G. W. Leibniz à J-L Marion," *Phainomena* 23, no. 88–89, http://www.sif-praha.cz/wp-content/uploads/2013/04/Cogito-me-cogitare.pdf.

51. Descartes, "Correspondence," in *The Philosophical Writings of Descartes*, vol. III, 357. French original, Oeuvres 5, Adam and Tannery, 221: "C'est une autre chose d'avoir de conscience de nos pensées au moment où nous pensons, et autre chose de s'en souvenir par après."

52. Descartes, Oeuvres, Adam and Tannery, 7, 481.

53. The earliest known translation as "I am thinking, therefore I am" is from 1872 by Charles Portenfield Krauth. The similar translation, "I am thinking, therefore I exist" of Descartes's correspondence in French ("*je pense, donc je suis*"), appears in *The Philosophical Writings of Descartes* by Cottingham et al.

54. G. W. F. Hegel, *Vorlesungen über die Geschichte der Philosophie* III, Werke 20 (Frankfurt am Main: Suhrkamp, 1986), 127; Hegel, *Lectures on the History of Philosophy III*, trans. R. F. Brown and J. M. Stewart with assistance of H. S. Harris (Berkeley: University of California Press, 1990), 131.

55. Hegel, *Lectures on the History of Philosophy III* (Berkeley: University of California Press, 1990). The English version translated *Bildung* as formation of reason, XXX.

56. Hegel, *Lectures on the History of Philosophy III* (Berkeley: University of California Press, 1990), 127.

57. This passage does not figure in the English translation, which should be in the middle of page 140. This is my own translation. The German reads as follows: "Aber das Denken als Subjekt ist das Denkende, und das ist Ich; das Denken ist das innere Beimirsein, die Unmittelbarkeit bei mir, - es ist das einfache Wissen selbst. Die Unmittelbarkeit ist aber eben dasselbe als was Sein heißt," G. W. F. Hegel, *Vorlesungen über die Geschichte der Philosophie* III, Werke 20 (Frankfurt am Main: Suhrkamp, 1986), 132.

58. G. W. F. Hegel, *Vorlesungen über die Geschichte der Philosophie* III, Werke 20 (Frankfurt am Main: Suhrkamp, 1986), 131, Eng. Hegel, *Lectures on the History of Philosophy III* (Berkeley: University of California Press, 1990), 140.

59. The Latin expression *ars cogitans* means "art of thinking." It was in fact this title that Antoine Arnaud and Pierre Nicole gave to their *Logic*, which represents an important Treatise of the Logic of Port-Royal, published in 1662 under the title *La logique ou l'art de penser*. Eng.

Antoine Arnaud and Pierre Nicole, *Logic or the Art of Thinking*, trans. Jill Vance Buroker (Cambridge: Cambridge University Press, 1996). This work received in the last decades a renewed attention mostly due to the importance Noam Chomsky attributed to it as a percursor of modern transformational generative grammar (see Noam Chomsky, *Cartesian Linguistics: A Chapter in the History of Rationalist Thought*, 3rd ed., edited with a new introduction by James McGilvray (Cambridge: Cambridge University Press, 2009). It differs, however, from the meaning we are giving to the expression "art of thought"; thus, what is being intended in our investigation is the way of thinking the act of thinking while it is taking place.

60. Descartes, "Principles of Philosophy," in *The Philosophical Writings of Descartes*, vol. III, 184.

61. Descartes, "Principles of Philosophy," in *The Philosophical Writings of Descartes*, vol. III, 184.

62. Descartes, "Principles of Philosophy," in *The Philosophical Writings of Descartes*, vol. III, 184.

63. Descartes, "Principles of Philosophy," in *The Philosophical Writings of Descartes*, vol. III, 185.

64. Cf. Christia Mercer, "Descartes's Debt to Teresa of Avila, or Why Should We Work on Women in the History of Philosophy," *Philosophical Studies* 174, no. 10 (2017).

65. Jacques Derrida, *Circonfession (La bibliothèque des Voix)* (Paris: des femmes, 2004).

66. Jean-François Lyotard, *The Confession of Augustine*, trans. Richard Beardsworth (Stanford, CA: Stanford University Press, 2000).

67. Descartes, "Meditations on First Philosophy," in *The Philosophical Writings of Descartes*, vol. II, 12.

68. Descartes, "Discourse on the Method," in *The Philosophical Writings of Descartes*, vol. I, 131.

69. Descartes, "Meditations on First Philosophy," in *The Philosophical Writings of Descartes*, vol. II, 53.

70. Descartes, "Meditations on First Philosophy," in *The Philosophical Writings of Descartes*, vol. II, 53.

71. Descartes, "Discourse on the Method," in *The Philosophical Writings of Descartes*, vol. I, 130–131.

72. Descartes, "Meditations on First Philosophy," in *The Philosophical Writings of Descartes*, vol. II, 13.

73. Descartes, "Meditations on First Philosophy," in *The Philosophical Writings of Descartes*, vol. II, 13.

74. See Derrida's discussions with Foucault about Descartes and madness in Derrida, "Cogito and the History of Madness," in *Writing and Difference*, trans. Alan Bass (London and New York: Routledge, 1978), 36–76. Originally published as "Cogito et histoire de la folie," *Revue de métaphysique et de morale* 68, no. 4 (October–December 1963): 460–494. See also Jean-Luc Nancy's "Mad Derrida: Ipso facto cogitans ac demens," in *Adieu, Derrida*, ed. Costas Douzinas (Basingstoke: Palgrave Macmillan, 2007).

75. Descartes, "Meditations on First Philosophy," in *The Philosophical Writings of Descartes*, vol. II, 13.

76. Martial Gueroult, *Descartes selon l'ordre des raisons* (Paris: Aubier, 1953).

77. Descartes, "Discourse on the Method," in *The Philosophical Writings of Descartes*, vol. I, 130.

78. Descartes, "Discourse on the Method," in *The Philosophical Writings of Descartes*, vol. I, 131.
79. Descartes, "Meditations on First Philosophy," in *The Philosophical Writings of Descartes*, vol. II, 13.
80. Descartes, "Meditations on First Philosophy," in *The Philosophical Writings of Descartes*, vol. II, 13.
81. Maurice Blanchot, *The Space of Literature*, trans. Ann Smock (Lincoln: University of Nebraska Press, 1989). See also my discussions about sleep in Aristotle in Sá Cavalcante Schuback, "The Hermeneutic Slumber: Aristotle's Reflections on Sleep," in *The Bloomsbury Companion to Aristotle*, ed. Claudia Baracchi (New York and London: Bloomsbury Academic, 2014).
82. Descartes, "Meditations on First Philosophy," in *The Philosophical Writings of Descartes*, vol. II, 15.
83. Descartes, "Meditations on First Philosophy," in *The Philosophical Writings of Descartes*, vol. II, 15.
84. Descartes, "Meditations on First Philosophy," in *The Philosophical Writings of Descartes*, vol. II, 15.
85. Descartes, "Meditations on First Philosophy," in *The Philosophical Writings of Descartes*, vol. II, 16.
86. Descartes, "Meditations on First Philosophy," in *The Philosophical Writings of Descartes*, vol. II, 17.
87. Dugald Murdoch, "Abstraction vs. Exclusion," in *The Cambridge Descartes Lexicon* (Cambridge: Cambridge University Press, 2015).
88. Descartes, "Meditations on First Philosophy," in *The Philosophical Writings of Descartes*, vol. II, 18.
89. Descartes, "Meditations on First Philosophy," in *The Philosophical Writings of Descartes*, vol. II, 18; see the Latin original: Oeuvres VII, Adam and Tannery, s. 27, Cogitare?, Hic invenio: cogitatio est; haec sola a me divelli nequit. Ego sum, ego existo; certum eft. Quandiu autem? Nempe quandiu cogito; nam forte etiam fieri posset, si cessarem ab omni cogitatione, ut illico totus efle definerem. Nihil nunc admitto nisi quod necessario sit verum; sum igitur praecise tantùm res cogitans, id est, mens, sive animus, sive intelledus, sive ratio, voces mihi prius significationis ignotae. Sum autem res vera, et vere existens; sed qualis res? Dixi, cogitans.
90. Descartes, "Meditations on First Philosophy," in *The Philosophical Writings of Descartes*, vol. II, 19.
91. Descartes, "Meditations on First Philosophy," in *The Philosophical Writings of Descartes*, vol. II, 24.
92. D. Arbib, ed., *Les Méditations métaphysiques, Objections et réponses de Descartes* (Paris: Vrin, 2019).
93. What Descartes presents here *in nuce*, Bergson developed later with his concept of *durée*, duration. H. Bergson, *Time and Free Will: An Essay on the Immediate Data of Consciousness* (Mineola, NY: Dover, 2001 [1913]).
94. Hegel, *Lectures on the History of Philosophy III* (Berkeley: University of California Press, 1990), 140.
95. Ibid.
96. Descartes, "Meditations on First Philosophy," in *The Philosophical Writings of Descartes*, vol. II, 21.

97. Descartes, "Meditations on First Philosophy," in *The Philosophical Writings of Descartes*, vol. II, 21.

3. Descartes's Performative *Cogito*

1. Descartes, "Discourse on Method," in *The Philosophical Writings of Descartes*, vol. I, 127.
2. Descartes, "Principles of Philosophy," in *The Philosophical Writings of Descartes*, vol. I, pt. 1, § 7, 194–195. (Latin:) Sic autem rejicientes illa omnia, de quibus aliquo modo possumus dubitare, ac etiam, falsa esse fingentes, facilè quidem, supponimus nullum esse Deum, nullum coelum, nulla corpora; nosque etiam ipsos, non habere manus, nec pedes, nec denique ullum corpus, non autem ideò nos qui talia cogitamus nihil esse: repugnat enim ut putemus id quod cogitat eo ipso tempore quo cogitat non existere. Ac proinde haec cognitio, *ego cogito, ergo sum*, est omnium prima & certissima, quae cuilibet ordine philosophanti occurrat.
3. Descartes, "Meditations on First Philosophy," in *The Philosophical Writings of Descartes*, vol. II, 17.
4. Kambouchner, *Descartes n'a pas dit*, 63.
5. Descartes, "The Search for Truth," in *The Philosophical Writings of Descartes*, vol. II, 418–419. The French original of this dialogue has disappeared; only a part could be found at Hannover's Library. Nevertheless, there exists a Latin translation from 1701 published at Amsterdam in Descartes's *Opuscula posthuma*. This part of the dialogue only exists in Latin. The French translation of the Latin translation reads as follows:

> Puisque Poliandre est content, je m'en tiens là également, et je ne pousserai pas plus loin la controverse. Cependant, je ne vois pas qu'il ait beaucoup progressé depuis deux heures que nous avons passes ici à raisonner. Tout ce qu'il a appris, grâce à cette belle method que vous prônez tant, c'est seulement qu'il doute, qu'il pense et qu'il est une chose pensante. Certes, c'est admirable! Voilà beaucoup de paroles pour bien peu de choses. Cela aurait pu être dit en quatre mots et nous aurions tous été d'accord. Quant à moi, si je devais dépenser autant de paroles et de temps pour apprendre une chose de si peu d'importance, j'aurais du mal à m'y résigner. Descartes, *Oeuvres et Lettres* (Paris: Pléiade, Gallimard, 1953), 900.

6. Descartes, "The Search for Truth," in *The Philosophical Writings of Descartes*, vol. II, 419.
7. Descartes, "Second Set of Replies," in *The Philosophical Writings of Descartes*, vol. II, 100.
8. J. L. Austin, *How to Do Things with Words?* (Oxford: Clarendon Press, 1962), 6.
9. Austin, *How to do things with words?* 99.
10. Jaako Hintikka, "'Cogito, ergo sum': Inference or Performance?" *Philosophical Review* 71, no. 2 (1962): 3–32. See also his response to critique made by Julius R. Weinberg and James D. Carney of this paper in "Ergo sum as Inference and a Performance," *Philosophical Review* 72, no. 4 (October 1963): 487–496.
11. Descartes, "Meditations on First Philosophy," in *The Philosophical Writings of Descartes*, vol. II, 16.
12. Jean Wahl, *Du rôle de l'idée de l'instant dans la philosophie de Descartes* (Paris: F. Alcan, 1920).

13. Descartes, "Meditations on First Philosophy," in *The Philosophical Writings of Descartes*, vol. II, 323.
14. Descartes, "Meditations on First Philosophy," in *The Philosophical Writings of Descartes*, vol. II, 323, original, Descartes, *Oeuvres* 7, Adam and Tannery, 481.
15. Descartes, "Meditations on First Philosophy," in *The Philosophical Writings of Descartes*, vol. II, 324, original, Descartes, *Oeuvres* 7, Adam and Tannery, 481.
16. Saint Augustine, *Confessions* (Oxford: Oxford University Press, 1998), 189.
17. See here the poetical meditation by Pascal Quignard, *Mourir de penser* (Paris: Bernard Grasset, 2014), 179.
18. Jean-Luc Nancy, *Ego sum*.
19. French original, *Oeuvres* 5, Adam and Tannery, 221: "C'est une autre chose d'avoir de conscience de nos pensées au moment où nous pensons, et autre chose de s'en souvenir par après"; Descartes, "Correspondence," in *The Philosophical Writings of Descartes*, vol. III, I, 357.
20. Ibid.
21. Descartes, "Rules for the Direction of the Mind," in *The Philosophical Writings of Descartes*, vol. I, 21.
22. Descartes, "Rules for the Direction of the Mind," in *The Philosophical Writings of Descartes*, vol. I, 15.
23. Descartes, "Six Sets of Replies," in *The Philosophical Writings of Descartes*, vol. II, 285.
24. The original title was "L'Homme de René Descartes, et un Traité de la Formation du Foetus du même auteur. Aved des Remarques de Louis de la Forge, Docteur en médicine, demeurant à La Flèche, sur le Traité de l'Homme de René descartes, et sur les Figures par lui inventés." The book was translated into Latin by Florent Schuyl and published in 1662 at Leyden. See the chapters by Cecilia Sjöholm in this book, "Descartes, Images and Drives" and "The Thinking Fetus."
25. Descartes, "Treatise on Man," in *The Philosophical Writings of Descartes*, vol. I, 108.
26. Descartes, "Rules for the Direction of the Mind," in *The Philosophical Writings of Descartes*, vol. I, 107–108.
27. Paul Valéry, "Leonard and the Philosophers," "Introduction to the Method of Leonardo da Vinci," in Complete works by Paul Valéry, vol. 8, Leonardo, Poe, Mallarmé, trans. Malcolm Cowley and James R. Lawler (New York: Princeton University press, 1972).
28. Cf. Leonardo da Vinci. Notebooks, vols. I and II.
29. Descartes, "Treatise on Man," in *The Philosophical Writings of Descartes*, vol. I, 106.
30. Descartes, "Treatise on Man," in *The Philosophical Writings of Descartes*, vol. I, 106.
31. Descartes, "Treatise on Man," in *The Philosophical Writings of Descartes*, vol. I, 100.
32. Descartes, "Treatise on Man," in *The Philosophical Writings of Descartes*, vol. I, 100–101.
33. For an account on the role of aesthetic forms in science and how this directly connected to Descartes philosophy, see Claus Zittel, *Theatrum philosophicum: Descartes und die Rolle ästhetischer Formen in der Wissenschaft* (Berlin: Akademie Verlag, 2009). See also C. Sjöholm in her chapters in this book.
34. Jacques Derrida, *Memoirs d'aveugle. L'autoportrait et autres ruines* (Paris: Editions de la Réunion des musées nationaux, 1990), trans. Pascal-Anne Brault and Michael Naas, *Memoirs of the Blind: The Self-Portrait and Other Ruins* (Chicago and London: University of Chicago Press, 1993).

35. Descartes, "Rules for the Direction of the Mind," in *The Philosophical Writings of Descartes*, vol. I, 29.
36. "Léonard est peintre: Je dis qu'il a la peinture pour philosophie," Paul Valéry, "Leonard et les philosophes," *Pleiade*, vol. 1 (Paris: Gallimard, 1957), 1259.
37. There are nonetheless different readings of Descartes's in Merleau-Ponty. See, for instance, his discussions on the cogito in *The Phenomenology of Perception*.
38. Claude Lefort, introduction from *L'oeil et l'esprit* (Paris: Gallimard, 1985), 26, for Merleau-Ponty's *Eye and Mind* in English. See Maurice Merleau-Ponty, *Eye and Mind* [L'Œil et l'esprit, Paris: Gallimard, 1961] trans. Carleton Dallery in *The Primacy of Perception*, ed. James Edie (Evanston, IL: Northwestern University Press, 1964), 159–190. Revised translation by Michael Smith in *The Merleau-Ponty Aesthetics Reader* (1993), 121–149.
39. Claude Lefort, introduction from *L'oeil et l'esprit*.
40. Merleau-Ponty, *L'oeil et l'esprit*, 18, Eng. version, 162.
41. Ibid., 21, Eng. 163.
42. 23, Eng. 164.
43. 27, Eng. 166.
44. 27–28, Eng. 166.
45. Daniel Giovannangelli, "Descartes et l'énigme de la vision," in *La fiction de l'être: Lectures de la philosophie moderne* (Paris: De Boeck, 1990), 9–18.
46. Merleau-Ponty, *Eye and the Spirit*, op. cit., 34.
47. Ibid., 34.
48. Robert Delaunay, Du cubisme à l'art abstratit, Bibliothèque générale de l'École pratique des hautes études. Section 6, Centre de recherches historiques, Paris, 1957.
49. Merleau-Ponty, *Eye and the Spirit*, op. cit., 34.
50. Cf. translation.
51. Henri Focillon, The Life of Forms in Art (New York: Zone, 1989 [1948]).
52. Merleau-Ponty, L'oeil et l'esprit, 38, Eng. version 170.
53. Merleau-Ponty, L'oeil et l'esprit, 39, Eng. 170.
54. Ikonografi.
55. Descartes, "Optics," in *The Philosophical Writings of Descartes*, vol. I, 165–166.
56. Descartes, "The World," in *The Philosophical Writings of Descartes*, vol. I, 81.
57. Descartes, "The World," in *The Philosophical Writings of Descartes*, vol. I, 81.
58. Lucien Vinciguerra, *La representation excessive: Descartes, Leibniz, Locke, Pascal* (Paris: Presses Universitaires du Septentrion, 2013).
59. M. Foucault, *The Order of Things: An Archaeology of the Human Sciences* (Repr. London: Tavistock/Routledge, 1989 [1974]).
60. Oeil l'esprit, 40, Eng. 171.
61. Ibid., 41, Eng. 171.
62. Ibid.
63. 42, Eng. 172.
64. Darren Hynes, "Parallel Traditions in the Image of Descartes: Iconography, Intention, and Interpretation" *International History Review* 32, no. 4 (December 2010): 575–597.
65. 43, Eng. 172.
66. Ibid.
67. Ibid.

68. "Comme tout serait plus limpide dans notre philosophie si l'on pouvait exorciser ces spectres, en faire des illusions ou des perceptions sans objet, en marge d'un monde sans équivoque! La Dioptrique de Descartes est cette tentative. C'est le bréviaire d'une pensée qui ne veut plus hanter le visible et décide de le reconstruire selon le modèle qu'elle s'en donne. Il vaut la peine de rappeler ce que fut cet essai, et cet échec."

69. Descartes, "Optics," in *The Philosophical Writings of Descartes*, vol. I, 165: "We should, however, recall that our mind can be stimulated by many things other than images—by signs and words, for example, which in no way resemble the things they signify." About the question of language in Descartes, see Pierre-Alain Cahné, *Un autre Descartes: Le philosophe et son langage* (Paris: Vrin, 1980).

70. Ibid.

71. As suggested by Lucien Vinciguerra, *La representation excessive*, 51–106.

72. Descartes, "Meditations on First Philosophy," in *The Philosophical Writings of Descartes*, vol. II, 13.

73. Descartes, "Meditations on First Philosophy," in *The Philosophical Writings of Descartes*, vol. II, 13.

74. Descartes, "Meditations on First Philosophy," in *The Philosophical Writings of Descartes*, vol. II, 13.

75. Descartes, "Meditations on First Philosophy," in *The Philosophical Writings of Descartes*, vol. II, 13.

76. Descartes, "Meditations on First Philosophy," in *The Philosophical Writings of Descartes*, vol. II, 14.

77. Merleau-Ponty, The Doubt of Cézanne in Sense and Non-sense, translated, with a preface, by Hubert L. Dreyfus and Patricia Allen Dreyfus (Evanston, IL: Northwestern University Press, 1982 [1964]), 18.

78. Original, AT VI, 41–42, Descartes, "Discourse on the Method," in *The Philosophical Writings of Descartes*, vol. I, 133.

4. Rhythms of Snow

1. Descartes, *Meteorology*. Throughout, the translation of Paul J. Olscamp will be used, and therefore I will abstain from using the alternative English translation of *Les Météores, The Meteors*, which is sometimes seen. *Discourse on Method, Optics, Geometry and Meteorology* (Indianapolis, IN: Hackett, 2001), 312, AT VI, 299.

2. Descartes, *Meteorology*, 313, AT VI, 300.

3. Steven Nadler, *The Philosopher, the Priest and the Painter* (Princeton, NJ: Princeton University Press, 2013), 20.

4. Descartes, *Meteorology*, 321, AT VI 311.

5. Descartes, *Meteorology*, 329, AT VI, 321.

6. In Maurice Merleau-Ponty's seminar on nature, Descartes is considered as an inventor of a modern concept of nature, closer to a positivist conception than a rationalist one. *La nature* (Paris: Editions du Seuil, 1995) 26, 31.

7. See, for instance, Daniel Dennett, *Content and Consciousness* (London: Routledge, 1999); Antonia Damasio, *Descartes Error: Emotion, Reason and the Human Brain* (London: Penguin, 2005).

8. See, for instance, Theo Verbeer, "The Invention of Nature," 149–168; Veronique Foti, "Descartes' Intellectual and Corporeal Memories," 591–604; Gordon Baker, "The Senses and Witnesses," 604–630; and Catherine Wilson, "Descartes and the Corporeal Mind; Some Implications of the Regius Affair," 659–680 in *Descartes' Natural Philosophy*, ed. Stephen Gaukroger.

9. Lucian Petrescu has shown how the matter analyzed is not considered in terms of the "real distinction" or the res extensa but is the result of a deduction following mechanical principles. "Cartesian Meteors and Scholastic Meteors: Descartes against the School in 1637," *Journal of the History of Ideas* 76, no. 1 (2015): 25–45.

10. Dennis Sepper has demonstrated the many varieties that this relation may take in Descartes's writings in a seminal book on *Descartes's Imagination: Proportion, Images and the Activity of Thinking* (Berkeley: University of California Press, 1996). Imagination is much more than the capacity of the mind to represent things as internal images outside of an empirical reality; it is also "phantasia," presented like an organ of the body in rule twelve in *Rules of the Direction of the Mind* (Sepper, 30); it is the mathematical-physical imagery of proportion, the representation of dreams, and so on.

11. Svante Nordin, *Filosofins historia: det västerländska förnuftets historia från Thales till postmodernismen* (Lund: Studentlitteratur, 2017), 100.

12. See, for example, the letter to Mersenne where Descartes says that he wishes to demonstrate nature's building blocks through the most beautiful examples. Letter to Mersenne, January 1630 *Oeuvres de Descartes*, ed. Charles Adam and Paul Tannery (Paris: Vrin, 1969), Tome III, 492 (the complete works in French will be referred to as AT). Cf. also *Principles of Philosophy* in *The Philosophical Writings of Descartes* I, ed. and trans. John Cottingham (Cambridge: Cambridge University Press, 1985), 288.

13. Descartes, *Meteorology*, 263, AT VI, 231.

14. Claus Zittel, *Theatrum Philosophicum Descartes und die Rolle ästhetischer Formen in die Wissenschaft* (Berlin: Akademie Verlag, 2009), 193. As Craig Martin has shown, the Aristotelian tradition is more present than Descartes admits when it comes to presenting what counts as the field of meteorology as such, especially in the work presented as part of *Le Monde*. In the version published in 1937, the atomist inclination is more stressed. *Renaissance Meteorology, Pomponazzi to Descartes* (Baltimore, MD: Johns Hopkins University Press, 2011), 135–147.

15. Merleau-Ponty, *La nature*, 26, 31.

16. Letter from October 2017, sent to Plempius to forward to his critique Fromondus, T I 402–409. As Descartes scholars have noted, *Principles of Philosophy* describes a methodological movement from presenting scientific "suppositions" in the *Meteorology* and *Optics*, to deductions of cosmological principles in the third part of *Principles*. Nadler, *Philosopher, the Priest and the Painter*, 122–124.

17. Descartes, *Rules for the Direction of the Mind*, 41, image 414.

18. Descartes, *Meteorology*, 283 AT VI, 260.

19. Descartes witnessed avalanches himself (*Meteorology*, 325) but also retold stories of augeries and supernatural phenomena.

20. Descartes speaks about this rapture as "wonder," *Meteorology*, 263, AT VI, 231.

21. Descartes to Huygens, July 15, 1636, AT I, 611. He sometimes calls for a good "artisan"—craftsman—and a mathematician, indicating that "painter" and "artisan" are not widely distinct here. See, for instance, the letter from Huygens to Descartes, June 15, 1636, AT

I, 344. Van Schooten also made the figures for *Principles of Philosophy*; Geneviève Rodis-Lewis, *Descartes* (Paris: Calmann-Lévy, 1995), 214, 300.

22. Descartes to Mersenne, March 1636, AT I, 339.

23. Descartes to Mersenne, January 1630, AT I, 492.

24. "A painter cannot represent all the different sides of a solid body equally well on his flat canvas, and so he chooses one of the principle ones, sets it facing the light, and shades the others so as to make them stand out only when viewed from the persoective of the chosen side. In just the same way, fearing that I could not put everything I had in my mind into my discourse, I undertook merely to expund quite fully what I understood about light." *Discourse on Method*, The Philosophical Writings of Descartes I, 132, AT VI, 42–43.

25. Antoine Furetière, *Dictionnaire universel* contenant generalement tous les mots françois, tant vieux que modernes, & les termes de toutes les sciences et des arts (1690).

26. Descartes to Mersenne, January 1630 AT I, 492.

27. This is the case throughout in the translation of *Meteorology*; see, for instance, AT VI where Descartes speaks of "figures & grosseurs," which in English becomes shapes and sizes. *Meteorology*, 264, AT VI, 232.

28. Cf. The translation into "diagram" in http://www.earlymoderntexts.com/assets/pdfs/descartes1619_1.pdf.

29. Sepper, *Descartes Imagination*, 51.

30. Sybille Krämer, "Epistemology of the Line. Reflections on the Diagrammatical Mind", in Alexander Gerner and Olga Pombo (Eds.), *Studies in Diagrammatology and Diagram Praxis* (London: College Publications, 2010), 13–38.

31. Jean-Luc Marion, *Sur l'Ontologie Grise de Descartes* (Paris: Vrin, 1981), 116–118.

32. Descartes, rule twelve in *Rules for the Direction of the Mind*, The Philosophical Writings of Descartes I, 38–40, AT X, 413. See also the discussion on figures of rhythm further below.

33. Descartes, rule nine in *Rules for the Direction of the Mind*, 33, AT X, 400.

34. Descartes, rule twelve in *Rules for the Direction of the Mind*, 43, AT X, 417.

35. Dennis Sepper has shown that Descartes's early notion of figures, for instance in the *Compendium on Music*, precedes his later metaphysics and therefore cannot be reduced to "ideas" of the mind, or representation. Figures can be conceived as parts of the whole, as minimal modes of representation, but they also refer to some kind of sensible experience— "all figuration requires activity—the minumum of which is like conceiving figures mentally or sizing up an object in a glance." *Descartes Imagination*, 51.

36. Cf. As Sybille Krämer ("Epistemology of the Line: Reflections on the Diagrammatical Mind," in *Studies in Diagrammatology and Diagram Praxis*, ed. Alexander Gerner and Olga Pombo [London: College Publications, 2010], 13–38) has argued, Descartes transforms geometry into a figurative "language of the eye" that not only represents the objects but constitutes them; the objects arise through the operation.

37. Descartes, rule fifteen in *Rules for the Direction of the Mind*, 65, AT X, 452.

38. Cf. Raz Chen-Moris and Ofer Gal, *Baroque Science* (Chicago: University of Chicago Press, 2013), 238.

39. Descartes to Mersenne, March 1636, AT I, 340, translation of author. A translation using "shapes" rather than figures is to be found in *The Philosophical Writings of Descartes* III, 51.

40. Gassendi was angry not to have been quoted on this phenomena, which Descartes took from Reneri. According to Rodis-Lewis (*Descartes* [Paris: Calmann-Lévy, 1995], 123–124), Descartes had decided to use this exceptional phenomenon for speculations on physics in general.

41. Descartes to Mersenne, March 1636, AT I, 340.

42. Susanna Berger has used this analogy in explaining the role of printed images in Descartes's work. *The Art of Philosophy: Visual Thinking in Europe from the Late Renaissance to the Early Enlightenment* (Princeton, NJ: Princeton University Press, 2017), 184–186. Helen Hattab has also noted the use of art in Descartes's physics, in conjunction with a move away from Aristotelian physics beginning from self-evident principles. Descartes assumes problems of physics to rest on geometrical forms, and he demonstrates this in his hypotheses of particles in the *Meteorology*. "Descartes Mechanical but Not Mechanistic Physics," in *The Oxford Handbook of Descartes and Cartesianism*, ed. Steven Nadler, Tad M. Schmaltz, and Delphine Antoine-Mahut (Oxford: Oxford University Press, 2019) 127–137. Hattab also shows that the natural philosophy does not rest on theories of extended forms present in the *Meditations*: "Applying geometrical principles enables the derivation of many diverse effects," 136.

43. René Descartes, *Optics*, in *Discourse on Method, Optics, Geometry and Meteorology*, transl. Paul J Olscamp (Cambridge: Hackett, 2001), 90.

44. Alain Baillet, *La Vie de Monsieur Descartes*, Tome I (Paris: 1691), 305.

45. Huygens to Descartes, October 28, 1635, AT I, 325–328.

46. This combination of skills also occurs in Descartes's plan for an academy of the arts in Paris—the teachers were to know arts, mathematics, and physics. It may have never come to fruition, but it makes its mark on his work. AT XI, 659. See also Alain Baillet, *La Vie de Monsieur Descartes*, Tome II, 433–434.

47. Descartes to Huygens, November 1, 1635, AT I, 331.

48. Descartes to Beeckman, April 23, 1619, *The Philosophical Writings of Descartes*, 3, AT X, 157. As Dennis Sepper has shown, there is a direct link between Descartes's concept of imagination—which Sepper sees as an overall key to his philosophy—and his use of figures. Therefore, there is a natural relation also between the figures of algebra and geometry and those of music, for instance. "Figuring Things Out: Figurate Problem-Solving in the Early Descartes," in *Descartes' Natural Philosophy*, 238–239. Cf. also Sybille Krämer, *Berechenbare Vernunft: Kalkül und Rationalismus im 17. Jahrhundert* (Berlin and New York: De Gruyter, 1991), 169–220.

49. See note 38. One may, as Dennis Sepper has done, confer the intelligibility of the universe to "analogies" of a divine source, which is also what makes algebra meaningful despite its lack of object. "Figuring Things Out: Figurate Problem-Solving in the Early Descartes," in *Descartes' Natural Philosophy*, 245.

50. Zittel has pointed this out, *Theatrum Philosophicum Descartes*, 206–208.

51. Descartes to Huygens, June 11, 1636, AT I, 605–606.

52. Huygens to Descartes, June 15, 1636, AT I, 344, 607.

53. Descartes to Mersenne, May 25, 1637, AT I, 378. Particles of different shapes and sizes are "never so well arrranged, nor so exactly joined together, that there do not remain many spaces around them." Descartes, *Meteorology*, 264, AT VI, 232.

54. Cf. Douglas Jesseph "Hobbes and Descartes," in *The Oxford Handbook of Descartes and* Cartesianism, ed. Steven Nadler, Tad M. Schmaltz, and Delphine Antoine-Mahut (Oxford: Oxford University Press, 2019), 623–624.

55. According to Daniel Garber, Descartes's notion of particulars develops over time and is used in different ways in different works. The essays are to be read and understood against *Principles of Philosophy*, where experience may lead up to conjectures of how things are constituted. The proof is then not measured against any notion of truth but rather how well it may work in future experiences and experimentation. *Descartes Embodied: Reading*

Cartesian Philosophy through Cartesian Science (Cambridge: Cambridge University Press, 2001), 122–127.

56. Descartes to Mersenne, January 9, 1639, AT I, 482–484.
57. Huygens to Descartes, October 28, 1635, AT I, 325–328.
58. Copy at Wrangelska biblioteket Roggebiblioteket, Strängnäs.
59. According to Christoph Lüthy ("Where Logical Necessity Becomes Visual Persuasion," in *Transmitting Knowledge: Words, Images and Instruments in Early Modern Europe*, ed. Sachiko Kusukawa and Ian Maclean [Oxford: Oxford University Press, 2006], 99), the readers of Descartes's own times may have thought of the images as proofs and the repetition would have underscored that.
60. Edmund Husserl, *Phantasy, Image Consciousness and Memory*, trans John B. Brough, *The Collected Works of Husserl*, vol. XI (Dordrecht: Springer, 2005), 646–647.
61. Descartes to Golius, May 19, 1635, *The Philosophical Writings of Descartes* III, 48–49, AT I, 318–320.
62. The English translation has "admirable," *Meteorology*, 263. The French original "admirable," however, is a concept that brings us to the passion of wonder, explored in *Les Passions de l'ame, Passions of the Soul*.
63. Descartes, *Passions of the Soul*, 52, AT XI, 373.
64. Descartes, *Passions of the Soul*, 58, AT XI, 381.
65. Descartes, *Meteorology*, 361, AT VI, 366.
66. Descartes, rule twelve in *Rules for the Direction of the Mind*, 49–50, AT X, 426–428.
67. Brown has argued that there is a difference between the specific practice of the *Wunderkammer* and the scientific ideals that were equally explored in Descartes, arguing that wonder may both raise the desire to acquire new knowledge and free us from "bad theories": "The test of a good theory is how well it unlocks the secrets and marvels of nature and frees us from wonder." Deborah J. Brown, *Descartes and the Passionate Mind* (Cambridge: Cambridge University Press, 2006), 145–150.
68. Craig Martin, *Renaissance Meteorology*, 127. As Martin has shown, "wonder" was a much used concept in renaissance meteorology, 132–134.
69. Descartes, *Principles of Philosophy*, 89, AT VIIIA.
70. Descartes to Reneri, June 2, 1631, AT I, 205.
71. Descartes, *Meteorology*, 264, AT VI, 232.
72. Descartes, *Meteorology*, 299–301, AT VI, 281–285.
73. See, for instance, fig. 1, Descartes, *Meteorology*, 270, AT VI, 242.
74. Descartes to Huygens, October 30, 1636, AT I, 614. Unfortunately, van Schooten did not altogether succeed in following that through since Hobbes had reason to complain about the placement of an image in *Optics*; Hobbes to Mersenne for Descartes, March 30, 1641, AT III, 348.
75. Descartes to Huygens, October 30, 1636, AT I, 614. Translation by author.
76. For an essay that has captured the precise observations on the discourse on salt, see Roger Ariew, *The A to Z of Descartes and Cartesian Philosophy*, Roger Ariew et al. (Lanham, MD: Scarecrow, 2010), 179.
77. *L'homme de Réne Descartes: Et un traitté de la formation du fotetus du mesme autheur. Avec les Remarques de Louys de la Forge sur le Traitté de l'homme de René Descartes; et sur les figures par luy inventée*s, Paris, 1664.
78. Descartes, *Meteorology*, 277–278, AT VI, 251–254.
79. Descartes, *Meteorology*, 275–276, AT VI, 249–251.
80. Descartes, *Meteorology*, 285, AT VI, 261–262.

81. Letter to Plempius, December 20, 1637, AT I, 475–477. *The Philosophical Writings of Descartes* III, 77.
82. Descartes, *Principles of Philosophy*, 288, AT VIIIA, 326.
83. See for instance Zittel, who calls the images a kind of "morphological alphabet." *Theatrum Philosophicum Descartes*, 241, 279.
84. Zittel, *Theatrum Philosophicum Descartes*, 299–300.
85. "It is in this twilight zone that Descartes illustration perform their illuminating function: where the indeterminacy of 'clear and distinct ideas' threatens to lead to an impasse, Descartes feeds the outer eye, and thanks to it the recipient mind, with a type of 'clarity' whose epistemological source is excitingly unclear." Lüthy, "Where Logical Necessity Becomes Visual Persuasion," 126. "The clarity and distinctness of the illustration serve to hide the problems in the argument, which is about as circular as the sling's motion," 111. Through the drawings, Descartes becomes what he is not: a mechanical atomist, Lüthy argues, 124.
86. After Descartes, speculations on atoms and particles became very popular in the 1660–1670s, leading to such reductionism. Lüthy, "Where Logical Necessity Becomes Visual Persuasion," 131.
87. Descartes, *Meteorology*, 321, AT VI, 311.
88. Descartes, rule twelve, *Rules for the Direction of the Mind*, *The Philosophical Writings of Descartes* I, 41, AT X, 413–414.
89. Descartes, *Meteorology*, 339, AT VI, 336.
90. Descartes, *Meteorology*, 338, AT VI, 335.
91. Descartes, rule twelve, *Rules for the Direction of the Mind*, *The Philosophical Writings of Descartes* I, 41, AT X, 413–414.
92. Descartes, rule twelve, *Rules for the Direction of the Mind*, *The Philosophical Writings of Descartes* I, 40, AT X, 413.
93. SERRES.
94. *Abrégé de musique* in *Oeuvres complètes*, ed. Jeanne-Marie Beyssade and Denis Kambouchner (Paris: Gallimard, 2016), 149. This is also the way Descartes approaches affects in *Passions of the Soul*. The translation of Robert has "physicist." *Compendium on Music*, 11, AT X, 89.
95. Descartes, *Compendium on Music*, 14–16. AT X, 95–96.
96. Mersenne to Descartes, December 1638, AT II, 465.
97. See Kasper Levin, Tone Roald, and Bjarne Sode Funch, "Visual Art and the Rhythm of Experience," *Journal of Aesthetics and Art Criticism* 77, no. 3, 281–293. The article argues that rhythm is immanent to the aesthetic domain and that it gathers the senses and actualizes modes of absorption in perception and affect.
98. Edmund Husserl, *Analyses Concerning Passive and Active Synthesis: Lectures on Transcendental Logic*, trans. Anthony Steinbock, *The Collected Works of Husserl* vol. IX (Dordrecht: Kluwer, 2001), 587.
99. See, for instance, Husserl, *Phantasy, Image, Consciousness and Memory*, 189–190.
100. Maurice Merleau-Ponty, *The World of Perception* (London Routledge, 2008), 57.
101. Merleau-Ponty, *World of Perception*, 57–58.
102. Glen Mazis, *Merleau-Ponty and the Face of the World: Silence, Ethics, Imagination, and Poetic Ontology* (Albany: State University of New York Press, 2016), 204.
103. Jessica Wiskus, *The Rhythm of Thought: Art, Literature, and Music after Merleau-Ponty* (Chicago: University of Chicago Press, 2013), 53.

104. She quotes Merleau-Ponty: "The contour of an object conceived as a line encircling the object belongs not to the visible world but to geometry. If one outlines the shape of an apple with a continuous line, one makes an object of the shape, whereas the contour is rather the ideal towards which the sides of the apple recede in depth. / . . . / That is why Cezanne follows the swelling in modulating colors and indicates several outlines in blue." Through Wiskus, *Rhythm of Thought*, 55.

105. Cf. Jamie Lorimer, "Aesthetics for Post-Human Worlds: Difference, Expertise and Ethics," *Dialogues in Human Geography* 2, no. 3 (2013): 284–287.

106. Descartes, rule fourteen, *Rules for the Direction of the Mind*, *The Philosophical Writings of Descartes* I, 62, AT X, 446.

107. Descartes, *Compendium on Music*, 14–15, AT X, 95.

108. Descartes, *Compendium on Music*, 51–52, AT X, 140–141.

109. Descartes, rule ten, *Rules for the Direction of the Mind*, *The Philosophical Writings of Descartes* I, 35, AT X, 404.

110. In this context I differ from Lüthy who says that Descartes first argues for an unimaginable res extensa, and then that he attempts to prove the solidity of the res extensa. As I have wanted to argue, the res extensa has a solidity that is not imagined, but figured—that is, made accessible through the senses. Cf. Lüthy, "Where Logical Necessity Becomes Visual Persuasion."

111. Descartes, *Principles of Philosophy*, *The Philosophical Writings of Descartes* I, 288, AT VIIIA, 325–326.

112. As Daniel Garber has remarked, the essays do not provide a natural philosophy where a knowledge of certainty is presented; instead, we are confronted with hypothesis concerning the nature of light, water, wind, and so on. Only in the eighth discourse in *Meteorology*, on the rainbow, is *Discourse on Method* referenced. Daniel Garber, *Descartes' Metaphysical Physics* (Chicago: University of Chicago Press, 1992), 45–46.

113. Note quoted through Renaud Barbaras, "Merleau-Ponty and Nature," *Research in Phenomenology* 31, no. 1 (2001): 22–38.

114. Barbaras, "Merleau-Ponty and Nature," 31.

115. With Descartes begins "the modern appropriation of feeling by thinking," Mario Perniola (*The Sex Appeal of the Inorganic*, trans. Massimo Verdicchio [London: Continuum, 2005], 8) argues, who sees that the mind-body dualism is not the most central problem but rather the "thing" that thinks beyond all substances.

116. Descartes, *Meteorology*, 321, AT VI, 311.

117. René Descartes, *Compendium on Music*, 14–15, AT X, 95–96.

118. Descartes rule twelve, *Rules for the Direction of the Mind*, *The Philosophical Writings of Descartes* I, 39, AT X, 411.

5. Thinking through Lines with Descartes

1. See Jurgis Baltrušaitis, *Anamorphic Art* (Cambridge: Chadwick-Healey, 1977). Baltrušaitis has in this book a chapter on Descartes, where he shows Descartes's interests in anamorphic or paradoxical perspective in connection with his thoughts on the automata, illusionary machines, optical illusions, toys, and constructions that produce extravagant and unnatural foreshortenings, optical diversions, flourishing tremendously at that time. See ibid., 61–70.

2. A. De Rosa, *Perspective, Catoptric and Artificial Magic*, ed. by Jean François Nicéron. With critical editions of *La Perspective Curieuse* (Paris, 1638) and of the *Thaumaturgus Opticus* (Paris, 1646), (Roma: Aracne edizioni, 2013).

3. In a letter to Mersenne dated April 30, 1639, AT II, 539–540, Descartes tells Mersenne that he has received Niceron's work and speaks of it with admiration.

4. Lucien Vinciguerra considers that anamorphosis is an image that suits better to Locke's understanding of confused ideas. He quotes a passage from § 29 from Locke's essays that reads: "The author takes anamorphosis for illusionary perspective that confuses the things for showing things. He does not consider that at stake here is indeed the movement of seeing and not in first place what is being showed." See Lucien Vinciguerra, *La représentation excessive: Descartes, Leibniz, Locke, Pascal* (Paris: Presses Universitaires du Septentrion, 2013), 19–120.

5. Bossuet, "Sermon sur la providence," prêché à Dijon, en la Sainte-Chapelle, le IIIe dimanche après Pâques, 7 mai 1656, Texte établi et annoté par Bernard Velat, Yvonne Champailler in *Sur la brièveté de la vie* (Paris: Gallimard, 2017), 19–53. In English it reads:

> When I consider in myself the arrangement of human things, confused, uneven, irregular, I often compare it to certain paintings that one finds quite usually in the libraries of the curious as a game of perspective. The first sight shows only shapeless features and a confused mixture of colors which seem to be either the trial of some apprentice or the play of some child rather than the work of a learned hand. But as soon as the one who knows the secret makes you look at it from a certain place, as soon as all the uneven lines come together in a certain way in our sight, all the confusion is unraveled, and you see a face appear with its lineaments and proportions, where it previously had no appearance of human form. It seems to me, Gentlemen, a rather natural picture of the world, of its apparent confusion and its hidden correctness, that we can never notice except by looking at it from a certain point that faith in Jesus Christ discovers.

6. Descartes, "Optics," in *The Philosophical Writings of Descartes* I, 213.

7. Descartes, AT X, 92, 94.

8. Jean Wahl, *Du rôle de l'idée de l'instant dans la philosophie de Descartes* (Paris: Felix Alcan, 1920): "c'est par un acte instantanée de la pensée que l'esprit pourra se délivrer de son doute."

9. Descartes, "Conversation with Burman," in *The Philosophical Writings of Descartes* III, 333.

10. Descartes, "Conversation with Burman," in *The Philosophical Writings of Descartes* III, 335.

11. Descartes, "Conversation with Burman," in *The Philosophical Writings of Descartes* III, 335.

12. Jean-Luc Nancy, *Ego sum*, trans. Marie-Eve Morin (New York: Fordham University Press, 2016), 23–24.

13. Descartes, "Optics," in *The Philosophical Writings of Descartes* I, 166.

14. Victor I. Stoichita, *A Short History of the Shadow* (London: Reaktion, 1997), specially chapter 3, "A Shadow on the Painting," 89–122.

15. André Gide, *Journal 1889–1939* (Paris: Gallimard, Pléiade, 1948), 41, cf. *Journals 1889–1949*, trans. J. O'Brien (London: Penguin, 198), 30–31.

In a work of art, I rather like to find thus transposed, at the level of the characters, the subject of the work itself. Nothing shed more light on the work or displays the proportions of the whole work more accurately. Thus, in paintings by Memling or Quentin Metzys, a small dark convex mirror reflects, in its turn, the interior of the room in which the action of the painting takes place. Thus, in a slightly different way, in Velazquez' *La Meninas*. Finally, in literature, there is the scene in which a play is acted in *Hamlet*; this also happens in many other plays. In *Wilhelm Meister*, there are the puppet shows and the festivities in the castle. In *The Fall of the House of Usher*, there is the piece that is read to Roderick, etc. one of these examples is absolutely accurate. What would be more accurate, and what would explain better what I'd wanted to do in my *Cahiers*, in *Narcisse* and in *La Tentative*, would be a comparison with the device from heraldry that involves putting a second representation of the original shield "en abyme" within it.

16. Allain Robbe-Grillet, *Pour un nouveau roman* (Paris: Editions de Minuit, 1963).

17. "Est mise en abyme toute enclave entretenant une relation de similitude avec l'eouvre qui la contient," Lucien Dällenbach, *Le récit spéculaire: Essai sur la misen en abyme* (Paris: editions du Seuil, 1977), 18, trans. Jeremy Whiteley with Emma Hughes, *The Mirror in the Text* (Cambridge: Polity, 1989), 8.

18. For a recent discussion of myse en abyme as central for post-Heideggerian philosophy, see Iddo Dickmann, *The Little Crystalline Seed: The Ontological Significance of Mise en Abyme in Post-Heideggerian Thought* (New York: SUNY Press, 2020).

19. Jean Wahl, *Du rôle de l'idée de l'instant dans la philosophie de Descartes*.

20. Jean Lafond, "Descartes philosophe et écrivain," *Revue Philosophique de la France Et de l'Etranger* 182, no. 4 (1992): 421–438.

21. Durs Grünbein, *Der Cartesische Taucher* (Frankfurt am Main: Suhrkamp Verlag, 2008).

22. Cf. Bruno Clément, "La langue claire de Descartes," Mis en ligne sur Cairn.info le 23/10/2009 https://doi.org/10.3917/rdes.065.0020.

23. Descartes, "Discourse on the Method," in *The Philosophical Writings of Descartes* I, 113–114.

24. Jacques Derrida, *Eyes of the University: Right to Philosophy 2*, trans. Jan Plug et al. (Stanford, CA: Stanford University Press, 2004).

25. Descartes, "Discourse on the Method," in *The Philosophical Writings of Descartes* I, 151.

26. Descartes, AT VI, 41–42, "Discourse on the Method," in *The Philosophical Writings of Descartes* I, 132.

27. In the Dialogue *Search for Truth*, Descartes puts in the mouth of Epistemon the view that "the intellect is like an excellent painter who is called upon to put the finishing touches to a bad picture sketched out by a young apprentice. It would be futile for him to employ the rules of his art in correcting the picture little by little, a bit here and a bit there, and in adding with his own hand all that is lacking in it, if, despite his best efforts, he could never remove every major fault, since the drawing was badly sketched from the beginning, the figures badly placed, and the proportions badly observed." "Search for Truth," in *The Philosophical Writings of Descartes* II, 406.

28. Nancy, *Ego sum*, Eng trans., 51.

29. In a much more general and different perspective, for an account about the relation between Descartes's philosophical views and Poussin's view on art and painting, see

Genevieve Rodis-Lewis, "Descartes et Poussin," *Boulletin de Société d'étude du XVII eme siècle* 23 (1953): 520–549.

30. Descartes. "Rules for the Direction of the Mind," in *The Philosophical Writings of Descartes* I, 41.

31. Nancy, *Ego sum*, Eng. trans., 31.

32. Ibid. Nancy notes that calamus is an ancient reed pen and that Descartes's portraying can be connected to Pascal's words in *Pensées* § 347 that reads: "Man is but a reed, the most feeble thing in nature; but he is a thinking reed."

33. Paul Valéry, Cahiers / 21, 1938–1939 (Paris: Centre National de la Recherche Scientifique, 1960), 164. Valéry speaks also of the oeil-tact in Cahiers / 29, 1944–1945 (Paris: Centre National de la Recherche Scientifique, 1961), 435.

34. Descartes, "Principles of Philosophy," in *The Philosophical Writings of Descartes* I, 197.

35. AT I, 137–138.

36. Descartes, "Principles of Philosophy," in *The Philosophical Writings of Descartes* I, 185.

37. Jacques Derrida, *Du droit à la philosophie* (Paris: Galilée, 1990), 336, Eng. trans. *Eyes of the University: Right to Philosophy 2*.

38. See, among others, Jonathan Rée, "Descartes's Commedy," in *Philosophical Tales: An Essay on Philosophy and Literature* (London: Methuen, 1987).

39. Maurice Muller, *De Descartes à Marcel Proust* (Paris: La Baconnière, 1947); Jeanne Marie Gagnebin, "Entre le rêve et la veille: Qui suis-je ?" in *Études théologiques et religieuses* 80, no. 2 (2005): 201–214.

40. On the relation between Beckett and Descartes, see Edward Bizub, *Beckett et Descartes dans l'œuf—Aux sources de l'œuvre beckettienne: de Whoroscope à Godot*; and Helena Martins, "Words (mis)trusted" in *Dis-orientations: Philosophy, Literature and the Lost Grounds of Modernity*, ed. Marcia Sá Cavalcante Schuback and Tora Lane (London: Rowman & Littlefield, 2015), 159–173.

41. Rée, *Philosphical Tales*.

42. AT VI, 4; I, 112.

43. AT XI, 31; I, 90.

44. Nancy, *Ergo sum*, 74.

45. Emile Benveniste, "Analytic Philosophy and Language," in *Problems of General Linguistics*, trans. Mary Elisabeth Meck (Miami, FL: University of Miami Press, 1971), I: 236; Nancy's comments, *Ego sum*, 84–86. See also J.-M. Beyssade, *La philosophie première de Descartes: le temps et la cohérence de la métaphysique* (Paris: Flammarion, 1979), 250–251, who points out how the cogito is not tacit but an autonomous moment in which its moment of articulation emerges.

46. Descartes, "Discourse on the Method," in *The Philosophical Writings of Descartes* I, 151.

47. Derrida, *Eyes of the University*, 317f.

48. Michel de Certeau, Dominique Julia, and Jacques Revel, *Une politique de la langue: la Révolution française et les patois: l'enquête de Grégoire* (Paris: Gallimard, 1975).

49. Letter to Pere Vatier, January 24, 1638.

50. See also here Derrida, *Eyes of the University*, on Descartes's thoughts on language.

51. This sounding connection between the French "je" (I) and the German "je," each time, is at the core of several meditation of Jean-Luc Nancy on the "Je," the "ego," as pure utterance.

52. Rée, *Philosophical Tales*, 19.

53. Cit. in Rée, *Philosophical Tales*, 26.

54. Descartes 1596–1650; Shakespeare 1564–1616; Cervantes 1547–1616.
55. Pierre Guenancia, "Le modèle du théâtre chez Descartes," *Revue de métaphysique et de moral* 2, no. 98 (2018): 199–214.
56. Descartes, "Principles of Philosophy," in *The Philosophical Writings of Descartes* I, 190.
57. Descartes, "Principles of Philosophy," in *The Philosophical Writings of Descartes* I, 190.
58. Descartes, "Principles of Philosophy," in *The Philosophical Writings of Descartes* I, 190.
59. Plato, 189 e, Plato in Twelve Volumes, vol. 12, trans. Harold N. Fowler (Cambridge, MA: Harvard University Press; London: William Heinemann, 1921).
60. AT VIII, 7, Descartes, "Principles of Philosophy," in *The Philosophical Writings of Descartes* I, n.9, 195.
61. Descartes, "Principles of Philosophy," in *The Philosophical Writings of Descartes* I, n.197, 284.
62. Descartes, "Principles of Philosophy," in *The Philosophical Writings of Descartes* I, n.197, 284.
63. Descartes, "Principles of Philosophy," in *The Philosophical Writings of Descartes* I, n.197, 284.
64. Descartes, "The Passions of the Soul," in *The Philosophical Writings of Descartes* I, n.70, 353.
65. Descartes, "The Passions of the Soul," in *The Philosophical Writings of Descartes* I, n.79, 356.
66. Descartes, "The Passions of the Soul," in *The Philosophical Writings of Descartes* I, n.79, 356.

6. The Gaze, Images, and Drives

1. Descartes, *Meditations, The Philosophical Writings of Descartes* II, 15, AT VII, 22–23.
2. It has been pointed out by Alexander Schlutz (*Mind's World* [Seattle: University of Washington Press, 2009], 36–80) that Descartes's imagination resembles Aristotle's *phantasia*: it entails the creation of mental representations of images and figures. It is the concept of imagination above all that offers a bridge between ancient systems of knowledge and modern conceptions of subjectivity. Here Descartes holds a key position.
3. Descartes, *Meditations, The Philosophical Writings of Descartes* II, 13, AT VII, 19.
4. Descartes, *Meditations, The Philosophical Writings of Descartes* II, 24, AT VII, 34.
5. Daniel Dennett, *Consciousness Explained* (New York: Little Brown & Co., 1991), 106.
6. As Jacques Lacan has noted, *Four Concepts of Psychoanalysis*, trans. Alan Sheridan (New York: Norton, 1986), 141.
7. Dumont, *Descartes et l'esthetique*, 62–69.
8. Lacan, *Four Concepts of Psychoanalysis*, 44.
9. See, for instance, Mladen Dolar, "Cogito as the Subject of the Unconscious," in *Cogito and the Unconsious*, ed. Slavoj Zizek (Cambridge, MA: MIT Press, 1998), 21.
10. *Les Olympique*, 22. The accuracy of these notes have been contested by Fernand Hallyn, *Les Olympiques de Descartes* (Genève: Librarie DROZ, 1995), 21.
11. Freud, "Some Dreams of Descartes': A Letter to Maxime Leroy." Standard Edition XXI, 203–204.
12. Sigmund Freud, *Interpretation of Dreams*, Standard Edition IV-V (London: Hogarth, 1953), 32.

13. Freud, *Interpretation of Dreams*, SE V, 540.
14. Freud, *Interpretation of Dreams*, SE V 540.
15. Descartes, *Passions of the Soul*, 43, AT XI, 362.
16. Descartes, *Passions of the Soul*, 33, AT XI, 348.
17. Descartes, *Passions of the Soul*, 31, AT XI, 346.
18. Descartes, *Passions of the Soul*, 29, AT XI, 344–345.
19. Descartes, *Passions of the Soul*, 33, AT XI, 348.
20. Merleau-Ponty, "Eye and Mind," in *The Primacy of Perception*, trans. Carleton Dallery, rev. Michael Smith (Evanston, IL: Northwestern University Press, 1964), 159–190.
21. Descartes, *Optics, The Philosophical Writings of Descartes* I, 165, AT VI, 113.
22. Husserl, *Phantasy, Image Consciousness and Memory*, 607.
23. Descartes, *Passions of the Soul*, 33, AT XI, 348.
24. Descartes, *Meditations, The Philosophical Writings of Descartes* II, 13, AT VII, 19–20.
25. Descartes, *Optics, The Philosophical Writings of Descartes* I, 165, AT VI, 112.
26. Maurice Merleau-Ponty: "Eye and Mind," in *The Merleau-Ponty Aesthetics Reader*, ed. Galen Johnson, trans. Michael Smith (Evanston, IL: Northwestern University Press, 1993), 132.
27. Descartes, *Passions of the Soul*, 30, AT XI, 345. As Pascal Dumont (*Descartes et l'esthéthique: l'art d'emerveiller*, 67–68) has pointed out, the images in dreams and imagination are both described as composites that derive from the activity of the mind, willful or not, but never from the external world. In this sense, they point to the existence of an "aesthetic faculty" in Descartes that he never fully develops.
28. Descartes, *Passions of the Soul*, 29, AT XI, 345.
29. Imagination, to Descartes, does not equal the internal, synthesizing production of images that Kant describes in terms of *Einbildungskraft* in *Critique of Pure Reason*. Here, imagination is a "blind though indispensible function of the soul, which we are seldom even conscious." Immanuel Kant, *Critique of Pure Reason*, trans. Paul Guyer and Allen W. Wood (New York: Cambridge University Press, 1998), B103, A78. Neither does it correspond to the joyful freeplay of the faculties presented in *Critique of Judgement*; it is rather conceived as an internal production of images by the will.
30. Descartes, *Discourse on Method, The Philosophical Writings of Descartes* I, 114, AT VI, 7.
31. Descartes, *Principles of Philosophy, The Philosophical Writings of Descartes* I, 284, AT VIIIA, 320.
32. Descartes, *Principles of Philosophy, The Philosophical Writings of Descartes* I, 284, AT VIIIA, 320.
33. Descartes, *Passions of the Soul*, 33, AT XI, 348.
34. As Schlutz (*Mind' World*, 43–37) has pointed out, imagination consistently belongs to a lower faculty of the soul than the pure intellect in Descartes's metaphysical writings. In *Passions*, however, it is not metaphysics that is at stake.
35. Descartes, rule twelve in *Rules for the Direction of the Mind, The Philosophical Writings of Descartes* I, 42, AT X, 415.
36. Descartes, *Treatise on Man, The Philosophical Writings of Descartes* I, 99, AT XI, 119. The introduction hints at a part of the manuscript being lost; the men "resembling us" are never introduced.
37. *Renatus Des Cartes de Homine, figuris et latinitate donatus a Florentio Schuyl, vgdvni Batavorvm, apud Petrvm Leffen & Franciscvm Moyardvm*, ed. (Paris: de Schuyl, 1662).

38. L'Homme de René Descartes et un traité de la formation de foetus avec remarques de Deforges sur le traitte de René Descartes et les figures par lui inventes, ed. Clerselier (Paris, 1664).
39. Cottingham, *Philosophical Writings of Descartes*, 1, 313.
40. Descartes, *L'Homme*, ed. Clerselier, 1664, 17–18.
41. Descartes, *L'Homme*, ed. Clerselier, 1664, figure 17.
42. See, for instance, Delphine Antoine-Mahut, "The Story of L'Homme," in *Descartes' Treatise on Man and Its Reception*, ed. Delphine Antoine-Mahut and Stephen Gaukroger (Cham: Springer International, 2016), 23.
43. Antoine-Mahut, "Story of L'Homme," 23.
44. Descartes to Mersenne, December 1632, *The Philosophical Writings of Descartes* III, 40, AT I, 263.
45. Descartes, *Optics, The Philosophical Writings of Descartes* I, 164–167, AT VI, 109–128.
46. Descartes, *Optics, The Philosophical Writings of Descartes* I, 167, AT VI, 130.
47. Descartes, *Optics, The Philosophical Writings of Descartes* I, 132, AT VI, 42–43.
48. Descartes, *Optics, The Philosophical Writings of Descartes* I, 165, AT VI, 113.
49. Cf. the reading of Maurice Merleau-Ponty in "The Relations of the Soul and the Body and the Problem of Perceptual Consciousness," in *The Merleau-Ponty Reader*. Cf. Merleau-Ponty, "Eye and Mind," 8, https://www.academia.edu/10572479/Merleau_Ponty_Eye_and_Mind_1961_.
50. Lacan, *Four Concepts of Psychoanalysis*, 87.
51. Joseph K Perloff, "Human Dissection and the Science and Art of Leonardo da Vinci," *American Journal of Cardiology* 111 (2013): 775–777.
52. Giorgio Vasari, *The Lives of the Artists*, trans. Guilia and Peter Bondanella (Oxford: Oxford University Press, 1991), 284–299.
53. Sigmund Freud, "Leonardo da Vinci and a Memory of His Childhood," in *The Standard Edition* XI, ed. James Strachey (London: Hogarth, 1957), 65–66.
54. Freud, SE XI, 70–71.
55. Freud SE XI, 95.
56. Leonardo da Vinci, *Skizzenbücher*, ed. Anna Suh (London: Parragon, 2005), 136. Cf. Clerselier foreword.
57. Descartes, *Description of the Human Body, The World and Other Writings* 172, AT XI, 227.
58. Descartes, *Treatise on Man, The World and Other Writings*, 103, AT XI, 126.
59. Descartes, *Description of the Human Body, The World and Other Writings*, 187, AT XI, 253.
60. Descartes, *Description of the Human Body, The World and Other Writings* 193, AT XI, 265.
61. Descartes, *Treatise on Man, The World and Other Writings* 102, AT XI, 124–125.
62. Lacan, *Four Concepts of Psychoanalysis*, 87.

7. The Thinking Fetus

1. See, for example, Freud's brief "Some Dreams of Descartes: A Letter to Maxime Leroy." SE 21, 203–204. In Freud's reading the dreams appear to be "from above"—that is, intellectual dreams—rather than of associative content.

2. See, for instance, Mladen Dolar, "Cogito as the Subject of the Unconscious," in *Cogito and the Unconsious*, ed. Slavoj Zizek (Cambridge, MA: MIT Press, 1998), 11–41; Joël Sipos, *Lacan et Descartes, La tentation métaphysique* (Paris: PUF, 1994), 275–306; Humphrey Morris, "Reflections of Lacan: His Origins in Descartes and Freud," *Psychoanalytic Quarterly* 57, no. 2 (1988): 186–208; Adrianna M. Paliyenko, "Postmodern Turns Against the Cartesian Subject: Descartes 'I,' Lacan's Other," in *Feminist Interpretations of René Descartes*, ed. Susan Bordo (Pittsburgh: Pennsylvania State University Press, 2000), 141–166.

3. Lewis S. Feuer ("Anxiety and Philosophy: The Case of Descartes," *American Imago* 20, no. 4 [1963]: 417) performs an analysis of Cartesian "anxiety" with reference to these personal experiences, adding also that the often-commented section in *Passions* about a husband secretly feeling relief at his wife's passing is referring to his father. See also Geneviève Rodis-Lewis (*Descartes* [Paris: Calmann-Lewy, 1995], 17–22) on the guilt associated with the maternal death.

4. Clerselier produced the 1664 illustrated edition of *L'Homme* that is included in the bigger work *Le Monde*. As Annie Bitbol-Hespériès (*Descartes' Treatise on Man and Its Reception*, ed. Delphine Antoine-Mahut and Stephen Gaukroger [Cham: Springer International, 2016], 33) has shown, no script was found that carries the title *La formation du foetus*.

5. Descartes, *Description of the Human Body, The Philosophical Writings of Descartes* I, 314, AT XI, 224.

6. Descartes, *Description of the Human Body, The World and Other Writings*, trans. Stephen Gaukroger (Cambridge: Cambridge University Press), 204, AT XI, 284.

7. Descartes, *The Treatise on Man, The World and Other Writings*, 150, AT X, 178; and *The Philosophical Writings of Descartes* I, 106, AT XI, 177.

8. Descartes, *Optics*, 100, AT VI, 128. See also Descartes to Mersenne, May 27, 1630, *The Philosophical Writings of Descartes* III, 26, where Descartes expresses doubt on this matter, AT I, 153.

9. Descartes to Elisabeth, June 28, 1643, *The Philosophical Writings of Descartes* III, 227–228, AT III, 691–694.

10. Arnauld, "Fourth Set of Objections," in *The Philosophical Writings of Descartes* II, 150, AT VII, 214.

11. Descartes, "Fourth Set of Replies," in *The Philosophical Writings of Descartes* II, 171–172, AT VII, 246.

12. Rebecka Wilkin ("Descartes, Individualism, and the Fetal Subject," *Differences: A Journal of Feminist Cultural Studies* 19, no. 1 [2008]: 96–127) has given an account of the exchange from this point of view, arguing that accounts of Descartes's argumentations concerning the fetus underline his overall argument that we usually, in our everyday lives, perceive of ourselves as beings of both body and mind. The shock of Descartes's considerations of the fetus, Wilkin (106) argues, historically related to his joining the idea of a biological entity and a thinking being—they had hitherto stemmed from two different ontologies and not been joined.

13. Arnauld, "Fifth Set of Objections," in *The Philosophical Writings of Descartes* II, 184, AT VII, 264.

14. Letter to Hyperaspistes, August 1641, *The Philosophical Writings of Descartes* III, 189, AT III, 423.

15. Letter to Hyperaspistes, *The Philosophical Writings of Descartes* III, 190, AT III, 424.

16. Letter to Hyperaspistes, *The Philosophical Writings of Descartes* III, 189, AT III, 424.

17. Letter to Hyperaspites, *The Philosophical Writings of Descartes* III, 190, AT III, 424.

18. Descartes, *Conversation with Burman*, trans. John Cottingham (Oxford: Clarendon, 1976), 8.
19. Descartes, *Conversation with Burman*, 8.
20. Descartes, *Principles of Philosophy*, *The Philosophical Writings of Descartes* I, 218, AT VIII 8A, 35. See also Letter to Hyperaspites, *The Philosophical Writings of Descartes* III, 189, AT III, 424.
21. Descartes, *Conversation with Burman*, 8.
22. Descartes, *Conversation with Burman*, 8. *The Philosophical Writings of Descartes* III, 190, AT III, 424.
23. Descartes to De Launey, July 22, 1641, *The Philosophical Writings of Descartes* III, 188, AT III, 420.
24. As André Gombray ("Sigmund Descartes?" *Philosophy* 83, no. 325 [2008]: 301) has noted, Freud and Descartes differ in the sense that Descartes does not find the mind of the child to be deficient in any way.
25. Marion, *On the Passive Thought of Descartes*, 139–140.
26. Lilli Alanen (*Descartes's Concept of Mind* [Cambridge: Harvard University Press, 2003], 64–65) has an interpretation of "confused thoughts" in Descartes that pertains to emotional cognition rather than psychic life. She describes the passions originating in the body as modes of thought, and the kind of knowledge that the passions may produce as inherently confused, since it belongs to the hybrid domain situated between body and mind.
27. Lilli Alanen (*Descartes's Concept of Mind* [Cambridge, MA: Harvard University Press, 2003], 172–178) has argued that passions in Descartes are modes of the mind, or thoughts, caused by modes of the body, and that Descartes implies that we may never assert the relation between body and mind through philosophical means. This, in turn, is a philosophical statement; individual histories will determine the way in which affects are produced and received in each unique person.
28. Descartes to Elisabeth, May 1646, AT IV, 407–413.
29. See John Sutton, "Controlling the Passions: Passion, Memory and the Moral Philosophy of the Self in Seventeenth Century Neurophilosophy," in *The Soft Underbelly of Reason: The Passions in the Seventeenth Century*, ed. Stephen Gaukroger (London: Routledge 1998), 147–165.
30. Cottingham, *Philosophy and the Good Life: Reason and the Passions in Greek, Cartesian and Psychoanalytic Ethics* (Cambridge: Cambridge University Press, 1998), 80–96.
31. Freud, "Project for a Scientific Psychology," SE I, 358–59.
32. Descartes, *Passions of the Soul*, 28, AT XI, 342.
33. Correspondence with Elisabeth of Boehmen, *Passions of the Soul*, 17. Descartes's notions of physiology in this work and others, such as de L'homme, were on the one hand inspired by physiological models such as Harvey's, but it also came to hold a canonical position in the teaching of medicine in Holland, and was widely spread within the scientific community in Europe. Koch, *Aesthetic Body*, 28–33.
34. Descartes, *Meditations*, *The Philosophical Writings of Descartes* II, 56–57, AT VII, 81–83.
35. Descartes, *Passions of the Soul*, 32, AT XI, 346–348.
36. Alanen has seen that the Cartesian account of passions is attached to an immediate somatic effect on the body; what we see makes us act and behave in a certain way. As perceptions, they are not object to judgment. See "The Psycho-Physiology of Passions," *Descartes's Concept of Mind*, 183–185.

37. *Descartes's Conversation with Burman*, 8; *The Philosophical Writings of Descartes* III, 190, AT III, 424.
38. Descartes to Chanut, February 1, 1647, *The Philosophical Writings of Descartes* III, 308, AT IV, 605.
39. Descartes to Chanut, February 1, 1647, *The Philosophical Writings of Descartes* III, 306, AT IV, 60. See discussion by Geneviève Rodis-Lewis, *Descartes* (Paris: Calmann-Lévy, 1995), 262–263.
40. Descartes to Chanut, February 1, 1647, *The Philosophical Writings of Descartes* III, 306, AT IV, 602; Denis Kambouchner, "La subjectivité cartésienne et l'amour." in *Les passions à l'âge classique: Théories et critiques des passions II*, ed. P. F. Moreau (Paris: PUF, 2006), 77–97; Alberto Frigo, "A Very Obscure Definition: Descartes's Account of Love in the Passions of the Soul and Its Scholastic Background," *British Journal for the History of Philosophy* 24, no. 6 (2016): 1097–1116.
41. Descartes to Chanut, February 1, 1647, *The Philosophical Writings of Descartes* III, 308, AT IV, 606.
42. Descartes to Chanut, February 1, 1647, *The Philosophical Writings of Descartes* III, 307, AT IV, 602.
43. Descartes to Chanut, February 1, 1647, *The Philosophical Writings of Descartes* III, 308, AT IV, 602.
44. Descartes to Elisabeth, May 1646, *The Philosophical Writings of Descartes* III, 286, AT IV, 409.
45. Descartes, *Passions of the Soul*, 77, AT XI, 408.
46. Descartes to Chanut, February 1, 1647, *The Philosophical Writings of Descartes* III, 308, AT IV, 605.
47. Descartes, *Passions of the Soul*, 62, AT XI, 387.
48. Melanie Klein, "Love, Guilt and Reparation," in *Love, Guilt and Reparation and Other Works* (London: Virago, 1988), 306.
49. Klein, *Love, Guilt and Reparation*, 326.
50. Klein, "Weaning," in *Love, Guilt and Reparation*, 295.
51. Freud, "Project for a Scientific Psychology," SE I, 358–359.
52. Klein, "Weaning," 294.
53. Klein, "Love, Guilt and Reparation," 308.
54. Klein, "A Contribution to the Psycho-Genesis of Manic-Depressive States," in *Love, Guilt and Reparation*, 263; "Weaning," 295.
55. Klein, *Envy and Gratitude* (London: Tavistock, 1957), 32.
56. Descartes, *Passions of the Soul* 74, AT XI, 409.
57. Descartes to Elisabeth of Bohemia, May 1646, *The Philosophical Writings of Descartes* III, 286, AT IV, 408.
58. Descartes to Chanut, February 1, 1647, *The Philosophical Writings of Descartes* III, 307, AT IV, 604.
59. Descartes, *Passions of the Soul*, 62, AT XI, 387.
60. Klein, *Love Guilt and Reparation*, 190.
61. Freud SE VII, 182.
62. Freud, *Three Essays on Sexuality*, SE VII, 197.
63. Jacques Lacan, *The Four Fundamental Concepts of Psychoanalysis*, Seminar X, trans. Alan Sheridan (New York: Norton, 1998), 177–178, 183.

64. Descartes, *The World*, *The Philosophical Writings of Descartes* I, 82, AT XI, 6; Cf. Freud SE XI, 107.

65. Descartes to Chanut, February 1, 1647, *The Philosophical Writings of Descartes* III, 307, AT IV, 603.

66. Descartes to Chanut, February 1, 1647, *The Philosophical Writings of Descartes* III, 308, AT IV, 606. Cf. Descartes, *Passions of the Soul*, 62–63, AT XI, 388.

67. Freud, "Instincts and Their Vicissitudes," SE XIV, 122.

68. Descartes, *Description of the Human Body*, *The World and Other Writings*, 198, AT XI, 274.

69. Descartes, *Description of the Human Body*, *The World and Other Writings*, 194, AT XI, 266.

70. Descartes, *The Treatise on Man*, *The World and Other Writings*, 141, AT X, 167.

71. Descartes to Chanut, February 1, 1647, *The Philosophical Writings of Descartes* III, 305–314, AT IV, 601–617.

72. Descartes, *Passions of the Soul*, 77, AT XI, 407.

73. Descartes, *Passions of the Soul*, 77, AT XI, 408.

74. Descartes, *Passions of the Soul*, 61, AT XI, 387.

75. Descartes, *Passions of the Soul*, 61, AT XI, 387.

76. Descartes, *Treatise on Man*, *The World and Other Writings*, 104, AT XI, 128.

77. John Sutton identifies the spirits as the radically new element in the Cartesian psychophysiology, which was otherwise based upon renaissance theories of bodies that were fluid and permeable at large. Gaukroger et al., *Descartes' Natural Philosophy*, 700–705.

78. Letter to Hyperaspites, *Philosophical Writings of Descartes* III, 190, AT III, 424–425.

79. Letter to Hyperaspites, *Philosophical Writings of Descartes* III, 190, AT III, 424.

80. Descartes, *Conversation with Burman*, 8.

81. Letter to Hyperaspites, August 1641, *Philosophical Writings of Descartes* III, 190, AT III, 424.

82. John Sutton, "The Body and the Brain," Gaukroger et al., *Descartes' Natural Philosophy*, 699.

83. Freud SE VII, 182.

84. Freud SE VII, 182.

85. Freud SE VII, 175.

86. Descartes to Chanut, February 1, 1647, *The Philosophical Writings of Descartes* III, 608, AT IV, 606.

87. Descartes, "Fourth Set of Replies," *The Philosophical Writings of Descartes* II, 171–172, AT VII, 246–247.

88. This has been noted by Cottingham (*Philosophy and the Good Life* [Cambridge: Cambridge University Press], 92), who sees in Descartes a new route for the "therapy" of passions; the "physicien" of passions does not avoid them but sorts them by reason.

89. AT IV, 407–413, Descartes to Elisabeth, May 1646, *The Philosophical Writings of Descartes* III, 285–288. See the discussion of Alanen, *Descartes's Concept of Mind*, 165–171.

90. Descartes to Elisabeth, May 1646, *The Philosophical Writings of Descartes* III, 286, AT IV, 408.

91. Descartes to Elisabeth, *The Philosophical Writings of Descartes* III, 286, AT IV, 408.

92. Descartes to Chanut, June 6, 1647, *The Philosophical Writings of Descartes* III, 336, AT V, 150.

93. Descartes, *Passions of the Soul*, 28, 43, AT XI, 342, 362.
94. Descartes, *Passions of the Soul*, 43, AT XI, 362.
95. Descartes, *Passions of the Soul*, 43, AT XI, 362.
96. Freud, *Interpretation of Dreams*, SE IV–V, 537–541. Freud describes the dream thought apparatus as a kind of accumulated resource of traces of perceptions rendered unconscious, that through certain association and stimulations might become preconscious and result in a motor discharge.
97. Descartes, *Passions of the Soul*, 91, AT XI, 429.
98. Descartes, *Passions of the Soul*, 91, AT XI, 429.
99. Chanut to Descartes, May 11, 1647, AT V, 21.
100. Descartes to Chanut, June 6, 1647, AT V, 57, *Philosophical Writings of Descartes* III, 322. Henri F. Ellenberger (*The Discovery of the Unconscious* [New York: Basic, 1970], 523) mentions this letter, as referring to an "unconscious or half-conscious memory."
101. Descartes, *Passions of the Soul*, 6, AT XI, 396.
102. Klein, *Love, Guilt and Reparation*, 326.
103. Freud SE VII, 222.
104. Descartes to Chanut, February 1, 1647, *The Philosophical Writings of Descartes* III, 308, AT IV, 606.
105. Mladen Dolar, "Cogito as the Subject of the Unconscious," in *Cogito and the Unconscious*, ed. Slavoj Zizek (Cambridge, MA: MIT Press, 1998), 11–41.
106. Jean-Luc Marion, "The Originary Otherness of the Ego: A Re-reading of Descartes's Second Meditation," in *On the Ego and on God: Further Cartesian Questions*, trans. Christina Geschwandtner (New York: Fordham University Press, 2007), 27.
107. Lacan, *Four Concepts of Psychoanalysis*, 168, 270–71.
108. Christia Mercer, "Descartes' Debt to Teresa of Ávila, or Why We Should Work on Women in the History of Philosophy," *Philosophical Studies* 174, no. 10 (2017): 2539–2555.
109. Descartes to Elisabeth, October/November 1646, *The Philosophical Writings of Descartes* III, 296–297, AT IV, 528–530.
110. Descartes, *Meditations*, *The Philosophical Writings of Descartes* II, 20, AT VII, 29.
111. Marion, *On the Ego and on God*, 12.
112. Marion, *On the Ego and on God*, 27.
113. Hannah Arendt, *Denktagebuch* II, ed. Ursula Ludz and Ingeborg Nordmann (München: Piper 2002), 761.

8. The Love between Body and Soul

1. Jean-Marie Beyssade, "Philosopher par lettres," introduction to *Descartes, Correspondance avec Elisabeth et autres lettres* (Paris: Flammarion, 1989), 23.
2. Jean-Marie Beyssade, "Philosopher par lettres," introduction to *Descartes, Correspondance avec Elisabeth et autres lettres*, 25.
3. Descartes, "Letter to Chanut, 1 February 1647," in *The Philosophical Writings of Descartes* III, 310.
4. Descartes, "Letter to Chanut, 1 February 1647," in *The Philosophical Writings of Descartes* III, 306.
5. Descartes, "Letter to Chanut, 1 February 1647," in *The Philosophical Writings of Descartes* III, 306.

6. Descartes, "Letter to Chanut, 1 February 1647," in *The Philosophical Writings of Descartes* III, 306.
7. Nancy, *Ergo sum*, 55.
8. Descartes, "Letter to Chanut, 1 February 1647," in *The Philosophical Writings of Descartes* III, 306–307.
9. Descartes, "Letter to Chanut, 1 February 1647," in *The Philosophical Writings of Descartes* III, 307.
10. Descartes, "Letter to Chanut, 1 February 1647," in *The Philosophical Writings of Descartes* III, 307.
11. Descartes, "Letter to Chanut, 1 February 1647," in *The Philosophical Writings of Descartes* III, 307.
12. Descartes, "Letter to Chanut, 1 February 1647," in *The Philosophical Writings of Descartes* III, 307.
13. Descartes, "Letter to Chanut, 1 February 1647," in *The Philosophical Writings of Descartes* III, 307.
14. Descartes, "Letter to Chanut, 1 February 1647," in *The Philosophical Writings of Descartes* III, 307.
15. Descartes, "Letter to Chanut, 6 June 1647," in *The Philosophical Writings of Descartes* III, 322.
16. Horatius Flaccus Q. Satires, Epistles and Ars poetica [Elektronisk resurs]. Rev. and repr. Cambridge, MA: Harvard University Press, 1929 [1926], II, ii, 79.
17. Descartes, "Letter to Chanut, 1 February 1647," in *The Philosophical Writings of Descartes* III, 309.
18. Descartes, "Letter to Chanut, 1 February 1647," in *The Philosophical Writings of Descartes* III, 309.
19. Descartes, "Letter to Chanut, 1 February 1647," in *The Philosophical Writings of Descartes* III, 310.
20. Descartes, "Letter to Chanut, 1 February 1647," in *The Philosophical Writings of Descartes* III, 310.
21. Descartes, "Letter to Chanut, 6 June 1647," in *The Philosophical Writings of Descartes* III.
22. Ibid., III, 322.
23. Descartes, "Letter to Chanut, 1 February 1647," in *The Philosophical Writings of Descartes* III, 312, 313.
24. Descartes, "Letter to Chanut, 1 February 1647," in *The Philosophical Writings of Descartes* III, 313.
25. Descartes, "Letter to Chanut, 1 February 1647," in *The Philosophical Writings of Descartes* III, 313.
26. Quoted by Descartes in "Letter to Chanut, 1 February 1647," in *The Philosophical Writings of Descartes* III, 313.
27. Descartes, "Letter to Chanut, 1 February 1647," in *The Philosophical Writings of Descartes* III, 314.
28. Descartes, "The Passions of the Soul," in *The Philosophical Writings of Descartes* I, 329.
29. Descartes, "The Passions of the Soul," in *The Philosophical Writings of Descartes* I, 340.
30. Descartes, "The Passions of the Soul," in *The Philosophical Writings of Descartes* I, 364.

31. About Descartes's views on involuntary bodily movements and their connection to the concept of bodily reflex, see Goerges Canguilhem, *La Formation du Concept de Réflexe aux XVIIe et XVIIIe siècles* (Paris: PUF, 1955).

32. Descartes, Description of the Human Body.

33. Descartes, AT XI, 124.

34. Jean-Luc Nancy, *Corpus*, trans. Richard A. Rand (New York: Fordham University Press, 2008).

35. Marguerite Duras, *Écrire* (Paris: Gallimard, 1993); "Ma chambre n'est pas un lit, ni ici, ni à Paris, ni à trouville. C'est une certaine fenêtre, une certaine table, des habitudes d'encre noire, de marques d'encres noires introuvables, c'est une certaine chaise," 15.

36. Duras, *Écrire*, 32.

37. La Feuille Blanche, English translation of *The Blank Sheet*.

> En vérité, une feuille blanche
> Nous déclare par le vide
> Qu'il n'est rien de si beau
> Que ce qui n'existe pas.
> Sur le miroir magique de sa blanche étendue,
> L'âme voit devant elle le lieu des miracles
> Que l'on ferait naître avec des signes et des lignes.
> Cette présence d'absence surexcite
> Et paralyse à la fois l'acte sans retour de la plume.
> Il y a dans toute beauté une interdiction de toucher,
> Il en émane je ne sais quoi de sacré
> Qui suspend le geste, et fait l'homme
> Sur le point d'agir se craindre soi-même.

38. Descartes, "Letter 21 May 1643," in *The Philosophical Writings of Descartes* III, 217.

39. Descartes, "Letter 21 May 1643," in *The Philosophical Writings of Descartes* III, 217.

40. Etienne de La Boétie uses the verb *s'entr'aimer* in his De la Servitude Volontaire, "*ils ne s'entr'aiment pas, mais ils s'entrecraignent; ils ne sont pas amis; mais ils sont complices,*" in *Les Discours de la servitude volontaire* (Paris: Petite Bibliothèque Payot, 2002), 180. Corneille employs this verb in his piece Attila III, 4: "*Et si ressemblance est par où l'on s'entr'aime. J'ai lieu de vous aimer comme un autre moi-même.*"

41. Descartes, "Letter 1 February 1647," in *The Philosophical Writings of Descartes* III, 311.

Bibliography

Descartes's Works

Descartes, René. *Abrégé de Musique: Conpendium Musicae*. Paris: PUF, 1987.
———. *Compendium on Music*, trans. Walter Robert. Rome: American Institute of Musicology, 1961.
———. *Discourse on Method, Optics, Geometry and Meteorology*. Translated by Paul Olscamp. Indianapolis, IN: Hackett, 2001.
———. *L'homme de Réne Descartes: Et un traitté de la formation du fotetus du mesme autheur. Avec les Remarques de Louys de la Forge sur le Traitté de l'homme de René Descartes; et sur les figures par luy inventées*, Clerselier, ed. Paris 1664.
———. *Meditations on First Philosophy: with Selections from the Objections and Replies*. 2nd ed. Edited by B. Williams. Cambridge: Cambridge University Press, 2017.
———. *Oeuvres completes*. Edited by Jeanne-Marie Beyssade and Denis Kambouchner. Paris: Gallimard, 2016.
———. *Oeuvres de Descartes*. Edited by Charles Adam and Paul Tannery. Paris: Vrin, 1969.
———. *Renatus Des Cartes de Homine, figuris et latinitate donatus a Florentio Schuyl, vgdvni Batavorvm, apud Petrvm Leffen & Franciscvm Moyardvm*, ed, de Schuyl, Paris, 1662.
———. *The Philosophical Writings of Descartes I-III*. Edited and translated by John Cottingham. Cambridge: Cambridge University Press, 1985—.
———. *The World and Other Writings*. Edited by Stephen Gaukruger. Cambridge: Cambridge University Press, 2004.
Descartes, René, and Charles Adam. *Œuvres de Descartes. T. 12, Vie & œuvres: étude historique*. Paris: Léopold Cerf, 1910.

Other Sources

Alanen, Lilli. *Descartes's Concept of the Mind*. Cambridge, MA: Harvard University Press, 2003.
Alquié, Ferdinand. "Descartes et l'immédiat." *Revue de Métaphysique et de Morale* 55, no. 4 (1950): 370–375.
Antoine-Mahut, Delphine, and Stephen Gaukroger, eds. *Descartes' Treatise on Man and Its Reception*. Cham: Springer International, 2016.
Arendt, Hannah. *Denktagebuch II*. München: Piper, 2002.
———. *Human Condition*. Chicago: University of Chicago Press, 1958.
Ariew, Roger. Dennis Des Chene, Douglas M. Jesseph, Tad M. Schmaltz, and Theo Verbeek. *The A to Z of Descartes and Cartesian Philosophy*. Lanham, MD: Scarecrow, 2003.
Arnaud, Antoine, and Pierre Nicole. *Logic or the Art of Thinking*. Translated by Jill Vance Buroker. Cambridge: Cambridge University Press, 1996.
Augustine. *Confessions*. Oxford: Oxford University Press, 1998.

Austin, J. L. *How to Do Things with Words*. Oxford: Clarendon, 1962.
Baillet, Alain. *La Vie de Monsieur Descartes*, Tome II, Paris: 1691. *The life of Monsieur Des Cartes*, containing the history of his philosophy and works: as also the most remarkable things that befell him during the whole course of his life. London: Printed for R. Simpson, 1693, vol. I, 80–86.
Baltrušaitis. Jurgis. *Anamorphic Art*. Cambridge: Chadwick-Healey, 1977.
Baracchi, Claudia, ed. *The Bloomsbury Companion to Aristotle*. New York, London: Bloomsbury Academic, 2014.
Barbaras, Renaud. "Merleau-Ponty and Nature." *Research in Phenomenology* 31, no. 1 (2001): 22–38.
Bataille, Georges. "Formless," *Documents #1* (Paris, 1929): 382. Translated by Allan Stoekl, Carl Lovitt, and Donald Leslie. *Georges Bataille: Vision of Excess: Selected Writings, 1927–1939*, Minneapolis: University of Minnesota Press, 1985.
Baumgarten, Alexander. *Metaphysics: A Critical Translation with Kant's Elucidations, Selected Notes and Related Materials*. Translated by Courtney D. Fugate and John Hymers. London: Bloomsbury, 2013.
Beardsley, Monroe. *The Aesthetic Point of View*. Ithaca, NY: Cornell University Press, 1982.
Benveniste, Emile. "Analytic Philosophy and Language." In *Problems of General Linguistics*, translated by Mary Elisabeth Meck. Coral Gables, FL: University of Miami Press, 1971.
Berger, Susanna. *Descartes Work: The Art of Philosophy: Visual Thinking in Europe from the Late Renaissance to the Early Enlightenment*. Princeton, NJ: Princeton University Press, 2017.
Bergson Henri. *Time and Free Will: An Essay on the Immediate Data of Consciousness*. Mineola, NY: Dover, 2001 [1913].
Beyssade, Jean-Marie. *Descartes au fil de l'ordre*. Paris: PUF, 2001.
———. *La philosophie première de Descartes: le temps et la cohérence de la métaphysique*. Paris: Flammarion, 1979.
Bizub, Edward. *Beckett et Descartes dans l'œuf—Aux sources de l'œuvre beckettienne: de Whoroscope à Godot*. Paris: Garnier, 2012.
Blanchot, Maurice. *The Space of Literature*. Translated by Ann Smock. Lincoln: University of Nebraska Press, 1989.
Bordo, Susan, ed. *Feminist Interpretations of René Descartes*. Pittsburgh: Pennsylvania State University Press, 2000.
Boros, Gábor. *Sur les émotions intellectuelles chez Descartes*. http://filozofiaiszemle.net/wp-content/uploads/2016/10/G%C3%A1bor-Boros-Sur-les-%C3%A9motions-intellectuelles-chez-Descartes.pdf.
Bossuet, Jacque-Bénigne. *Sur la brièveté de la vie* (2017). Paris: Gallimard, 2017.
Bottici, Chiara. *Imaginal Politics: Images beyond Imagination and the Imaginary*. New York: Columbia University Press, 2014.
Brown, Deborah J. *Descartes and the Passionate Mind*. Cambridge: Cambridge University Press, 2006.
Cahné, Pierre-Alain. *Un autre Descartes: Le philosophe et son langage*. Paris: Vrin, 1980.
Canguilhem, Georges. *La Formation du Concept de Réflexe aux XVIIe et XVIIIe siècles*. Paris: PUF, 1955.
Certeau, Michel, Dominique Julia, and Jacques Revel. *Une politique de la langue: la Révolution française et les patois: l'enquête de Grégoire*. Paris: Gallimard, 1975.

Chen-Moris, Raz, and Ofer Gal. *Baroque Science*. Chicago: University of Chicago Press, 2013.
Chomsky, Noam. *Cartesian Linguistics: A Chapter in the History of Rationalist Thought*. 3rd ed. Edited by James McGilvray. Cambridge: Cambridge University Press, 2009.
Clément, Bruno. "La langue claire de Descartes." *Dans Rue Descartes* 3, no. 65 (2009): 20–34. https://doi.org/10.3917/rdes.065.0020.
Consoli, Gianluca. "A Cognitive Theory of the Aesthetic Experience." *Contemporary Aesthetics* 10 (2012).
Cottingham, John. *Philosophy and the Good Life: Reason and the Passions in Greek, Cartesian and Psychoanalytic Ethics*. Cambridge: Cambridge University Press, 1998.
Courtine, Jean-François. "Les méditations cartésiennes de Martin Heidegger." *Les Études Philosophiques* 1 (2009).
Craig, Martin. *Renaissance Meteorology: Pomponazzi to Descartes*. Baltimore, MD: Johns Hopkins University Press, 2011.
Dällenbach, Lucien. *Le récit spéculaire: Essai sur la misen en abyme*. Paris: editions du Seuil, 1977. Translated by Jeremy Whiteley with Emma Hughes. *The Mirror in the Text*. Cambridge: Polity, 1989.
Damasio, Antonio. *Descartes Error: Emotion, Reason and the Human Brain*. London: Penguin, 2005.
Da Vinci, Leonardo. *Skizzenbücher*. Edited by Anna Suh. London: Parragon, 2005.
Delaunay, Robert. Du cubisme à l'art abstratit, Bibliothèque générale de l'École pratique des hautes études. Section 6, Centre de recherches historiques. Paris, 1957.
Dennett, Daniel. *Consciousness Explained*. New York: Little, Brown & Company, 1991.
———. *Content and Consciousness*. London: Routledge, 1999.
Derrida, Jacques. *Circonfession (La bibliothèque des Voix)*. Paris: des femmes.
———. 1978. "Cogito and the History of Madness." In *Writing and Difference*, translated by Alan Bass. London and New York: Routledge, 36–76. Originally published as "Cogito et histoire de la folie." *Revue de métaphysique et de morale* 68, no. 4 (1963): 460–494.
———. *Du droit à la philosophie*. Paris: Galilée, 1990.
———. *Eyes of the University: Right to Philosophy 2*. Translated by Jan Plug et al. Stanford, CA: Stanford University Press, 2004.
———. *Memoirs d'aveugle: L'autoportrait et autres ruines*. Paris: Editions de la Réunion des musées nationaux, 1990. English translation by Pascal-Anne Brault and Michael Naas. *Memoirs of the Blind: The Self-Portrait and Other Ruins*. Chicago and London: University of Chicago Press, 1993.
Dickmann, Iddo. *The Little Crystalline Seed: The Ontological Significance of Mise en Abyme in Post-Heideggerian Thought*. New York: SUNY Press, 2020.
Douzinas, Costas, ed. *Adieu, Derrida*. Basingstoke: Palgrave Macmillan, 2007.
Dumont, Pascal. *Descartes et l'esthétique: L'art d'emerveiller*. Paris: PUF, 1997.
Ebbersmeyer, Sabina, ed. *Emotional Minds: The Passions and the Limits of Pure Inquiry in Early Modern Philosophy*. Berlin [u.a.]: De Gruyter, 2012.
Feuer, Lewis S. "Anxiety and Philosophy: The Case of Descartes." *American Imago* 20, no. 4 (1963): 2–36.
Focillon, Henri. *The Life of Forms in Art*. New York: Zone, 1989 [1948].
Foucault, Michel. *The Order of Things: An Archaeology of the Human Sciences*. London: Tavistock/Routledge, 1989 [1974].

Freud, Sigmund. *Complete Psychological Works of Sigmund Freud*, vol. 21 (1927–1931): The Future of an Illusion, Civilization and Its Discontents, and Other Works, Unspecified. 1961.
———. *Standard Edition*. Edited by James Strachey. London: Hogarth, 1953.
Frigo, Alberto. "A Very Obscure Definition: Descartes's Account of Love in the Passions of the Soul and Its Scholastic Background." *British Journal for the History of Philosophy* 24, no. 6 (2016).
Furetière, Antoine. *Dictionnaire universel contenant generalement tous les mots françois, tant vieux que modernes, & les termes de toutes les sciences et des arts* (1690).
Gagnebin, Jeanne Marie. "Entre le rêve et la veille: Qui suis-je?" *Études théologiques et religieuses* 80, no. 2 (2005): 201–214.
Garber, Daniel. *Descartes Embodied: Reading Cartesian Philosophy through Cartesian Science*. Cambridge: Cambridge University Press, 2001.
———. *Descartes' Metaphysical Physics*. Chicago: University of Chicago Press, 1992.
Gasché, Rodolphe. *The Tain of the Mirror: Derrida and the Philosophy of Reflection*. Cambridge, MA: Harvard University Press, 1986.
Gaukroger, Stephen, ed. *The Soft Underbelly of Reason: The Passions in the Seventeenth Century*. London: Routledge, 1998.
Gaukroger, Stephen, John Andrew Schuster, and John Sutton, eds. *Descartes' Natural Philosophy*. Cambridge: Cambridge University Press, 2002.
Gide, André. *Journals 1889–1939*. Paris: Gallimard, Pléiade, 1948.
———. *Journals 1889–1949*. Translated by J. O'Brien. London: Penguin, 1981.
Giovannangelli, Daniel. *La fiction de l'être: Lectures de la philosophie modern*. Paris: De Boeck, 1990.
Gobert, Darren. *The Mind-Body Stage: Passion and Interaction in the Cartesian Theatre*. Stanford, CA: Stanford University Press, 2013.
Gregg, Melissa, and Gregory Seigworth, eds. *The Affect Theory Reader*. Durham, NC: Duke University Press, 2009.
Guenancia, Pierre. "Le modèle du théâtre chez Descartes." *Revue de métaphysique et de moral* 2, no. 98 (2018): 199–214.
———. *L'intelligence du sensible: Essai sur le dualisme cartésien*. Paris: Gallimard, 1998.
Gueroult, Martial. *Descartes selon l'ordre des raisons*. Paris: Aubier, 1953.
Grünbein, Durs. *Der Cartesische Taucher*. Frankfurt am Main: Suhrkamp Verlag, 2008.
Hallyn, Fernand. *Les Olympiques de Descartes*. Genève: Librairie Droz S. A, 1995.
Hamerton, Katharine J. *Journal of the History of Ideas* 69, no. 4 (2008).
Hegel, G. W. F. *Lectures on the History of Philosophy III*, Berkeley: University of California Press, 1990.
———. *Vorlesungen über die Geschichte der Philosophie III*, Werke 20, Frankfurt am Main: Suhrkamp, 1986.
Heidegger, Martin. *Being and Time*. Translated by Joan Stambaugh. Albany: State University of New York Press, 1996.
———. *Die Grundprobleme der* Phänomenologie, GA 24. Frankfurt am Main: Vittorio Klostermann, 1997.
Heinämaa, Sara, and Timo Kaitaro. "Descartes's Notion of the Mind-Body Union and Its Phenomenological Expositions." In *The Oxford Handbook of the History of Phenomenology*, edited by Dan Zahavi. Oxford: Oxford University Press, 2018.

Hintikka, Jaako. "'Cogito, ergo sum': Inference or Performance?" *Philosophical Review* 71, no. 2 (1962): 3–32.
Hoffman, Paul. *Essays on Descartes*. Oxford: Oxford University Press, 2009.
Horatius Flaccus, Q. *Horace: Satires, Epistles, and Ars poetica* [Elektronisk resurs]. Rev. and repr. Cambridge, MA: Harvard University Press, 1929 [1926], II, ii, 79.
Hughes, Fiona. *Kant's Aesthetic Epistemology: Form and World*. Edinburgh: Edinburgh University Press, 2007.
Husserl, Edmund. *Analyses Concerning Passive and Active Synthesis: Lectures on Transcendental Logic*. Translated by Anthony Steinbock. Collected Works of Husserl, vol. 9. Dordrecht: Kluwer, 2001.
———. *Phantasy, Image Consciousness and Memory*. Translated by John B. Brough. Collected Works of Husserl, vol. 11. Dordrecht: Springer, 2005.
Hynes, Darren. "Parallel Traditions in the Image of Descartes: Iconography, Intention, and Interpretation." *International History Review* 32, no. 4 (2010): 575–597.
Ishizu, Tomohiro, and Semir Zeki. "Toward a Brain-Based Theory of Beauty." *PLoS ONE* 6, no. 7 (2011): e21852. doi:10.1371/journal.pone.0021852.
Jaquet, Chantal. *Affects, Actions and Passions in Spinoza: The Unity of Body and Mind*. Translated by Tatiana Reznichenko. Edinburgh: Edinburgh University Press, 2018.
Johnson, Gale, ed. *The Merleau-Ponty Aesthetics Reader*. Evanston, IL: Northwestern University Press, 1993.
Jorgensen, Larry. "Descartes on Music: Between the Ancient and the Aestheticians." *British Journal of Aesthetics* 52, no. 4 (2012).
Kambouchner, Denis. *Descartes n'a pas dit*. Paris: Les Belles Lettres, 2015.
Kant, Immanuel. "Werkausgabe" 12 Bänden. Bd 4 Kritik der reinen Vernunft. 2. Frankfurt am Main: Suhrkamp; 1976, Eng. version Critique of Pure Reason. Translated by Paul Guyer and Allen W. Wood. Cambridge: Cambridge University Press, 1998.
Keiling, Tobias. "Ars Cogitans: Überlegungen mit Descartes und Husserl zum Ursprung des Kunstwerks." *Kalliope, Zeitschrift für Literatur und Kunst*, Heft I (2009): 72.
Klein Melanie. *Love, Guilt and Reparation: And Other Works 1921–1945*. London: Virago, 1988.
Koch, Erec R. *The Aesthetic Body: Passion, Sensibility and Corporeality in 17th Century France*. Newark: University of Delaware Press, 2010.
Koyré, Alexandre. *From the Closed World to the Infinite Universe*. Baltimore, MD: Johns Hopkins Press, 1957.
Krämer, Sybille, and Christina Ljungberg, eds. *Thinking with Diagrams*. Berlin: De Gruyter Mouton, 2016.
Krämer, Sybille. *Berechenbare Vernunft: Kalkül und Rationalismus* im 17. Jahrhundert. Berlin: Walter De Gruyter, 1991.
———. "Epistemology of the Line: Reflections on the Diagrammatical Mind." In *Studies in Diagrammatology and Diagram Praxis*, edited by Olga Pombo and Alexander Gerner. London: College Publications, 2010, 13–38.
Krantz, Emile. *Essai sur l'esthétique de Descartes*. Paris: Baillière & Ciem, 1898 [1882].
Kristeva, Julia. *Powers of Horror*. Translated by Leon Roudiez. New York: Columbia University Press, 1982.
Kusukawa, Sashiko, and Ian Maclean, eds. *Transmitting Knowledge: Words, Images and Instruments in Early Modern Europe*. Oxford: Oxford University Press, 2006.

La Boétie, Etienne de. *Les Discours de la servitude volontaire*. Paris: Petite Bibliothèque Payot, 2002.
Lacan, Jacques. *Four Concepts of Psychoanalysis*. Trans by Alan Sheridan. New York: Norton; London: Karnac, 2004.
Lafond, Jean. "Descartes philosophe et écrivain." *Revue Philosophique de la France Et de l'Etranger* 182, no. 4 (1992): 421–438.
Laporte, Jean-Marc, S. J. "Husserl's Critique of Descartes." *Philosophy and Phenomenological Research* 23, no. 3 (1963).
Larsen, Erik. "Le baroque et l'esthétique de Descartes." *Baroque* [En ligne] 6 (1973). http://journals.openedition.org/baroque/416; DOI: 10.4000/baroque.416.
Leibniz. *New Essays on Human Understanding*. Translated by Peter Remnant and Jonathan Bennett. Cambridge: Cambridge University Press, 1996.
Levin, Kasper, Tone Roald, and Bjarne Sode Funch. "Visual Art and the Rhythm of Experience." *Journal of Aesthetics and Art Criticism* 77, no. 3 (2019): 281–293.
Lorimer, Jamie. "Aesthetics for Post-Human Worlds: Difference, Expertise and Ethics." *Dialogues in Human Geography* 2, no. 3 (2013): 284–287.
Lyotard, Jean-François. *The Confession of Augustine*. Translated by Richard Beardsworth. Stanford, CA: Stanford University Press, 2000.
Marion, Jean-Luc. *Cartesian Questions: Method and Metaphysics*. Chicago, University of Chicago Press, 1999.
———. *On Descartes' Passive Thought: The Myth of Cartesian Dualism*. Translated by Christina M. Gschwandtner. Chicago: University of Chicago Press, 2018.
———. *On the Ego and on God: Further Cartesian Questions*. Translated by Christina M. Gschwandtner. New York: Fordham University Press, 2007.
Massironi, Manfredo. *The Psychology of Graphic Images: Seeing, Drawing, Communicating*. London: Routledge, 2010.
Mazis, Glen. *Merleau-Ponty and the Face of the World: Silence, Ethics, Imagination, and Poetic Ontology*. Albany: State University of New York Press, 2016.
McQuillan, Colin. *Early Modern Aesthetics*. London: Rowman & Littlefield, 2011.
Mercer, Christia. "Descartes's Debt to Teresa of Avila, or Why Should We Work on Women in the History of Philosophy." *Philosophical Studies* 174, no. 10 (2017).
Merleau-Ponty, Maurice. *L'oeil et l'esprit*, (Paris: Gallimard, 1985), Eng. translation by Maurice Merleau-Ponty, *Eye and Mind* [L'Œil et l'esprit, Paris: Gallimard, 1961] translated by Carleton Dallery in *The Primacy of Perception*, edited by James Edie (Evanston, IL: Northwestern University Press, 1964), 159–190. Revised translation by Michael Smith in *The Merleau-Ponty Aesthetics Reader* (1993), 121–149.
———. *Phenomenology of Perception*. Translated by Taylor Carman. London: Routledge, 2002 [1962].
———. *Sense and Non-sense*. Translated by Hubert L. Dreyfus and Patricia Allen Dreyfus. Evanston, IL: Northwestern University Press, 1982 [1964].
———. *The World of Perception*. London: Routledge, 2008.
Moreau, Pierre-François. *Théories et critiques des passions II à l'âge classique*. Paris: Presses Universitaires de France, 2006.
Morris, Humphrey. "Reflections of Lacan: His Origins in Descartes and Freud." *Psychoanalytic Quarterly* 57, no. 2 (1988): 186–208.
Muller, Maurice. *De Descartes à Marcel Proust*. Paris: La Baconnière, 1947.

Murdoch, Dugald. "Abstraction vs. Exclusion." In *The Cambridge Descartes Lexicon*. Cambridge: Cambridge University Press, 2015.
Nadler, Steven. *The Philosopher, the Priest, and the Painter*. Princeton, NJ: Princeton University Press, 2013.
Nadler, Steven, Tad Schmaltz, and Delfine Antoine-Mahut. *The Oxford Handbook of Descartes and Cartesianism*. Oxford: Oxford University Press, 2019.
Nancy, Jean-Luc. *Corpus*. New York: Fordham University Press, 2008.
———. *Ego sum: corpus, anima, fabula*. Translated by Marie-Eve Morin. New York: Fordham University Press, 2016.
Nordin, Svante. *Filosofins historia: det västerländska förnuftets historia från Thales till postmodernismen*. Lund: Studentlitteratur, 2017.
Olscamp, Paul J. *Discourse on Method, Optics, Geometry and Meteorology*, Indianapolis, IN: Hackett, 2001.
Orden, Kate van. "Descartes of Musical Training and the Body." In *Music Sensation and Sensuality*, Linda Phyllis Austern. London: Routledge, 2002.
Ott, Walter. *Descartes, Malebranche, and the Crisis of Perception*. Oxford: Oxford University Press, 2017.
Perler, Dominik. *Feelings Transformed: Philosophical Theories of the Emotions, 1270–1670*. Translated by Tony Crawford. New York: Oxford University Press, 2018.
Perloff, Joseph K. "Human Dissection and the Science and Art of Leonardo da Vinci." *American Journal of Cardiology* 111 (2013): 775–777.
Perniola, Mario. *The Sex Appeal of the Inorganic*. Translated by Massimo Verdicchio. London: Continuum, 2004.
Perrin, Christophe. "Cogito me cogitare: Note pour servir la généalogie et la téléologie d'une formule clé de G. W. Leibniz à J-L Marion." *Phainomena* 23, no. 88–89. http://www.sif-praha.cz/wp-content/uploads/2013/04/Cogito-me-cogitare.pdf.
Petrescu, Lucian. "Cartesian Meteors and Scholastic Meteors: Descartes against the School in 1637." *Journal of the History of Ideas* 76, no. 1 (2015): 25–45.
Plato. *Plato in Twelve Volumes*, vol. 12. Translated by Harold N. Fowler. Cambridge, MA: Harvard University Press; London: William Heinemann Ltd., 1921.
Quignard, Pascal. *Mourir de penser*. Paris: Bernard Grasset, 2014.
Rancière, Jacques. *The Politics of Aesthetics*. London: Bloomsbury, 2002.
Rée, Jonathan. *Philosphical Tales: An Essay on Philosophy and Literature*. London: Methuen, 1987.
Revault d'Allones, O. "L'esthétique de Descartes." *Revue des Sciences Humaines*, no. 61 (1951).
Robbe-Grillet, Alain. *Pour un nouveau roman*. Paris: Editions de Minuit, 1963.
Rodis-Lewis, Geneviève. *Descartes*. Paris: Calmann-Lévy, 1995.
———. "Descartes et Poussin" in *Boulletin de Société d'étude du XVII eme siècle*, vol. 23, 1953, 520–549.
Rosa, A. De. *Perspective, Catoptric and Artificial Magic*, edited by Jean François Nicéron, with critical editions of *La Perspective Curieuse* (Paris, 1638) and of the *Thaumaturgus Opticus* (Paris, 1646), Roma: Aracne edizioni, 2013.
Sá Cavalcante Schuback, Marcia, and Tora Lane, eds., *Dis-orientations: Philosophy, Literature and the Lost Grounds of Modernity*. London: Rowman & Littlefield, 2015.
Sartre, Jean-Paul. "La liberté cartésienne," in *Descartes 1596–1650*. Introduction et choix par J.-P. Sartre (Genève-Paris: Trois Collines, coll. "Les Classiques de la Liberté," 1946),

10–11. Eng. version by Annette Michelson, "Cartesian Freedom" in *Literary Philosophical and Essays*. New York: Collier, 1962, 180–198.
Schlutz, Alexander. *Mind's World*. Seattle: University of Washington Press, 2009.
Sepper, Dennis. *Descartes's Imagination: Proportion, Images and the Activity of Thinking*. Berkeley: University of California Press, 1996.
Shusterman, Richard. "The End of Aesthetic Experience." *Journal of Aesthetics and Art Criticism* 55, no. 1 (1997).
———. "Aesthetic Experience: From Analysis to Eros," *Journal of Aesthetics and Art Criticism* 64, no. 2 (2006): 217–229.
Sipos, Joël. *Lacan et Descartes, La tentation métaphysique*. Paris: PUF, 1994.
Sobchak, Vivian. *Carnal Thoughts: Embodiment and Moving Image Culture*. Berkeley: University of California Press, 2004.
Springbord, Patricia, ed., *The Cambridge Companion to Hobbes's Leviathan*. Cambridge: Cambridge University Press, 2007.
Stoichita, Victor I. *A Short History of the Shadow*. London: Reaktion, 1997.
Valéry, Paul. Cahiers / 21, 1938–1939. Paris: Centre National de la Recherche Scientifique; 1960. Valéry speaks also of the oeil-tact in Cahiers / 29, 1944–1945. Paris: Centre National de la Recherche Scientifique; 1961, 435.
———. *Collected Works of Paul Valéry, Masters and Friends*, vol. 9. Translated by Martin Turnell. Princeton, NJ: Princeton University Press, 1968.
———. *The Complete Works by Paul Valéry*, volume 8, Leonardo, Poe, Mallarmé, transl by Malcolm Cowley and James R. Lawler (Princeton, NJ: Princeton University Press, 1972).
———. *Vues*. Paris: La table ronde, 1948.
Van Wymeersch, Brigitte. "L'esthétique musicale de Descartes et le cartésianisme." *Revue Philosophique de Luvain* 94, no. 2 (1996): 271–293.
Vasari, Giorgio. *The Lives of the Artists*. Translated by Guilia and Peter Bondanella. Oxford: Oxford University Press, 1991, 284–299.
Vinciguerra, Lucien. *La representation excessive: Descartes, Leibniz, Locke, Pascal*. Paris: Presses Universitaires du Septentrion, 2013.
Voss, Stephen. *Passions of the Soul*. Cambridge: Hackett, 1995.
Wahl, Jean. *Du rôle de l'idée de l'instant dans la philosophie de Descartes*. Paris: F. Alcan, 1920.
Watson, Richard A. *Descartes's Ballet, His Doctrine of the Will and His Political Philosophy* (with a transcript and English translation of *La Naissance de la Paix*), South Bend, IN: St. Augustine's Press, 2007.
Wilkin, Rebecka. "Descartes, Individualism, and the Fetal Subject." *differences: A Journal of Feminist Cultural Studies* 19, no. 1 (2008): 96–127.
Wiskus, Jessica. *The Rhythm of Thought: Art, Literature, and Music after Merleau-Ponty*. Chicago: University of Chicago Press, 2013.
Zittel, Claus. *Theatrum philosophicum: Descartes und die Rolle ästhetischer Formen in der Wissenschaft*, Berlin: Akademie Verlag, 2009.
Zizek, Slavoj, ed. *Cogito and the Unconsious*. Cambridge, MA: MIT Press, 1998.

Subject Index

abduction, 51
abjection, 12
abhorrence, 7, 11, 12, 31, 33, 176, 193
abyss, 5, 64
achronic, 105
actualism, 102
aerography, 63
aesthetics, aesthetic, vii, 1, 4–7, 10–11, 13–15, 17, 19, 21, 23–25, 27, 29, 31, 33–35, 70, 77, 99, 108, 124, 137, 174, 186, 192–193, 198, 209, 211–214; visceral aesthetics, 6, 10–13, 15, 17, 19, 21, 24–25, 124, 137, 174; baroque aesthetics, 1, 5–7, 27–28; theory of, 1
affects, 5, 9–13, 17–28, 33, 35, 77, 83, 93, 127, 130, 132, 133, 146, 149, 150–153, 156–160, 192, 201, 211
alienation, 5
amnesia, 157–158, 161
anaclasis, 65, 100
anamorphosis, anamorphic, 8, 98–100, 103, 105, 107, 137, 142, 169, 193–194, 208
anatomy, 1, 4–5, 11–12, 19, 20, 24, 32, 123, 137–139, 142, 146; visceral anatomy, 1; anatomical writing, 7, 145; anatomical images, 22; anatomical imagery, 11; anatomical sketches, 133
anthropomorphic, 76–77, 93
anxiety, 136, 200, 209
après-coup, 132, 160
apostrophe, 170–171; apostrophic love, 171
apparatus, psychic, 129, 159
Aristotelian worldview, 125
arithmetic, 4, 14, 82, 84, 90
art; nonrepresentational art, 70; abstract art, 76; works of, 129, 130, 136
artisan, 14, 81, 82, 188

artist, 12, 14, 19, 22–23, 32, 65, 71, 81–82, 105, 111, 135, 171
as if, 49
as long as, 52, 58
asexuality, 139
association, 129, 131–132, 145, 159, 165
associative flow, 129–130
atmosphere, 8, 76, 80, 82, 85, 91, 93
attention, 59, 105, 107, 108; sudden attention, 121
attraction, 11, 28–31, 136, 160
autoanalysis, 1, 145
autobiography, 110, 113–114, 117
autoerotic, 155–156
automimesis, 105–107
awareness, 45, 58, 60, 66, 107–108, 110, 148; sensory awareness, 149; internal awareness, 60, 100

baroque, 10, 12, 14, 25, 31–33, 80, 137, 167
beautiful, 7, 10–14, 27–30, 32, 36, 63, 65, 78, 91, 169
beauty, 6, 7, 10–12, 14, 27, 28–32, 44, 78, 136–137, 159, 163, 169
benevolence, 160
birth, 19, 22, 32, 142, 145–149, 151–153, 165–166, 169
birthmark, 147
blindness, 63, 64, 69
blind spot, 64
blood, 24, 29, 32, 51, 62, 63, 75, 133, 140, 142, 152, 154, 156–157, 164, 167–168
body, 1, 4, 6, 8–10, 12, 13, 14, 15, 17, 18, 19, 20, 22–29, 32–36, 48, 51–53, 55, 59, 61–63, 65–69, 71–73, 76, 80, 83, 84, 91, 94–95, 105, 110–112, 118, 121–124, 126, 128, 130, 132–139, 142, 145–171, 173–170; body-thought, 11; maternal body, 9, 128, 145, 147, 150–162

215

brain 8, 10, 17–19, 24–25, 32, 38, 48, 59, 62–63, 80–81, 84, 121, 123, 126, 129, 134–135, 139, 140, 142, 144, 157, 158, 156–160, 167; brain-vulva, 142, 144
breast, 151–155, 160; maternal breast, 128, 153; breastfeeding, 151–152, 155, 157

castration, 136–137, 139, 142
cartography, 112
catastrophic, 171
certainty, 10, 50–52, 60, 76, 96, 127–128, 137
chasm, 162
child, 6, 12, 28, 139, 142, 146–160
chaogito, 59, 164
cinematic perception, 21
circulation, 24, 62–63, 129, 130, 168
climate, 8, 75, 82; climate crisis, 74
clitoris-heart, 142, 144
cloud-drawing, 65
cogitans, 41–42, 44–45, 49, 52, 58–59, 61, 75, 76, 79, 80, 95, 115, 117, 125, 157
cogito, 7–9, 24, 40–44, 52, 54–55, 57–60, 64–66, 98, 101–103, 105–108, 115, 117–118, 123, 125–128, 145, 148, 150–151, 157, 160–162; *cogito designans*, 65; split cogito, 9, 145; performative cogito, 7, 55–59, 65, 108, 118
cogitography, 117
cognition, 150; process of, 82
cognitive function, 10
cognitive pluralism, 90
color, 15, 18, 50, 69–72, 77–80, 90–93, 110, 125, 130–131, 136–137
community, 120
concept, 6–7, 9, 14, 39–40, 66, 69, 79, 93, 100, 104, 107, 129, 132, 136–7, 146, 150, 155–6
conception, 4, 8–9, 13, 60, 70, 76–78, 126–127, 133, 139–140, 142, 147–148, 158–159, 163
condensation, 127
conglomerate, 90, 97
consonance, 14
consciousness, 1, 21, 28, 40–42, 29, 90–91, 93, 106, 127, 128, 129, 130, 136, 154, 157; streams of, 131; states of, 6, 7, 9, 10, 12, 27, 38, 51, 123, 126; forms of, 124
convulsions, aesthetic, 13
corporeality, 127–128

crystallization, 87, 90

dance, 14–15, 17, 85, 95
dead, 32, 137, 139
decipherment, 131
deprivation, 152–153
depth, 20, 68–70, 80, 93, 136
description, 7, 8, 12, 20, 22, 24, 77, 98, 115, 123, 132, 134, 137, 139, 142, 146, 153, 173; graphic description, 19, 142; prephenomenological descriptions, 136 optical descriptions, 4
descriptor, 76, 91, 93, 96, abstract descriptor, 103
design, 113; Baroque design of thought, 11
desire, 5–7, 9–10, 13, 17, 25, 27–30, 33, 122, 126–127, 135, 138–139, 145, 155, 157–162, 164, 166–167
devotion, 122, 163–164
dialogue, 56, 117–119; dramatic dialogue, 119
differences, 76, 78, 90–91, 95, 151; production of differences, 76, 78, 90
differentiation, 76, 81–82, 84–85, 91, 94–95, 97
digestion, 61
displacement, 127, 168
dissection, 123, 133, 135, 136, 137, 138, 139, 142; eye of dissection, 125; method of dissection, 123, 146
doubt, 24, 33, 38–39, 47–48, 51–52, 55–56, 58, 60, 102, 125–126, 148, 153, 161–162, 170; sensual doubt, 48
drawing, 8, 25, 62–64, 69, 70, 76, 82, 94–96, 98, 106, 112, 133, 139, 192, 195, 212; act of drawing, 113; anamorphic drawing, 99, 169; anatomical drawings, 24; birth of drawing, 169; cloud-drawing, 65; drawing pen; hand drawing, 105; line drawing, 107, 108; rhythmic drawings, 93
dreams, 6, 13, 17, 19, 33, 35–39, 45, 49–51, 60, 125, 127–132, 145, 151, 153, 159
drive, 6, 8, 9, 11–12, 14, 27, 29, 32, 123, 124, 126–127, 145–146, 150, 155–157; scopic drive, 7, 30, 33, 137, 142, 144
duration, 61, 84, 105, 107–108, 115, 183

écart, 168–169

ego, 4–5, 11, 19, 32–33, 40–44, 52, 55, 57, 59, 65, 76, 78, 85, 93, 116, 118, 127–128, 137, 150–153, 156, 161–162, 171
eksaiphnes, 104
embodiment, 12, 20, 27, 29, 137
e-motion, 115, 119, 165
emotion, 4–7, 9, 11–14, 18, 22, 24–28, 30, 33–35, 39, 44–45, 60, 76–77, 84, 87, 93, 94, 112, 115, 120–123, 129, 131–133, 136, 145, 149, 150–153, 156–160, 163, 165, 171; archaic emotions, 153; philosophical emotion, 4, 6, 7, 34, 35, 39, 44–45; emotion of the soul, 7; catalog of emotions, 25
enigma, 66–67
engraving, 1, 3, 19, 25, 36, 63, 68–70, 82–83, 97, 99, 112, 130
enjoyment, 10, 32, 151–157
enthusiasm, 38, 45, 60, 66, 98, 128, 135, 179
epistolography, 169
epistrophic, 171
eureka, 35, 38, 45, 105
exchange, 4, 23–24, 104, 118, 132, 148, 152, 159
existence, 5, 9, 43, 50–56, 58, 60, 67, 82, 90, 107, 110, 112, 115, 121, 124, 126, 127, 135, 146, 161, 162
experience, 1, 4, 5, 6, 7, 9–14, 17, 18, 20–22, 26–33, 40, 42–44, 46, 53, 58–60, 63–64, 69, 75–82, 84, 85, 87, 90, 91, 93, 95–97, 103–104, 107–108, 113, 115–119, 121, 122, 126, 129, 132, 136, 148, 151–154, 156, 159, 162, 166, 169, 174–177, 189–190, 192, 200, 209, 212, 214; aesthetic experience, 1, 6, 7, 11–14, 27, 30–33, 81, 84, 90–91, 209, 214
expression, 5, 25, 32, 34, 41, 56, 59, 74, 91, 93, 95, 96, 107, 108, 116, 132, 145, 155, 157, 163, 166, 170, 181–182
eye, 5, 7–8, 19–21, 24, 28–33, 36–37, 51, 54, 63–71, 78–82, 87–91, 96, 98, 99, 112, 123, 125, 126, 130, 131, 133–137, 142, 144, 160

fable, 1, 10, 114–116, 120, 164, 168, 169
falsity, 37
fantasmatic life, 153
fantasy, 9, 12, 83, 126, 133, 145, 146, 151, 153–155
fascination, 7, 8, 12, 30–32, 61, 74, 77, 98, 123, 136, 137, 139
fascinum, 32, 137
fear, 15, 21, 22, 25, 31, 37, 73, 77, 95, 133, 139, 153–155, 169, 189
fetus, 6, 12, 139, 142, 144, 146, 147, 148, 156, 157; fetal state, 145, 149, 155; thinking fetus, 9, 29, 146, 148, 149, 152, 154, 156, 158, 160–162
fictions, 50, 51
figure, 1, 4, 14, 15, 20, 22, 24, 25, 49, 52, 53, 61, 62, 64, 65, 70, 72, 75, 76, 77, 78, 79, 80, 81, 84, 85, 87, 90, 91, 94, 95, 96, 97, 99, 110, 113, 116, 126, 128, 133, 135, 139, 142, 144, 152, 166; aesthetic, 75; narrative, 76, 77
figurability, 91
fire, 22, 37, 48, 82, 87, 126, 142, 167–170
flow, 8, 17, 27, 28, 31–33, 42, 47, 50, 60, 77, 93, 94, 117, 121, 123, 128–133, 142, 153–159, 167, 170–171
fluidity, 90
fluids, 17, 63, 87, 140, 145; bodily fluids, 7, 27
focal point, 64
form, 6, 8, 9, 13, 20, 21, 26–31, 33, 36, 38, 56, 60, 62, 75, 79, 80, 87, 90, 91, 93, 95, 97, 114, 115, 117, 118, 119, 124, 126–131, 136, 142, 145, 147, 148, 151, 153, 154, 155, 156, 157, 158, 160, 161, 170
formation, 9, 44, 74, 85, 90, 91, 94, 95, 98, 123, 127, 134, 140, 142, 144, 146, 147, 148, 150, 151, 155, 156, 158, 181, 185, 191, 199, 200, 206, 207, 208; active formation, 127
frankness, 114, 117
frigidity, 139
function, 10, 53, 62, 80, 90, 126, 133, 137, 151, 160

gap, 75, 116, 136
gaze, 5, 8, 11, 23, 24, 30, 33, 123, 124, 133–138, 140, 142, 144; of fascination, 5, 11, 30; of curiosity, 123; of learning, 123, 136
genealogy, 133, 151, 156
geometric, 14, 61, 80, 85, 90, 91
geometry, 19, 76, 77, 79, 94
gerundive mode, 7, 44, 49
gland, 28, 29, 62, 63
graphic, 19, 24, 25, 74, 110, 135, 140, 142, 169
graphology, 112
graphomancy, 112

hallucination, 151, 153
hands, 1, 3, 8, 48, 51, 55, 64, 68, 69, 71, 106, 126, 140, 169, 170; writing hand, 8, 169
hate, 6, 24, 25, 52, 77, 152–156, 158, 161
heart, 8, 24, 29, 32, 61, 69, 123, 139, 140, 142, 152, 156, 164, 165, 167, 168, 169, 170, 171; beating of, 61, 168
heat, 79, 87, 140, 149, 152, 156, 164, 165, 167, 168, 169, 170
homunculus, 126
hyperbole, 80

illusions, 39, 47, 48, 131, 137
illustration, 8, 63, 75, 77, 82, 90, 132, 135
images, 5, 6, 8, 10, 11, 14, 20, 22, 24, 25, 50, 53, 62, 64, 66, 70, 71, 73, 75, 77, 78, 79, 80, 81, 82, 83, 84, 85, 87, 90, 93, 94, 95, 96, 99; inner images, 1, 13; physical images, 19; thought-images, 75, 76, 90; mental images, 123, 126, 156
imagination, 1, 14, 17, 18, 19, 22, 23, 24, 31, 33, 37, 53, 59, 61, 62, 63, 68, 76, 79, 80, 82, 84, 90, 95, 97, 123, 125, 126, 128, 129, 130, 131, 132, 135, 147, 148, 162; scientific imagination, 20; experimental imagination, 97; corporeal imagination, 132
impression, 19, 25, 61, 62, 63, 80, 121, 122, 129, 130, 131, 135, 140, 147, 148, 167
imprints, 35, 62, 63, 127, 129, 130, 131, 142, 158, 159, 160, 161
impulse, 153–154, 156, 158; destructive impulse, 153
in-between, 5, 6, 12, 13, 15, 61, 115, 123, 156
infancy, 7, 145, 149
infant, 9, 18, 139, 140, 145–162
intellect, 10, 28, 34, 38, 44, 76, 77, 97, 136, 148; rational intellect, 4, 5, 44
intelligible, 5, 54
instinct, 5, 6, 11, 94, 133, 145, 149, 150, 152, 153, 154, 155, 156, 157, 158, 160, 161
immediacy, 39, 44, 45
immediate, 7, 39–41, 43, 45, 51, 55, 59, 60, 78, 79, 151, 152, 154
infinite, 8, 39, 60, 74, 75, 77, 78, 82, 85, 90, 91, 96, 108, 137, 166
inspiration, 24, 34, 36, 37

instant, 36, 45, 58, 66, 98, 100, 101, 102, 104, 105, 107, 115, 117, 121, 122
intensity, 60, 121
introspection, 46
intuition, 29, 56–60, 100; intuition of the mind, 58; thinking intuition, 59, 60, 100, 103; mental intuition, 61; sensuous intuition, 60
"it", 161
isolation, 41, 42

je, 44, 55, 57
joy, 15, 18, 25, 27, 112, 121, 132, 152, 154, 155, 164, 165; exuberant, 32; intellectual, 34
judgment, 10, 198; act of judgment, 4; aesthetic judgment, 10, 14

kinesthesis, 132
knowledge, 4, 14, 25, 26, 39, 41, 55, 56, 60, 78, 79, 80, 82, 84, 95, 96, 97, 113, 125, 127, 133, 138, 148, 151, 161, 164, 191, 193, 197, 201, 211; human, 35; marvelous, 36; moral, 29, reflective, 100; self-, 157; truth, 111

lactation, 157
landscape, 62, 74, 85, 93, 130, 136; internal landscape, 33; subcutaneous landscape, 63
language, 24, 32, 44, 57, 59, 66, 70, 79, 85, 95, 108, 110, 116, 127, 128, 129, 131, 132, 159, 162, 165, 169, 187, 189, 196, 208; invention of a language, 5; dream language, 127; native language, 108, 116; of the eye, 79; poetic language, 131; visceral language, 24
life, 5, 9, 35, 36, 37, 42, 52, 60, 63, 71, 84, 93, 119, 148, 150, 154, 158, 159, 160, 169, 177, 178, 179, 186, 201, 203, 208, 209; biological life, 124; embryonic, 165; everyday, 95; joy of, 32; human, 142; infantile, 145, 146, 151, 152, 157, 162; mental, 153; origin of, 144; psychic life, 155, 161; pregnant, 165, 167; sense of, 31; subjective life, 13; waking, 49
ligaments, 62, 63
light, 7, 14, 15, 20, 33, 36, 40, 48, 56, 58, 61, 62, 63, 68, 69, 72, 73, 74

lines, 7, 8, 14, 46, 52, 62, 63, 65, 69, 70, 72, 76, 79, 80, 81, 82, 93, 94, 95, 98, 99, 103, 104, 108, 110, 112, 113, 116, 130, 146, 167, 169, 170
love, 5, 6, 9, 13, 24, 25, 27, 28, 29, 30, 52, 112, 121, 122, 132, 145, 152, 153, 154, 155, 156, 157, 158, 159, 160, 161, 163, 164, 165, 166, 167, 168, 169, 170, 171; Cartesian love, 9, 164, 168, 171; immoderate love, 152, 164, 166; love of literature, 169; love letters, 9

machine, 11, 62, 63, 168, 193; aesthetic machine, 1, 6, 11, 12, 17, 18, 20, 22, 25, 33; human machine, 62; of the earth, 11
materiality, 112, 136
maternal symbiosis, 145
maternal sphere, 149
masculinity, 139
mathesis universalis, 4, 66
measure, 66, 105, 108, 156
medical imagery, 24
melancholia, 48, 161
memory, 17, 18, 29, 31, 60, 61, 64, 102, 115, 123, 135, 139, 148, 157, 158, 160; memory traces, 1, 129; childhood memories, 138, 139; repressed memories, 17; corporeal memory, 13, 83
metamorphosis, 67, 69
metaphysics, 1, 4, 5, 6, 11, 69, 72, 76, 81, 94, 123, 124, 135, 149, 150, 156, 161
metaphysics of thought, 5
metaphysical solipsism, 5
method, 35, 38, 49, 52, 56, 66, 74, 75, 76, 80, 84, 114, 116, 117, 123, 146, 161
mind-body dualism, 5, 6, 33
mineral, 7, 74, 77, 84
mirror, 63, 65, 67, 68, 69, 81, 107, 108, 130, 135, 169
mise en Abyme, 106, 107
moods, 15, 17, 18, 33, 151, 157
motion, 15, 20, 75, 77, 78, 79, 94-97, 110, 142, 157, 164, 165, 168
movement, 6, 7, 8, 15, 17, 18, 20, 26, 27, 28, 29, 30, 34-35, 40, 47, 49-52, 56, 57, 59, 60-65, 67, 75, 81-82, 85, 87, 90-91, 93-95, 98, 100, 104, 112-113, 115, 118, 121-122, 128, 131-133, 135-136, 138-139, 142, 154, 156, 158, 160, 164, 166-169, 170; thinking movement, 6-8, 47, 50, 52, 56-57, 59, 60-62, 98, 100, 104, 112-113, 115, 118, 121-122, 166
music, 8, 10, 13, 14, 15, 17, 22, 25, 27, 28, 31, 58, 62, 76, 82, 91, 93, 95, 97, 101
muscles, 62, 121, 130, 133, 135, 138, 154, 156, 168
multisensorial, 21
mystery, 145

natural philosophy, 1, 4, 6, 8, 11, 23, 76, 77, 78, 81, 82, 91, 97, 123, 136, 145, 151
navel, 156
negativity, 127; radical negativity, 127
nerve, 19, 22, 28, 29, 63, 80, 82, 87, 135, 140, 142, 152, 154, 158, 164, 171
nervosity, 22
nervous system, 8, 24, 25, 123, 133, 134
neuroaesthetics, 10
newborn, 152, 158
novel, 46, 113, 114, 119; philosophical novel, 120, 168

object, 7, 10-12, 14, 17-19, 20, 27-30, 32-33, 39-43, 45, 53, 56, 58, 60-62, 64, 68-70, 78-81, 83, 87, 90-91, 96, 106-107, 110, 118, 121-123, 126-127, 130-131, 135, 145-146, 148-149, 152-155, 157-167; object relations, 145, 153; internalized object, 154; object attachment, 151; *objet à*, 137, 161-162
ongoing, 44, 61, 107, 154
ontology, 75, 84, 97
optical, 4, 48, 99, 100; optical descriptions, 4
organ, 20, 24, 61, 62, 84, 121, 123, 124, 133, 139, 142, 146, 155; bodily organs, 17, 28; artificial organ, 68; sexual organ, 139; female sexual organ, 144
organism, 10, 11, 156; Baroque organism, 10
organization, 8, 75, 76
origin, 4, 6, 7, 11, 13, 23, 25, 27, 28, 29, 38, 40, 42, 74, 78, 81, 96, 107, 108, 115, 123, 133, 137, 138, 139, 142, 144, 146, 151, 152, 154, 155, 157, 158, 160, 161, 162, 167; archaic origins, 133
other, 166
overwhelming, 48, 59, 102, 105, 115, 117

painting, 1, 5, 7, 8, 12, 19, 20, 32, 47, 50, 62, 64–73, 76, 78, 93, 98, 99, 107, 110, 130, 131, 136, 137; imaginative painting, 71; figurative painting, 70; unrealistic painting, 71
paralysis, 128
passions, 6, 17, 26, 29, 33, 34, 35, 38, 61, 91, 95, 121, 123, 145, 150, 152, 154, 156, 158, 165, 167; passion of sadness, 95, 165
pedagogy, 139; aesthetic, 24
perception, 7, 12, 13, 17, 18, 19, 20, 21, 22, 24, 28, 31, 33, 34, 39, 40, 48, 51, 52, 53, 54, 66, 67, 70, 80, 81, 82, 83, 84, 90, 93, 97, 123, 124, 125, 126, 129, 130, 131, 132, 133, 135, 136, 137, 144, 146, 147, 150, 151, 158, 159, 162; act of perceiving, 53
performative, 3
performative thinking gesture, 7
performativity, 25, 64, 114, 117
perspective, 4, 5, 8, 12, 19, 61, 65, 67, 68, 70, 72, 98, 99, 100, 105, 107, 130, 137, 142, 146
phantom, 36, 48, 83
phenomenology, 5, 20, 41, 42, 43, 93
phenomena, 11–15, 28, 31, 32, 75, 77, 78, 79, 80, 81, 87, 97, 127, 136, 151, 188, 189; atmospheric phenomena, 74, 75, 76, 77, 90; aesthetic phenomena, 7, 11, 14, 76
philosophical diary, 117
physicien, 23, 24, 91, 137
physiological, 27, 62
pictorial eyes, 20
pictorial imagination, 19, 20, 22, 62
pleasure, 6, 7, 10–12, 14, 17, 18, 28, 30, 44, 91, 101, 112, 121, 131, 149, 150, 151, 152–158, 167, 178
poets, 29, 30, 34, 37, 78, 128, 131, 160
poetry, 10, 13, 36, 95, 128, 131, 132
point, 4, 7, 9, 24, 25, 28, 35, 37, 60, 61, 63, 64, 65, 66, 67, 93, 99, 110, 116, 117, 127, 137, 138, 144, 146, 150, 153; breaking point, 30, 33, 125; point-instant, 98, 100
polymorphous perversity, 155
portrait, 1, 5, 22, 34, 36, 37, 63, 67, 68, 106, 120, 137; self-portrait, 110
pregnancy, 165, 166
pre-history, 159, 161; archaic prehistory, 13

private, 69, 118, 119
problem, 5, 25, 28, 42, 53, 65, 66, 69, 80, 82, 90, 111, 119, 126, 128, 129, 135, 145, 148, 149, 150, 156, 160, 162, 166; criterial problem, 49
proportion, 15, 79, 80, 81, 85, 91
prose, 108
prosthesis, 63
psychoanalysis, 8, 9, 28, 124, 127, 136, 142, 145, 146, 150, 161, 162
psychoanalytical, 5, 8, 151
psychoanalytic criticism, 7
psychoanalytic theory, 8, 9, 133, 136, 145, 146, 153
psychography, 117
public, 118, 119
pulsion, 171
putrification, 12

rainbow, 78, 80, 84, 90
reading, 22, 46, 82, 112, 113, 118, 119, 121
reason, 1, 4, 5, 8, 10, 14, 20, 22, 25, 28, 29, 31, 33, 37, 38, 39, 44, 47, 49, 51, 52, 59, 68, 74, 75, 76, 77, 80, 81, 85, 90, 91, 94, 96, 102, 113, 114, 116, 119, 125, 128, 146, 151, 160, 162, 163, 168; limits of reason, 8
reciprocity, 166
reflection, 5, 6, 10, 11, 25, 27, 28, 40, 41, 42, 43, 55, 60, 62, 64, 65, 72, 81, 82, 93, 100, 106, 112, 125, 146, 148, 150, 155, 162
reflexivity, 7, 35, 39, 40, 42, 43, 67, 69
refraction, 32, 62, 65
reification, 41, 42
relation, 4, 9, 10, 14, 19, 24, 25, 34, 35, 40, 41, 43, 49, 52, 53, 57, 58, 61, 67, 70, 72, 74, 75, 78, 80, 82, 85, 87, 90, 91, 95, 96, 97, 111, 113, 117, 123, 133, 134, 135, 137, 142, 145, 146, 147, 148, 151, 152, 153, 154, 155, 159, 160, 161, 162, 165, 166, 167, 168; symbiotic relation, 145, 152, 155; object relations, 9, 145, 146, 153
representation, 27, 29, 40, 41, 52, 70, 77, 79, 80, 83, 93, 107, 108, 126, 130, 131, 154, 158, 159; musical representation, 27
repression, 9, 146, 157, 158; pre-psychoanalytic theory of repression, 146
resemblance, 50, 68, 69, 70, 130

return of the oppressed, 5
revulsion, 11, 29, 30, 31
rhythm, 8, 11, 14, 15, 17, 65, 72, 75, 76, 77, 91, 93, 94, 95, 96, 97, 110, 154; rhythmic figuration, 8, 75; rhythmic conception, 8; structural rhythm, 72
romance, 29, 30, 160

saying, 37, 57, 58, 108, 117, 170
science, 4, 20, 22, 38, 41, 44, 47, 55, 56, 66, 78, 80, 99, 100, 128, 139, 159; wonderful science, 38, 56
seed, 37, 128, 140, 142, 157
sensation, 11, 12, 13, 17, 18, 20, 22, 27, 29, 31, 33, 34, 48, 52, 68, 79, 83, 97, 112, 121, 145, 149, 151, 153, 155, 160, 160, 165; internal sensation, 13, 17
senses, 1, 4, 5, 7, 11, 12, 13, 14, 20, 21, 27–31, 34, 39, 47, 48, 51, 52, 59, 61, 62, 63, 66, 67, 74–81, 84, 87, 90, 91, 93, 96, 97, 101, 110, 112, 126, 135, 146, 147, 159
sensible, 5, 6, 13, 33, 36, 37, 54, 58, 64, 66, 67, 79, 84
sensibility, 4, 5, 24, 33, 34, 35, 39, 44, 45, 54, 151, 163; aesthetic sensibility, 1, 33; philosophical sensibility, 34, 35, 39, 44, 45, 163
sentiment, 31, 61, 160, 170
sensual experience, 4, 8, 12, 20, 32, 33, 76, 77, 78, 85, 96, 126, 136
sexual satisfaction, 155
sexuality, 127, 139, 153, 155, 157, 160
simulacra, 81, 131, 135
signs, 70, 93, 112, 130, 131, 132, 136, 169
shadow, 31, 62, 106, 130, 131, 160, 169
shape, 8, 14, 15, 20, 30, 50–52, 65, 68, 70–72, 74–80, 82, 84, 85, 87, 90, 91, 93–96, 100, 110, 125, 126, 140, 142, 155, 160; cosmological shapes, 14
shock, 6, 12, 78
singular, 55, 96, 108, 114, 115, 116
sketches, 11, 19, 48, 79, 81, 85, 96, 133
sky, 51, 63, 98, 125, 166, 182
sleep, 1, 9, 17, 36, 37, 39, 43, 49, 50, 59, 61, 123, 128, 131, 132, 136, 145, 148, 149, 155, 183
snow, 8, 11, 74, 75, 77, 78, 80, 85, 90, 91, 95
soliloquy, 118

solipsism, 5, 118
solitude, 37, 46, 119, 120, 168
soul, 1, 4, 5, 7, 9, 11, 12, 15, 18, 22, 24, 24–31, 34, 35, 41, 51, 52, 59, 61, 62, 63, 65, 66, 69, 72, 81, 84, 102, 111, 117, 118, 119, 121, 122, 124, 129, 130, 132, 133, 139, 145, 146, 148, 149, 150, 152, 156, 163, 164, 165, 166, 167, 168, 169
stickiness, 128, 136–138
storyteller, 114
strophic, 171
subjectivity, 9, 44, 126, 127, 145, 146, 158, 162
split, 9, 28, 87, 123, 125, 126, 128, 137, 145, 146, 153, 156, 158, 161, 162
sound, 10, 11, 14, 15, 17, 18, 31, 40, 51, 57, 58, 61, 62, 95, 105, 108, 125, 136, 162, 170
spectacle, 67
salt, 80, 85, 87, 90, 95
spirits, 34, 62, 121, 122, 129, 135, 156, 167; flow of, 17, 156; animal spirits, 17, 29, 63, 140, 154, 157, 168
stimulation, 25, 128, 153, 158
stimuli, 22, 25, 26, 29, 131, 133, 135, 151, 156
subject, 4, 6–11, 13, 22, 24, 26, 29, 32, 33, 35, 40–45, 48, 53, 60, 74, 76, 78, 79, 82, 91, 95, 107, 110, 116, 124–131, 136, 137, 142, 144, 145, 146, 148, 151, 153, 154, 155, 156, 157, 158, 159, 160, 161, 162, 164, 168; embodied subject, 10, 136; aesthetic subject, 11
sublime, 85
sublimity, 12, 17
substantiality, 41, 42, 53
sum, 40, 42, 43, 44, 55, 58, 59
surfaces, 20, 62, 80, 85
syllogism, 45, 56, 59, 103
symmetry, 90
synteresis, 37

tailles-douces, 68, 69
taste, 1, 10, 11, 12, 14, 17, 31, 61, 78, 79, 87, 90; aesthetic taste, 1
theater, 5, 25–27, 107, 123, 126, 127, 129; inner theater, 127, 129; Cartesian theatre, 27, 123, 126, 127
therapy, 150, 203
thickness, 43, 44, 60

222 | Subject Index

thing, 5, 22, 24, 29, 31, 35, 37, 39, 41, 42, 44, 45, 46, 49, 50, 51, 52, 56, 58, 64, 66, 67, 69, 70, 71, 78, 79, 80, 87, 91, 93, 94, 99, 106, 107, 117, 122, 123, 126, 127, 131, 132, 133, 136, 146, 149, 157, 159, 161, 162, 163, 166

thinking, 4, 6, 7, 8, 9, 10, 12, 13, 29, 33, 34, 35, 39, 40, 41, 42, 43, 44, 45, 46, 47, 48, 49, 50, 51, 52, 53, 54, 55, 56, 57, 58, 59, 60, 61, 62, 65, 66, 67, 68, 70, 98, 100, 101, 102, 103, 104, 105, 106, 107, 108, 110, 111, 112, 113, 115, 116, 117, 118, 119, 120, 121, 122, 126, 128, 133, 145, 146, 148, 151, 152, 154, 156, 157, 158, 160, 161, 162, 165, 166, 168, 169

third eye, 126

thought, 1, 5, 6, 7, 8, 9, 11, 12, 13, 19, 20, 24, 25, 28, 34, 35, 36, 38, 39, 40, 41, 42, 43, 44, 46, 47, 49, 50, 52, 53, 55, 56, 57, 59, 60, 61, 62, 63, 64, 66, 67, 68, 69, 70, 71, 73, 75, 76, 77, 80, 81, 84, 85, 90, 95, 96, 103, 104, 108, 112, 113, 115, 116, 117, 118, 119, 120, 126, 127, 128, 129, 131, 132, 140, 145, 146, 147, 148, 149, 150, 151, 152, 154, 155, 156, 157, 158, 159, 160, 161, 162, 163, 164, 165, 166, 167, 170, 173, 175, 177, 179, 182, 191, 192, 193, 195, 196, 201, 204, 209, 212, 214; aesthetic (of) thought, 6, 35, 108; confused thoughts, 6, 13, 25, 28, 112, 146, 149, 150, 151, 152, 153, 156, 158, 160, 161, 162, 164, 166, 201; figural thought, 80

time-space, 61

touch, 11, 20, 21, 30, 31, 53, 61, 64, 68, 72, 79, 90, 91, 112, 150, 169

traces, 1, 5, 7, 17, 18, 27–32, 62, 127, 129, 130, 131, 138, 146, 147, 152, 157, 158, 159, 160, 161, 170; traces of perception, 7, 18, 129

transcription, 5

transgression, 32

translation, 5, 36, 40, 44, 58, 66, 72, 78, 91, 108

transport, 8, 24, 123

trauma, 145

trompe l'œil, 33, 137, 142, 144

truth, 37, 38, 39, 46–48, 51, 52, 55, 59, 69, 97, 103, 111, 115, 116, 117, 118, 169

tubes, 12, 17, 24, 62, 133, 158; tubes of transport, 8, 24, 123

ugly, 7, 11–13, 27, 29–33

uncanny, 136, 139

unknown, 13, 20, 34, 84, 114, 127, 148, 161, 162

uniqueness, 115, 117

universal, 4, 10, 13, 20, 66, 67, 69, 78, 114–116

unreal, 49, 50, 71

untouchability, 112

uprooting, 38, 47, 52

vague, 76, 132

vanishing point, 33, 123, 137, 138, 142, 144

velocity, 170

vestige, 35, 107, 160, 161

violence, 13, 30, 112, 121, 132

viscerality, 22; visceral domain, 17; visceral material, 22; visceral drives, 27; visceral form, 29; visceral conflict, 128

visibility, 66, 112, 165

visual culture, 19, 18

visual enchantment, 98

vision, 7, 11, 14, 20, 28, 31, 37, 39, 44, 50, 53, 56, 63–70, 75–77, 79, 80, 98, 99, 107, 129, 135, 136, 137, 138

voice, 15, 27, 114, 161, 162, 170; inner voice, 161; voices of deceit, 161; voice of the self, 161; voice of an originary interlocution, 162

volition, 156, 157

weather, 7, 8, 74, 75, 77, 78, 82, 84, 90, 93, 95, 96, 142

whileness, 52, 105, 112, 115

will to attention, 4

wind, 36, 37, 62, 63, 74, 75, 77, 78, 80, 85, 87, 91, 128, 140, 168, 170, 193

womb, 18, 28, 133, 139, 140, 142, 146, 147, 148, 149, 156, 159

wonder, 6, 12, 25, 27, 31, 37, 66, 78, 84, 85, 105, 121, 121, 161, 164, 168, 170

writing, 1, 5, 6, 7, 8, 34, 57, 58, 64, 74, 75, 76, 107, 108, 110, 111, 112, 113, 114, 115, 116, 117, 118, 119, 120, 121, 131, 132, 164, 168, 169, 170; philosophical writing, 34; philosophical writer, 108, 115; physics of writing, 112

Names Index

Abbé Gregoire, 116
Arendt, Hannah, 4, 162, 173, 204, 207
Aristotle, 57, 63, 105, 122, 183, 197, 208
Arnauld, Antoine, 43, 59, 148, 158, 200
Augustine, St, 46, 59, 110, 175, 182, 185, 207, 212, 214
Aurelius, Marcus, 110
Ausonius, 36, 178
Avila, Teresa of, 161, 182, 212

Bataille, George, 12, 31, 32, 176, 177, 208
Baudelaire, 7, 12, 31
Baumgarten, Alexander, 14, 40, 180, 208
Beck, David, 2, 22, 23
Beckett, Samuel, 113, 196, 208
Benveniste, Émile, 115, 196, 208
Blanchot, Maurice, 50, 183, 208
Bossuet, Jacques-Bénigne Lignel, 98, 194, 208
Burman, Frans, 103, 104, 149, 157, 194, 201, 202, 203

Cézanne, Paul, 19, 20, 31, 71, 93, 175, 187
Chanut, Pierre, 152, 159, 163, 164, 171, 176, 202, 203, 204, 205
Clerselier, Claude, 134, 135, 139, 146, 199, 200, 207

Da Vinci, Leonardo, 62, 65, 66, 67, 70, 82, 99, 103, 138, 139, 142, 155, 185, 199, 209, 213
Delaunay, Robert, 67, 186, 209
Deleuze, Gilles, 5
Dennett, Daniel, 126, 130, 187, 197, 209
Derrida, Jacques, 46, 63, 64, 113, 116, 180, 182, 185, 195, 196, 209, 210

El Greco, 106
Elisabeth, Princess of Bohemia, 5, 118, 119, 120, 121, 148, 152, 158, 161, 163, 164, 170, 171, 200, 201, 202, 203, 204

Focillon, Henri, 68, 186, 209
Freud, Sigmund, 9, 36, 124, 127, 128, 129, 131, 137, 138, 139, 142, 145, 146, 150, 151, 153, 154, 155, 156, 157, 158, 159, 160, 179, 197, 198, 199, 200, 201, 202, 203, 204, 210, 212

Gide, André, 8, 107, 108, 194, 210
Gobert, Stephen, 26
Grünbein, Durs, 108, 195, 210
Gueroult, Martial, 49, 182, 210
Gutschoven, Gérard von, 135

Hals, Frans, 1, 2
Händel, Georg Friedrich, 27
Harvey, William, 24, 201
Hegel, Georg Wilhelm Friedrich, 44, 45, 53, 181, 183, 210
Heidegger, Martin, 41, 42, 116, 180, 181, 209, 210
Heemskreck, Merten van, 105, 106
Henriot, Émile, 107
Hobbes, Thomas, 10, 53, 82, 175, 190, 191, 214
Holbein, Hans, 32, 99
Horace, 166, 211
Husserl, Edmund, 41, 42, 43, 59, 83, 91, 93, 130, 162, 181, 191, 192, 198, 211, 212
Huygens, Constantijn, 81, 82, 85, 171, 175, 188, 190, 191

Kafka, Franz, 4, 116, 173
Kant, Immanuel, 10, 14, 31, 40, 41, 174, 180, 198, 208, 211
Klee, Paul, 66, 72, 73
Klein, Melanie, 9, 146, 153, 154, 155, 160, 202, 204, 211
Krämer, Sybille, 79, 175, 189, 190, 211
Kristeva, Julia, 12, 32, 177, 211

Lacan, Jacques, 9, 127, 136, 137, 138, 142, 145, 155, 161, 197, 199, 200, 202, 204, 212, 214

Names Index

La Forge, Louis de, 87, 135, 185, 191, 207
Le Brun, Charles, 26, 81
Lefort, Claude, 66, 186
Leibniz, 5, 10, 35, 40, 128, 180, 181, 186, 194, 212
Lyotard, Jean-François, 46, 182, 212

Marion, Jean-luc, 79, 161, 162, 173, 177, 179, 181, 196, 201, 204, 208, 212, 213
Margolles, Teresa, 32
Massumi, Brian, 22, 175
Memling, 107, 195
Merleau-Ponty, 7, 12, 19, 20, 43, 66, 67, 68, 69, 70, 93, 96, 130, 131, 136, 173, 175, 181, 186, 187, 188, 192, 193, 198, 199, 208, 212, 214
Mersenne, Marin, 14, 17, 78, 91, 109, 113, 135, 148, 174, 175, 188, 189, 190, 191, 192, 194, 199, 200
Metzys, Quentin, 107, 195

Nancy, Jean-Luc, v, 59, 105, 110, 111, 112, 113, 114, 115, 164, 168, 173, 182, 185, 194, 195, 196, 205, 206, 213

Palotti, Alphonsus, 133
Perniola, Mario, 33, 177, 193, 213
Poussin, Nicolas, 110, 111, 195, 196, 213
Proust, Marcel, 113, 168, 196, 212
Pythagoras, 37, 178

Rameau, Jean-Philippe, 27
Rembrandt, 47, 137, 138
Robbe-Grillet, Alain, 107, 195, 213
Rousseau, Jean-Jacques, 46

Schooten, Franz van, 78, 189, 191
Schuyl, Florentio, 133, 135, 139, 142, 185, 198, 207
Sepper, Dennis, 79, 175, 188, 189, 190, 214
Serrano, Andres, 32
Shakespeare, 107, 118, 197
Sherman, Cindy, 32
Sobchack, Vivian, 21, 175
Spinoza, 10, 211
Stoichita, Victor I, 105, 194, 214
Suyderhoff, Jonas, 1, 3

Twombly, Cy, 93, 94

Valéry, Paul, 34, 62, 65, 66, 67, 70, 112, 168, 177, 180, 185, 186, 196, 214
Vasari, Giorgio, 138, 199, 214
Van Zurck, 133
Velasquez, 107
Viau, Théophile de, 167

Wahl, Jean, 102, 108, 184, 194, 195, 214
Warhol, Andy, 32
Weenix, Jan Baptist de, 1, 3, 110
Wiskus, Jessica, 93, 192, 193, 214
women, 116, 119, 163, 182, 204, 212

CECILIA SJÖHOLM is Professor of Aesthetics at Södertörn University. Her books include *Doing Aesthetics with Arendt: How to See Things*, *Kristeva and the Political*, *Regionality/Mondiality* (editor with Charlotte Bydler), and *The Antigone Complex: Ethics and the Invention of Feminine Desire*.

MARCIA SÁ CAVALCANTE SCHUBACK is Professor of Philosophy at Södertörn University. Her books include *The Fascism of Ambiguity*; *Time in Exile: In Conversation with Heidegger, Blanchot, and Lispector*; *The End of the World* (editor with Susanna Lindberg); and *Dis-orientations: Philosophy, Literature and the Lost Grounds of Modernity*.

For Indiana University Press

Lesley Bolton, Project Manager/Editor
Tony Brewer, Artist and Book Designer
Brian Carroll, Rights Manager
Gary Dunham, Acquisitions Editor and Director
Anna Francis, Assistant Acquisitions Editor
Brenna Hosman, Production Coordinator
Katie Huggins, Production Manager
Dan Pyle, Online Publishing Manager
Stephen Williams, Marketing and Publicity Manager
Jennifer L. Witzke, Senior Artist and Book Designer

www.ingramcontent.com/pod-product-compliance
Lightning Source LLC
Chambersburg PA
CBHW021353300426
44114CB00012B/1203